# CONSUMER GUIDE

# NEW CAR

## PRICE GUIDE

### 1998 EDITION

C0-AYR-526

# CONTENTS

# INTRODUCTION

The 1998 edition of the *New Car Price Guide* contains the latest prices and specifications for more than 130 passenger cars, minivans, and sport-utility vehicles that are available in the U.S.

In most cases, the editors were able to provide dealer invoice prices. In some cases, only the suggested retail prices were available. In all cases, the prices are subject to change by the manufacturers.

The dealer invoice prices are what the dealer pays the manufacturer for the car, including its factory- or port-installed options. The dealer's cost of preparing a car for delivery to the consumer is included in the invoice price of all domestic cars. On some imported vehicles, this cost may not be included in the dealer invoice.

Cash rebates and dealer incentives are not included because they change so frequently.

While we have done all we can to see that the prices in this issue are accurate, car companies are free to change their prices at any time.

Many dealers tell our readers that the prices we publish are incorrect so they can eliminate dealer-invoice price from consideration. Once they accomplish that, then they're back in the driver's seat on price negotiations. If a dealer claims our prices are incorrect or the information in this book doesn't match what you see in showrooms, contact us and we'll do our best to help.

The address is listed on page 9.

## Destination Charges

The destination charge—the cost of shipping the car to the dealer—is not included in the base price of most cars. This charge must be added to the total price of the car and optional equipment. Dealers do not receive a discount on the destination charge. If the manufacturer's price sticker lists a $500 destination charge, that is what the dealer paid—and you will, too.

On the other hand, the destination charges listed in our price charts (and on the manufacturer's price sticker) are the only *legitimate* shipping charges. Don't let a dealer trick you into paying a bogus charge.

## Advertising Fees and Taxes

Advertising fees are not included in the price lists because they vary greatly in different parts of the country and not all dealers try to charge their customers for advertising. We think it's unfair for consumers to reimburse dealers for their advertising expenses, so we strongly suggest you argue against paying such a fee. It's their cost of doing business, not yours.

Two federal taxes affect car prices. First, a gas-guzzler tax is levied on cars that average less than 22.5 mpg in combined city/highway mileage based on EPA estimates. (This does not apply to light trucks, including SUVs.) Some manufacturers include the gas-guzzler tax in the base prices; others list it separately. Guzzler taxes range from $1000 to more than $3000, so they can have a substantial impact on the purchase price.

Second, an seven percent "luxury tax" is levied

on cars selling for more than $36,000. The tax applies only to the amount over $36,000, so a car that sells for $40,000 will be taxed $320 and one that sells for $50,000 will be taxed $1120. The tax applies to the *transaction* or sale price of the vehicle, not the suggested retail price. In addition, the tax is figured on the full purchase price before any trade-in value is deducted.

The editors invite your questions and comments. Address them to:

Consumer Guide™
7373 N. Cicero Ave.
Lincolnwood, IL 60646

## Key to Specifications

Specifications are supplied by the manufacturers. **Body styles: notchback** = coupe or sedan with a separate trunk; **hatchback** = coupe or sedan with a rear liftgate. **Wheelbase** = distance between the front and rear wheels. **Curb weight** = weight of base models, not including optional equipment. **Engines: ohv** = overhead valve; **ohc** = overhead camshaft; **dohc** = dual overhead camshafts; **I** = inline cylinders; **V** = cylinders in V configuration; **flat** = horizontally opposed cylinders; **rpm** = revolutions per minute. **OD** = overdrive transmission. **NA** = not available.

# ACURA CL

*Acura 2.3CL*

## SPECIFICATIONS

| | 2-door coupe |
|---|---|
| Wheelbase, in. | 106.5 |
| Overall length, in. | 190.0 |
| Overall width, in. | 70.1 |
| Overall height, in. | 54.7 |
| Curb weight, lbs. | 3009 |
| Cargo vol., cu. ft. | 12.0 |
| Fuel capacity, gals. | 17.1 |
| Seating capacity | 4 |
| Front head room, in. | 37.4 |
| Max. front leg room, in. | 42.9 |
| Rear head room, in. | 35.9 |
| Min. rear leg room, in. | 31.0 |

## ENGINES

| | ohc I-4 | ohc V-6 |
|---|---|---|
| Size, liters/cu. in. | 2.3/137 | 3.0/183 |
| Horsepower @ rpm | 150@ 5700 | 200@ 5000 |
| Torque (lbs./ft.) @ rpm | 152@ 4800 | 195@ 4800 |
| Availability | S[1] | S[2] |

**EPA city/highway mpg**

| | | |
|---|---|---|
| 5-speed OD manual | 25/31 | |
| 4-speed OD automatic | 23/29 | 20/28 |

1. 2.3CL. 2. 3.0CL.

| Acura CL | Retail Price | Dealer Invoice |
|---|---|---|
| 2.3CL 2-door coupe, 5-speed | $22310 | $20159 |
| 2.3CL 2-door coupe, automatic | 23110 | 20882 |
| 2.3CL 2-door coupe w/Premium Pkg., 5-speed | 23360 | 21108 |
| 2.3CL 2-door coupe w/Premium Pkg., automatic | 24160 | 21831 |

| | Retail Price | Dealer Invoice |
|---|---|---|
| 3.0CL 2-door coupe, automatic ...................................... | $25310 | $22870 |
| 3.0CL 2-door coupe w/Premium Pkg., automatic ............................................. | 26660 | 24090 |
| Destination charge ........................................................ | 435 | 435 |

## STANDARD EQUIPMENT:

**2.3CL:** 2.3-liter 4-cylinder engine, 4-speed automatic or 5-speed manual transmission, driver- and passenger-side air bags, anti-lock 4-wheel disc brakes, variable-assist power steering, tilt steering wheel, leather-wrapped steering wheel, cruise control, air conditioning w/automatic climate control, moquette front bucket seats, 6-way power driver seat w/manual recliner, manual walk-in front seats, center storage armrest w/CD tray, rear center armrest, rear trunk pass-through, cupholders, door pockets, courtesy and map lights, power windows, power door locks, remote keyless entry, power mirrors, power moonroof, 6-speaker AM/FM/CD player, steering-wheel mounted radio controls, integrated antenna, digital clock, rear defogger, illuminated visor mirrors, variable intermittent wipers, remote decklid and fuel-door release, theft-deterrent system, front mud guards, front and rear stabilizer bars, 205/55VR16 tires, alloy wheels.

**2.3CL w/Premium Pkg.** adds: leather upholstery, seatback pocket, universal garage door opener.

**3.0CL** adds: 3.0-liter V-6 engine, 4-speed automatic transmission, 8-way power driver seat w/power recliner, power walk-in driver seat, Bose sound system, heated outside mirrors, deletes leather upholstery, seatback pocket.

**3.0CL w/Premium Pkg.** adds: leather upholstery, heated front seats, seatback pocket.

**Options** are available as dealer-installed accessories.

# ACURA INTEGRA

## SPECIFICATIONS

| | 2-door coupe | 4-door sedan |
|---|---|---|
| Wheelbase, in. ...................................... | 101.2 | 103.1 |
| Overall length, in. ................................. | 172.4 | 178.1 |
| Overall width, in. ................................... | 67.3 | 67.3 |
| Overall height, in. ................................. | 52.6 | 53.9 |
| Curb weight, lbs. ................................... | 2529 | 2628 |
| Cargo vol., cu. ft. ................................. | 13.3 | 11.0 |
| Fuel capacity, gals. .............................. | 13.2 | 13.2 |
| Seating capacity .................................... | 4 | 5 |
| Front head room, in. ............................. | 38.6 | 38.9 |
| Max. front leg room, in. ........................ | 42.7 | 42.2 |

*Prices are accurate at time of publication; subject to manufacturer's change.*

*Acura Integra LS sedan*

|  | 2-door coupe | 4-door sedan |
|---|---|---|
| Rear head room, in. | 35.0 | 36.0 |
| Min. rear leg room, in. | 28.1 | 32.7 |

## ENGINES

|  | dohc I-4 | dohc I-4 | dohc I-4 |
|---|---|---|---|
| Size, liters/cu. in. | 1.8/112 | 1.8/110 | 1.8/110 |
| Horsepower @ rpm | 142@ 6300 | 170@ 7600 | 195@ 8000 |
| Torque (lbs./ft.) @ rpm | 127@ 5200 | 128@ 6200 | 130@ 7500 |
| Availability | S[1] | S[2] | S[3] |
| **EPA city/highway mpg** | | | |
| 5-speed OD manual | 25/31 | 25/31 | 23/28 |
| 4-speed OD automatic | 24/31 | | |

*1. RS, LS, GS. 2. GS-R. 3. Type R.*

| Acura Integra | Retail Price | Dealer Invoice |
|---|---|---|
| RS 2-door hatchback, 5-speed | $16200 | $14475 |
| RS 2-door hatchback, automatic | 17000 | 15190 |
| LS 2-door hatchback, 5-speed | 19200 | 17155 |
| LS 2-door hatchback, automatic | 20000 | 17870 |
| LS 4-door sedan, 5-speed | 20000 | 17870 |
| LS 4-door sedan, automatic | 20800 | 18585 |
| GS 2-door hatchback, 5-speed | 20850 | 18630 |
| GS 2-door hatchback, automatic | 21650 | 19345 |
| GS 4-door sedan, 5-speed | 21400 | 19121 |
| GS 4-door sedan, automatic | 22000 | 19836 |
| GS-R 2-door hatchback, 5-speed | 21300 | 19032 |
| GS-R 2-door hatchback w/leather, 5-speed | 22100 | 19747 |
| GS-R 4-door sedan, 5-speed | 21600 | 19300 |
| GS-R 4-door sedan w/leather, 5-speed | 22400 | 20014 |
| Type R prices not yet available. | | |
| Destination charge | 435 | 435 |

## STANDARD EQUIPMENT:

**RS:** 1.8-liter dohc 140-horsepower 4-cylinder engine, 5-speed manual or 4-speed automatic transmission, driver- and passenger-side air bags, 4-wheel disc brakes, variable-assist power steering, tilt steering column, cloth reclining front bucket seats w/driver-side lumbar adjustment, 50/50 split folding rear seat, center console w/armrest, power windows, power mirrors, tachometer, coolant temperature gauge, AM/FM/CD player w/six speakers, power antenna, remote fuel-door and decklid/hatch releases, rear defogger, rear wiper/washer, intermittent wipers, cargo cover, tinted glass, fog lights, 195/60HR14 tires, wheel covers.

**LS** adds: anti-lock brakes, air conditioning, cruise control, tilt/height-adjustable driver seat, one-piece folding rear seat (4-door), power moon-roof, power door locks, map lights, color-keyed bodyside moldings, Michelin 195/60HR14 tires, alloy wheels, deletes cargo cover and rear wiper/washer (4-door).

**GS** adds: leather upholstery, rear spoiler (hatchback), 195/55VR15 tires.

**GS-R** adds to LS: 1.8-liter dohc VTEC 170-horsepower engine, wood-grain console (4-door), rear spoiler (hatchback), 195/55VR15 tires.

**GS-R w/leather** adds: leather upholstery, leather-wrapped steering wheel and shift knob.

Options are available as dealer-installed accessories.

# ACURA RL

*Acura 3.5RL*

## SPECIFICATIONS

| | 4-door sedan |
|---|---|
| Wheelbase, in. | 114.6 |
| Overall length, in. | 195.1 |
| Overall width, in. | 71.3 |
| Overall height, in. | 56.6 |
| Curb weight, lbs. | 3660 |
| Cargo vol., cu. ft. | 14.0 |

*Prices are accurate at time of publication; subject to manufacturer's change.*

| | 4-door sedan |
|---|---|
| Fuel capacity, gals. | 18.0 |
| Seating capacity | 5 |
| Front head room, in. | 38.6 |
| Max. front leg room, in. | 42.2 |
| Rear head room, in. | 36.7 |
| Min. rear leg room, in. | 35.5 |

## ENGINES

| | ohc V-6 |
|---|---|
| Size, liters/cu. in. | 3.5/212 |
| Horsepower @ rpm | 210@ 5200 |
| Torque (lbs./ft.) @ rpm | 224@ 2800 |
| Availability | S |

**EPA city/highway mpg**

| | |
|---|---|
| 4-speed OD automatic | 19/25 |

| Acura RL | Retail Price | Dealer Invoice |
|---|---|---|
| Base 3.5RL 4-door sedan | $41200 | $35980 |
| Base 3.5RL 4-door sedan w/Navigation System | 43200 | 37727 |
| Base 3.5RL 4-door sedan w/Premium Pkg. | 44000 | 38425 |
| Base 3.5RL 4-door sedan w/Premium Pkg. and Navigation System | 46000 | 40172 |
| Destination charge | 435 | 435 |

Navigation System not available in some areas.

## STANDARD EQUIPMENT:

**Base:** 3.5-liter V-6 engine, 4-speed automatic transmission, driver- and passenger-side air bags, anti-lock 4-wheel disc brakes, automatic air conditioning w/front and rear controls, interior air filter, variable-assist power steering, tilt/telescopic steering wheel w/memory, leather-wrapped steering wheel and shifter, cruise control, leather upholstery, power front seats w/memory, driver-seat lumbar support, center console, cupholders, rear-seat trunk pass-through, rear armrest, power moonroof, heated power mirrors w/memory, power windows, power door locks, remote keyless entry, Acura/Bose 8-speaker AM/FM/cassette player w/anti-theft, digital clock, integrated antenna, maintenance interval reminder, automatic headlights, rear defogger, remote fuel-door and decklid releases, speed-sensitive intermittent wipers, illuminated visor mirrors, map lights, rear reading lights, tinted glass, theft-deterrent system, fog lamps, mudguards, 215/60R16 tires, alloy wheels.

**Navigation System models** add: Global Positioning System, dashboard-mounted LCD screen.

**Premium Pkg. models** add: traction control, heated front seats, burled walnut interior trim, trunk pass-through ski sleeve.

Options are available as dealer-installed accessories.

# ACURA SLX

*Acura SLX Sport*

## SPECIFICATIONS

| | 4-door wagon |
|---|---|
| Wheelbase, in. | 108.7 |
| Overall length, in. | 187.8 |
| Overall width, in. | 72.2 |
| Overall height, in. | 72.2 |
| Curb weight, lbs. | 4615 |
| Cargo vol., cu. ft. | 90.2 |
| Fuel capacity, gals. | 22.5 |
| Seating capacity | 5 |
| Front head room, in. | 39.4 |
| Max. front leg room, in. | 53.7 |
| Rear head room, in. | 37.8 |
| Min. rear leg room, in. | 39.1 |

## ENGINES

| | dohc V-6 |
|---|---|
| Size, liters/cu. in. | 3.5/214 |
| Horsepower @ rpm | 215@ 5400 |
| Torque (lbs./ft.) @ rpm | 230@ 3000 |
| Availability | S |
| **EPA city/highway mpg** | |
| 4-speed OD automatic | 14/18 |

*Prices are accurate at time of publication; subject to manufacturer's change.*

## Acura SLX

|  | Retail Price | Dealer Invoice |
|---|---|---|
| Base 4WD 4-door wagon ................................ | $36300 | $32251 |
| Destination charge ......................................... | 435 | 435 |

## STANDARD EQUIPMENT:

**Base:** 3.5-liter dohc V-6 engine, 4-speed automatic transmission, part-time 4-wheel drive, limited-slip differential, driver- and passenger-side air bags, anti-lock 4-wheel disc brakes, variable-assist power steering, leather-wrapped tilt steering wheel, cruise control, air conditioning, rear heat ducts, heated power reclining front bucket seats with folding arm-rests, leather upholstery, 60/40 split folding rear seats, center storage console with cupholders, rear storage compartment, electronic multi-meter (compass, altimeter, outside temperature display, barometer), map lights, AM/FM/CD/cassette with six speakers, digital clock, power door locks, remote keyless entry, power windows, heated power fold-in outside mirrors, power moonroof, rear defogger, tachometer, coolant temperature and oil pressure gauges, voltmeter, trip odometer, cargo lights, illuminated visor mirrors, tinted windows, theft-deterrent system, fog lights, cornering lights, rear step bumper, rear air deflector, mud guards, front and rear stabilizer bars, skid plates, full-size spare tire, 245/70R16 all season tires, alloy wheels.

**Options** are available as dealer-installed accessories.

# ACURA TL

*Acura 3.2TL*

## SPECIFICATIONS

| | 4-door sedan |
|---|---|
| Wheelbase, in. ................................................. | 111.8 |

|  | 4-door sedan |
|---|---|
| Overall length, in. | 191.5 |
| Overall width, in. | 70.3 |
| Overall height, in. | 55.3 |
| Curb weight, lbs. | 3252 |
| Cargo vol., cu. ft. | 14.1 |
| Fuel capacity, gals. | 17.2 |
| Seating capacity | 5 |
| Front head room, in. | 39.1 |
| Max. front leg room, in. | 43.7 |
| Rear head room, in. | 36.9 |
| Min. rear leg room, in. | 35.2 |

## ENGINES

|  | ohc I-5 | ohc V-6 |
|---|---|---|
| Size, liters/cu. in. | 2.5/152 | 3.2/196 |
| Horsepower @ rpm | 176@ 6300 | 200@ 5300 |
| Torque (lbs./ft.) @ rpm | 170@ 3900 | 210@ 4500 |
| Availability | S[1] | S[2] |
| **EPA city/highway mpg** | | |
| 4-speed OD automatic | 20/25 | 19/24 |

1. 2.5TL.  2. 3.2TL.

## Acura TL

|  | Retail Price | Dealer Invoice |
|---|---|---|
| 2.5TL 4-door sedan | $30700 | $27431 |
| 3.2TL 4-door sedan | 33150 | 29619 |
| Destination charge | 435 | 435 |

## STANDARD EQUIPMENT:

**2.5:** 2.5-liter 5-cylinder engine, 4-speed automatic transmission, driver- and passenger-side air bags, anti-lock 4-wheel disc brakes, variable-assist power steering, leather-wrapped tilt steering wheel, cruise control, air conditioning w/automatic climate control, leather upholstery, reclining front bucket seats, 8-way power driver seat w/lumbar adjuster, front console with armrest, rear armrest, trunk pass-through, power windows, power door locks, remote keyless entry, heated power mirrors, power moonroof, AM/FM/cassette/CD player, rear defogger, variable intermittent wipers, map lights, illuminated visor mirrors, tinted glass, theft-deterrent system, fog lights, 205/60HR15 tires, alloy wheels.

**3.2** adds: 3.2-liter V-6 engine, heated front seats, power passenger seat, leather-wrapped shift knob, 205/65VR15 tires.

**Options** are available as dealer-installed accessories.

*Prices are accurate at time of publication; subject to manufacturer's change.*

# AUDI A4

*Audi A4 2.8*

## SPECIFICATIONS

| | 4-door sedan | 4-door wagon |
|---|---|---|
| Wheelbase, in. | 103.0 | 103.0 |
| Overall length, in. | 178.0 | 176.7 |
| Overall width, in. | 68.2 | 68.2 |
| Overall height, in. | 55.8 | 56.7 |
| Curb weight, lbs. | 3087 | 3289 |
| Cargo vol., cu. ft. | 13.7 | NA |
| Fuel capacity, gals. | 16.4 | 16.4 |
| Seating capacity | 5 | 5 |
| Front head room, in. | 38.1 | 38.1 |
| Max. front leg room, in. | 41.3 | NA |
| Rear head room, in. | 36.8 | 37.8 |
| Min. rear leg room, in. | 33.4 | NA |

## ENGINES

| | Turbo dohc I-4 | dohc V-6 |
|---|---|---|
| Size, liters/cu. in. | 1.8/107 | 2.8/169 |
| Horsepower @ rpm | 150@ 5700 | 190@ 6000 |
| Torque (lbs./ft.) @ rpm | 155@ 1750 | 207@ 3200 |
| Availability | S[1] | S[2] |
| **EPA city/highway mpg** | | |
| 5-speed OD manual | 23/32[3] | 20/29[4] |
| 5-speed OD automatic | 21/31[3] | 18/29[4] |

1. A4 1.8T. 2. A4 2.8 and Avant. 3. 21/29 and 19/27 w/Quattro. 4. 19/27 and 17/27.

| Audi A4 | Retail Price | Dealer Invoice |
|---|---|---|
| 1.8T 4-door sedan | $23790 | $20942 |
| 2.8 4-door sedan | 28390 | 24944 |
| Avant 4-door wagon | 30465 | 26839 |

| | Retail Price | Dealer Invoice |
|---|---|---|
| Avant Quattro 4-door wagon | $31040 | $27464 |
| Destination charge | 500 | 500 |

## STANDARD EQUIPMENT:

**1.8T:** 1.8-liter turbocharged 4-cylinder engine, 5-speed manual transmission, Electronic Differential Lock, driver- and passenger-side air bags, front side-impact air bag, anti-lock 4-wheel disc brakes, automatic air conditioning, interior air filter, power steering, tilt/telescoping steering wheel, leather-wrapped shifter and boot, cruise control, reclining front seats with height adjustment, 60/40 split folding rear seat, velour or leatherette upholstery, front storage console w/cupholders, folding rear storage armrest, tachometer, trip odometer, coolant-temperature and oil-temperature gauges, voltmeter, outside temperature display, service interval indicator, analog clock, 8-speaker AM/FM/cassette, integrated antenna, power windows, power door locks, heated power outside mirrors, rear defogger, remote decklid and fuel-door releases, intermittent wipers, illuminated visor mirrors, front and rear reading lights, floormats, tinted glass, theft-deterrent system, headlight washers, front and rear fog lights, 205/65R15 tires, alloy wheels.

**2.8** adds: 2.8-liter V-6 engine, 8-way power driver seat w/lumbar adjustment, leather-wrapped steering wheel, jacquard satin or leatherette upholstery, adjustable front armrest, cellular phone prewiring, interior wood trim, 205/55HR16 tires.

**Avant** adds: 5-speed Tiptronic automatic transmission, roof rails, ski sack.

**Avant Quattro** adds: permanent 4WD, 5-speed manual transmission, deletes 5-speed Tiptronic automatic transmission.

## OPTIONAL EQUIPMENT:

### Major Packages

| | | |
|---|---|---|
| All-Weather Package, 1.8T, 2.8 | 630 | 548 |
| Avant, Avant Quattro | 470 | 409 |
| *Includes heated driver-side door lock, heated front seats, heated windshield washer nozzles, ski sack (1.8T, 2.8).* | | |
| Sport Pkg., 1.8T | 750 | 653 |
| 2.8, Avant, Avant Quattro | 400 | 348 |

### Powertrains

| | | |
|---|---|---|
| 5-speed Tiptronic automatic transmission, 1.8T, 2.8, Avant Quattro | 1075 | 1025 |
| *Std. Avant.* | | |
| Quattro IV all-wheel-drive system, 1.8T, 2.8 | 1650 | 1650 |

### Comfort and Convenience

| | | |
|---|---|---|
| Audi/Bose 8-speaker sound system, 2.8 | 660 | 574 |

*Prices are accurate at time of publication; subject to manufacturer's change.*

| | Retail Price | Dealer Invoice |
|---|---|---|
| 6-disc CD changer | $1200 | $1044 |
| *Includes Audi/Bose sound system.* | | |
| Leather upholstery | 1320 | 1148 |
| *NA 1.8T.* | | |
| Leather-wrapped sport steering wheel | 160 | 139 |
| Trip computer | 250 | 218 |
| Power sunroof and remote keyless entry | 1190 | 1035 |

## Appearance and Miscellaneous

| | | |
|---|---|---|
| Pearlescent metallic paint | 570 | 496 |
| Cool Shades paint | 460 | 400 |
| Metallic/mica paint, 1.8T | 460 | 400 |
| 2.8 | NC | NC |

# AUDI A6

*Audi A6 sedan*

## SPECIFICATIONS

| | 4-door sedan |
|---|---|
| Wheelbase, in. | 108.7 |
| Overall length, in. | 192.0 |
| Overall width, in. | 71.3 |
| Overall height, in. | 57.2 |
| Curb weight, lbs. | 3473 |
| Cargo vol., cu. ft. | 17.2 |
| Fuel capacity, gals. | 18.5 |
| Seating capacity | 5 |
| Front head room, in. | 39.3 |
| Max. front leg room, in. | 41.3 |
| Rear head room, in. | 37.9 |

| | 4-door sedan |
|---|---|
| Min. rear leg room, in. ........................................................ | 37.3 |

## ENGINES

| | dohc V-6 |
|---|---|
| Size, liters/cu. in. ................................................................ | 2.8/169 |
| Horsepower @ rpm ............................................................. | 200@ 6000 |
| Torque (lbs./ft.) @ rpm ....................................................... | 207@ 3200 |
| Availability .......................................................................... | S |

**EPA city/highway mpg**

| | |
|---|---|
| 5-speed OD automatic............................................................ | 17/28[1] |

*1. 17/26 w/Quattro.*

| Audi A6 | Retail Price | Dealer Invoice |
|---|---|---|
| A6 4-door sedan ............................................. | $33750 | $29697 |
| A6 4-door wagon ............................................. | 34400 | 30250 |
| Destination charge ......................................... | 500 | 500 |

Wagon requires Quattro Value Pkg.

## STANDARD EQUIPMENT:

**Sedan:** 2.8-liter V-6 engine, 5-speed automatic transmission, Electronic Differential Lock, driver- and passenger-side air bags, front side-impact air bags, anti-lock 4-wheel disc brakes, automatic air conditioning w/dual zone controls, speed-sensitive power steering, tilt/telescoping steering column, leather-wrapped steering wheel, cruise control, Jacquard satin cloth upholstery, reclining front bucket seats with height and lumbar adjustments, 8-way power driver seat, center storage console with cupholders, adjustable front storage armrest, split folding rear seat, rear folding armrest, walnut interior trim, outside-temperature indicator, tachometer, oil-temperature and coolant-temperature gauge, trip odometer, analog clock, service-interval indicator, Active Auto Check System, power windows, power door locks, heated power mirrors, remote fuel-door and decklid release, AM/FM/cassette, integrated antenna, reading lights, illuminated visor mirrors, rear defogger, rear heat ducts, intermittent wipers, ski sack, floormats, tinted glass, theft-deterrent system, front and rear fog lights, 195/65R15 tires, alloy wheels.

**Wagon** adds: quattro all-wheel drive, power moonroof, 2-place rear seat, roof-mounted antenna, rear wiper/washer, remote tailgate release, retractable rear window sunshade, cargo-area cover and net, roof rack, 205/55R16 tires.

## OPTIONAL EQUIPMENT:
### Major Packages

| | | |
|---|---|---|
| Quattro Value Pkg............................................... | 2490 | 2360 |

*Quattro all-wheel-drive system, power sunroof, 205/55R16 tires.*

*Prices are accurate at time of publication; subject to manufacturer's change.*

| | Retail Price | Dealer Invoice |
|---|---|---|
| Comfort and Convenience Pkg., wagon ........................ | $860 | $748 |

*Power front passenger seat, memory driver seat and outside mirrors, remote keyless entry.*

| | | |
|---|---|---|
| Convenience Pkg., sedan .............................................. | 1500 | 1305 |

*Memory mirrors, automatic day/night rearview and driver-side mirror, power sunroof.*

| | | |
|---|---|---|
| Enhanced Security Pkg., sedan ..................................... | 950 | 827 |

*Rear side-impact air bags, Xenon headlights.*

| | | |
|---|---|---|
| Warm Weather Pkg., sedan............................................ | 1800 | 1566 |

*Insulated glass, power rear sun shade, manual rear side shade, solar panel sunroof.*

| | | |
|---|---|---|
| Cold Weather Pkg., sedan.............................................. | 750 | 653 |

*Heated front seats, heated steering wheel, ski sack.*

| | | |
|---|---|---|
| All-Weather Pkg., wagon................................................ | 520 | 452 |

*Heated front seats, heated windshield washer nozzles, heated front door locks, headlight washers.*

## Powertrains

| | | |
|---|---|---|
| Quattro IV all-wheel-drive system, sedan ...................... | 1650 | 1650 |

## Comfort and Convenience

| | | |
|---|---|---|
| Power moonroof, sedan.................................................. | 1000 | 870 |
| Leather upholstery......................................................... | 1550 | 1349 |
| Audi/Bose audio system, wagon .................................... | 660 | 574 |
| 6-disc CD changer, sedan.............................................. | 1300 | 1131 |

*Includes Audi/Bose sound system.*

## Appearance and Miscellaneous

| | | |
|---|---|---|
| Pearlescent metallic paint, sedan.................................... | 600 | 522 |
| Pearlescent metallic paint, wagon ................................... | 570 | 496 |
| 16-inch alloy wheels, sedan............................................ | 225 | 196 |

*Includes 205/55R16 tires.*

# AUDI A8

## SPECIFICATIONS

| | 4-door sedan |
|---|---|
| Wheelbase, in. ..................................................... | 113.0 |
| Overall length, in. ................................................ | 198.2 |
| Overall width, in. ................................................. | 74.0 |
| Overall height, in. ................................................ | 56.7 |
| Curb weight, lbs. ................................................. | 3682 |
| Cargo vol., cu. ft. ................................................ | 17.6 |
| Fuel capacity, gals. ............................................. | 23.7 |

*Audi A8 3.7*

| | 4-door sedan |
|---|---|
| Seating capacity | 5 |
| Front head room, in. | 38.9 |
| Max. front leg room, in. | 41.3 |
| Rear head room, in. | 38.2 |
| Min. rear leg room, in. | 38.4 |

## ENGINES

| | dohc V-8 | dohc V-8 |
|---|---|---|
| Size, liters/cu. in. | 3.7/226 | 4.2/255 |
| Horsepower @ rpm | 230@ 5500 | 300@ 6000 |
| Torque (lbs./ft.) @ rpm | 235@ 2700 | 295@ 3300 |
| Availability | S[1] | S[2] |
| **EPA city/highway mpg** | | |
| 5-speed OD automatic | 17/26 | 17/25 |

1. 3.7.  2. 4.2 Quattro.

| Audi A8 | Retail Price | Dealer Invoice |
|---|---|---|
| 3.7 4-door sedan | $57400 | $50183 |
| 4.2 4-door sedan | 65000 | 56795 |
| Destination charge | 500 | 500 |

## STANDARD EQUIPMENT:

**3.7:** 3.7-liter dohc V-8 engine, 5-speed Tiptronic automatic transmission, Electronic Differential Lock, Anti-Slip Regulation system, driver- and passenger-side air bags, front and rear side-impact air bags, anti-lock 4-wheel disc brakes, dual-zone automatic air conditioning w/air filter, speed-sensitive power steering, power tilt/telescoping steering wheel, leather-wrapped steering wheel and shifter, cruise control, leather upholstery, 14-way power front bucket seats w/lumbar adjustment and power headrests, memory functions (driver seat, outside mirrors, center storage console with cupholders, two adjustable front armrests, rear folding armrest, walnut interior trim, power sunroof, trip computer, outside-temperature indicator, tachometer, coolant-temperature gauge, trip odometer, digital clock, ser-

## AUDI • BMW

vice-interval indicator, Active Auto Check System, power windows, power door locks, heated power mirrors w/automatic day/night, automatic day/night rearview mirror, remote keyless entry, remote fuel-door and decklid release, Audi/Bose AM/FM/cassette, power antenna, reading lights, dual pane acoustic glass, illuminated visor mirrors, rear defogger, rear heat ducts, intermittent wipers, floormats, tinted glass, theft-deterrent system, heated washer nozzles, headlight washers, front and rear fog lights, 225/60HR16 tires, alloy wheels.

**4.2** adds: 4.2-liter dohc V-8 engine, Quattro all-wheel-drive system.

## OPTIONAL EQUIPMENT:

|  | Retail Price | Dealer Invoice |
|---|---|---|
| **Major Packages** | | |
| Warm Weather Pkg. | $2000 | $1740 |
| *Power solar sunroof, insulated glass, power rear-window sunshade, manual rear-side-window sunshades.* | | |
| Cold Weather Pkg. | 1000 | 870 |
| *Heated front and rear seats, heated steering wheel, ski sack.* | | |
| Electronics Group | 700 | 609 |
| *Automatic day/night mirrors, power rear seat lumbar support and headrests.* | | |
| **Comfort and Convenience** | | |
| Audi/Bose 6-disc CD changer, 3.7 | 1400 | 1218 |
| 6-disc CD changer, 4.2 | 540 | 470 |
| **Appearance and Miscellaneous** | | |
| Pearlescent metallic paint | 600 | 522 |
| Polished alloy wheels and 225/55R17 tires | 1000 | 870 |

# BMW 3-SERIES

*BMW 323is 2-door*

| SPECIFICATIONS | 2-door hatchback | 2-door coupe | 4-door sedan | 2-door conv. |
|---|---|---|---|---|
| Wheelbase, in. | 106.3 | 106.3 | 106.3 | 106.3 |

| | 2-door hatchback | 2-door coupe | 4-door sedan | 2-door conv. |
|---|---|---|---|---|
| Overall length, in. | 165.7 | 174.5 | 174.5 | 174.5 |
| Overall width, in. | 66.9 | 67.3 | 66.9 | 67.3 |
| Overall height, in. | 54.8 | 53.8 | 54.8 | 53.1 |
| Curb weight, lbs. | 2745 | 2976 | 2976 | 3131 |
| Cargo vol., cu. ft. | 15.0 | 9.2 | 10.3 | 8.9 |
| Fuel capacity, gals. | 13.7 | 16.4 | 16.4 | 16.4 |
| Seating capacity | 5 | 5 | 5 | 4 |
| Front head room, in. | 38.7 | 37.8 | 38.1 | 38.1 |
| Max. front leg room, in. | 41.1 | 41.2 | 41.1 | 41.2 |
| Rear head room, in. | 37.0 | 36.6 | 37.3 | 36.3 |
| Min. rear leg room, in. | 32.6 | 32.7 | 34.0 | 28.1 |

## ENGINES

| | dohc I-4 | dohc I-6 | dohc I-6 | dohc I-6 |
|---|---|---|---|---|
| Size, liters/cu. in. | 1.9/116 | 2.5/152 | 2.8/170 | 3.2/192 |
| Horsepower @ rpm | 138@ 6000 | 168@ 5550 | 190@ 5300 | 240@ 6000 |
| Torque (lbs./ft.) @ rpm | 133@ 4300 | 181@ 3950 | 206@ 3950 | 225@ 3800 |
| Availability | S[1] | S[2] | S[3] | S[4] |

### EPA city/highway mpg

| | | | | |
|---|---|---|---|---|
| 5-speed manual | 23/32 | 20/30 | 20/28 | 20/28 |
| 4-speed OD automatic | 22/31 | 19/27 | 18/26 | |
| 5-speed OD automatic | | | | 19/28 |

1. 318i models. 2. 323i models. 3. 328i models. 4. M3 models.

| BMW 3-Series | Retail Price | Dealer Invoice |
|---|---|---|
| 318ti 2-door hatchback | $21390 | $19225 |
| 318i 4-door sedan | 26150 | 22930 |
| 323is 2-door coupe | 28700 | 25160 |
| 323i 2-door convertible | 34700 | 30410 |
| 328i 4-door sedan | 33100 | 29010 |
| 328is 2-door coupe | 33200 | 29095 |
| 328i 2-door convertible | 41500 | 36355 |
| M3 4-door sedan | 39700 | 34780 |
| M3 2-door coupe | 39700 | 34780 |
| Destination charge | 570 | 570 |

## STANDARD EQUIPMENT:

**318 models:** 1.9-liter dohc 4-cylinder engine, 5-speed manual transmission, All Season Traction, driver- and passenger-side air bags, front side-impact air bags (318i), anti-lock 4-wheel disc brakes, variable-assist power steering, air conditioning, automatic dual climate control (318i), cruise control (318i), cloth upholstery (318ti), leatherette upholstery (318i), 6-way manual reclining bucket seats with height/tilt adjustments, split folding rear

# BMW

seat (2-door), cupholders, front seatback storage nets, power windows, power door locks, heated power mirrors, 10-speaker AM/FM/cassette, heated windshield washer jets, diversity antenna (318i), tachometer, trip odometer, digital clock, fuel-economy indicator (318i), outside temperature indicator (318i), speed-sensitive intermittent wipers, rear defogger, Service Interval Indicator, map lights (318i), rear reading lights, cargo-area storage box, tool kit, full-size spare tire (318i), 185/65TR15 tires, wheel covers.

**323 models** add: 2.5-liter dohc 6-cylinder engine, leather-wrapped steering wheel and shifter, rear storage armrest w/rear cupholders (323i convertible), manual folding top (323i convertible), fog lights, 205/60HR15 tires, alloy wheels.

**328 models** add: 2.8-liter dohc 6-cylinder engine, Active Check Control system, front reading lights, rear reading lights, 8-way power front seats, front center armrest, fully automatic power folding top (328i convertible).

**M3** adds: 3.2-liter dohc 6-cylinder engine, limited-slip differential, leather upholstery, 8-way manual sport seats (4-door), 12-way manual sport seats (2-door), upgraded brakes, sport suspension, 225/45ZR17 front tires, 245/40ZR17 rear tires, M double-spoke alloy wheels, deletes 8-way power front seats, front center armrest, cruise control.

## OPTIONAL EQUIPMENT:
## Major Packages

| | Retail Price | Dealer Invoice |
|---|---|---|
| Active Pkg., 318ti | $1350 | $1150 |
| *Cruise control, leather-wrapped steering wheel and shifter, remote keyless entry, theft-deterrent system, onboard computer, 205/60HR15 tires, alloy wheels, metallic paint. NA with Sports Pkg.* | | |
| 318ti Sports Pkg., 318ti | 2940 | 2500 |
| *Sport suspension, cloth/leather upholstery, sport seats, leather-wrapped steering wheel and shifter, fog lights, M-Aerodynamic bumpers and rocker panels, 225/50ZR16 tires, alloy wheels. NA with Active Pkg.* | | |
| 323 Sports Pkg., 323is | 990 | 820 |
| 323i conv. | 750 | 625 |
| *Fog lights, sport suspension (323i), 225/50ZR16 tires, cross-spoke alloy wheels.* | | |
| 328 Sports Pkg., 328i 4-door, 328is | 2125 | 1750 |
| 328i conv. | 1775 | 1465 |
| *Leather sport seats, sport suspension (328i 4-door, 328is), 225/50ZR16 tires, double-spoke alloy wheels.* | | |
| 318i Premium Pkg., 318i | 1900 | 1575 |
| *Leather-wrapped steering wheel and shifter, front armrest, remote keyless entry, theft-deterrent system, power sunroof, alloy wheels.* | | |
| 323 Premium Pkg., 323is | 2125 | 1765 |
| 323i conv. | 2750 | 2285 |
| *Leather upholstery, front armrest, power sunroof (323is), power convertible top (323i conv.), remote keyless entry, theft-deterrent system.* | | |

| | Retail Price | Dealer Invoice |
|---|---|---|
| 328 Premium Pkg., 328i, 328is | $2125 | $1765 |
| 328i conv. | 1600 | 1330 |

*Leather upholstery, wood trim, power sunroof (328i, 328is), remote keyless entry, theft-deterrent system.*

## Powertrains

| | | |
|---|---|---|
| 4-speed automatic transmission | 975 | 925 |

*NA on M3.*

| | | |
|---|---|---|
| 5-speed automatic transmission, M3 4-door | 1200 | 1140 |

## Safety Features

| | | |
|---|---|---|
| Rollover Protection System, convertible | 1450 | 1190 |

## Comfort and Convenience

| | | |
|---|---|---|
| Cruise control, 318ti, M3 | 475 | 390 |
| Leather upholstery, 318, 323, 328 | 1450 | 1190 |

*318ti and 318i 4-door include leather-wrapped steering wheel and shifter. 4-doors include rear storage armrest with cupholders when not ordered with split folding rear seat. 328 includes wood interior trim (NA with 328 Sports Pkg.) and onboard computer. NA 318ti Sports Pkg.*

| | | |
|---|---|---|
| Power front seats, M3 | 945 | 775 |
| Heated front seats | 500 | 410 |

*M3 includes heated mirrors.*

| | | |
|---|---|---|
| Split folding rear seat, 318i 4-door, 328i 4-door, M3 4-door | 300 | 245 |

*NA w/ski sack.*

| | | |
|---|---|---|
| Ski sack, 318i 4-door, 328i 4-door | 300 | 245 |

*NA w/folding rear seat.*

| | | |
|---|---|---|
| Harman Kardon audio system | 975 | 800 |

*Includes CD changer. NA 318ti.*

| | | |
|---|---|---|
| Fog lights, 318i, 323is, 323i conv. | 260 | 215 |
| Onboard computer, 318ti | 300 | 250 |
| 328, 323, M3 | 500 | 415 |
| Power sunroof | 950 | 780 |

## Appearance and Miscellaneous

| | | |
|---|---|---|
| Metallic paint, M3 | NC | NC |
| Hardtop, convertible | 2295 | 1885 |
| California top, 318ti | 1600 | 1380 |
| Metallic paint, 318, 323, 328 | 475 | 390 |
| Rear spoiler, M3 | 650 | 535 |
| Sport suspension, 318i | 350 | 290 |

*318i 4-door requires 205/60R15 tires and alloy wheels.*

| | | |
|---|---|---|
| Alloy wheels, 318i | 850 | 700 |
| Forged alloy wheels, M3 | 1450 | 1190 |
| M-Contour alloy wheels, M3 | NC | NC |

*Prices are accurate at time of publication; subject to manufacturer's change.*

# BMW 5-SERIES

*BMW 540i*

## SPECIFICATIONS

| | 4-door sedan |
|---|---|
| Wheelbase, in. | 111.4 |
| Overall length, in. | 188.0 |
| Overall width, in. | 70.9 |
| Overall height, in. | 56.5 |
| Curb weight, lbs. | 3450 |
| Cargo vol., cu. ft. | 11.0 |
| Fuel capacity, gals. | 18.5 |
| Seating capacity | 5 |
| Front head room, in. | 37.4 |
| Max. front leg room, in. | 41.7 |
| Rear head room, in. | 37.5 |
| Min. rear leg room, in. | 34.2 |

## ENGINES

| | dohc I-6 | dohc V-8 |
|---|---|---|
| Size, liters/cu. in. | 2.8/170 | 4.4/268 |
| Horsepower @ rpm | 190@ 5300 | 282@ 5700 |
| Torque (lbs./ft.) @ rpm | 207@ 3950 | 310@ 3900 |
| Availability | S[1] | S[2] |
| **EPA city/highway mpg** | | |
| 5-speed manual | 20/28 | |
| 6-speed OD manual | | 15/24 |
| 4-speed OD automatic | 18/26 | |
| 5-speed OD automatic | | 18/24 |

1. 528i. 2. 540i.

| BMW 5-Series | Retail Price | Dealer Invoice |
|---|---|---|
| 528i 4-door sedan | $38900 | $34490 |
| 540i 4-door sedan, 6-speed manual transmission | 53300 | 46675 |

| | Retail Price | Dealer Invoice |
|---|---|---|
| 540i 4-door sedan, 5-speed automatic transmission .... | $50500 | $44225 |
| Destination charge ........................................ | 570 | 570 |

540i w/6-speed manual transmission adds $1300 Gas Guzzler Tax.

## STANDARD EQUIPMENT:

**528i:** 2.8-liter dohc 6-cylinder engine, 5-speed manual transmission, All Season Traction, driver- and passenger-side air bags, front side-impact air bags, side head protection system, anti-lock 4-wheel disc brakes, variable-assist power steering, power tilt/telescopic steering wheel, leather-wrapped steering wheel, shift knob and hand brake, steering-wheel-mounted radio and telephone controls, cruise control, air conditioning with dual automatic climate controls, filtered ventilation, 10-way power front seats (with power head restraints and memory driver's seat, steering wheel and outside mirrors), leatherette upholstery, rear center storage armrest, cupholders, 10-speaker anti-theft AM/FM stereo cassette, diversity antenna, power windows, power door locks, heated power mirrors, power sunroof, tachometer, trip odometer, outside temperature display, onboard computer, theft-deterrent system, map lights, intermittent wipers, remote decklid release, rear defogger, seatback and door storage, front and rear reading lights, Service Interval Indicator, Active Check Control system, fuel economy indicator, illuminated visor mirrors, tool kit, 225/60HR15 tires, alloy wheels.

**540i** adds: 4.4-liter dohc V-8 engine, 5-speed automatic transmission, Dynamic Stability Control, 14-way power front seats, leather upholstery, burl walnut interior trim, power moonroof, automatic day/night rearview mirror, remote keyless entry, upgraded onboard computer, metallic paint, 225/55HR16 tires, deletes Active Check Control System.

**540i 6-speed** adds: 6-speed manual transmission, front sport seats, Shadowline exterior trim, sport suspension, 235/45WR17 tires, 7-spoke composite alloy wheels, deletes Dynamic Stability Control.

## OPTIONAL EQUIPMENT:
### Major Packages
| | | |
|---|---|---|
| Premium Pkg., 528i ........................................ | 3450 | 2520 |

*Leather upholstery, wood interior trim, metallic paint, cross-spoke alloy wheels. NA with Sport Pkg.*

| | | |
|---|---|---|
| 528i Sport Pkg., 528i ........................................ | 3450 | 2865 |

*Leather upholstery, Technical Surfaca interior trim, metallic paint, Shadowline exterior trim, sport suspension, cross-spoke alloy wheels, 235/45WR17 tires.*

| | | |
|---|---|---|
| 540 Sport Pkg., 540i automatic........................ | 3115 | 2585 |

*Sport seats, Shadowline exterior trim, sport suspension, cross-spoke alloy wheels, 235/45WR17 tires.*

*Prices are accurate at time of publication; subject to manufacturer's change.*

## Powertrains

| | Retail Price | Dealer Invoice |
|---|---|---|
| 4-speed automatic transmission, 528i | $975 | $925 |

## Safety Features

| | | |
|---|---|---|
| Rear side-impact air bags | 385 | 320 |

## Comfort and Convenience

| | | |
|---|---|---|
| Power moonroof, 528i | 1050 | 865 |
| Navigation system, 528i | 2690 | 2420 |
| 540i | 2500 | 2250 |
| *528i includes wood interior trim.* | | |
| Comfort 16-way power front seats | 1200 | 965 |
| *Includes power lumbar support. 528i requires Premium Pkg.* | | |
| Power lumbar support, 528i, 540i automatic | 400 | 325 |
| *NA with sport seats.* | | |
| Sport seats, 540i automatic | NC | NC |
| *Requires Sport Pkg.* | | |
| Split folding rear seat | 575 | 470 |
| *Includes ski sack. 528i requires Premium Pkg.* | | |
| 14-speaker audio system | 1500 | 1240 |
| *Includes upgraded amplifier and digital signal processor.* | | |
| Heated front seats | 500 | 410 |
| Heated front seats and steering wheel | 650 | 535 |
| Power rear and manual rear side sunshades | 575 | 470 |

## Appearance and Miscellaneous

| | | |
|---|---|---|
| Metallic paint, 528i | 475 | 390 |
| 540i | NC | NC |
| Sport alloy wheels, 540i manual | 300 | 245 |

# BMW 7-SERIES

*BMW 740iL*

## SPECIFICATIONS

| | 4-door sedan | 4-door sedan |
|---|---|---|
| Wheelbase, in. | 115.4 | 120.9 |

| | 4-door sedan | 4-door sedan |
|---|---|---|
| Overall length, in. | 196.2 | 201.7 |
| Overall width, in. | 73.3 | 73.3 |
| Overall height, in. | 56.5 | 56.1 |
| Curb weight, lbs. | 4255 | 4288 |
| Cargo vol., cu. ft. | 13.0 | 13.0 |
| Fuel capacity, gals. | 22.5 | 22.5 |
| Seating capacity | 5 | 5 |
| Front head room, in. | 37.7 | 37.7 |
| Max. front leg room, in. | 41.9 | 41.9 |
| Rear head room, in. | 38.1 | 38.1 |
| Min. rear leg room, in. | 36.7 | 41.9 |

## ENGINES

| | dohc V-8 | ohc V-12 |
|---|---|---|
| Size, liters/cu. in. | 4.4/268 | 5.4/328 |
| Horsepower @ rpm | 282@ 5700 | 322@ 5000 |
| Torque (lbs./ft.) @ rpm | 310@ 3900 | 361@ 3900 |
| Availability | S[1] | S[2] |
| **EPA city/highway mpg** | | |
| 5-speed OD automatic | 17/24 | 15/20 |

1. 740i, 740iL. 2. 750iL.

| BMW 7-Series | Retail Price | Dealer Invoice |
|---|---|---|
| 740i 4-door sedan | $61500 | $54495 |
| 740iL 4-door sedan | 65500 | 57345 |
| 750iL 4-door sedan | 92100 | 80610 |
| Destination charge | 570 | 570 |

750iL adds $1700 Gas Guzzler Tax.

## STANDARD EQUIPMENT:

**740i:** 4.4-liter dohc V-8 engine, 5-speed automatic transmission w/Adaptive Transmission Control, All Season Traction, driver- and passenger-side air bags, front side-impact air bags, side head protection system, anti-lock 4-wheel disc brakes, variable-assist power steering, power tilt/telescopic steering wheel with memory, cruise control, air conditioning, automatic climate control system with dual controls, interior air filtration system, 14-way power front seats with driver-side memory system, 4-way lumbar support adjustment, leather upholstery, walnut interior trim, door and seatback pockets, folding rear seatback, power windows, power door locks, heated power mirrors with 3-position memory, remote keyless entry, remote decklid release, variable intermittent wipers, heated windshield-washer jets, heated driver-side door lock, rear head rests, front and rear storage armrests, automatic day/night rearview mirror, front and rear reading lamps, illuminated visor mirrors, tachometer, trip odometer, Service Interval Indicator, Active Check Control system, onboard computer, rear defogger, power moonroof, 10-speaker AM/FM/cassette with diversity antenna and steering wheel controls, cargo net, Electronic Damping Control, theft-deterrent system, tinted glass, fog lamps, tool kit, 235/60HR16 tires, cast alloy wheels.

**740iL** adds: 16-way power Comfort Seats, 6-inch longer wheelbase.

**750iL** adds: 5.4-liter V-12 engine, ASC+T traction control with Dynamic Stability Control, heated seats, heated steering wheel, power rear seats with power lumbar adjustment, power rear headrests, cellular telephone, 14-speaker premium sound system w/CD and digital sound processor, 6-disc CD changer, power rear sunshade, parking distance control, ski sack, self-leveling rear suspension, ventilated rear disc brakes, Xenon headlamps, headlight washers, forged alloy wheels.

## OPTIONAL EQUIPMENT:

| | Retail Price | Dealer Invoice |
|---|---|---|
| **Major Packages** | | |
| Cold Weather Pkg., 740i, 740iL | $825 | $685 |
| *Heated steering wheel, headlight washers, ski sack.* | | |
| **Safety Features** | | |
| Rear side-impact air bags | 385 | 320 |
| Break-resistant security glass, 740iL, 750iL | 2600 | 2160 |
| **Comfort and Convenience** | | |
| Heated front seats, 740i, 740iL | 500 | 410 |
| 16-way power Comfort Seats, 740i | 1200 | 965 |
| *Includes 2-way power upper backrest adjustment, power lumbar support.* | | |
| Navigation system | 2500 | 2250 |
| 14-speaker premium sound system, 740i, 740iL | 2100 | 1745 |
| *Includes CD player and digital sound processor.* | | |
| Parking distance control, 740iL | 900 | 750 |
| Power rear sunshade, 740iL | 740 | 615 |
| **Appearance and Miscellaneous** | | |
| Self-leveling rear suspension, 740iL | 1100 | 915 |
| Electronic Damping Control, 740i, 740iL | 2000 | 1660 |

# BUICK CENTURY

## SPECIFICATIONS

| | 4-door sedan |
|---|---|
| Wheelbase, in. | 109.0 |

*Buick Century Limited*

| | 4-door sedan |
|---|---|
| Overall length, in. | 194.6 |
| Overall width, in. | 72.7 |
| Overall height, in. | 56.6 |
| Curb weight, lbs. | 3335 |
| Cargo vol., cu. ft. | 16.7 |
| Fuel capacity, gals. | 17.0 |
| Seating capacity | 6 |
| Front head room, in. | 39.3 |
| Max. front leg room, in. | 42.4 |
| Rear head room, in. | 37.4 |
| Min. rear leg room, in. | 37.5 |

## ENGINES

| | ohv V-6 |
|---|---|
| Size, liters/cu. in. | 3.1/191 |
| Horsepower @ rpm | 160@ 5200 |
| Torque (lbs./ft.) @ rpm | 185@ 4000 |
| Availability | S |

**EPA city/highway mpg**

| | |
|---|---|
| 4-speed OD automatic | 20/29 |

| **Buick Century** | Retail Price | Dealer Invoice |
|---|---|---|
| Custom 4-door sedan | $18215 | $17031 |
| Limited 4-door sedan | 19575 | 18303 |
| Destination charge | 550 | 550 |

## STANDARD EQUIPMENT:

**Custom:** 3.1-liter V-6 engine, 4-speed automatic transmission, driver- and passenger-side air bags, anti-lock brakes, daytime running lamps, power steering, tilt steering wheel, air conditioning, cloth reclining 55/45 front bench seat, front storage armrest w/cupholders, rear armrest w/cupholders, automatic power door locks, power windows, power mirrors, coolant-temperature gauge, trip odometer, AM/FM radio, digital clock, rear defogger, interior air filter, remote keyless entry, variable intermittent wipers, visor mirrors, rear heat ducts, tinted glass, solar-control windshield and rear window, Pass-Key theft-deterrent system, 205/70R15 tires, wheel covers.

**Limited** adds: variable-assist power steering, dual automatic climate control, body-colored heated power mirrors, illuminated visor mirrors, retained accessory power, rear courtesy/reading lights, floormats, striping.

## OPTIONAL EQUIPMENT:

| | Retail Price | Dealer Invoice |
|---|---|---|

### Major Packages

Popular Pkg. SB, Custom .............................................. $330    $283
*Cruise control, cargo net, map lights on inside rearview mirror, floormats.*

Premium Pkg. SC, Custom............................................ 830    714
*Popular Pkg SB plus 6-way power driver seat, cassette player.*

Luxury Pkg. SE, Limited................................................ 525    452
*Cruise control, rear storage armrest with cupholders, cassette player, map lights on inside rearview mirror, cargo net.*

Prestige Pkg. SF, Limited............................................. 1620    1393
*Luxury Pkg. SE plus dual automatic climate control, 6-way power driver and passenger seats, upgraded cassette player with automatic tone control and anti-theft feature, Concert Sound II speakers, steering-wheel radio controls, integrated antenna, automatic day/night inside mirror.*

### Safety Features

Integrated child seat, Custom ......................................... 100    86

### Comfort and Convenience

OnStar System............................................................. 895    761
*Includes Global Positioning System, voice-activated cellular telephone, roadside assistance, emergency services. Requires dealer installation charge and monthly service charges.*

Dual automatic climate control,
   Custom w/Pkg. SC ..................................................... 45    39

Leather upholstery, Limited ............................................. 550    473
*Includes leather-wrapped steering wheel.*

6-way power driver seat................................................. 305    262

Cruise control .............................................................. 225    194

Power glass sunroof...................................................... 695    598
*Custom requires Premium Pkg. SC, automatic day/night inside mirror, and illuminated visor mirrors. Limited requires Prestige Pkg. SF.*

Automatic day/night inside mirror, Custom ..................... 217    187
   Limited ...................................................................... 80    69
*Custom includes illuminated visor mirrors. Custom requires Premium Pkg. SC. Limited requires Luxury Pkg. SE.*

| | Retail Price | Dealer Invoice |
|---|---|---|
| Heated power mirrors, Custom....................................... | $58 | $50 |
| *Requires option pkg.* | | |
| Illuminated visor mirrors, Custom w/Pkg. SC ............... | 137 | 118 |
| Rear storage armrest with cupholders, Limited.............. | 45 | 39 |
| Cassette player ............................................................. | 195 | 168 |
| Upgraded cassette player, | | |
|    Custom w/Pkg. SB, Limited ....................................... | 220 | 189 |
|    Custom w/Pkg. SC, Limited w/Pkg. SE ...................... | 25 | 22 |
|    *Includes automatic tone control and anti-theft feature. Requires Concert Sound II speakers.* | | |
| CD player, Custom w/Pkg. SB, Limited.......................... | 320 | 275 |
|    Custom w/Pkg. SC, Limited w/Pkg. SE ...................... | 125 | 108 |
|    Limited w/Pkg. SF........................................................ | 100 | 86 |
|    *Includes automatic tone control and anti-theft feature. Requires Concert Sound II speakers.* | | |
| CD/cassette player, Custom w/Pkg. SB, Limited............ | 420 | 361 |
|    Custom w/Pkg. SC, Limited w/Pkg. SE ...................... | 225 | 194 |
|    Limited w/Pkg. SF........................................................ | 200 | 172 |
|    *Includes automatic tone control and anti-theft feature. Requires Concert Sound II speakers.* | | |
| Concert Sound II speakers ............................................ | 70 | 60 |
|    *Custom requires option pkg.* | | |
| Integrated antenna........................................................ | 40 | 34 |
|    *Requires option pkg.* | | |
| Steering-wheel radio controls....................................... | 125 | 108 |
|    *Requires upgraded cassette player, CD player, or cassette/CD player. Requires cruise control. Custom requires option pkg.* | | |
| Trunk-mounted CD changer prep pkg. .......................... | 50 | 43 |
|    *Requires upgraded cassette player, CD player, or cassette/CD player. Custom requires option pkg.* | | |
| Cargo net...................................................................... | 30 | 26 |
| Floormats, Custom ........................................................ | 45 | 39 |

## Appearance and Miscellaneous

| | | |
|---|---|---|
| Striping, Custom ........................................................... | 75 | 65 |
| Alloy wheels .................................................................. | 375 | 323 |
| 205/70R15 whitewall tires .............................................. | 150 | 129 |

# BUICK LeSABRE

## SPECIFICATIONS

| | 4-door sedan |
|---|---|
| Wheelbase, in. .......................................................... | 110.8 |

*Prices are accurate at time of publication; subject to manufacturer's change.*

# BUICK

*Buick LeSabre Limited*

|  | 4-door sedan |
| --- | --- |
| Overall length, in. | 200.8 |
| Overall width, in. | 74.4 |
| Overall height, in. | 55.6 |
| Curb weight, lbs. | 3441 |
| Cargo vol., cu. ft. | 17.0 |
| Fuel capacity, gals. | 18.0 |
| Seating capacity | 6 |
| Front head room, in. | 38.8 |
| Max. front leg room, in. | 42.6 |
| Rear head room, in. | 37.8 |
| Min. rear leg room, in. | 40.4 |

## ENGINES

|  | ohv V-6 |
| --- | --- |
| Size, liters/cu. in. | 3.8/231 |
| Horsepower @ rpm | 205@ 5200 |
| Torque (lbs./ft.) @ rpm | 230@ 4000 |
| Availability | S |

**EPA city/highway mpg**

| 4-speed OD automatic | 19/30 |
| --- | --- |

| **Buick LeSabre** | Retail Price | Dealer Invoice |
| --- | --- | --- |
| Custom 4-door sedan | $22465 | $20555 |
| Limited 4-door sedan | 25790 | 23598 |
| Destination charge | 605 | 605 |

## STANDARD EQUIPMENT:

**Custom:** 3.8-liter V-6 engine, 4-speed automatic transmission, driver- and passenger-side air bags, anti-lock brakes, air conditioning, power steering, tilt steering wheel, cruise control, 55/45 cloth seats, front storage armrest with cupholders, manual front seatback recliners, power door locks, power windows, AM/FM radio with clock, intermittent wipers, color-keyed left remote and right manual mirrors, rear defogger, instrument panel courtesy lights, trip odometer, visor mirrors, Twilight Sentinel headlamp control,

Pass-Key theft-deterrent system, solar-control tinted glass, daytime running lights, 205/70R15 all-season tires, wheel covers.

**Limited** adds: front and rear automatic climate control with front dual temperature controls, remote keyless entry, memory door locks, power remote decklid release, 6-way power driver and passenger seats, voltmeter, tachometer, oil pressure and coolant temperature gauges, oil level/change monitor, cassette player, Concert Sound II speakers, rear armrest, heated power mirrors, illuminated visor mirrors, front- and rear-door courtesy lights, front and rear reading lights, floormats, trunk net, striping, 205/70R15 all-season whitewall tires, alloy wheels.

## OPTIONAL EQUIPMENT:

|  | Retail Price | Dealer Invoice |
|---|---|---|
| **Major Packages** | | |
| Luxury Pkg. SD, Custom | $716 | $616 |
| *Includes cassette player, cargo net, floormats, striping, 205/70R15 all-season whitewall tires, alloy wheels.* | | |
| Prestige Pkg. SE, Custom | 1668 | 1434 |
| Limited | 659 | 567 |
| *Luxury Pkg. SD plus 6-way power driver's seat, memory door locks, remote keyless entry, voltmeter, tachometer, oil-pressure and coolant-temperature gauges, oil-life and oil-level monitor, power mirrors, Lighting Pkg. (illuminated visor mirrors, map lights), power remote decklid release, Concert Sound II speakers, door-edge guards.* | | |
| Gran Touring Pkg., Custom w/Pkg. SE, Limited | 512 | 440 |
| Limited w/Pkg. SE | 337 | 290 |
| *Includes variable-assist power steering, Gran Touring Suspension, 3:06 axle ratio, automatic level control, leather-wrapped steering wheel, 215/60R16 touring tires, alloy wheels. Requires traction control.* | | |

### Powertrains

| | | |
|---|---|---|
| Traction control system, Custom w/Pkg. SE, Limited | 175 | 151 |

### Comfort and Convenience

| | | |
|---|---|---|
| OnStar System | 895 | 761 |
| *Includes Global Positioning System, voice activated cellular telephone, roadside assistance, emergency services. Requires dealer installation charge and monthly service charges.* | | |
| Leather upholstery, Custom | 995 | 856 |
| Limited | 550 | 473 |
| *Custom requires option pkg. Custom with Luxury Pkg. SD requires power mirrors, 6-way power driver's seat, remote keyless entry, memory door locks, remote decklid release.* | | |
| 6-way power driver's seat, Custom | 305 | 262 |
| *Requires power mirrors and cruise control. With Luxury Pkg. SD, requires power mirrors, remote keyless entry, memory door locks, remote decklid release.* | | |

*Prices are accurate at time of publication; subject to manufacturer's change.*

|  | Retail Price | Dealer Invoice |
|---|---|---|
| 6-way power passenger seat, Custom w/Pkg. SE ......... | $305 | $262 |
| Power mirrors, Custom.................................................. | 78 | 67 |
| *Requires 6-way power driver's seat and cruise control. With Luxury Pkg. SD, requires 6-way power driver's seat, remote keyless entry, memory door locks, and remote decklid release.* | | |
| Automatic day/night mirror, Limited ............................... | 70 | 60 |
| *Includes compass.* | | |
| Lighting Pkg., Custom w/Pkg. SD ................................. | 116 | 100 |
| *Map lights, illuminated visor mirrors.* | | |
| Power remote decklid release, Custom w/Pkg. SD ....... | 60 | 52 |
| *Requires remote keyless entry, 6-way power driver's seat, power mirrors, and memory door locks.* | | |
| Remote keyless entry, Custom w/Pkg. SD .................... | 135 | 116 |
| *Requires remote decklid release, 6-way power driver's seat, power mirrors, and memory door locks.* | | |
| Memory door locks, Custom w/Pkg. SD ........................ | 25 | 22 |
| *Requires remote decklid release, remote keyless entry, 6-way power driver's seat, and power mirrors.* | | |
| UN6 audio system, Custom............................................ | 195 | 168 |
| *Includes cassette player with clock.* | | |
| UL0 audio system, Custom w/Pkg. SE, Limited............. | 150 | 129 |
| *Includes cassette player with clock, automatic tone control, and steering-wheel radio controls.* | | |
| UN0 audio system, Custom w/Pkg. SE, Limited ............ | 250 | 215 |
| Limited w/Pkg. SE ................................................... | 100 | 86 |
| *Includes CD player with clock, automatic tone control, and steering-wheel radio controls.* | | |
| UP0 audio system, Custom w/Pkg. SE, Limited ............ | 350 | 301 |
| Limited w/Pkg. SE ................................................... | 200 | 172 |
| *UN0 audio system plus cassette player.* | | |
| Floormats, Custom ........................................................ | 45 | 39 |

## Appearance and Miscellaneous

|  | Retail Price | Dealer Invoice |
|---|---|---|
| Starter interrupt, Limited ............................................... | 159 | 137 |
| Cornering lamps, Limited .............................................. | 60 | 52 |
| Engine block heater...................................................... | 18 | 15 |
| Automatic level control, Custom w/Pkg. SE, Limited ..... | 175 | 151 |
| Alloy wheels, Custom .................................................... | 325 | 280 |
| Locking wire wheel covers, | | |
| Custom w/option pkg., Limited................................... | NC | NC |
| *NA with Gran Touring Pkg.* | | |
| 205/70R15 whitewall tires, Custom ............................... | 76 | 65 |
| *NA with Gran Touring Pkg.* | | |
| 205/70R15 self-sealing whitewall tires, Custom ............ | 226 | 194 |
| Custom w/option pkg., Limited................................... | 150 | 129 |

# BUICK PARK AVENUE

*Buick Park Avenue Ultra*

## SPECIFICATIONS

|  | 4-door sedan |
|---|---|
| Wheelbase, in. | 113.8 |
| Overall length, in. | 206.8 |
| Overall width, in. | 74.7 |
| Overall height, in. | 57.4 |
| Curb weight, lbs. | 3740 |
| Cargo vol., cu. ft. | 19.1 |
| Fuel capacity, gals. | 18.5 |
| Seating capacity | 6 |
| Front head room, in. | 39.8 |
| Max. front leg room, in. | 42.4 |
| Rear head room, in. | 38.0 |
| Min. rear leg room, in. | 41.1 |

## ENGINES

|  | ohv V-6 | Super ohv V-6 |
|---|---|---|
| Size, liters/cu. in. | 3.8/231 | 3.8/231 |
| Horsepower @ rpm | 205@ 5200 | 240@ 5200 |
| Torque (lbs./ft.) @ rpm | 230@ 4000 | 280@ 3600 |
| Availability | S[1] | S[2] |
| **EPA city/highway mpg** | | |
| 4-speed OD automatic | 19/28 | 18/27 |

*1. Base model. 2. Ultra.*

| Buick Park Avenue | Retail Price | Dealer Invoice |
|---|---|---|
| Base 4-door sedan | $30675 | $27761 |
| Ultra 4-door sedan | 35550 | 32173 |

*Prices are accurate at time of publication; subject to manufacturer's change.*

# BUICK

|                      | Retail Price | Dealer Invoice |
|----------------------|--------------|----------------|
| Destination charge ....................................................... | $665 | $665 |

## STANDARD EQUIPMENT:

**Base:** 3.8-liter V-6 engine, 4-speed automatic transmission, driver- and passenger-side air bags, anti-lock 4-wheel disc brakes, daytime running lights, air conditioning w/automatic climate control with dual temperature controls, rear-seat climate controls, interior air filtration, power steering, tilt steering wheel, cruise control, 10-way power 55/45 cloth front seat, front storage armrest with cupholders, rear armrest with cupholders, rear head restraints, rear seat pass-through, power windows with passenger lockout, power door locks, power mirrors, remote keyless entry with perimeter lighting, overhead console, rear defogger, tachometer, trip odometer, coolant-temperature gauge, AM/FM/cassette player, Concert Sound II speakers, rear-window antenna, remote decklid and fuel-door releases, front and rear reading and courtesy lights, illuminated visor mirrors, intermittent wipers, Twilight Sentinel headlamp control, cargo net, floormats, automatic level-control suspension, Pass-Key theft-deterrent system with starter interrupt, solar-control tinted glass, cornering lamps, 225/60R16 tires, alloy wheels.

**Ultra** adds: supercharged 3.8-liter V-6 engine, traction-control system, leather upholstery, memory driver seat and memory mirrors w/parallel park assist passenger-side mirror, memory climate control and radio presets, heated mirrors w/driver-side automatic day/night mirror, Seating Pkg. (power lumbar adjustment, heated front seats, power front and manual rear articulating headrests), rear-seat storage armrest with cupholders, leather-wrapped steering wheel, cellular phone readiness pkg., moisture-sensing windshield wipers, driver information center (tire- and oil-pressure warning, oil-life and oil-level monitors, low-washer-fluid, low-coolant, and door-ajar indicators, and trip computer), CD player with automatic tone control and steering-wheel controls, rear illuminated vanity mirrors, wood door trim, Concert Sound III speakers, 4-note horn.

## OPTIONAL EQUIPMENT:
### Major Packages

| | | |
|---|---|---|
| SE Prestige Pkg., Base.................................................... | 890 | 765 |

*Memory driver-seat and mirrors w/parallel park assist passenger-side mirror, heated mirrors, automatic day/night driver-side mirror, automatic day/night rearview mirror, universal garage door opener, UL0 audio system (AM/FM/cassette player with clock, seek and scan, automatic tone control, and steering-wheel radio controls), moisture-sensing windshield wipers, driver information center (tire- and oil-pressure warning; volt, oil-life, and oil-level monitors; low-washer-fluid, low-coolant, and door-ajar indicators; and trip computer).*

| | Retail Price | Dealer Invoice |
|---|---|---|
| Gran Touring Pkg., Base w/SE Pkg. | $240 | $206 |
| Ultra | 105 | 90 |

*Includes Gran Touring suspension, aluminum wheels, and 225/60R16 touring tires. Base w/option pkg. also includes 3.05 axle ratio and leather-wrapped steering wheel. Base also includes variable-assist power steering. Requires automatic day/night mirror. Base also requires traction control.*

## Powertrains

| | | |
|---|---|---|
| Traction-control system, Base w/SE Pkg. | 175 | 151 |

## Comfort and Convenience

| | | |
|---|---|---|
| OnStar System | 895 | 761 |

*Includes Global Positioning System, voice-activated cellular telephone, roadside assistance, emergency services. Requires dealer installation charge and monthly service charges.*

| | | |
|---|---|---|
| UL0 audio system, Base | 150 | 129 |

*Includes AM/FM/cassette player with clock, seek and scan, automatic tone control, and steering-wheel radio controls.*

| | | |
|---|---|---|
| UN0 audio system, Base | 250 | 215 |
| Base w/Pkg. SE | 100 | 86 |

*Includes AM/FM/CD player with clock, seek and scan, automatic tone control, and steering-wheel radio controls.*

| | | |
|---|---|---|
| UP0 audio system, Base | 350 | 301 |
| Base w/SE Pkg. | 200 | 172 |
| Ultra | 100 | 86 |

*UN0 audio system plus cassette player.*

| | | |
|---|---|---|
| Trunk-mounted CD changer, Ultra | 595 | 512 |
| Concert Sound III speakers, Base w/SE Pkg. | 250 | 215 |
| Automatic day/night rearview mirror w/compass | 70 | 60 |

*Base requires SE Pkg.*

| | | |
|---|---|---|
| Electric sliding sunroof | 995 | 856 |

*Base requires SE Prestige Pkg.*

| | | |
|---|---|---|
| Seating Pkg., Base | 380 | 327 |

*Power lumbar adjustment, heated front seats, and power front articulating headrest.*

| | | |
|---|---|---|
| Convenience Console/Five Person Seating Pkg. | 185 | 159 |

*Bucket seats, console with writing surface and accommodations for phone and fax, cupholders, and auxiliary power outlets. Base requires leather upholstery, rear storage armrest, Cellular Phone Readiness Pkg.*

| | | |
|---|---|---|
| Leather upholstery, Base | 600 | 516 |
| Rear storage armrest, Base | 50 | 43 |

*Requires leather upholstery.*

| | | |
|---|---|---|
| Cellular Phone Readiness Pkg., Base | 75 | 65 |

*Requires optional radio.*

| | Retail Price | Dealer Invoice |
|---|---|---|
| Eyecue Head-up display | $275 | $237 |

*Base requires cellular phone readiness pkg., SE Prestige Pkg.*

## Appearance and Miscellaneous

| | | |
|---|---|---|
| Four-note horn, Base w/SE Pkg. | 28 | 24 |
| Engine-block heater | 18 | 15 |
| Chrome-plated alloy wheels | 695 | 598 |
| 225/60R16 whitewall tires, Base | 85 | 73 |

*NA with Gran Touring Pkg.*

# BUICK REGAL

*Buick Regal GS*

## SPECIFICATIONS

| | 4-door sedan |
|---|---|
| Wheelbase, in. | 109.0 |
| Overall length, in. | 196.2 |
| Overall width, in. | 72.7 |
| Overall height, in. | 56.6 |
| Curb weight, lbs. | 3447 |
| Cargo vol., cu. ft. | 16.7 |
| Fuel capacity, gals. | 17.0 |
| Seating capacity | 5 |
| Front head room, in. | 39.3 |
| Max. front leg room, in. | 42.4 |
| Rear head room, in. | 37.4 |
| Min. rear leg room, in. | 36.9 |

## ENGINES

| | ohv V-6 | Super ohv V-6 |
|---|---|---|
| Size, liters/cu. in. | 3.8/231 | 3.8/231 |
| Horsepower @ rpm | 195@ 5200 | 240@ 5200 |
| Torque (lbs./ft.) @ rpm | 220@ 4000 | 280@ 3600 |
| Availability | S[1] | S[2] |

**EPA city/highway mpg**

| | | |
|---|---|---|
| 4-speed OD automatic | 19/30 | 17/27 |

1. LS. 2. GS.

| Buick Regal | Retail Price | Dealer Invoice |
|---|---|---|
| LS 4-door sedan | $20945 | $19165 |
| GS 4-door sedan | 23690 | 21676 |
| Destination charge | 550 | 550 |

## STANDARD EQUIPMENT:

**LS:** 3.8-liter V-6 engine, 4-speed automatic transmission, traction control, driver- and passenger-side air bags, anti-lock 4-wheel disc brakes, daytime running lamps with Twilight Sentinel, magnetic variable assist power steering, leather-wrapped tilt steering wheel, cruise control, air conditioning, dual zone manual climate control, air filtration system, cloth reclining front bucket seats, front console w/dual cupholders and auxiliary power outlet, rear armrest w/dual cupholders, remote keyless entry, programmable automatic power door locks, lockout protection, power windows w/driver's express down feature, trip odometer, tachometer, temperature gauge, warning lights for door ajar and trunk ajar, intermittent wipers, Pass-Key theft-deterrent system, color-keyed heated power mirrors, rear defogger, rear seat pass-through, courtesy/map lights on inside rearview mirror, visor vanity mirrors, AM/FM/cassette player with clock, retained accessory power, low fuel reminder tone, solar-control tinted glass, integral fog lamps, 215/70R15 tires, wheel covers.

**GS** adds: supercharged 3.8-liter V-6 engine, heavy-duty 4-speed automatic transmission with driver selectable shift control, traction control, leather seats, power driver seat, front and rear floormats, rear courtesy and reading lamps, automatic radio tone control, Concert Sound II speakers, dual illuminated visor vanity mirrors, driver information center (oil change monitor, oil level, fuel/engine information), Gran Touring suspension, bright exhaust outlets, 225/60R16 touring tires, alloy wheels.

## OPTIONAL EQUIPMENT:
### Major Packages

| | | |
|---|---|---|
| Luxury Pkg. SB, LS | 587 | 505 |

*Includes front and rear floormats, reading/map lights, dual illuminated visor vanity mirrors, 6-way power driver's seat, integrated rear window antenna, trunk convenience net.*

| | | |
|---|---|---|
| Prestige Pkg. SC, LS | 887 | 763 |

*Luxury Pkg. plus automatic day/night rearview mirror, cassette player, steering-wheel-mounted radio controls, automatic radio tone control, Concert Sound II speakers.*

*Prices are accurate at time of publication; subject to manufacturer's change.*

# BUICK

|  | Retail Price | Dealer Invoice |
|---|---|---|
| Luxury Pkg. SE, GS ..................................................... | $330 | $284 |

*Includes dual zone automatic climate control, steering-wheel-mounted radio controls, integrated radio antenna, reading/map lights, illuminated visor mirrors, trunk convenience net.*

| Prestige Pkg. SF, GS.................................................... | 915 | 787 |

*Luxury Pkg. SE plus cassette/CD player with automatic tone control, automatic day/night rearview mirror, 6-way power passenger's seat.*

| Gran Touring Pkg., LS ................................................. | 552 | 475 |

*Consists of Gran Touring suspension and 225/60R16 blackwall tires, alloy wheels. Requires option pkg.*

## Safety Features

| Integrated rear child safety seat...................................... | 100 | 86 |

## Comfort and Convenience

| OnStar System............................................................. | 895 | 761 |

*Includes Global Positioning System, voice-activated cellular telephone, roadside assistance, emergency services. Requires dealer installation charge and monthly service charges.*

| Cellular phone prewire package ....................................... | 75 | 64 |
| Driver information center, LS w/Pkg. SC......................... | 75 | 65 |

*Includes oil change monitor, oil level, fuel/engine information center.*

| Steering-wheel-mounted radio controls, LS.................... | 125 | 108 |
| CD player prep package ................................................. | 50 | 43 |
| ULO audio system, LS .................................................. | 95 | 82 |

*Includes automatic tone control and Concert Sound II speakers.*

| UPO audio system, LS .................................................. | 295 | 254 |
| LS w/Pkg. SC, GS...................................................... | 200 | 172 |

*Includes CD/cassette player and Concert Sound II speakers.*

| Power moonroof ............................................................ | 695 | 597 |

*Includes automatic day/night rearview mirror, map lights. Requires option pkg.*

| Leather bucket seats, LS ............................................... | 600 | 516 |

*Requires option pkg.*

| Heated front seats ........................................................ | 225 | 193 |

*LS requires leather seats.*

| 6-way power driver's seat, LS........................................ | 305 | 262 |
| 6-way power passenger's seat, LS ................................. | 305 | 262 |

*Requires Prestige Pkg. SC.*

| Electrochromatic rearview mirror .................................... | 80 | 69 |

*LS requires Luxury Pkg. SB.*

| Floormats, LS................................................................ | 45 | 38 |

## Appearance and Miscellaneous

| Engine block heater....................................................... | 18 | 15 |

| | Retail Price | Dealer Invoice |
|---|---|---|
| Alloy wheels, LS | $375 | $323 |
| 16-inch chrome alloy wheels | 650 | 559 |

LS requires Gran Touring Pkg.

# BUICK RIVIERA

*Buick Riviera*

## SPECIFICATIONS

| | 2-door coupe |
|---|---|
| Wheelbase, in. | 113.8 |
| Overall length, in. | 207.2 |
| Overall width, in. | 75.0 |
| Overall height, in. | 54.6 |
| Curb weight, lbs. | 3699 |
| Cargo vol., cu. ft. | 17.4 |
| Fuel capacity, gals. | 20.0 |
| Seating capacity | 5 |
| Front head room, in. | 38.2 |
| Max. front leg room, in. | 42.6 |
| Rear head room, in. | 36.2 |
| Min. rear leg room, in. | 37.1 |

## ENGINES

| | Super ohv V-6 |
|---|---|
| Size, liters/cu. in. | 3.8/231 |
| Horsepower @ rpm | 240@ 5200 |
| Torque (lbs./ft.) @ rpm | 280@ 3600 |
| Availability | S |

*Prices are accurate at time of publication; subject to manufacturer's change.*

**EPA city/highway mpg**
4-speed OD automatic.................................................... 18/27

| **Buick Riviera** | Retail Price | Dealer Invoice |
|---|---|---|
| 2-door coupe .................................................. | $32500 | $29413 |
| Destination charge ......................................... | 665 | 665 |

## STANDARD EQUIPMENT:

**Base:** 3.8-liter supercharged V-6 engine, 4-speed automatic transmission, driver- and passenger-side air bags, anti-lock 4-wheel disc brakes, variable-assist power steering, leather-wrapped tilt steering wheel, cruise control, automatic air conditioning with dual climate controls, rear-seat heating vents, leather upholstery, cloth 6-way power front bucket seats with power recliners, front storage armrest with cupholders, rear-seat armrest, power windows, power heated mirrors, automatic power door locks, remote keyless entry system (w/perimeter lighting, security feedback and instant alarm), tachometer, coolant-temperature gauge, illuminated passenger-side visor mirror, remote fuel door and decklid releases, AM/FM/cassette/CD player with clock, Concert Sound II speakers, power antenna, intermittent wipers, rear defogger, front and rear reading and courtesy lights, Twilight Sentinel headlamp control, cargo net, automatic level control suspension, Pass-Key theft-deterrent system, trip odometer, solar-control tinted glass, daytime running lights, 225/60R16 all-season tires, alloy wheels.

## OPTIONAL EQUIPMENT:

### Major Packages

SE Prestige Pkg............................................... 1145 985

*Traction-control system, driver-seat and passenger-seat power lumbar adjustment, automatic day/night rearview and driver-side mirrors, steering-wheel-mounted radio controls, driver-side illuminated visor mirror, theft-deterrent system, universal garage door opener, cornering lamps, striping.*

### Comfort and Convenience

OnStar System................................................. 895 761

*Includes Global Positioning System, voice-activated cellular telephone, roadside assistance, emergency services. Requires dealer installation charge and monthly service charges.*

Power sunroof with sunshade.......................... 995 856
Memory/heated front seats .............................. 415 357

*Includes memory outside mirrors.*

Automatic day/night rearview mirror ............... 70 60

*Includes compass. Requires SE Prestige Pkg.*

| **Appearance and Miscellaneous** | Retail Price | Dealer Invoice |
|---|---|---|
| Bright white diamond paint | $395 | $340 |
| Engine block heater | 18 | 15 |
| Chrome alloy wheels | 695 | 598 |

# CADILLAC CATERA

Cadillac Catera

## SPECIFICATIONS

| | 4-door sedan |
|---|---|
| Wheelbase, in. | 107.4 |
| Overall length, in. | 194.0 |
| Overall width, in. | 70.3 |
| Overall height, in. | 56.3 |
| Curb weight, lbs. | 3770 |
| Cargo vol., cu. ft. | 14.5 |
| Fuel capacity, gals. | 18.0 |
| Seating capacity | 5 |
| Front head room, in. | 38.7 |
| Max. front leg room, in. | 42.2 |
| Rear head room, in. | 38.4 |
| Min. rear leg room, in. | 37.5 |

## ENGINES

| | dohc V-6 |
|---|---|
| Size, liters/cu. in. | 3.0/181 |
| Horsepower @ rpm | 200@ 6000 |
| Torque (lbs./ft.) @ rpm | 192@ 3600 |
| Availability | S |
| **EPA city/highway mpg** | |
| 4-speed OD automatic | 18/24 |

| **Cadillac Catera** | Retail Price | Dealer Invoice |
|---|---|---|
| Base 4-door sedan | $29995 | $28880 |

*Prices are accurate at time of publication; subject to manufacturer's change.*

# CADILLAC

|  | Retail Price | Dealer Invoice |
|---|---|---|
| Base 4-door sedan w/leather interior | $33610 | $31244 |
| Destination charge | 640 | 640 |

## STANDARD EQUIPMENT:

**Base:** 3.0-liter dohc V-6 engine, 4-speed automatic transmission, dual exhaust, traction control, driver- and passenger-side air bags, anti-lock 4-wheel disc brakes, daytime running lamps, air conditioning w/dual-zone automatic climate control, back seat air conditioning vent, variable-assist steering, leather-wrapped tilt steering wheel, cruise control, cloth front bucket seats, 8-way power driver seat with power recliner, passenger-seat w/power height adjuster and manual recliner, split folding rear bench seat, front and rear articulating head-rests, front console w/storage armrest and cupholders, rear armrests, power windows, automatic power door locks, remote-keyless entry system, heated power mirrors, AM/FM/cassette with eight speakers and Theftlock, integrated rear window antenna, steering-wheel radio controls, intermittent wipers, Driver Information Center, analog instrument cluster, tachometer, coolant-temperature and oil-pressure gauge, voltmeter, trip odometer, outside temperature display, remote fuel-door and decklid release, rear defogger, automatic day/night rearview mirror, illuminated visor mirrors, front and rear reading lights, illuminated entry, automatic parking-brake release, automatic head-lights, wiper-activated headlights, trunk mat and cargo net, floormats, tinted glass, theft-deterrent system, cornering lamps, fog lights, load-leveling suspension, full-size spare, 225/55HR16 tires, alloy wheels.

**Base w/leather upholstery** adds: leather upholstery, 8-way power passenger seat, memory seats and mirrors, universal garage door opener, theft deterrent system w/alarm.

## OPTIONAL EQUIPMENT:
### Comfort and Convenience

| | | |
|---|---|---|
| OnStar System | 895 | 761 |

*Includes Global Positioning System, voice-activated cellular telephone, roadside assistance, emergency services. Requires dealer installation charge and monthly service charges.*

| | | |
|---|---|---|
| Heated front and rear seats | 400 | 340 |
| Power sunroof | 995 | 846 |
| Cassette/CD player | 973 | 827 |

*Includes weatherband, 8-speaker Bose sound system.*

| | | |
|---|---|---|
| Power rear sunshade | 295 | 251 |

### Appearance and Miscellaneous

| | | |
|---|---|---|
| Chrome alloy wheels | 795 | 507 |

# CADILLAC DeVILLE

*Cadillac DeVille*

## SPECIFICATIONS

| | 4-door sedan |
|---|---|
| Wheelbase, in. | 113.8 |
| Overall length, in. | 209.7 |
| Overall width, in. | 76.5 |
| Overall height, in. | 56.0 |
| Curb weight, lbs. | 4012 |
| Cargo vol., cu. ft. | 20.0 |
| Fuel capacity, gals. | 20.0 |
| Seating capacity | 6 |
| Front head room, in. | 38.5 |
| Max. front leg room, in. | 42.6 |
| Rear head room, in. | 38.4 |
| Min. rear leg room, in. | 43.3 |

## ENGINES

| | dohc V-8 | dohc V-8 |
|---|---|---|
| Size, liters/cu. in. | 4.6/279 | 4.6/279 |
| Horsepower @ rpm | 275@ 5600 | 300@ 6000 |
| Torque (lbs./ft.) @ rpm | 300@ 4000 | 295@ 4400 |
| Availability | S[1] | S[2] |
| **EPA city/highway mpg** | | |
| 4-speed OD automatic | 17/26 | 17/26 |

*1. Base, d'Elegance. 2. Concours.*

| Cadillac DeVille | Retail Price | Dealer Invoice |
|---|---|---|
| Base 4-door sedan | $37695 | $34646 |
| d'Elegance 4-door sedan | 41295 | 37940 |
| Concours 4-door sedan | 42295 | 38855 |
| Destination charge | 665 | 665 |

*Prices are accurate at time of publication; subject to manufacturer's change.*

# CADILLAC

## STANDARD EQUIPMENT:

**Base:** 4.6-liter dohc V-8 275-horsepower engine, 4-speed automatic transmission, traction control, driver- and passenger-side air bags, front side-impact air bags, anti-lock 4-wheel disc brakes, daytime running lamps, dual-zone automatic climate control w/outside temperature indicator, Magnasteer variable-assist steering, tilt steering wheel, leather-wrapped steering wheel, cruise control, cloth 8-way power front seats with power recliners, front storage armrest w/cupholders, front and rear articulating headrests, overhead storage compartment, power windows, programmable power locks w/valet lockout, remote-keyless entry system, illuminated entry, heated power mirrors w/driver-side automatic day/night, AM/FM/cassette with six speakers and Theftlock, power antenna, steering-wheel radio and climate controls, driver-side visor storage, illuminated front visor mirrors, intermittent wipers, Driver Information Center, trip odometer, power decklid release and pulldown, remote fuel-door release, rear defogger, Pass-Key II theft-deterrent system, automatic day/night inside rearview mirror, front and rear reading lights, Integrated Chassis Control System, automatic parking-brake release, Twilight Sentinel headlamp control, wiper-activated headlights, trunk mat and cargo net, floormats, automatic level-control suspension, tinted glass, cornering lamps, striping, 225/60R16 all-season whitewall tires, alloy wheels.

**d'Elegance** adds: Comfort/Convenience Pkg. (heated seats, Memory Pkg. [memory seats, mirrors, climate control and radio presets], dual power lumbar adjustment), leather upholstery, Zebrano wood trim, Active Audio System with cassette/CD player and 11 speakers, automatic windshield wipers, rear illuminated visor mirrors, gold trim/badging, chrome alloy wheels.

**Concours** adds: 4.6-liter dohc V-8 300-horsepower engine, dual exhaust, front bucket seats, front floor console, rear storage armrest w/cupholders, analog instrument cluster, tachometer, coolant-temperature gauge, fog lights, continuously variable Road-Sensing Suspension, Stabilitrak, 225/60HR16 blackwall tires, deletes: front storage armrest, gold trim/badging, striping, chrome alloy wheels.

## OPTIONAL EQUIPMENT:

### Major Packages

| | Retail Price | Dealer Invoice |
|---|---|---|
| Comfort/Convenience Pkg., Base ..................................... | $867 | $737 |
| *Heated seats, Memory Pkg. (memory seats, mirrors, climate control, radio presets), dual power lumbar adjustment.* | | |
| Safety/Security Pkg., Base, d'Elegance .......................... | 752 | 639 |
| Concours ......................................................................... | 502 | 427 |
| *Electronic compass, StabiliTrak (Base, d'Elegance), universal garage-door opener, theft-deterrent system.* | | |
| 3000-lb. Trailer Towing Pkg. ............................................. | 110 | 94 |
| *Includes trailer wiring harness, engine oil cooler.* | | |

## Comfort and Convenience

| | Retail Price | Dealer Invoice |
|---|---|---|
| OnStar System...................................................... | $895 | $761 |
| *Includes Global Positioning System, voice-activated cellular telephone, roadside assistance, emergency services. Requires dealer installation charge and monthly service charges.* | | |
| Leather upholstery, Base............................... | 785 | 667 |
| Power sunroof.................................................. | 1550 | 1318 |
| *Concours, d'Elegance delete rear visor mirrors.* | | |
| U1R Active Audio Sound System, Base .......................... | 670 | 570 |
| *AM/FM/cassette/CD with 11 speakers.* | | |
| UM5 Active Audio Sound System, Base.......................... | 770 | 655 |
| d'Elegance, Concours ............................... | 100 | 85 |
| *Includes AM/FM/cassette/CD, digital signal processing, and 11 speakers.* | | |
| 12-disc CD changer............................................. | 595 | 506 |
| Trunk storage system ......................................... | 265 | 225 |

## Appearance and Miscellaneous

| | | |
|---|---|---|
| White diamond or pearl red paint ...................... | 500 | 425 |
| Chrome alloy wheels, Base, Concours.......................... | 795 | 507 |

# CADILLAC ELDORADO

*Cadillac Eldorado Touring Coupe*

## SPECIFICATIONS

| | 2-door coupe |
|---|---|
| Wheelbase, in. ................................................. | 108.0 |
| Overall length, in. ............................................ | 200.6 |
| Overall width, in. .............................................. | 75.5 |
| Overall height, in. ............................................ | 53.6 |
| Curb weight, lbs. .............................................. | 3843 |
| Cargo vol., cu. ft. ............................................. | 15.3 |
| Fuel capacity, gals. .......................................... | 20.0 |
| Seating capacity ............................................... | 5 |
| Front head room, in. ......................................... | 37.8 |

*Prices are accurate at time of publication; subject to manufacturer's change.*

# CADILLAC

|  | 2-door coupe |
|---|---|
| Max. front leg room, in. | 42.6 |
| Rear head room, in. | 38.3 |
| Min. rear leg room, in. | 35.5 |

## ENGINES

|  | dohc V-8 | dohc V-8 |
|---|---|---|
| Size, liters/cu. in. | 4.6/279 | 4.6/279 |
| Horsepower @ rpm | 275@ 5600 | 300@ 6000 |
| Torque (lbs./ft.) @ rpm | 300@ 4000 | 295@ 4400 |
| Availability | S[1] | S[2] |
| **EPA city/highway mpg** | | |
| 4-speed OD automatic | 17/26 | 17/26 |

*1. Base. 2. Touring Coupe.*

| Cadillac Eldorado | Retail Price | Dealer Invoice |
|---|---|---|
| Base 2-door notchback | $38495 | $35378 |
| Touring Coupe 2-door notchback | 42695 | 39221 |
| Destination charge | 665 | 665 |

## STANDARD EQUIPMENT:

**Base:** 4.6-liter dohc V-8 275-horsepower engine, 4-speed automatic transmission, traction control, dual exhaust, anti-lock 4-wheel disc brakes, driver- and passenger-side air bags, daytime running lamps, wiper-activated headlights, Magnasteer variable-assist steering, leather-wrapped steering wheel with controls for radio and climate, tilt steering wheel, automatic climate control air conditioning, cruise control, cloth 8-way power front bucket seats, center console with armrest and storage bins, overhead storage compartment, power windows, automatic power locks, remote keyless entry system, heated power mirrors w/driver-side automatic day/night, rear defogger, automatic day/night rearview mirror, AM/FM/cassette player with six speakers, power antenna, remote fuel-door and decklid release, power decklid pull-down, trip odometer, tachometer, Driver Information Center, Zebrano wood trim, driver-side visor storage flap, intermittent wipers, automatic parking-brake release, Twilight Sentinel headlamp control, illuminated entry, reading lights, illuminated visor mirrors, floormats, trunk mat and cargo net, Integrated Chassis Control System, automatic level control, solar-control tinted glass, valet lockout, Pass-Key II theft-deterrent system, fog lamps, cornering lamps, 225/60R16 tires, alloy wheels.

**Touring Coupe** adds: Comfort/Convenience Pkg. (Memory Pkg. [memory seats, mirrors, climate control, and radio presets], power lumbar adjustment, heated front seats), high-output 4.6-liter dohc V-8 300-horsepower engine, CD player w/Bose sound system, leather upholstery, rear-seat storage armrest with cupholders, analog instrument cluster, coolant-temperature gauge, automatic windshield wiper system, theft-deterrent system w/alarm, continuously-variable Road-Sensing Suspension, Stabilitrak, 225/60HR16 tires.

## OPTIONAL EQUIPMENT:

| | Retail Price | Dealer Invoice |
|---|---|---|

### Major Packages

| | Retail Price | Dealer Invoice |
|---|---|---|
| Comfort/Convenience Pkg., Base | $867 | $737 |
| *Memory Pkg. (memory seats, mirrors, climate control, and radio presets), power lumbar support, heated front seats.* | | |
| Safety/Security Pkg., Base | 502 | 427 |
| Touring Coupe | 207 | 176 |
| *Electronic compass, universal garage-door opener, theft-deterrent system w/alarm (Base).* | | |

### Comfort and Convenience

| | Retail Price | Dealer Invoice |
|---|---|---|
| OnStar System | 895 | 761 |
| *Includes Global Positioning System, voice-activated cellular telephone, roadside assistance, emergency services. Requires dealer installation charge and monthly service charges.* | | |
| Power sunroof | 1550 | 1318 |
| U1R Bose Sound System, Base | 1119 | 951 |
| *Includes AM/FM/cassette/CD player, four Bose amplified speakers, Theftlock.* | | |
| UM5 Bose Sound System, Base | 1219 | 1036 |
| Touring Coupe | 100 | 85 |
| *Includes AM/FM/weatherband/cassette/CD player, digital signal processing, and four Bose amplified speakers, Theftlock.* | | |
| 12-disc CD player | 595 | 506 |
| Leather upholstery, Base | 785 | 667 |
| Trunk storage system, Touring Coupe | 265 | 225 |

### Appearance and Miscellaneous

| | Retail Price | Dealer Invoice |
|---|---|---|
| White diamond or red pearl paint | 500 | 425 |
| Striping, Base | 75 | 64 |
| StabiliTrak, Base | 250 | 213 |
| 225/60ZR16 tires, Touring Coupe | 250 | 213 |
| Chrome alloy wheels | 795 | 507 |

# CADILLAC SEVILLE

## SPECIFICATIONS

| | 4-door sedan |
|---|---|
| Wheelbase, in. | 112.2 |

*Prices are accurate at time of publication; subject to manufacturer's change.*

*Cadillac Seville STS*

|  | 4-door sedan |
| --- | --- |
| Overall length, in. | 201.0 |
| Overall width, in. | 75.0 |
| Overall height, in. | 55.7 |
| Curb weight, lbs. | 3972 |
| Cargo vol., cu. ft. | 15.7 |
| Fuel capacity, gals. | 18.5 |
| Seating capacity | 5 |
| Front head room, in. | 38.1 |
| Max. front leg room, in. | 42.5 |
| Rear head room, in. | 38.0 |
| Min. rear leg room, in. | 38.2 |

## ENGINES

|  | dohc V-8 | dohc V-8 |
| --- | --- | --- |
| Size, liters/cu. in. | 4.6/279 | 4.6/279 |
| Horsepower @ rpm | 275@ 5600 | 300@ 6000 |
| Torque (lbs./ft.) @ rpm | 300@ 4000 | 295@ 4400 |
| Availability | S[1] | S[2] |
| **EPA city/highway mpg** | | |
| 4-speed OD automatic | 17/26 | 17/26 |

1. SLS. 2. STS.

| Cadillac Seville | Retail Price | Dealer Invoice |
| --- | --- | --- |
| SLS 4-door sedan | $42495 | $39038 |
| STS 4-door sedan | 46995 | 43155 |
| Destination charge | 665 | 665 |

## STANDARD EQUIPMENT:

**SLS:** 4.6-liter dohc V-8 275 horsepower engine, 4-speed automatic transmission, traction control, driver- and passenger-side air bags, front side-impact air bags, anti-lock 4-wheel disc brakes, daytime running lights, air conditioning w/dual zone climate control, outside temperature display, interior air filter, rear heat/air conditioning outlet with fan, Magnasteer variable-assist steering, leather-wrapped steering wheel with controls for radio and climate system, cruise control, leather upholstery, 8-way power front seats with power recliners, front and rear articulating headrests w/power height adjustment for front headrests, center storage console with armrest, rear armrest w/storage, overhead console, Zebrano wood interior trim, power windows, programmable power door locks, valet lockout, remote keyless entry, illuminated entry, heated power mirrors w/driver-side automatic day/night, automatic day/night rearview mirror, Bose AM/FM/cassette/CD with eight speakers and Theftlock, diversity antenna, map lights, illuminated visor mirrors, visor storage flaps, Driver Information Center, tachometer, coolant-temperature gauge, trip odometer, automatic parking brake release, remote fuel door and decklid releases, trunk pass through, intermittent wipers, wiper-activated headlights, automatic headlights, rear defogger, floormats, trunk mat and cargo net, cornering lights, Pass Key III theft-deterrent system, solar-control tinted glass, continuously variable Road-Sensing suspension, Stabilitrak, automatic level control, 235/60R16 tires, alloy wheels.

**STS** adds: 4.6-liter dohc V-8 300 horsepower engine, Performance Shift Algorithm, Memory Pkg. (two-driver memory seats, mirrors, climate control, and radio presets), power lumbar adjusters, power tilt and telescoping steering wheel, Curb-View passenger-side mirror, Rainsense automatic wipers, compass, universal garage door opener, sound system with digital signal processing/weatherband/automatic volume control, fog lights, STS suspension tuning, 235/60HR16 tires.

## OPTIONAL EQUIPMENT:

| | Retail Price | Dealer Invoice |
|---|---|---|
| **Major Packages** | | |
| Convenience Pkg., SLS | $596 | $508 |
| *Includes power lumbar support for front seats, Rainsense automatic wipers, compass, universal garage door opener.* | | |
| Personalization Pkg., SLS | 1698 | 1443 |
| *Convenience Pkg. plus Memory Pkg. (two-driver memory for seats, mirrors, climate control, and radio presets), heated front and rear seats, power tilt and telescoping steering wheel.* | | |
| Heated Seat Pkg., STS | 632 | 537 |
| *Heated front and rear seats, compass, universal garage door opener. NA with Adaptive Seat Pkg.* | | |
| Adaptive Seat Pkg., STS | 1202 | 1022 |
| *Adaptive front seats, compass, universal garage door opener.* | | |
| **Comfort and Convenience** | | |
| OnStar System | 895 | 761 |
| *Includes Global Positioning System, voice-activated cellular telephone, roadside assistance, emergency services. Requires dealer installation charge and monthly service charges.* | | |
| Power sunroof | 1550 | 1318 |

*Prices are accurate at time of publication; subject to manufacturer's change.*

| | Retail Price | Dealer Invoice |
|---|---|---|
| UM4 AM/FM/cassette/mini CD player, SLS | $300 | $255 |
| UM5 Bose sound system, SLS | 950 | 808 |
| *Includes AM/FM/weatherband/cassette/CD with digital signal processing, automatic volume control.* | | |
| UM9 Bose sound system, SLS | 1250 | 1063 |
| STS | 300 | 255 |
| *Includes AM/FM/weatherband/cassette/mini CD player with digital signal processing, automatic volume control.* | | |
| 6-disc CD player | 500 | 425 |
| Wood Trim Pkg. | 495 | 421 |
| *Wood trimmed steering wheel and shift knob.* | | |
| Trunk storage system | 265 | 225 |

### Appearance and Miscellaneous

| | | |
|---|---|---|
| Engine block heater | 18 | 15 |
| Striping, SLS | 75 | 64 |
| Special paint | 500 | 425 |
| Chrome alloy wheels | 795 | 507 |
| 235/60ZR16 tires, STS | 250 | 213 |

# CHEVROLET ASTRO

*Chevrolet Astro LT AWD*

## SPECIFICATIONS

| | 3-door van |
|---|---|
| Wheelbase, in. | 111.2 |
| Overall length, in. | 189.8 |
| Overall width, in. | 77.5 |
| Overall height, in. | 76.0 |
| Curb weight, lbs. | 4197 |
| Cargo vol., cu. ft. | 170.4 |

| | 3-door van |
|---|---|
| Fuel capacity, gals. | 25.0 |
| Seating capacity | 8 |
| Front head room, in. | 39.2 |
| Max. front leg room, in. | 41.6 |
| Rear head room, in. | 37.9 |
| Min. rear leg room, in. | 36.5 |

## ENGINES

| | ohv V-6 |
|---|---|
| Size, liters/cu. in. | 4.3/262 |
| Horsepower @ rpm | 190@ 4400 |
| Torque (lbs./ft.) @ rpm | 250@ 2800 |
| Availability | S |

**EPA city/highway mpg**

| | |
|---|---|
| 4-speed OD automatic | 16/21[1] |

1. 15/19 w/AWD.

| Chevrolet Astro | Retail Price | Dealer Invoice |
|---|---|---|
| 2WD 3-door Cargo van | $19340 | $17503 |
| AWD 3-door Cargo van | 21740 | 19675 |
| 2WD 3-door Standard van | 20074 | 18167 |
| AWD 3-door Standard van | 22374 | 20248 |
| Destination charge | 585 | 585 |

## STANDARD EQUIPMENT:

**Cargo:** 4.3-liter V-6 engine, 4-speed automatic transmission, driver- and passenger-side air bags, anti-lock brakes, daytime running lamps, front air conditioning, variable-assist power steering, black rubber floormat, reclining highback vinyl front bucket seats, coolant-temperature and oil-pressure gauges, voltmeter, trip odometer, intermittent wipers, AM/FM radio, digital clock, remote fuel-door release, front and rear auxiliary power outlets, Passlock theft-deterrent system, solar-control tinted glass, dual manual outside mirrors, 215/75R15 tires.

**AWD models** add: permanent 4-wheel drive.

**Standard** adds: 5-passenger seating with 3-passenger rear bench seat, carpeting, cloth door trim, visor mirrors, cloth headliner, rear heat ducts, swing-out rear side windows, rear storage compartments.

**AWD models** add: permanent 4-wheel drive.

## OPTIONAL EQUIPMENT:
### Major Packages

| | | |
|---|---|---|
| Preferred Equipment Group 1SB, Standard | 2055 | 1767 |

*Prices are accurate at time of publication; subject to manufacturer's change.*

# CHEVROLET

|  | Retail Price | Dealer Invoice |
|---|---|---|
| Manufacturer's discount price ......................................... | $1455 | $1251 |

Includes 8-passenger seating (front bucket seats, second- and third-row bench seats), tilt steering wheel, cruise control, power windows and door locks, reading lights, Seat Pkg. (inboard and outboard armrests, manual lumbar support, map pocket), floormats, cargo net, bodyside moldings, deep-tinted glass, styled steel wheels.

| | | |
|---|---|---|
| LS Preferred Equipment Group 3 1SC, Standard ..................................................................... | 3336 | 2869 |
| Manufacturer's discount price ......................................... | 2636 | 2267 |

LS Pkg. (cruise control, tilt steering wheel, 8-passenger seating, Seat Pkg., power door locks, power windows, power mirrors, deep-tinted glass, swing-out rear door windows, reading lamps, lower bodyside cladding, chrome-accent grille, cargo net, chrome styled steel wheels, floormats), front seat storage compartment, overhead console, illuminated visor mirrors.

| | | |
|---|---|---|
| LS Preferred Equipment Group 1SD, Standard ............ | 3877 | 3334 |
| Manufacturer's discount price ......................................... | 3177 | 2732 |

LS Preferred Equipment Pkg. 1SC plus remote keyless entry, 6-way power driver seat, roof rack, alloy wheels.

| | | |
|---|---|---|
| LT Preferred Equipment Pkg. 1SE, Standard ................ | 5542 | 4766 |
| Manufacturer's discount price ......................................... | 4742 | 4078 |

LS Preferred Equipment Group 1SD plus upgraded cloth upholstery, split folding center bench w/console and additional cupholders, leather-wrapped steering wheel, compass, outside temperature indicator.

| | | |
|---|---|---|
| Seat Pkg., Cargo ............................................................ | 168 | 144 |

Front seat armrests, map pocket, manual driver-seat lumbar support. Requires cloth upholstery.

| | | |
|---|---|---|
| Convenience Pkg., Cargo ................................................ | 383 | 329 |

Tilt steering wheel, cruise control.

| | | |
|---|---|---|
| Convenience Group, Cargo .............................................. | 474 | 408 |

Power windows and door locks.

| | | |
|---|---|---|
| Trailering Special Equipment ........................................... | 309 | 266 |

Platform trailer hitch, 8-lead wiring harness.

## Safety Features

| | | |
|---|---|---|
| Dual integrated child seats, Standard ............................ | 240 | 206 |

Requires cloth upholstery. NA with LT Group or 7-passenger seating.

## Comfort and Convenience

| | | |
|---|---|---|
| Rear air conditioning, Standard ...................................... | 523 | 450 |
| Air conditioning delete, Cargo (credit) ............................ | (845) | (727) |
| Rear heater .................................................................... | 205 | 176 |
| Dutch doors .................................................................... | 364 | 313 |
| Standard w/LS or LT Group ........................................ | 305 | 262 |

Includes rear wiper/washer and electric release.

| | Retail Price | Dealer Invoice |
|---|---|---|
| 7-passenger seating, Standard | $969 | $833 |
| Standard w/Group 1SB | 406 | 349 |
| Standard w/LS Group | 318 | 273 |
| Standard w/LT Group | NC | NC |
| *Front- and second-row bucket seats, third-row bench seat, Seat Pkg.* | | |
| 8-passenger seating, Standard | 395 | 340 |
| *Front bucket seats, second- and third-row bench seats.* | | |
| Manual lumbar adjusters for second-row bucket seats, Standard | 100 | 86 |
| 6-way power driver seat, Standard | 240 | 206 |
| *Requires Preferred Equipment Group and cloth upholstery.* | | |
| 6-way power passenger seat, Standard | 240 | 206 |
| *Requires 6-way power driver seat. Requires Preferred Equipment Group.* | | |
| Leather seat trim, Standard | 950 | 817 |
| *Requires LT Group.* | | |
| Rear defogger | 154 | 132 |
| *Requires dutch doors.* | | |
| Power door locks | 223 | 192 |
| Leather-wrapped steering wheel, Standard w/LS Group | 54 | 46 |
| Remote keyless entry | 150 | 129 |
| *Requires power door locks.* | | |
| Power mirrors, Standard | 98 | 84 |
| *Requires Preferred Equipment Group 1SB.* | | |
| Homelink garage-door opener, Standard | 115 | 98 |
| *Requires LS or LT Group.* | | |
| Cassette player | 147 | 126 |
| Cassette player w/automatic tone control | 307 | 264 |
| *Cargo requires Convenience Group. Standard requires Preferred Equipment Group.* | | |
| CD player w/automatic tone control | 407 | 350 |
| *Cargo requires Convenience Group. Standard requires Preferred Equipment Group.* | | |
| Cassette and CD players w/automatic tone control | 507 | 436 |
| *Cargo requires Convenience Group. Standard requires Preferred Equipment Group.* | | |
| Rear radio controls, Standard | 158 | 136 |
| *Requires LS or LT Group.* | | |
| Dome/map lights, Cargo | 33 | 28 |
| Floormats, Standard | 47 | 40 |
| Standard w/7- or 8-passenger seating | 69 | 59 |

## Appearance and Miscellaneous

| | | |
|---|---|---|
| Glass Pkg., Cargo | 368 | 316 |
| *Complete rear cargo area glass.* | | |

*Prices are accurate at time of publication; subject to manufacturer's change.*

| | Retail Price | Dealer Invoice |
|---|---|---|
| Deep tinted glass, Cargo | $262 | $225 |
| *Requires Glass Pkg.* | | |
| Deep-tinted glass, Standard | 290 | 249 |
| Chrome accent grille | 150 | 129 |
| Bodyside moldings | 121 | 104 |
| Roof rack, Standard | 126 | 108 |
| 2-tone paint, Standard | NC | NC |
| *Requires LS or LT Group.* | | |
| Cold Climate Pkg. | 46 | 40 |
| *Includes engine-block heater, coolant protection.* | | |
| Locking differential, Standard | 252 | 217 |
| Touring Suspension Pkg., Standard 2WD | 306 | 263 |
| *Gas shock absorbers, rear stabilizer bar, 235/65R15 white outline letter tires.* | | |
| 215/75R15 white outline letter tires | 88 | 76 |
| Alloy wheels, Standard | 365 | 314 |
| Standard w/Group 1SB | 273 | 235 |
| Standard w/LS Group | 25 | 22 |
| Chrome styled steel wheels, Standard | 340 | 292 |
| Standard w/Group 1SB | 248 | 213 |
| Standard w/LT Group (credit) | (25) | (22) |
| Styled steel wheels | 92 | 79 |

# CHEVROLET BLAZER

*Chevrolet Blazer LT 4WD 4-door*

## SPECIFICATIONS

| | 2-door wagon | 4-door wagon |
|---|---|---|
| Wheelbase, in. | 100.5 | 107.0 |
| Overall length, in. | 176.8 | 183.3 |

|                          | 2-door wagon | 4-door wagon |
| ------------------------ | ------------ | ------------ |
| Overall width, in.       | 67.8         | 67.8         |
| Overall height, in.      | 64.9         | 64.3         |
| Curb weight, lbs.        | 3515         | 3685         |
| Cargo vol., cu. ft.      | 66.9         | 74.1         |
| Fuel capacity, gals.     | 19.0         | 18.0         |
| Seating capacity         | 4            | 6            |
| Front head room, in.     | 39.6         | 39.6         |
| Max. front leg room, in. | 42.5         | 42.4         |
| Rear head room, in.      | 38.2         | 38.2         |
| Min. rear leg room, in.  | 36.3         | 36.3         |

## ENGINES

|                                | ohv V-6    |
| ------------------------------ | ---------- |
| Size, liters/cu. in.           | 4.3/262    |
| Horsepower @ rpm               | 190@ 4400  |
| Torque (lbs./ft.) @ rpm        | 250@ 2800  |
| Availability                   | S          |

### EPA city/highway mpg

| 5-speed OD manual      | 17/23[1] |
| ---------------------- | -------- |
| 4-speed OD automatic   | 16/21[2] |

*1. 16/21 w/4WD. 2. 16/20 w/4WD.*

| Chevrolet Blazer     | Retail Price | Dealer Invoice |
| -------------------- | ------------ | -------------- |
| 2-door wagon, 2WD    | $21663       | $19605         |
| 2-door wagon, 4WD    | 23651        | 21404          |
| 4-door wagon, 2WD    | 23188        | 20985          |
| 4-door wagon, 4WD    | 25176        | 22784          |
| Destination charge   | 515          | 515            |

## STANDARD EQUIPMENT:

**2-door:** 4.3-liter V-6 engine, 4-speed automatic transmission, driver- and passenger-side air bags, anti-lock 4-wheel disc brakes, daytime running lights, power steering, air conditioning, cloth front bucket seats with manual lumbar adjustment and console, split folding rear bench seat, trip odometer, coolant-temperature and oil-pressure gauges, voltmeter, automatic day/night rearview mirror, AM/FM radio, digital clock, automatic headlights, cupholders, intermittent wipers, floormats, cargo-area tie down hooks, Passlock theft-deterrent system, solar-control tinted glass, dual outside mirrors, bright grille, 5-lead trailer wiring harness, Smooth Ride suspension, 205/75R15 all-season tires, **4WD adds:** Insta-Trac part-time 4WD, electronic-shift transfer case, tow hooks.

**4-door adds:** cloth 60/40 split front bench seat with storage armrest, **4WD adds:** Insta-Trac part-time 4WD, electronic-shift transfer case, tow hooks.

## OPTIONAL EQUIPMENT:
### Major Packages

| | Retail Price | Dealer Invoice |
|---|---|---|
| Preferred Equipment Group 1SB | $643 | $553 |
| *Manufacturer's discount price, (credit)* | (57) | (49) |
| *Cassette player, tilt steering wheel, cruise control.* | | |
| LS Preferred Equipment Group 1SC, 2-door | 2855 | 2455 |
| *Manufacturer's discount price* | 1455 | 1251 |
| *Group 1SB plus cassette player with automatic tone control, map lights, illuminated visor mirrors, leather-wrapped steering wheel, overhead console, tachometer, 2 power outlets, power windows and door locks, heated power mirrors, deep-tinted tailgate glass, rear defogger, rear wiper/washer, power tailgate release, color-keyed grille and front bumper, touring suspension, 235/70R15 tires, alloy wheels.* | | |
| LS preferred Equipment Group 1SC, 4-door | 3556 | 3058 |
| *Manufacturer's discount price* | 2156 | 1854 |
| *Group 1SB plus cassette player with bucket seats, automatic tone control, map lights, illuminated visor mirrors, leather-wrapped steering wheel, overhead console, tachometer, 2 power outlets, power windows and door locks, heated power mirrors, liftgate, deep-tinted tailgate glass, rear defogger, rear wiper/washer, power tailgate release, color-keyed grille and front bumper, bodyside moldings, rear cargo shade, Premium Ride Suspension Pkg., 235/70R15 tires, alloy wheels.* | | |
| LS Preferred Equipment Group 1SD, 2-door | 3490 | 3001 |
| *Manufacturer's discount price* | 2090 | 1797 |
| *2-door Group 1SC plus 6-way driver seat, remote keyless entry, Homelink universal garage door opener.* | | |
| LT Preferred Equipment Group 1SD, 4-door | 5529 | 4859 |
| *Manufacturer's discount price, 4-door* | 4129 | 3551 |
| *4-door Group 1SC plus 6-way power driver seat, front power lumbar adjustors, leather upholstery, remote keyless entry, Homelink universal garage door opener, front air dam, fog lights.* | | |
| Convenience Pkg. | 395 | 340 |
| *Cruise control, tilt steering wheel.* | | |
| Convenience Group, 2-door | 535 | 460 |
| 4-door | 710 | 611 |
| *Power windows, door locks, and mirrors.* | | |
| Rear-Window Convenience Pkg. | 322 | 277 |
| *Rear defogger, remote tailgate release, rear wiper/washer.* | | |
| ZR2 Wide Stance Performance Pkg., 2-door 4WD | 1850 | 1591 |
| *Heavy-duty wide stance chassis, heavy-duty suspension, Bilstein shock absorbers, Shield Pkg., heavy-duty differential gears and axles, fender flares, 31x10.5R15 tires, full-size spare. Requires LS Group, limited slip differential. NA w/Trailering Special Equipment.* | | |
| Off-road suspension, 2-door 4WD | 634 | 545 |

| | Retail Price | Dealer Invoice |
|---|---|---|
| 2-door 4WD with Group 1SC or 1SD.......................... | $245 | $211 |

*Includes gas shock absorbers, uprated torsion bar, jounce stabilizer bar, full-size spare tire, 235/75R15 on/off-road white outline letter tires (w/o Group 1SC or 1SD).*

| | | |
|---|---|---|
| Trailering Special Equipment ........................................... | 210 | 181 |

*Includes platform hitch, heavy-duty flasher. 2WD models require automatic transmission.*

## Powertrains

| | | |
|---|---|---|
| 5-speed manual transmission, 2-door (credit) ............... | (890) | (765) |

*Requires tachometer.*

| | | |
|---|---|---|
| Locking differential ................................................................ | 252 | 217 |

## Comfort and Convenience

| | | |
|---|---|---|
| 6-way power driver seat, w/Group 1SC ......................... | 240 | 206 |

*Requires remote keyless entry.*

| | | |
|---|---|---|
| Heated front seats, 4-door ................................................ | 225 | 194 |

*Requires leather upholstery.*

| | | |
|---|---|---|
| Cloth upholstery, 4-door w/LT Group (credit) ................. | (600) | (516) |
| Power sunroof ......................................................................... | 695 | 598 |

*Requires overhead console.*

| | | |
|---|---|---|
| Homelink universal garage-door opener....................... | 130 | 112 |

*Includes trip computer, compass, outside-temperature indicator. Requires overhead console.*

| | | |
|---|---|---|
| Remote keyless entry system...................................... | 150 | 129 |

*Requires Group 1SC and 6-way power driver seat.*

| | | |
|---|---|---|
| Overhead console................................................................ | 147 | 126 |

*NA with bench seat. Requires power sunroof when ordered without a Preferred Equipment Group or with Group 1SB.*

| | | |
|---|---|---|
| Tachometer............................................................................... | 59 | 51 |
| Cassette player ...................................................................... | 122 | 105 |
| CD player ................................................................................. | 100 | 86 |

*Requires Group 1SC or 1SD.*

| | | |
|---|---|---|
| Cassette/CD player................................................................ | 200 | 172 |

*Requires Group 1SC or 1SD.*

| | | |
|---|---|---|
| Rear cargo shade, 2-door 4WD with LS Decor Group.. | 69 | 59 |

*Requires exterior spare-tire carrier.*

## Appearance and Miscellaneous

| | | |
|---|---|---|
| Roof rack ................................................................................. | 126 | 108 |
| Fog lights, 2WD, 4WD 4-door............................................ | 115 | 99 |
| Rear liftgate, 4-door ............................................................. | NC | NC |

*Requires ZQ6 convenience group and rear-window convenience pkg. when ordered without a Preferred Equipment Group or with Group 1SB.*

| | | |
|---|---|---|
| Custom 2-tone paint, 4-door ............................................. | 197 | 169 |

*Requires LS Decor Group or LT Decor Group.*

*Prices are accurate at time of publication; subject to manufacturer's change.*

|  | Retail Price | Dealer Invoice |
|---|---|---|
| Cold Climate Pkg. | $89 | $77 |

*Includes heavy duty battery, engine block heater.*

## Special Purpose, Wheels and Tires

|  | | |
|---|---|---|
| Shield Pkg., 4WD | 126 | 108 |

*Includes transfer case and front differential skid plates, fuel tank and steering linkage shields. NA with all-wheel drive.*

|  | | |
|---|---|---|
| Heavy-duty battery | 56 | 48 |
| Smooth Riding suspension (credit) | (275) | (237) |

*Requires Group 1SC or 1SD.*

|  | | |
|---|---|---|
| Touring suspension | 197 | 169 |
| w/Group 1SC or 1SD. | NC | NC |

*Includes gas shock absorbers.*

|  | | |
|---|---|---|
| Premium suspension, 4-door | 197 | 169 |
| 4-door w/Group 1SC or 1SD. | NC | NC |

*Includes gas shock absorbers.*

|  | | |
|---|---|---|
| Exterior spare-tire carrier, 2-door 4WD | 159 | 137 |

*Includes full-size spare tire and cover.*

|  | | |
|---|---|---|
| Alloy wheels | 280 | 241 |
| 205/75R15 all-season white letter tires | 121 | 104 |
| 235/70R15 all-season tires | 192 | 165 |
| 235/70R15 all-season white letter tires | 325 | 280 |
| w/Group 1SC or1SD. | 133 | 114 |
| 235/75R15 on/off-road white letter tires, 4WD | 335 | 288 |
| 4WD w/Preferred Equipment Group | 143 | 123 |

# CHEVROLET CAMARO

*Chevrolet Camaro Z28 hatchback*

## SPECIFICATIONS

|  | 2-door hatchback | 2-door conv. |
|---|---|---|
| Wheelbase, in. | 101.1 | 101.1 |

|  | 2-door hatchback | 2-door conv. |
| --- | --- | --- |
| Overall length, in. | 193.5 | 193.5 |
| Overall width, in. | 74.1 | 74.1 |
| Overall height, in. | 51.3 | 52.0 |
| Curb weight, lbs. | 3331 | 3468 |
| Cargo vol., cu. ft. | 12.9 | 7.6 |
| Fuel capacity, gals. | 15.5 | 15.5 |
| Seating capacity | 4 | 4 |
| Front head room, in. | 37.2 | 38.0 |
| Max. front leg room, in. | 42.9 | 42.9 |
| Rear head room, in. | 35.3 | 39.0 |
| Min. rear leg room, in. | 26.8 | 26.8 |

## ENGINES

|  | ohv V-6 | ohv V-8 | ohv V-8 |
| --- | --- | --- | --- |
| Size, liters/cu. in. | 3.8/231 | 5.7/346 | 5.7/346 |
| Horsepower @ rpm | 200@ 5200 | 305@ 5200 | 320@ 5200 |
| Torque (lbs./ft.) @ rpm | 225@ 4000 | 335@ 4000 | 345@ 4400 |
| Availability | S[1] | S[2] | S[3] |

### EPA city/highway mpg

|  | | | |
| --- | --- | --- | --- |
| 5-speed OD manual | 19/30 | | |
| 6-speed OD manual | | 18/27 | 18/27 |
| 4-speed OD automatic | 19/29 | 17/25 | 17/25 |

1. Base. 2. Z28. 3. SS.

| Chevrolet Camaro | Retail Price | Dealer Invoice |
| --- | --- | --- |
| Base 2-door hatchback | $16625 | $15212 |
| Base 2-door convertible | 22125 | 20244 |
| Z28 2-door hatchback | 20470 | 18730 |
| Z28 2-door convertible | 27450 | 25117 |
| Destination charge | 525 | 525 |

## STANDARD EQUIPMENT:

**Base:** 3.8-liter V-6 engine, 5-speed manual transmission, driver- and passenger-side air bags, anti-lock 4-wheel disc brakes, daytime running lamps, air conditioning, power steering, tilt steering wheel, cloth reclining front bucket seats with 4-way adjustable driver seat, center storage console with cupholders and auxiliary power outlet, folding rear seatback, automatic headlights, intermittent wipers, AM/FM/cassette, digital clock, day/night rearview mirror with dual reading lights, tachometer, voltmeter, oil-pressure and coolant-temperature gauges, trip odometer, low-oil-level indicator, visor mirrors, front floormats, solar-control tinted glass, left remote and right manual sport mirrors, Pass-Key theft-deterrent system, rear spoiler, 215/60R16 all-season tires, wheel covers.

*Prices are accurate at time of publication; subject to manufacturer's change.*

# CHEVROLET

**Base convertible** adds: rear defogger, premium speakers, power folding top, 3-piece hard boot with storage bag.

**Z28** adds to Base hatchback: 5.7-liter V-8 engine, 6-speed manual transmission or 4-speed automatic transmission, limited-slip differential, 2-way adjustable driver seat, low-coolant indicator system, performance ride and handling suspension, black roof and mirrors, 235/55R16 tires, alloy wheels.

**Z28 convertible** adds: rear defogger, premium speakers, 4-way adjustable driver seat, rear floormats, power folding top, 3-piece hard boot with storage bag, color-keyed power mirrors.

## OPTIONAL EQUIPMENT:
### Major Packages

|  | Retail Price | Dealer Invoice |
|---|---|---|
| Preferred Equipment Group 1SB, Base hatchback ....... | $565 | $486 |
| *Includes cruise control, remote hatch release, power door lock, fog lights.* | | |
| Preferred Equipment Group 1SC, Base hatchback ....... | 1231 | 1059 |
| *Pkg. 1SB plus power windows, power mirrors, leather-wrapped steering wheel, remote keyless entry, illuminated entry, theft-deterrent system.* | | |
| Preferred Equipment Group 1SE, Base convertible ...... | 1306 | 1123 |
| *Includes cruise control, remote decklid release, power door locks and windows, power mirrors, leather-wrapped steering wheel, remote keyless entry, illuminated entry, theft-deterrent system, bodyside moldings, rear floormats, fog lights.* | | |
| Preferred Equipment Group 1SG/H, Z28 hatchback ..... | 1576 | 1355 |
| Z28 convertible ............................................................. | NC | NC |
| *Includes cruise control, power door locks and windows, power mirrors, 6-way power driver seat, remote hatch/decklid release, leather-wrapped steering wheel, rear floormats, remote keyless entry, illuminated entry, theft-deterrent system, bodyside moldings, fog lights.* | | |
| Appearance Pkg., Base ................................................. | 1755 | 1509 |
| Z28.............................................................................. | 1480 | 1272 |
| *Front and rear body moldings, 235/55R16 tires (Base), alloy wheels (Base).* | | |
| Performance Handling Pkg., Base .................................. | 225 | 194 |
| *Limited slip differential, performance axle ratio (w/automatic transmission), dual exhaust, sport steering ratio. Requires option pkg., 235/55R16 tires, and alloy wheels.* | | |
| Performance Pkg., Z28 hatchback.................................. | 1175 | 1011 |
| *Larger stabilizer bars, stiffer springs and bushings, dual adjustable shock absorbers, power steering fluid cooler. Requires 245/50ZR16 performance tires, performance axle ratio w/automatic transmission. NA w/removable roof panels.* | | |

### Powertrains

|  | | |
|---|---|---|
| 4-speed automatic transmission, Base ........................... | 815 | 701 |

| | Retail Price | Dealer Invoice |
|---|---|---|
| Traction control, Z28 .................................................. | $450 | $387 |
| *Requires Preferred Equipment Group.* | | |
| Performance axle ratio, Z28 .......................................... | 300 | 258 |
| *Requires automatic transmission and 245/50ZR16 tires.* | | |

## Comfort and Convenience

| | | |
|---|---|---|
| AM/FM/cassette with automatic tone control, hatchback | 350 | 301 |
| convertible | 215 | 185 |
| AM/FM/CD with automatic tone control, hatchback ....... | 450 | 387 |
| convertible .......................................................................... | 315 | 271 |
| 12-disc CD changer .......................................................... | 595 | 512 |
| *Requires AM/FM/cassette with automatic tone control.* | | |
| Remote keyless entry, Base hatchback .......................... | 225 | 194 |
| *Includes theft-deterrent system. Requires Preferred Equipment Group 1SB.* | | |
| 6-way power driver seat, Base ........................................ | 270 | 232 |
| Leather bucket seats ....................................................... | 499 | 429 |
| *Z28 hatchback requires preferred equipment group.* | | |
| Rear defogger, hatchback ................................................ | 170 | 146 |
| Removable roof panels, hatchback ................................. | 995 | 856 |
| *Includes locks, storage provisions, and sun shade. NA Performance Pkg.* | | |
| Rear floormats, Base hatchback ..................................... | 15 | 13 |

## Appearance and Miscellaneous

| | | |
|---|---|---|
| Engine-block heater .......................................................... | 20 | 17 |
| Color-keyed bodyside moldings, Base hatchback ......... | 60 | 52 |
| 235/55R16 tires, Base ..................................................... | 132 | 114 |
| *Requires alloy wheels.* | | |
| 245/50ZR16 performance tires, Z28 .............................. | 225 | 194 |
| 245/50ZR16 all-season performance tires, Z28 ............. | 225 | 194 |
| Alloy wheels, Base ........................................................... | 275 | 237 |
| *Requires 235/55R16 tires.* | | |
| Chrome alloy wheels, Base ............................................. | 775 | 667 |
| Z28 .................................................................................... | 500 | 430 |

# CHEVROLET CAVALIER

| SPECIFICATIONS | 2-door coupe | 2-door conv. | 4-door sedan |
|---|---|---|---|
| Wheelbase, in. ..................................... | 104.1 | 104.1 | 104.1 |
| Overall length, in. .............................. | 180.7 | 180.3 | 180.7 |
| Overall width, in. ................................ | 68.7 | 67.4 | 67.9 |

*Prices are accurate at time of publication; subject to manufacturer's change.*

# CHEVROLET

*Chevrolet Cavalier LS sedan*

|  | 2-door coupe | 2-door conv. | 4-door sedan |
|---|---|---|---|
| Overall height, in. | 53.0 | 53.9 | 54.7 |
| Curb weight, lbs. | 2584 | 2899 | 2630 |
| Cargo vol., cu. ft. | 13.2 | 10.5 | 13.2 |
| Fuel capacity, gals. | 15.2 | 15.2 | 15.2 |
| Seating capacity | 5 | 4 | 5 |
| Front head room, in. | 37.6 | 38.1 | 38.9 |
| Max. front leg room, in. | 42.3 | 42.4 | 42.3 |
| Rear head room, in. | 36.6 | 37.6 | 37.2 |
| Min. rear leg room, in. | 32.7 | 32.6 | 34.4 |

## ENGINES

|  | ohv I-4 | dohc I-4 |
|---|---|---|
| Size, liters/cu. in. | 2.2/134 | 2.4/146 |
| Horsepower @ rpm | 115@ 5000 | 150@ 5600 |
| Torque (lbs./ft.) @ rpm | 135@ 3600 | 155@ 4400 |
| Availability | S[1] | S[2] |

### EPA city/highway mpg

|  | ohv I-4 | dohc I-4 |
|---|---|---|
| 5-speed OD manual | 24/34 | 22/33 |
| 3-speed automatic | 23/31 | |
| 4-speed OD automatic | 25/34 | 22/32 |

1. Base, RS, LS. 2. Z24; optional, LS.

| Chevrolet Cavalier | Retail Price | Dealer Invoice |
|---|---|---|
| Base 2-door notchback | $11610 | $10855 |
| Base 4-door sedan | 11810 | 11042 |
| RS 2-door notchback | 12870 | 12033 |
| LS 4-door sedan | 14250 | 13324 |
| Z24 2-door notchback | 15710 | 14689 |
| Z24 2-door convertible | 19410 | 18148 |
| Destination charge | 500 | 500 |

## STANDARD EQUIPMENT:

**Base:** 2.2-liter 4-cylinder engine, 5-speed manual transmission, driver-

and passenger-side air bags, anti-lock brakes, daytime running lights, power steering, cloth and vinyl reclining front bucket seats, folding rear seat, storage console with armrest, AM/FM radio, digital clock, intermittent wipers, tinted glass, left remote and right manual mirrors, theft-deterrent system, 195/70R14 tires, wheel covers.

**RS** adds: cruise control, tilt steering wheel, easy-entry front passenger seat, tachometer, trip odometer, visor mirrors, variable intermittent wipers, remote decklid release, floormats, trunk net, color-keyed fascias and body-side moldings, front mud guards, rear decklid spoiler, 195/65R15 tires.

**LS** adds to Base: 4-speed automatic transmission, traction control, tilt steering wheel, cruise control, air conditioning, cloth upholstery, tachometer, trip odometer, cassette player, digital clock, visor mirrors, front reading lamps, variable intermittent wipers, remote decklid release, floormats, trunk net, color-keyed fascias and bodyside moldings, 195/65R15 tires.

**Z24** adds: 2.4-liter dohc 4-cylinder engine, 5-speed manual transmission, easy-entry front passenger seat, power windows, power door locks, power mirrors, power top (convertible), rear defogger (convertible), dual map lights, sport suspension, rear decklid spoiler, fog lights, 205/55R16 tires, alloy wheels, deletes 4-speed automatic transmission, traction control, and mudguards.

## OPTIONAL EQUIPMENT:

| | Retail Price | Dealer Invoice |
|---|---|---|
| **Major Packages** | | |
| Preferred Equipment Group 1, Base 2-door | $515 | $464 |
|   Base 4-door | 498 | 448 |

*Remote decklid release, variable intermittent wipers, visor mirrors, color-keyed fascias and body moldings, front mud guards, cargo net, floormats, 195/65R15 tires, special wheel covers. 2-door adds easy-entry front passenger seat.*

| | | |
|---|---|---|
| Preferred Equipment Group 2, Base 2-door | 990 | 881 |

*Group 1 plus cruise control, tilt steering wheel, power mirrors.*

| | | |
|---|---|---|
| Preferred Equipment Group 1, RS | 714 | 643 |
|   LS | 819 | 737 |

*Power windows and door locks, remote keyless entry, power mirrors, power decklid release.*

### Powertrains

| | | |
|---|---|---|
| 2.4-liter dohc 4-cylinder engine, LS | 450 | 405 |
| 3-speed automatic transmission, Base | 600 | 540 |

*NA with Preferred Equipment Group 2.*

| | | |
|---|---|---|
| 4-speed automatic transmission, Base, RS, Z24 | 780 | 702 |

*Includes traction control. Base 2-door requires Preferred Equipment Group 1.*

### Comfort and Convenience

| | | |
|---|---|---|
| Air conditioning, Base, RS | 795 | 716 |

*Prices are accurate at time of publication; subject to manufacturer's change.*

| | Retail Price | Dealer Invoice |
|---|---|---|
| Vinyl bucket seats, convertible | NC | NC |
| Adjustable lumbar support, convertible | $50 | $45 |
| *Requires vinyl bucket seats.* | | |
| Rear defogger | 180 | 162 |
| *Std. convertible.* | | |
| Power sunroof, 2-door notchback | 595 | 535 |
| *Includes mirror-mounted front map light. Base requires Preferred Equipment Group.* | | |
| Power door locks, Base 2-door, RS | 220 | 198 |
| Base 4-door, LS | 260 | 234 |
| AM/FM/cassette, Base, RS | 165 | 149 |
| AM/FM/cassette with automatic tone control, | | |
| Base, RS | 220 | 198 |
| LS, Z24 | 55 | 50 |
| *Includes premium speakers.* | | |
| AM/FM/CD player with automatic tone control, | | |
| Base, RS | 320 | 288 |
| *Includes premium speakers.* | | |
| AM/FM CD player with automatic tone control, LS, Z24 | 155 | 140 |
| *Includes premium speakers.* | | |

## Appearance and Miscellaneous

| | | |
|---|---|---|
| Rear spoiler, LS | 125 | 113 |
| Engine block heater | 30 | 27 |
| Alloy wheels, RS, LS | 295 | 263 |

# CHEVROLET CORVETTE

*Chevrolet Corvette convertible*

## SPECIFICATIONS

| | 2-door hatchback | 2-door conv. |
|---|---|---|
| Wheelbase, in. | 104.5 | 104.5 |
| Overall length, in. | 179.7 | 179.7 |
| Overall width, in. | 73.6 | 73.6 |

| | 2-door hatchback | 2-door conv. |
|---|---|---|
| Overall height, in. | 47.7 | 47.7 |
| Curb weight, lbs. | 3245 | 3246 |
| Cargo vol., cu. ft. | 24.8 | 13.9 |
| Fuel capacity, gals. | 19.1 | 19.1 |
| Seating capacity | 2 | 2 |
| Front head room, in. | 37.8 | 37.6 |
| Max. front leg room, in. | 42.7 | 42.8 |
| Rear head room, in. | — | — |
| Min. rear leg room, in. | — | — |

## ENGINES

| | ohv V-8 |
|---|---|
| Size, liters/cu. in. | 5.7/350 |
| Horsepower @ rpm | 345@ 5600 |
| Torque (lbs./ft.) @ rpm | 350@ 4400 |
| Availability | S |

**EPA city/highway mpg**

| | |
|---|---|
| 6-speed OD manual | 18/28 |
| 4-speed OD automatic | 17/25 |

| Chevrolet Corvette | Retail Price | Dealer Invoice |
|---|---|---|
| 2-door hatchback | $37495 | $32808 |
| 2-door convertible | 44425 | 38872 |
| Destination charge | 565 | 565 |

## STANDARD EQUIPMENT:

**Base:** 5.7-liter V-8 engine, 4-speed automatic transmission, Acceleration Slip Regulation traction control, limited slip differential, driver- and passenger-side air bags, heavy-duty anti-lock 4-wheel disc brakes, daytime running lights, low tire-pressure warning system, air conditioning, Magnasteer variable-assist power steering, leather-wrapped tilt steering wheel, cruise control, oil-level indicator, cupholder, remote keyless entry, remote hatch/decklid release, analog gauges, digital driver information center in 4 languages, AM/FM/cassette, integrated antenna (hatchback), power antenna (convertible), rear defogger, reclining leather bucket seats, power driver's seat, center console, auxiliary power outlet, heated power mirrors, power windows with driver and passenger express down, power door locks, intermittent wipers, rearview mirror with reading lights, Pass-Key theft-deterrent system, solar-control tinted glass, body-color removable roof panel (hatchback), manually folding top (convertible), Goodyear Eagle GS-C extended mobility tires (245/45ZR17 front, 275/40ZR18 rear), alloy wheels.

*Prices are accurate at time of publication; subject to manufacturer's change.*

## OPTIONAL EQUIPMENT:
### Major Packages

|  | Retail Price | Dealer Invoice |
|---|---|---|
| Memory package | $150 | $129 |

*Includes settings for driver's seat, exterior mirrors, radio presets, and climate control.*

| Performance Handling Package | 350 | 301 |
|---|---|---|

*Sport suspension (Bilstein shock absorbers, stiffer springs, stabilizer bars and bushings), special wheels. Automatic transmission requires performance axle ratio. NA with Continuously Variable Real Time Damping Suspension.*

### Powertrains

| 6-speed manual transmission | 815 | 701 |
|---|---|---|
| Performance axle ratio | 100 | 86 |

### Comfort and Convenience

| Dual zone air conditioning controls | 365 | 314 |
|---|---|---|
| Perforated leather sport seats | 625 | 538 |
| 6-way power passenger seat | 305 | 262 |
| AM/FM/CD player | 100 | 86 |
| 12-disc CD changer | 600 | 516 |
| Luggage shade and parcel net, hatchback | 50 | 43 |
| Floormats | 25 | 22 |

### Appearance and Miscellaneous

| Transparent roof panel, hatchback | 650 | 559 |
|---|---|---|
| Dual roof option, hatchback | 950 | 817 |

*Standard solid removable roof panels and transparent roof panels.*

| Color-keyed bodyside moldings | 75 | 65 |
|---|---|---|
| Fog lamps | 69 | 59 |
| Front license plate frame | 15 | 13 |
| Continuous Variable Real Time Damping Suspension | 1695 | 1458 |
| Magnesium wheels | 3000 | 2580 |

# CHEVROLET LUMINA

## SPECIFICATIONS

|  | 4-door sedan |
|---|---|
| Wheelbase, in. | 107.5 |
| Overall length, in. | 200.9 |
| Overall width, in. | 72.5 |
| Overall height, in. | 55.2 |
| Curb weight, lbs. | 3330 |
| Cargo vol., cu. ft. | 15.5 |

*Chevrolet Lumina LTZ*

|  | 4-door sedan |
|---|---|
| Fuel capacity, gals. | 16.6 |
| Seating capacity | 6 |
| Front head room, in. | 38.4 |
| Max. front leg room, in. | 42.4 |
| Rear head room, in. | 37.4 |
| Min. rear leg room, in. | 36.6 |

## ENGINES

|  | ohv V-6 | ohv V-6 |
|---|---|---|
| Size, liters/cu. in. | 3.1/191 | 3.8/231 |
| Horsepower @ rpm | 160@ 5200 | 200@ 5200 |
| Torque (lbs./ft.) @ rpm | 185@ 4000 | 225@ 4000 |
| Availability | S | O[1] |

**EPA city/highway mpg**

|  | | |
|---|---|---|
| 4-speed OD automatic | 20/29 | 19/30 |

1. LTZ.

| Chevrolet Lumina | Retail Price | Dealer Invoice |
|---|---|---|
| Base 4-door sedan | $17245 | $15779 |
| LS 4-door sedan | 19245 | 17609 |
| LTZ 4-door sedan | 19745 | 18067 |
| Destination charge | 550 | 550 |

## STANDARD EQUIPMENT:

**Base:** 3.1-liter V-6 engine, 4-speed automatic transmission, driver- and passenger-side air bags, daytime running lamps, air conditioning, power steering, tilt steering wheel, 60/40 cloth reclining front seat with center armrest and 4-way manual driver seat, seatback storage pocket, cupholder, AM/FM radio with digital clock, power door locks, visor mirrors, reading lights, trip odometer, intermittent wipers, Pass-Key theft-deterrent system, tinted glass, left remote and right manual mirrors, color-keyed grille, bodyside moldings, 205/70R15 touring tires, wheel covers.

*Prices are accurate at time of publication; subject to manufacturer's change.*

# CHEVROLET

**LS** adds: anti-lock brakes, power windows, power mirrors, custom cloth upholstery, tachometer, cassette player with automatic tone control, illuminated passenger-side visor mirror, cargo net, QNX 225/60R16 touring tires, alloy wheels.

**LTZ** adds: rear spoiler, color-keyed outside mirrors, sport alloy wheels.

## OPTIONAL EQUIPMENT:

| | Retail Price | Dealer Invoice |
|---|---|---|
| **Major Packages** | | |
| Preferred Equipment Group 1, Base | $758 | $675 |
| LS | 645 | 574 |
| LTZ | 816 | 726 |
| *Power windows and mirrors, cruise control, power decklid release, cargo net, floormats.* | | |
| Sport Performance Pkg., LTZ | 500 | 445 |
| *3.8-liter V-6 engine, ride and handling suspension, 4-wheel disc brakes, sport alloy wheels, 225/60R16 tires.* | | |
| **Safety Features** | | |
| Anti-lock brakes, Base | 575 | 512 |
| Integrated child safety seat | 125 | 111 |
| *Base requires custom cloth 60/40 seat.* | | |
| **Comfort and Convenience** | | |
| OnStar System | 895 | 761 |
| *Includes Global Positioning System, voice-activated cellular telephone, roadside assistance, emergency services. Requires dealer installation charge and monthly service charges.* | | |
| Power windows, Base | 328 | 292 |
| Rear defogger | 170 | 151 |
| Cruise control | 225 | 200 |
| Remote keyless entry, Base, LS | 220 | 196 |
| *Base requires Preferred Equipment Group 1.* | | |
| Cassette player, Base | 232 | 206 |
| *Includes automatic tone control.* | | |
| CD player, Base | 325 | 289 |
| LS, LTZ | 93 | 83 |
| *Includes automatic tone control.* | | |
| Steering-wheel-mounted radio controls, LS | 171 | 152 |
| *Includes leather-wrapped steering wheel. Requires Preferred Equipment Group 1.* | | |
| Power driver seat | 305 | 271 |
| Front bucket seats w/center console, LTZ | 200 | 178 |
| Leather 60/40 seat, LS, LTZ | 645 | 574 |
| *Requires Preferred Equipment Group 1.* | | |
| Leather front bucket seats, LTZ | 695 | 619 |
| *Requires Preferred Equipment Group 1.* | | |

| | Retail Price | Dealer Invoice |
|---|---|---|
| Power sunroof | $700 | $623 |
| *LTZ requires a Preferred Equipment Group. NA Base.* | | |
| Front floormats | 20 | 18 |
| Rear floormats | 20 | 18 |

## Appearance and Miscellaneous

| | | |
|---|---|---|
| Engine block heater | 20 | 18 |
| QNX 225/60R16 touring tires, Base | 175 | 156 |
| *Requires alloy wheels.* | | |
| Chrome wheel covers, Base | 100 | 89 |
| White alloy wheels, LTZ | NC | NC |
| *Requires white paint.* | | |
| Alloy wheels, Base | 300 | 267 |
| *Requires QNX 225/60R16 touring tires.* | | |

# CHEVROLET MALIBU

*Chevrolet Malibu*

## SPECIFICATIONS

| | 4-door sedan |
|---|---|
| Wheelbase, in. | 107.0 |
| Overall length, in. | 190.4 |
| Overall width, in. | 69.4 |
| Overall height, in. | 56.4 |
| Curb weight, lbs. | 3100 |
| Cargo vol., cu. ft. | 17.0 |
| Fuel capacity, gals. | 15.0 |
| Seating capacity | 5 |
| Front head room, in. | 39.4 |
| Max. front leg room, in. | 41.9 |
| Rear head room, in. | 37.6 |
| Min. rear leg room, in. | 38.0 |

## ENGINES

| | dohc I-4 | ohv V-6 |
|---|---|---|
| Size, liters/cu. in. | 2.4/146 | 3.1/191 |

*Prices are accurate at time of publication; subject to manufacturer's change.*

# CHEVROLET

| | dohc I-4 | ohv V-6 |
|---|---|---|
| Horsepower @ rpm | 150@ 5600 | 155@ 4800 |
| Torque (lbs./ft.) @ rpm | 155@ 4400 | 180@ 3200 |
| Availability | S[1] | S[2] |
| **EPA city/highway mpg** | | |
| 4-speed OD automatic | 23/32 | 20/29 |

1. Base. 2. LS; optional, base.

| Chevrolet Malibu | Retail Price | Dealer Invoice |
|---|---|---|
| Base 4-door sedan | $15670 | $14338 |
| LS 4-door sedan | 18470 | 16900 |
| Destination charge | 525 | 525 |

## STANDARD EQUIPMENT:

**Base:** 2.4-liter 4-cylinder engine, 4-speed automatic transmission, driver- and passenger-side air bags, anti-lock brakes, daytime running lights, air conditioning, power steering, tilt steering wheel, cloth upholstery, reclining front bucket seats, storage console w/armrest, cupholder, tachometer, coolant-temperature gauge, trip odometer, AM/FM radio, digital clock, intermittent wipers, visor mirrors, remote decklid release, auxiliary power outlet, rear heat ducts, dual outside mirrors w/driver-side remote, tinted glass, Passlock II theft-deterrent system, 215/60R15 tires, bolt-on wheel covers.

**LS** adds: 3.1-liter V-6 engine, cruise control, custom cloth upholstery, power driver seat, split folding rear seat, power windows, power door locks, remote keyless entry, power outside mirrors, cassette player, rear defogger, illuminated passenger-side visor mirror, dual reading lamps, passenger assist handles, cargo net, floormats, fog lamps, alloy wheels.

## OPTIONAL EQUIPMENT:

### Major Packages

| | | |
|---|---|---|
| Preferred Equipment Group 1, Base | 700 | 630 |
| *Power windows and door locks, power outside mirrors.* | | |
| Preferred Equipment Group 2, Base | 1100 | 990 |
| *Group 1 plus cruise control, remote keyless entry, dual reading lamps.* | | |

### Powertrains

| | | |
|---|---|---|
| 3.1-liter V-6 engine, Base | 495 | 446 |

### Comfort and Convenience

| | | |
|---|---|---|
| Cruise control, Base | 225 | 203 |
| *Requires Preferred Equipment Group 1.* | | |
| Power sunroof, Base | 635 | 572 |

CONSUMER GUIDE™

| | Retail Price | Dealer Invoice |
|---|---|---|
| LS................................................................................ | $595 | $536 |

*Includes reading lights, passenger-side illuminated visor mirror (Base). Base requires Preferred Equipment Group 2.*

| | | |
|---|---|---|
| Custom cloth upholstery, Base ......................................... | 225 | 203 |

*Includes split folding rear seat, cargo net. Requires Preferred Equipment Group.*

| | | |
|---|---|---|
| Leather upholstery, LS.................................................... | 475 | 428 |

*Includes leather-wrapped steering wheel.*

| | | |
|---|---|---|
| Power driver seat, Base ................................................. | 310 | 279 |
| Cassette player, Base..................................................... | 220 | 198 |
| CD player, Base ............................................................. | 320 | 288 |
| LS.......................................................................... | 100 | 90 |
| CD/cassette player, Base ............................................... | 420 | 378 |
| LS.......................................................................... | 200 | 180 |
| Remote keyless entry, Base ........................................... | 150 | 135 |

*Requires Preferred Equipment Group.*

| | | |
|---|---|---|
| Rear defogger, Base........................................................ | 180 | 162 |
| Floormats, Base.............................................................. | 40 | 36 |

## Appearance and Miscellaneous

| | | |
|---|---|---|
| Mud guards ................................................................... | 60 | 54 |

*Base requires Preferred Equipment Group.*

| | | |
|---|---|---|
| Alloy wheels, Base.......................................................... | 310 | 572 |

*Requires Preferred Equipment Group.*

# CHEVROLET METRO

| SPECIFICATIONS | 2-door hatchback | 4-door sedan |
|---|---|---|
| Wheelbase, in. ............................................... | 93.1 | 93.1 |
| Overall length, in. .......................................... | 149.4 | 164.0 |
| Overall width, in. ........................................... | 62.6 | 62.6 |
| Overall height, in. .......................................... | 54.7 | 55.4 |
| Curb weight, lbs. ........................................... | 1895 | 1984 |
| Cargo vol., cu. ft. .......................................... | 22.5 | 10.3 |
| Fuel capacity, gals. ....................................... | 10.6 | 10.3 |
| Seating capacity............................................. | 4 | 4 |
| Front head room, in. ....................................... | 39.1 | 39.3 |
| Max. front leg room, in. .................................. | 42.5 | 42.5 |
| Rear head room, in. ....................................... | 36.0 | 37.3 |
| Min. rear leg room, in. .................................... | 32.2 | 32.2 |

| ENGINES | ohc I-3 | ohc I-4 |
|---|---|---|
| Size, liters/cu. in. .......................................... | 1.0/61 | 1.3/79 |

*Prices are accurate at time of publication; subject to manufacturer's change.*

# CHEVROLET

*Chevrolet Metro LSi 4-door*

|  | ohc I-3 | ohc I-4 |
|---|---|---|
| Horsepower @ rpm | 55 @ 5700 | 79 @ 6000 |
| Torque (lbs./ft.) @ rpm | 58 @ 3300 | 75 @ 3000 |
| Availability | S[1] | S[2] |
| **EPA city/highway mpg** | | |
| 5-speed OD manual | 44/49 | 39/43 |
| 3-speed automatic | | 30/34 |

1. Base. 2. LSi.

| Chevrolet Metro | Retail Price | Dealer Invoice |
|---|---|---|
| Base 2-door hatchback | $8655 | $8153 |
| LSi 2-door hatchback | 9455 | 8812 |
| LSi 4-door sedan | 10055 | 9371 |
| Destination charge | 340 | 340 |

## STANDARD EQUIPMENT:

**Base:** 1.0-liter 3-cylinder engine, 5-speed manual transmission, driver- and passenger-side air bags, daytime running lights, cloth/vinyl reclining front bucket seats, folding rear seat, console with cupholders and storage tray, coolant-temperature gauge, dual outside mirrors, 155/80R13 tires.

**LSi** adds: 1.3-liter 4-cylinder engine, upgraded cloth/vinyl upholstery, intermittent wipers, trip odometer, passenger-side visor mirror, color-keyed bumpers, bodyside moldings, wheel covers.

## OPTIONAL EQUIPMENT:
### Major Packages

| | | |
|---|---|---|
| Preferred Equipment Group 2, Base | 179 | 159 |

*Easy-entry passenger seat, remote outside mirrors, bodyside moldings, floormats, wheel covers.*

| | Retail Price | Dealer Invoice |
|---|---|---|
| Preferred Equipment Group 3, Base | $1294 | $1152 |
| *Group 2 plus air conditioning, AM/FM radio with digital clock.* | | |
| Preferred Equipment Group 2, LSi 2-door | 1375 | 1224 |
| LSi 4-door | 1665 | 1482 |
| *Air conditioning, AM/FM/cassette with digital clock, floormats.* | | |
| Convenience Pkg., LSi | 125 | 111 |
| *Easy-entry passenger seat (2-door), split folding rear seat (4-door), remote outside mirrors, remote decklid release (4-door), cargo cover (2-door), trunk light (4-door).* | | |

## Powertrains

| | | |
|---|---|---|
| 3-speed automatic transmission, LSi | 595 | 530 |

## Safety Features

| | | |
|---|---|---|
| Anti-lock brakes | 565 | 503 |

## Comfort and Convenience

| | | |
|---|---|---|
| Air conditioning | 785 | 699 |
| Power steering, 4-door | 290 | 258 |
| AM/FM radio | 330 | 294 |
| *Includes seek and scan, digital clock, four speakers.* | | |
| AM/FM/cassette | 550 | 490 |
| Base w/Group 3 | 220 | 196 |
| AM/FM/CD player | 650 | 579 |
| Base w/Preferred Group 3 | 320 | 285 |
| LSi w/Preferred Group 2 | 100 | 89 |
| Radio provisions | 100 | 89 |
| *Includes speakers, antenna.* | | |
| Power door locks, 4-door | 220 | 196 |
| Rear defogger | 160 | 142 |
| Rear wiper/washer, LSi 2-door | 125 | 111 |
| *Requires rear defogger.* | | |
| Tachometer | 70 | 62 |
| *Includes trip odometer on base.* | | |

# CHEVROLET MONTE CARLO

## SPECIFICATIONS

| | 2-door coupe |
|---|---|
| Wheelbase, in. | 107.5 |
| Overall length, in. | 200.7 |
| Overall width, in. | 72.5 |

*Prices are accurate at time of publication; subject to manufacturer's change.*

*Chevrolet Monte Carlo Z34*

|  | 2-door coupe |
|---|---|
| Overall length, in. | 200.7 |
| Overall width, in. | 72.5 |
| Overall height, in. | 53.8 |
| Curb weight, lbs. | 3239 |
| Cargo vol., cu. ft. | 15.5 |
| Fuel capacity, gals. | 16.6 |
| Seating capacity | 6 |
| Front head room, in. | 37.9 |
| Max. front leg room, in. | 42.4 |
| Rear head room, in. | 36.9 |
| Min. rear leg room, in. | 34.9 |

## ENGINES

| | ohv V-6 | ohv V-6 |
|---|---|---|
| Size, liters/cu. in. | 3.1/191 | 3.8/231 |
| Horsepower @ rpm | 160@ 5200 | 200@ 5200 |
| Torque (lbs./ft.) @ rpm | 185@ 4000 | 225@ 4000 |
| Availability | S[1] | S[2] |
| **EPA city/highway mpg** | | |
| 4-speed OD automatic | 20/29 | 19/30 |

1. LS. 2. Z34.

| Chevrolet Monte Carlo | Retail Price | Dealer Invoice |
|---|---|---|
| LS 2-door notchback | $17795 | $16282 |
| Z34 2-door notchback | 20295 | 18570 |
| Destination charge | 550 | 550 |

## STANDARD EQUIPMENT:

**LS:** 3.1-liter V-6 engine, 4-speed automatic transmission, driver- and passenger-side air bags, anti-lock brakes, daytime running lamps, air conditioning, power steering, tilt steering wheel, 60/40 custom cloth reclining front seat with center armrest and 4-way manual driver seat, seatback storage pocket, split fold-down rear seat, cupholder, AM/FM/cassette with automatic tone control, digital clock, power windows, power door locks, power mirrors, illuminated passenger-side visor mirror, reading lights, trip odometer, tachometer, intermittent wipers, floormats, chrome grille, Pass-Key theft-deterrent system, tinted glass, color-keyed grille, bodyside moldings, 205/70R15 touring tires, wheel covers.

**Z34** adds: 3.8-liter V-6 engine, custom cloth front bucket seats with center console, cruise control, dual zone automatic air conditioning controls, steering-wheel radio controls, leather-wrapped steering wheel, power decklid release, remote keyless entry, cargo net, 4-wheel disc brakes, QNX 225/60R16 touring tires, alloy wheels.

## OPTIONAL EQUIPMENT:

| | Retail Price | Dealer Invoice |
|---|---|---|
| **Major Packages** | | |
| Preferred Equipment Group 1, LS | $635 | $565 |
| *Cruise control, remote keyless entry, dual heater/air conditioner controls, power decklid release, trunk net.* | | |
| **Comfort and Convenience** | | |
| OnStar System | 895 | 761 |
| *Includes Global Positioning System, voice-activated cellular telephone, roadside assistance, emergency services. Requires dealer installation charge and monthly service charges.* | | |
| Rear defogger | 170 | 151 |
| Cruise control, LS | 225 | 200 |
| CD player | 93 | 83 |
| *Includes automatic tone control.* | | |
| Steering-wheel-mounted radio controls, LS | 171 | 152 |
| *Includes leather-wrapped steering wheel.* | | |
| Power driver seat | 305 | 271 |
| Front bucket seats w/center console, LS | 200 | 178 |
| Leather front bucket seats, LS | 695 | 619 |
| Z34 | 645 | 574 |
| Power sunroof | 700 | 623 |
| *LS requires a Preferred Equipment Group.* | | |
| **Appearance and Miscellaneous** | | |
| Rear spoiler | 175 | 156 |
| Engine block heater | 20 | 18 |
| QNX 225/60R16 touring tires, LS | 175 | 156 |
| *Requires alloy wheels.* | | |
| Alloy wheels, LS | 300 | 267 |
| *Requires QNX 225/60R16 touring tires.* | | |

*Prices are accurate at time of publication; subject to manufacturer's change.*

# CHEVROLET PRIZM

*Chevrolet Prizm*

## SPECIFICATIONS

| | 4-door sedan |
|---|---|
| Wheelbase, in. | 97.0 |
| Overall length, in. | 174.2 |
| Overall width, in. | 66.7 |
| Overall height, in. | 53.7 |
| Curb weight, lbs. | 2359 |
| Cargo vol., cu. ft. | 12.1 |
| Fuel capacity, gals. | 13.2 |
| Seating capacity | 5 |
| Front head room, in. | 39.3 |
| Max. front leg room, in. | 42.5 |
| Rear head room, in. | 36.9 |
| Min. rear leg room, in. | 33.2 |

## ENGINES

| | dohc I-4 |
|---|---|
| Size, liters/cu. in. | 1.8/110 |
| Horsepower @ rpm | 120@ 5600 |
| Torque (lbs./ft.) @ rpm | 122@ 4400 |
| Availability | S |

### EPA city/highway mpg

| | |
|---|---|
| 5-speed OD manual | 31/37 |
| 3-speed automatic | 28/33 |
| 4-speed OD automatic | 28/36 |

| Chevrolet Prizm | Retail Price | Dealer Invoice |
|---|---|---|
| Base 4-door sedan | $12043 | $11465 |
| LSi 4-door sedan | 14614 | 13474 |

|  | Retail Price | Dealer Invoice |
|---|---|---|
| Destination charge ........................................................... | $420 | $420 |

## STANDARD EQUIPMENT:

**Base:** 1.8-liter dohc engine, 5-speed manual transmission, driver- and passenger-side air bags, daytime running lights, power steering, cloth reclining front bucket seats, center console with storage tray and cupholders, intermittent wipers, dual trip odometer, automatic headlights, visor mirrors, remote fuel door and decklid release, rear heat ducts, left remote and right manual mirrors, tinted glass, bodyside moldings, 175/65R14 tires.

**LSi** adds: power mirrors, air conditioning, power door locks, remote keyless entry, AM/FM/cassette, upgraded cloth upholstery, split folding rear seat, floormats, wheel covers.

## OPTIONAL EQUIPMENT:

### Major Packages

| | | |
|---|---|---|
| Preferred Equipment Group 2, Base............................. | 1222 | 1051 |
| *Air conditioning, AM/FM radio with digital clock, floormats, wheel covers.* | | |
| Preferred Equipment Group 3, Base............................. | 1847 | 1588 |
| *Preferred Equipment Group 2 plus power door locks, cassette player, cruise control.* | | |
| Preferred Equipment Group 3, LSi .............................. | 550 | 473 |
| *Power windows, cruise control, CD player, tilt steering wheel, Handling Pkg. (front stabilizer bar, 185/65R14 tires).* | | |
| Handling Pkg., LSi ...................................................... | 70 | 60 |
| *Front stabilizer bar, 185/65R14 tires.* | | |

### Powertrains

| | | |
|---|---|---|
| 3-speed automatic transmission...................................... | 495 | 426 |
| 4-speed automatic transmission...................................... | 800 | 688 |

### Safety Features

| | | |
|---|---|---|
| Anti-lock brakes................................................................ | 645 | 555 |
| Front side-impact air bags................................................ | 295 | 254 |
| Integrated child safety seat, LSi...................................... | 125 | 108 |

### Comfort and Convenience

| | | |
|---|---|---|
| Air conditioning, Base...................................................... | 795 | 684 |
| Cruise control .................................................................. | 185 | 159 |
| Tilt steering wheel ........................................................... | 80 | 69 |
| Rear defogger .................................................................. | 180 | 155 |
| Power door locks, Base ................................................... | 220 | 189 |
| Power sunroof.................................................................. | 675 | 581 |
| Tachometer...................................................................... | 70 | 60 |
| *Includes outside temperature gauge.* | | |

*Prices are accurate at time of publication; subject to manufacturer's change.*

| | Retail Price | Dealer Invoice |
|---|---|---|
| AM/FM radio | $335 | $288 |
| *Includes seek/scan, digital clock, and four speakers.* | | |
| AM/FM/cassette, Base | 555 | 477 |
| *Includes seek/scan, digital clock, four speakers.* | | |
| AM/FM/CD player, Base | 655 | 563 |
| LSi | 100 | 86 |
| *Includes seek/scan, digital clock, four speakers.* | | |
| Floormats, Base | 40 | 34 |

## Appearance and Miscellaneous

| | | |
|---|---|---|
| Wheel covers, Base | 52 | 45 |
| Alloy wheels | 335 | 288 |

# CHEVROLET TRACKER

*Chevrolet Tracker 2WD 4-door*

| SPECIFICATIONS | 2-door conv. | 4-door wagon |
|---|---|---|
| Wheelbase, in. | 86.6 | 97.6 |
| Overall length, in. | 143.7 | 158.7 |
| Overall width, in. | 64.2 | 64.4 |
| Overall height, in. | 64.3 | 65.7 |
| Curb weight, lbs. | 2339 | 2747 |
| Cargo vol., cu. ft. | 32.9 | 45.9 |
| Fuel capacity, gals. | 11.1 | 14.5 |
| Seating capacity | 4 | 4 |
| Front head room, in. | 39.5 | 40.6 |
| Max. front leg room, in. | 42.1 | 42.1 |
| Rear head room, in. | 39.0 | 40.0 |
| Min. rear leg room, in. | 31.7 | 32.7 |

## ENGINES

| | ohc I-4 |
|---|---|
| Size, liters/cu. in. | 1.6/97 |
| Horsepower @ rpm | 95 @ 5600 |
| Torque (lbs./ft.) @ rpm | 98 @ 4000 |
| Availability | S |

**EPA city/highway mpg**

| | |
|---|---|
| 5-speed OD manual | 23/26 |
| 3-speed automatic | 23/24 |
| 4-speed OD automatic | 22/26 |

| Chevrolet Tracker | Retail Price | Dealer Invoice |
|---|---|---|
| 2-door convertible, 2WD | $13655 | $13000 |
| 2-door convertible, 4WD | 14665 | 13952 |
| 4-door wagon, 2WD | 14860 | 14147 |
| 4-door wagon, 4WD | 15605 | 14856 |
| Destination charge | 340 | 340 |

## STANDARD EQUIPMENT:

**Base:** 1.6-liter 4-cylinder engine, 5-speed manual transmission, driver- and passenger-side air bags, daytime running lights, power steering (wagon), rear defogger (wagon), cloth/vinyl reclining front bucket seats, folding rear bench seat (convertible), split folding rear bench seat (wagon), center console with storage tray and cupholders, tachometer, trip odometer, passenger-side visor mirror, intermittent wipers, dual outside mirrors, fuel-tank skid plate, full-size lockable spare tire, spare-tire cover, front and rear tow hooks, 195/75R15 tires, 4WD models add: part-time 4WD, manually locking front hubs, power steering (convertibles), 205/75R15 tires.

## OPTIONAL EQUIPMENT:
### Major Packages

| | | |
|---|---|---|
| Preferred Group 2, 2WD convertible | 1644 | 1463 |
|    4WD convertible | 1354 | 1205 |
|    wagon | 1366 | 1216 |

*Air conditioning, AM/FM radio with digital clock, power steering (2WD convertible), bodyside moldings, floormats.*

| | | |
|---|---|---|
| Preferred Group 3, | | |
|    2WD wagon | 2121 | 1888 |
|    4WD wagon | 2321 | 2066 |

*Group 2 plus automatic locking front hubs (4WD), Convenience Pkg. (power windows and door locks, power mirrors).*

| | | |
|---|---|---|
| Expression Color-appearance Pkg., convertible | 249 | 222 |

*Prices are accurate at time of publication; subject to manufacturer's change.*

|  | Retail Price | Dealer Invoice |
|---|---|---|
| Expression Appearance Pkg., convertible with Preferred Group | $164 | $146 |
| *Adjustable rear bucket seats, custom upholstery, bodyside moldings, special tan exterior color treatments.* | | |
| Convenience Pkg., wagon | 580 | 516 |
| *Power windows and door locks, power mirrors.* | | |

## Powertrains

|  |  |  |
|---|---|---|
| 3-speed automatic transmission, convertibles | 625 | 556 |
| 4-speed automatic transmission, wagons | 1000 | 890 |
| Automatic locking front hubs, 4WD | 200 | 178 |

## Safety Features

|  |  |  |
|---|---|---|
| Anti-lock brakes | 595 | 530 |

## Comfort and Convenience

|  |  |  |
|---|---|---|
| Air conditioning | 935 | 832 |
| Power steering, 2WD convertible | 290 | 258 |
| Cruise control | 175 | 156 |
| AM/FM radio | 306 | 272 |
| *Includes digital clock.* | | |
| AM/FM/cassette | 526 | 468 |
| with Preferred Group | 220 | 196 |
| AM/FM/CD player | 626 | 557 |
| AM/FM/cassette and CD players, with Preferred Group | 320 | 284 |
| Rear wiper/washer, wagon | 125 | 111 |
| Floormats, convertible | 28 | 25 |
| wagon | 40 | 36 |

## Appearance and Miscellaneous

|  |  |  |
|---|---|---|
| Bodyside moldings | 85 | 76 |

## Special Purpose, Wheels and Tires

|  |  |  |
|---|---|---|
| Transfer-case and front-differential skid plates, 4WD | 75 | 67 |
| Alloy wheels | 365 | 325 |

# CHEVROLET VENTURE

| SPECIFICATIONS | 3-door van | 3-door van |
|---|---|---|
| Wheelbase, in. | 112.0 | 120.0 |
| Overall length, in. | 186.9 | 200.9 |
| Overall width, in. | 72.0 | 72.0 |
| Overall height, in. | 67.4 | 68.1 |

*Chevrolet Venture*

| | 3-door van | 3-door van |
|---|---|---|
| Curb weight, lbs. | 3699 | 3838 |
| Cargo vol., cu. ft. | 126.6 | 148.3 |
| Maximum payload, lbs. | 1658 | 1519 |
| Fuel capacity, gals. | 20.0 | 25.0 |
| Seating capacity | 7 | 7 |
| Front head room, in. | 39.9 | 39.9 |
| Max. front leg room, in. | 39.9 | 39.9 |
| Rear head room, in. | 39.3 | 39.3 |
| Min. rear leg room, in. | 36.9 | 39.0 |

## ENGINES

| | ohv V-6 |
|---|---|
| Size, liters/cu. in. | 3.4/207 |
| Horsepower @ rpm | 180@ 5200 |
| Torque (lbs./ft.) @ rpm | 205@ 4000 |
| Availability | S |

**EPA city/highway mpg**

| | |
|---|---|
| 4-speed OD automatic | 18/25 |

| Chevrolet Venture | Retail Price | Dealer Invoice |
|---|---|---|
| Cargo Extended 3-door van | $20169 | $18253 |
| Cargo Extended 4-door van | 20759 | 18787 |
| Passenger SWB 3-door van | 20249 | 18325 |
| Passenger Extended 3-door van | 21669 | 19610 |
| Passenger LS SWB 4-door van | 21429 | 19393 |
| Passenger LS Extended 4-door | 22259 | 20144 |
| Destination charge | 570 | 570 |

SWB denotes short wheelbase.

## STANDARD EQUIPMENT:

**Cargo:** 3.4-liter V-6 engine, 4-speed automatic transmission, driver- and

*Prices are accurate at time of publication; subject to manufacturer's change.*

# CHEVROLET

passenger-side air bags, anti-lock brakes, daytime running lamps, front air conditioning, power steering, tilt steering column, 2-passenger seating (vinyl front bucket seats), rubber floor covering, center storage console, overhead consolette, front cupholders, automatic headlights, interior air filter, intermittent wipers, rear wiper/washer, AM/FM radio, digital clock, power door locks, power mirrors, visor mirrors, front auxiliary power outlets, Passlock theft-deterrent, tinted glass, Sungate solar-coated windshield with integrated antenna, dual horn, 215/70R15 tires, wheel covers.

**Passenger SWB 3-door** adds: 7-passenger seating (cloth front bucket seats, center and rear solid bench seats), seatback tray, carpeting, floormats, cargo net, rear cupholders, rear power outlet, intermittent rear wiper/washer, 205/70R15 tires.

**Passenger Extended 3-door** adds: center and rear split folding bench seats, 215/70R15 tires.

**Passenger LS SWB 4-door** adds: driver-side sliding door, cruise control, LS trim (driver-side lumbar support, adjustable headrests, upgraded interior trim and upholstery), power windows, cassette player with automatic tone control, remote keyless entry, interior roof-rail lighting, additional sound insulation, liftgate cargo net.

**Passenger LS Extended 4-door** adds: 215/70R15 tires.

## OPTIONAL EQUIPMENT:

| | Retail Price | Dealer Invoice |
|---|---|---|
| **Major Packages** | | |
| Preferred Equipment Group 1 | $650 | $559 |
| *Power windows, cruise control, remote keyless entry.* | | |
| LS Preferred Equipment Group 2, SWB 3-door | 1540 | 1324 |
| Passenger Extended 3-door, 4-door | 1205 | 1036 |
| *Group 1 plus power rear vent windows, custom cloth seats, center and rear split folding bench seats (SWB), front lumbar adjusters, adjustable headrests, cassette player w/automatic tone control.* | | |
| LS Preferred Equipment Group 3, Passenger Extended | 2401 | 2065 |
| *Group 2 plus power driver seat, overhead console, rear defogger, deep-tinted glass, roof rack.* | | |
| Safety and Security Pkg., Passenger | 285 | 245 |
| Passenger w/Touring Suspension | 210 | 181 |
| *Theft-deterrent system including alarm, self-sealing tires.* | | |
| Trailering Pkg. | 150 | 129 |
| *Includes heavy-duty engine and transmission oil cooling.* | | |
| **Powertrains** | | |
| Traction control | 195 | 168 |
| **Safety Features** | | |
| Integrated child seat, Passenger | 125 | 108 |
| *NA with captain's seats.* | | |

| | Retail Price | Dealer Invoice |
|---|---|---|
| Dual integrated child seats, Passenger.......................... | $225 | $194 |

*NA with captain's seats.*

## Comfort and Convenience

| | | |
|---|---|---|
| OnStar System............................................................ | 895 | 761 |

*Includes Global Positioning System, voice-activated cellular telephone, roadside assistance, emergency services. Requires dealer installation charge and monthly service charges.*

| | | |
|---|---|---|
| Rear air conditioning, Passenger Extended ................. | 450 | 387 |

*Requires deep-tinted glass and rear defogger. 3-door requires a preferred equipment group.*

| | | |
|---|---|---|
| Rear heater, Cargo...................................................... | 205 | 176 |
| Power passenger-side sliding door, SWB...................... | 435 | 374 |
| Passenger Extended.............................................. | 385 | 331 |

*Includes power rear vent windows. SWB requires Group 1. Extended requires Group 1 or 2.*

| | | |
|---|---|---|
| 6-way power driver seat, Passenger............................. | 270 | 232 |

*3-door requires Group 2.*

| | | |
|---|---|---|
| Cloth upholstery, Cargo............................................... | 185 | 159 |
| Center and rear split folding bench seats, SWB 3-door | 335 | 288 |

*Requires Group 1.*

| | | |
|---|---|---|
| Center row captain's seats, Passenger......................... | 265 | 228 |
| Rear bucket seats, Passenger..................................... | 115 | 99 |

*Requires Group 2 or 3.*

| | | |
|---|---|---|
| Rear defogger............................................................. | 170 | 146 |
| Cassette player, Cargo............................................... | 165 | 141 |
| Cassette player w/automatic tone control, SWB 3-door ......................................................... | 232 | 220 |
| CD player, Passenger ................................................. | 370 | 318 |
| Passenger w/Group 2 or 3...................................... | 100 | 86 |

*Includes automatic tone control, coaxial speakers, anti-theft feature.*

| | | |
|---|---|---|
| Cassette/CD player, Passenger................................... | 470 | 404 |
| Passenger w/Group 2 or 3...................................... | 200 | 172 |

*Includes automatic tone control, coaxial speakers, anti-theft feature.*

| | | |
|---|---|---|
| Rear-seat audio controls, Passenger ........................... | 120 | 103 |

*Includes headphone jacks. 3-door requires Group 2 or 3.*

| | | |
|---|---|---|
| Overhead console, Passenger ...................................... | 271 | 233 |

*Driver information center, illuminated visor mirrors.*

## Appearance and Miscellaneous

| | | |
|---|---|---|
| Roof rack.................................................................... | 175 | 151 |
| Engine-block heater.................................................... | 20 | 17 |
| Deep-tinted glass, Passenger...................................... | 275 | 237 |

*Includes blackout center pillar w/most exterior colors. Requires rear defogger.*

*Prices are accurate at time of publication; subject to manufacturer's change.*

|  | Retail Price | Dealer Invoice |
|---|---|---|
| Deep-tinted glass w/rear defogger, Cargo | $445 | $383 |
| Theft-deterrent system, Cargo | 60 | 51 |
| *Requires Preferred Equipment Group.* |  |  |
| Touring Suspension, Cargo | 195 | 167 |
| Passenger SWB | 285 | 245 |
| Passenger Extended w/Group 2 | 245 | 211 |
| Passenger Extended W/Group 3 | 210 | 181 |
| *Load-leveling suspension, auxiliary air inflator (passenger), 215/70R15 tires (SWB).* |  |  |
| 215/70R15 tires, SWB 3-door, LS SWB 4-door | 75 | 65 |
| 215/70R15 touring tires, Cargo Extended | 35 | 30 |
| *3-door requires a Preferred Equipment Group.* |  |  |
| Self-sealing tires, Cargo, Extended | 185 | 159 |
| SWB | 225 | 194 |
| Alloy wheels, Passenger | 295 | 254 |

# CHRYSLER CIRRUS

*Chrysler Cirrus LXi*

## SPECIFICATIONS

|  | 4-door sedan |
|---|---|
| Wheelbase, in. | 108.0 |
| Overall length, in. | 187.0 |
| Overall width, in. | 71.7 |
| Overall height, in. | 52.5 |
| Curb weight, lbs. | 3181 |
| Cargo vol., cu. ft. | 15.7 |
| Fuel capacity, gals. | 16.0 |
| Seating capacity | 5 |
| Front head room, in. | 38.1 |
| Max. front leg room, in. | 42.3 |
| Rear head room, in. | 36.8 |
| Min. rear leg room, in. | 37.8 |

## ENGINES

| | ohc V-6 |
|---|---|
| Size, liters/cu. in. | 2.5/152 |
| Horsepower @ rpm | 168@ 5800 |
| Torque (lbs./ft.) @ rpm | 170@ 4350 |
| Availability | S |
| **EPA city/highway mpg** | |
| 4-speed OD automatic | 18/28 |

| Chrysler Cirrus | Retail Price | Dealer Invoice |
|---|---|---|
| LXi 4-door sedan | $19460 | $17794 |
| Destination charge | 535 | 535 |

## STANDARD EQUIPMENT:

**LXi:** 2.5-liter V-6 engine, 4-speed automatic transmission, anti-lock brakes, driver- and passenger-side air bags, variable-assist power steering, tilt steering column, leather-wrapped steering wheel, air conditioning, cloth reclining front bucket seats with driver-side manual height and lumbar adjusters, folding rear bench seat, console, AM/FM/cassette with six speakers, digital clock, trip odometer, oil-pressure and coolant-temperature gauges, voltmeter, tachometer, cruise control, rear defogger, power windows, speed-sensitive power door locks, heated power mirrors, speed-sensitive intermittent wipers, illuminated remote keyless entry, remote decklid release, universal garage-door opener, reading lights, auxiliary power outlet, color-keyed bodyside moldings, illuminated visor mirrors, floormats, tinted glass with solar-control windshield, fog lights, 195/65R15 tires, alloy wheels.

## OPTIONAL EQUIPMENT:
### Major Packages

| | | |
|---|---|---|
| Gold Pkg. | 500 | 315 |
| *Gold trim and badging, chrome alloy wheels with gold accents.* | | |

### Comfort and Convenience

| | | |
|---|---|---|
| Leather upholstery | 1000 | 890 |
| *Manufacturer's discount price* | NC | NC |
| *Includes 8-way power driver seat.* | | |
| Premium cassette player | 340 | 303 |
| *Includes eight speakers, power amplifier, CD changer controls.* | | |
| Premium cassette and 6-disc CD changer | 550 | 490 |
| Theft-deterrent system w/security alarm | 150 | 134 |
| Power sunroof | 580 | 516 |
| Smoker's Pkg. | 20 | 18 |

*Prices are accurate at time of publication; subject to manufacturer's change.*

## Appearance and Miscellaneous

| | Retail Price | Dealer Invoice |
|---|---|---|
| Metallic candy-apple-red paint | $200 | $178 |
| Full-size spare tire | 125 | 111 |
| Engine block and battery heater | 30 | 27 |

# CHRYSLER CONCORDE

*Chrysler Concorde LXi*

## SPECIFICATIONS

| | 4-door sedan |
|---|---|
| Wheelbase, in. | 113.0 |
| Overall length, in. | 209.1 |
| Overall width, in. | 74.4 |
| Overall height, in. | 55.9 |
| Curb weight, lbs. | 3430 |
| Cargo vol., cu. ft. | 18.7 |
| Fuel capacity, gals. | 17.0 |
| Seating capacity | 6 |
| Front head room, in. | 38.3 |
| Max. front leg room, in. | 42.2 |
| Rear head room, in. | 37.2 |
| Min. rear leg room, in. | 41.6 |

## ENGINES

| | dohc V-6 | ohc V-6 |
|---|---|---|
| Size, liters/cu. in. | 2.7/167 | 3.2/197 |
| Horsepower @ rpm | 200@ 5800 | 225@ 6300 |
| Torque (lbs./ft.) @ rpm | 190@ 4850 | 225@ 3800 |
| Availability | S[1] | S[2] |

| **EPA city/highway mpg** | | |
|---|---|---|
| 4-speed OD automatic | NA | 19/29 |

1. LX. 2. LXi.

## Chrysler Concorde

| | Retail Price | Dealer Invoice |
|---|---|---|
| Base 4-door sedan | $21305 | $19511 |
| Destination charge | 550 | 550 |

Prices not available at time of publication.

## STANDARD EQUIPMENT:

**Base:** 2.7-liter dohc V-6 engine, 4-speed automatic transmission, driver- and passenger-side air bags, 4-wheel disc brakes, air conditioning, rear air conditioning ducts, power steering, tilt steering wheel, cruise control, cloth front bucket seats w/power driver seat, floor console, cupholders, trunk pass-through, power mirrors, power windows, power door locks, remote keyless entry, tachometer, trip odometer, coolant-temperature gauge, AM/FM/cassette with four speakers, illuminated visor mirrors, rear defogger, variable intermittent wipers, power decklid release, reading lights, floormats, solar-control glass, 205/70R15 tires, wheel covers.

## OPTIONAL EQUIPMENT:
### Major Packages

| | | |
|---|---|---|
| LX Pkg. 22D | 1090 | 970 |

*Eight-speaker sound system, overhead trip computer, 8-way power passenger seat, 225/60R16 tires.*

| | | |
|---|---|---|
| LXi Pkg. 24F | 3380 | 3008 |
| Manufacturer's discount price | 2935 | 2612 |

*LX Pkg. plus anti-lock brakes, traction control, leather upholstery, leather-wrapped steering wheel and shift knob, automatic temperature control, CD changer controls, nine Infinity speakers, automatic day/night rearview mirror, universal garage-door opener, theft-deterrent system, full-size spare tire.*

### Powertrains

| | | |
|---|---|---|
| 3.2-liter V-6 engine | 500 | 445 |

*Requires LXi Pkg.*

| | | |
|---|---|---|
| Traction control | 175 | 156 |

*Requires LX Pkg.*

### Safety Features

| | | |
|---|---|---|
| Anti-lock brakes | 600 | 534 |

### Comfort and Convenience

| | | |
|---|---|---|
| Power moonroof | 795 | 708 |

*Requires LXi Pkg.*

| | | |
|---|---|---|
| CD player | 435 | 387 |

*Includes CD changer controls, eight speakers.*

| | | |
|---|---|---|
| CD player, ordered w/LX Pkg. | 145 | 129 |

*Includes CD changer controls, eight speakers.*

*Prices are accurate at time of publication; subject to manufacturer's change.*

| | Retail Price | Dealer Invoice |
|---|---|---|
| CD player w/Infinity speakers ...................................... | 145 | 129 |
| *Includes CD changer controls, nine Infinity speakers. Requires LXi Pkg.* | | |
| CD/cassette player ..................................................... | 300 | 267 |
| *Includes nine Infinity speakers. Requires LXi Pkg.* | | |

## Appearance and Miscellaneous

| | Retail Price | Dealer Invoice |
|---|---|---|
| Metallic paint .............................................................. | 200 | 178 |
| 16-inch wheel and Tire Group........................................ | 200 | 178 |
| *Includes 225/60R16 tires* | | |
| Alloy wheels ............................................................... | 365 | 325 |
| *Requires LXi Pkg.* | | |

# CHRYSLER SEBRING

*Chrysler Sebring JXi*

## SPECIFICATIONS

| | 2-door coupe | 2-door conv. |
|---|---|---|
| Wheelbase, in. ............................................... | 103.7 | 106.0 |
| Overall length, in. .......................................... | 190.9 | 192.6 |
| Overall width, in. ........................................... | 69.7 | 70.1 |
| Overall height, in. .......................................... | 53.0 | 54.8 |
| Curb weight, lbs. ........................................... | 2959 | 3344 |
| Cargo vol., cu. ft. .......................................... | 13.1 | 11.3 |
| Fuel capacity, gals. ........................................ | 16.9 | 16.0 |
| Seating capacity............................................ | 5 | 5 |
| Front head room, in. ...................................... | 39.1 | 38.7 |
| Max. front leg room, in. .................................. | 43.3 | 42.4 |
| Rear head room, in. ....................................... | 36.5 | 37.0 |
| Min. rear leg room, in. .................................... | 35.0 | 35.2 |

## ENGINES

| | dohc I-4 | dohc I-4 | ohc V-6 | ohc V-6 |
|---|---|---|---|---|
| Size, liters/cu. in. ............ | 2.0/122 | 2.4/148 | 2.5/152 | 2.5/152 |

| | dohc I-4 | dohc I-4 | ohc V-6 | ohc V-6 |
|---|---|---|---|---|
| Horsepower @ rpm ........ | 140@ 6000 | 150@ 5200 | 163@ 5500 | 168@ 5800 |
| Torque (lbs./ft.) @ rpm .... | 130@ 4800 | 167@ 4000 | 170@ 4350 | 170@ 4350 |
| Availability ....................... | S[1] | S[2] | S[3] | O[4] |
| **EPA city/highway mpg** | | | | |
| 5-speed OD manual ........ | 22/31 | | | |
| 4-speed OD automatic..... | 21/30 | 21/30 | 19/28 | 19/28[5] |

1. LX. 2. JX and JXi. 3. LXi, optional LX. 4. JX and JXi. 5. 19/29 w/Autostick.

| Chrysler Sebring | Retail Price | Dealer Invoice |
|---|---|---|
| LX 2-door coupe ................................................................ | $16840 | $15498 |
| LXi 2-door coupe ............................................................... | 20775 | 19000 |
| JX 2-door convertible ........................................................ | 20575 | 18892 |
| JXi 2-door convertible ....................................................... | 25040 | 22866 |
| Destination charge ............................................................ | 535 | 535 |

## STANDARD EQUIPMENT:

**LX:** 2.0-liter dohc 4-cylinder engine, 5-speed manual transmission, driver- and passenger-side air bags, variable-assist power steering, tilt steering column, air conditioning, cloth front bucket seats, console with storage armrest and cupholders, rear defogger, split folding rear seat, rear headrests, AM/ FM/cassette player, digital clock, trip odometer, coolant-temperature gauges, tachometer, variable intermittent wipers, remote fuel-door and decklid releases, visor mirrors, map lights, color-keyed front and rear fascias, floormats, tinted glass, remote outside mirrors, fog lights, 195/70R14 tires, wheel covers.

**LXi** adds: 2.5-liter V-6 engine, 4-speed automatic transmission, 4-wheel disc brakes, power windows, power door locks, heated power mirrors, upgraded cloth upholstery and driver-seat lumbar support, leather-wrapped steering wheel, AM/FM/cassette/CD player, cruise control, remote keyless entry system w/security alarm, oil-pressure gauge, automatic day/night rearview mirror, compass, illuminated visor mirrors, Homelink universal garage-door opener, trunk net, rear spoiler, bright exhaust tips, 215/50HR17 tires, alloy wheels.

**JX:** 2.4-liter dohc 4-cylinder engine, 4-speed automatic transmission, driver- and passenger-side air bags, variable-assist power steering, tilt steering column, air conditioning, front bucket seats, vinyl upholstery, console with storage armrest, visor mirrors, power windows, rear defogger, AM/FM radio, digital clock, trip odometer, oil-pressure gauge, coolant-temperature gauge, tachometer, variable intermittent wipers, map lights, vinyl convertible top with glass rear window, tinted glass, dual remote mirrors, 205/65R15 tires, wheel covers.

**JXi** adds: anti-lock brakes, cruise control, Firm Feel power steering, leather/vinyl seats, 6-way power front seats, programmable power door locks, heated power mirrors, leather-wrapped steering wheel and shifter,

# CHRYSLER

trip computer, cassette player with six Infinity speakers, power antenna, remote-keyless entry, illuminated entry, illuminated visor mirrors, remote decklid release, floormats, touring suspension, cloth convertible top with glass rear window, theft-deterrent system, fog lamps, 215/55HR16 touring tires, alloy wheels.

## OPTIONAL EQUIPMENT:

| | Retail Price | Dealer Invoice |
|---|---|---|

### Major Packages

| | Retail Price | Dealer Invoice |
|---|---|---|
| Pkg. 21H/24H, LX | $780 | $694 |

*Cruise control, power windows, door locks, and mirrors, illuminated visor mirrors, trunk net.*

| | | |
|---|---|---|
| Pkg. 24K, LXi | 626 | 557 |

*Manufacturer's discount price* ..... NC NC
*Leather upholstery, power driver seat.*

| | | |
|---|---|---|
| Pkg. 24B/26B, JX | 1585 | 1411 |

*Power Convenience Group (programmable door locks, heated power mirrors), cassette player and CD control, 6-way power driver seat, cruise control, remote keyless entry, delay off headlamps, remote decklid release, illuminated entry, illuminated visor mirrors, additional trunk trim, floormats.*

| | | |
|---|---|---|
| Pkg. 26C, JX | 1780 | 1584 |

*Pkg. 24B/26B plus Autostick 4-speed automatic transmission. Requires 2.5-liter V-6 engine.*

| | | |
|---|---|---|
| Pkg. 26E, JXi | 195 | 174 |

*Autostick 4-speed automatic transmission.*

| | | |
|---|---|---|
| Pkg. 26G, JXi | 1550 | 1380 |

*Includes 4-wheel disc brakes, traction control, Autostick shifter, Limited Decor Group (leather seats, luxury floormats, color-keyed grille, chrome alloy wheels), Luxury Convenience Group (universal garage door opener, automatic day/night inside mirror, map light).*

| | | |
|---|---|---|
| Luxury Convenience Group, JX, JXi | 175 | 156 |

*Universal garage-door opener, automatic day/night rearview mirror, map light. JX requires option pkg.*

| | | |
|---|---|---|
| Power Convenience Group, JX | 360 | 320 |

*Programmable power door locks, heated power mirrors.*

| | | |
|---|---|---|
| Security Group, JX | 175 | 156 |

*Alarm system, programmable power door locks. Requires Pkg. 24B/26B.*

### Powertrains

| | | |
|---|---|---|
| 2.5-liter V-6 engine, LX | 830 | 739 |
| JX | 1365 | 1215 |
| JXi | 800 | 712 |

*LX includes 4-wheel disc brakes, upgraded suspension, heavy-duty battery, oil pressure gauge, bright dual exhaust outlets, 205/55HR16 tires. LX requires 4-speed automatic transmission, Pkg. 24H. JX includes antilock brakes, bright dual exhaust outlets. JX requires option pkg.*

|  | Retail Price | Dealer Invoice |
|---|---|---|
| 4-speed automatic transmission, LX | $695 | $619 |
| Traction control, JX | 790 | 703 |
| JX w/2.5-liter engine, JXi | 225 | 200 |

*Includes 4-wheel disc brakes. JX w/2.4-liter engine includes anti-lock brakes.*

## Safety Features

|  |  |  |
|---|---|---|
| Anti-lock brakes, LX, LXi | 600 | 534 |
| JX | 565 | 503 |

*LX, LXi include 4-wheel disc brakes. LX requires Pkg. 21H/24H.*

## Comfort and Convenience

|  |  |  |
|---|---|---|
| Cruise control, JX | 240 | 214 |
| Power sunroof, LX, LXi | 640 | 570 |

*LX requires Pkg. 21H/24H.*

|  |  |  |
|---|---|---|
| CD/cassette player, LX w/Pkg. 21H/24H | 435 | 387 |

*Includes graphic equalizer.*

|  |  |  |
|---|---|---|
| CD/cassette player with Infinity speakers and equalizer, LX w/Pkg. 21H/24H | 760 | 676 |
| CD/cassette player with eight Infinity speakers and equalizer, LXi | 325 | 289 |
| Cassette player, JX | 275 | 245 |

*Includes CD changer control.*

|  |  |  |
|---|---|---|
| Cassette player w/amplifier, JX | 355 | 316 |

*Includes six Infinity speakers, CD changer controls. Requires Pkg. 24B/26B.*

|  |  |  |
|---|---|---|
| CD player, JX | 445 | 396 |
| JX w/option pkg. | 170 | 151 |
| CD/cassette player w/amplifier, JX | 695 | 619 |
| JXi | 340 | 303 |

*Includes six Infinity speakers, power antenna. JX requires Pkg. 24B/26B.*

|  |  |  |
|---|---|---|
| 6-disc CD changer, JX, JXi | 500 | 445 |

*JX requires cassette player. NA with CD/cassette player.*

|  |  |  |
|---|---|---|
| Power driver seat, LX, LXi | 205 | 182 |

*LX requires Pkg. 21H/24H.*

|  |  |  |
|---|---|---|
| Premium cloth upholstery, JX | 95 | 85 |
| JXi (credit) | (250) | (223) |
| Remote keyless entry w/security alarm, LX w/Pkg. 21H/24H | 290 | 258 |
| Smoker's group, JX, JXi | 20 | 18 |

## Appearance and Miscellaneous

|  |  |  |
|---|---|---|
| Engine block heater, JX, JXi | 35 | 30 |
| Candy-apple-red metallic paint, JX, JXi | 200 | 178 |

*Prices are accurate at time of publication; subject to manufacturer's change.*

| | Retail Price | Dealer Invoice |
|---|---|---|
| 16-inch Wheel Group, LX | $490 | $436 |
| LX w/2.5-liter engine | 335 | 298 |
| *Alloy wheels, 205/55HR16 tires.* | | |
| 16-inch Touring Group, JX | 495 | 441 |
| *Firm Feel power steering, touring suspension, 215/55R16 touring tires, alloy wheels.* | | |

# CHRYSLER TOWN & COUNTRY

*Chrysler Town & Country*

## SPECIFICATIONS

| | 4-door van | 4-door van |
|---|---|---|
| Wheelbase, in. | 113.3 | 119.3 |
| Overall length, in. | 186.4 | 199.7 |
| Overall width, in. | 76.8 | 76.8 |
| Overall height, in. | 68.7 | 68.7 |
| Curb weight, lbs. | 3958 | 4082 |
| Cargo vol., cu. ft. | 138.5 | 162.9 |
| Fuel capacity, gals. | 20.0 | 20.0 |
| Seating capacity | 7 | 7 |
| Front head room, in. | 39.8 | 39.8 |
| Max. front leg room, in. | 40.6 | 40.6 |
| Rear head room, in. | 40.5 | 39.6 |
| Min. rear leg room, in. | 35.0 | 37.2 |

## ENGINES

| | ohv V-6 | ohv V-6 |
|---|---|---|
| Size, liters/cu. in. | 3.3/202 | 3.8/231 |
| Horsepower @ rpm | 158@ 4850 | 180@ 4400 |
| Torque (lbs./ft.) @ rpm | 203@ 3250 | 240@ 3200 |
| Availability | S[1] | S[2] |

**EPA city/highway mpg**
4-speed OD automatic.................................... 18/24    17/24[3]

*1. SX and LX. 2. LXi; optional, SX and LX. 3. 16/23 w/AWD.*

| Chrysler Town & Country | Retail Price | Dealer Invoice |
|---|---|---|
| SX 4-door van, short wheelbase, FWD ......................... | $26680 | $24218 |
| LX 4-door van, FWD ...................................... | 27135 | 24619 |
| LX 4-door van, AWD ...................................... | 30135 | 27259 |
| LXi 4-door van, FWD ...................................... | 31720 | 28654 |
| LXi 4-door van, AWD ...................................... | 34095 | 30744 |
| Destination charge ....................................... | 580 | 580 |

LX AWD requires an option pkg. AWD denotes all-wheel drive. FWD denotes front-wheel drive.

## STANDARD EQUIPMENT:

**LX:** 3.3-liter V-6 engine (FWD), 3.8-liter V-6 engine (AWD), 4-speed automatic transmission, traction control (FWD), driver- and passenger-side air bags, anti-lock brakes, power steering, tilt steering column, air conditioning with dual controls, dual sliding side doors, cruise control, seven passenger seating (cloth reclining front bucket seats with manual lumbar adjustment, reclining and folding middle bucket seats, rear-seat recliner and headrests), passenger-side underseat storage drawer, leather-wrapped steering wheel, overhead console with compass and trip computer, AM/FM/cassette, digital clock, tachometer, coolant-temperature gauge, trip odometer, power windows, power door locks, remote keyless entry, heated power mirrors, variable intermittent wipers, variable intermittent rear wiper/washer, windshield wiper de-icer, rear defogger, reading lights, front and rear auxiliary power outlets, illuminated visor mirrors, floormats, tinted glass, fog lights, load-leveling suspension (AWD), 215/65R16 tires, striping, alloy wheels.

**LXi** adds: 3.8-liter V-6 engine (FWD/AWD), rear air conditioning and heater, 8-way power front bucket seats with driver-side memory, leather upholstery, CD player with 10-speaker Infinity sound system and equalizer, automatic day/night inside mirror and driver-side outside mirror, outside heated memory mirrors, automatic headlights, universal garage door opener, rear reading lights, load-leveling suspension (FWD and AWD), sunscreen/solar tinted windshield, rear privacy glass, security alarm, roof rack, full-size spare tire.

## OPTIONAL EQUIPMENT:
### Major Packages

| | | |
|---|---|---|
| Pkg. 25R/28R/29R, LX..................................... | 1230 | 1046 |
| *Manufacturer's discount price......................... | 85 | 73 |

*Sunscreen/solar glass, 10-speaker Infinity sound system, equalizer, CD changer controls, 8-way power driver seat.*

*Prices are accurate at time of publication; subject to manufacturer's change.*

# CHRYSLER

|  | Retail Price | Dealer Invoice |
|---|---|---|
| Pkg. 25H/28H/29H, SX | $1515 | $1288 |
| *Manufacturer's discount price* | 245 | 208 |

*Sunscreen/solar glass, 10-speaker Infinity sound system, equalizer, CD changer control, 8-way power driver seat, roof rack, windshield wiper de-icer, full-size spare tire.*

| Climate Control Group III, LX | 405 | 344 |
|---|---|---|

*Rear air conditioning and heater. Requires option pkg.*

| Convenience Group VI, LX, SX | 240 | 204 |
|---|---|---|

*Universal garage door opener, theft-deterrent system. Requires option pkg.*

| Loading and Towing Group II, LX | 180 | 153 |
|---|---|---|
| LX with Wheel/Handling Group II | 145 | 123 |

*Includes Heavy Load/Firm Ride Suspension and full-size spare. Requires option pkg. NA with AWD.*

| Loading & Towing Group III, LX | 380 | 323 |
|---|---|---|

*Heavy-duty battery, heavy-duty brakes, Heavy Load/Firm Ride Suspension, and full-size spare. Requires option pkg. NA with AWD.*

| Trailer Tow Group, LXi | 270 | 230 |
|---|---|---|

*Heavy-duty battery, brakes, suspension, and radiator, heavy-duty transmission oil cooler; trailer wiring harness.*

| Wheel/Handling Group II, LX | 470 | 400 |
|---|---|---|
| LX w/Loading & Towing Group III | 435 | 370 |

*Touring suspension, front and rear stabilizer bars, 16-inch alloy wheels.*

## Powertrains

| 3.8-liter V-6 engine, LX, SX | 335 | 285 |
|---|---|---|

*Requires option pkg.*

## Safety Features

| Integrated child seats, LX, LXi | NC | NC |
|---|---|---|

*Reclining and folding middle bench seat with two integrated child seats replaces middle bucket seats. LX requires option pkg. NA with leather upholstery on LX.*

## Comfort and Convenience

| Leather bucket seats, LX, SX | 890 | 757 |
|---|---|---|

*NA with integrated child seats. Requires option pkg.*

| Heated front seats, LXi | 250 | 213 |
|---|---|---|
| Cassette/CD player with equalizer, LX, SX | 310 | 264 |

*Requires option pkg.*

| Smoker's Group | 20 | 17 |
|---|---|---|

*Cigarette lighter, ashtrays.*

## Appearance and Miscellaneous

| Load-leveling suspension, LX | 290 | 247 |
|---|---|---|

*Requires option pkg. NA with AWD.*

| | Retail Price | Dealer Invoice |
|---|---|---|
| Roof rack, LX | $175 | $149 |
| *Requires option pkg.* | | |
| Metallic paint | 200 | 170 |
| Engine block heater | 35 | 30 |
| Full size spare tire, LX, SX | 110 | 94 |
| *Requires option pkg.* | | |
| Alloy wheels, LX with option pkg. | 410 | 349 |

# DODGE AVENGER

*Dodge Avenger ES*

## SPECIFICATIONS

| | 2-door coupe |
|---|---|
| Wheelbase, in. | 103.7 |
| Overall length, in. | 190.2 |
| Overall width, in. | 69.1 |
| Overall height, in. | 53.0 |
| Curb weight, lbs. | 2888 |
| Cargo vol., cu. ft. | 13.1 |
| Fuel capacity, gals. | 16.9 |
| Seating capacity | 5 |
| Front head room, in. | 39.1 |
| Max. front leg room, in. | 43.3 |
| Rear head room, in. | 36.5 |
| Min. rear leg room, in. | 35.0 |

## ENGINES

| | dohc I-4 | ohc V-6 |
|---|---|---|
| Size, liters/cu. in. | 2.0/122 | 2.5/152 |
| Horsepower @ rpm | 140@ 6000 | 163@ 5500 |
| Torque (lbs./ft.) @ rpm | 130@ 4800 | 170@ 4350 |
| Availability | S | O |

*Prices are accurate at time of publication; subject to manufacturer's change.*

# DODGE

**EPA city/highway mpg**

| | | |
|---|---|---|
| 5-speed OD manual | 22/32 | |
| 4-speed OD automatic | 21/30 | 19/28 |

| **Dodge Avenger** | Retail Price | Dealer Invoice |
|---|---|---|
| Base 2-door notchback | $14930 | $13738 |
| ES 2-door notchback | 17310 | 15856 |
| Destination charge | 535 | 535 |

## STANDARD EQUIPMENT:

**Base:** 2.0-liter dohc 4-cylinder engine, 5-speed manual transmission, driver- and passenger-side air bags, variable-assist power steering, cloth reclining front bucket seats, console with storage armrest and cupholders, split folding rear seat, rear headrests, rear defogger, tilt steering column, AM/FM radio w/four speakers, trip odometer, coolant-temperature gauges, tachometer, intermittent wipers, map lights, visor mirrors, tinted glass, dual remote mirrors, 195/70HR14 tires, wheel covers.

**ES** adds: 4-wheel disc brakes, air conditioning, upgraded cloth upholstery and driver-seat lumbar support, leather-wrapped steering wheel, cruise control, cassette player w/six speakers, floormats, cargo nets and hooks, handling suspension, decklid spoiler, fog lights, 215/50HR17 tires, alloy wheels.

## OPTIONAL EQUIPMENT:

### Major Packages

| | | |
|---|---|---|
| Pkg. 21C/22C, Base w/2.0-liter engine | 1850 | 1647 |

*Air conditioning, cruise control, cassette player w/six speakers, power windows and door locks, power mirrors, floormats, trunk net. Pkg. 22C requires 4-speed automatic transmission.*

| | | |
|---|---|---|
| Pkg. 24S, Base w/2.5-liter engine | 2545 | 2265 |

*Pkg. 21C/22C plus 16-inch Wheel Group (alloy wheels, 205/55HR16 tires), sport badging, leather-wrapped steering wheel, rear spoiler.*

| | | |
|---|---|---|
| Pkg. 21F/24F, ES | 1375 | 1224 |

*Power windows and door locks, power mirrors, illuminated passenger visor mirror, cassette/CD player, universal garage-door opener, remote keyless entry, theft-deterrent system. Pkg. 24F requires 2.5-liter engine.*

### Powertrains

| | | |
|---|---|---|
| 2.5-liter V-6 engine, Base w/Pkg. 24S | 675 | 601 |
| ES | 610 | 543 |

*Includes 4-wheel disc brakes, upgraded suspension, oil pressure gauge, dual exhaust outlets, 205/55HR16 tires (base), 215/50HR17 tires (ES). Requires 4-speed automatic transmission.*

| | | |
|---|---|---|
| 4-speed automatic transmission | 695 | 619 |

*NA with ES 2.0-liter engine.*

CONSUMER GUIDE™

| Safety Features | Retail Price | Dealer Invoice |
|---|---|---|
| Anti-lock brakes | $600 | $534 |
| *Base requires option pkg.* | | |

## Comfort and Convenience

| | | |
|---|---|---|
| Air conditioning, Base w/option pkg. | 790 | 703 |
| Leather upholstery, ES | 630 | 561 |
| *Manufacturer's discount price* | NC | NC |
| *Includes power driver seat.* | | |
| Power driver seat, Base, ES | 205 | 182 |
| *Base requires pkg. 24S. ES requires pkg. 21F/24F.* | | |
| Cassette player, Base | 255 | 227 |
| CD/cassette player, Base w/option pkg. | 435 | 387 |
| CD/cassette player with eight Infinity speakers and equalizer, ES w/Pkg. 21F/24F | 325 | 289 |
| Remote keyless entry, Base | 290 | 258 |
| *Includes theft-deterrent system. Requires option pkg.* | | |
| Power sunroof | 640 | 570 |
| *Requires option pkg.* | | |

## Appearance and Miscellaneous

| | | |
|---|---|---|
| 16-inch Wheel Group, Base | 490 | 436 |
| *Alloy wheels, 205/55HR16 tires. Requires option pkg.* | | |

# DODGE CARAVAN

*Dodge Caravan*

| SPECIFICATIONS | 3-door van | 4-door van |
|---|---|---|
| Wheelbase, in. | 113.3 | 119.3 |
| Overall length, in. | 186.3 | 199.6 |
| Overall width, in. | 76.8 | 76.8 |

*Prices are accurate at time of publication; subject to manufacturer's change.*

# DODGE

|  | 3-door van | 4-door van |
|---|---|---|
| Overall height, in. | 68.5 | 68.5 |
| Curb weight, lbs. | 3517 | 3684 |
| Cargo vol., cu. ft. | 142.9 | 168.5 |
| Fuel capacity, gals. | 20.0 | 20.0 |
| Seating capacity | 7 | 7 |
| Front head room, in. | 39.8 | 39.8 |
| Max. front leg room, in. | 40.6 | 40.6 |
| Rear head room, in. | 41.0 | 40.0 |
| Min. rear leg room, in. | 42.3 | 36.6 |

## ENGINES

|  | dohc I-4 | ohc V-6 | ohv V-6 | ohv V-6 |
|---|---|---|---|---|
| Size, liters/cu. in. | 2.4/148 | 3.0/181 | 3.3/202 | 3.8/231 |
| Horsepower @ rpm | 150@ 5200 | 150@ 5200 | 158@ 4850 | 180@ 4400 |
| Torque (lbs./ft.) @ rpm | 167@ 4000 | 176@ 4000 | 203@ 3250 | 240@ 3200 |
| Availability | S[1] | S[2] | S[3] | S[4] |

**EPA city/highway mpg**

|  | | | | |
|---|---|---|---|---|
| 3-speed automatic | 20/26 | 19/24 | | |
| 4-speed OD automatic | 18/25 | 18/26 | 18/24 | 17/24[5] |

1. Base SWB. 2. Base Grand and SE; optional on Base. 3. LE and ES; optional on Base and SE. 4. AWD; optional on LE and ES. 5. 16/23 w/AWD.

| Dodge Caravan | Retail Price | Dealer Invoice |
|---|---|---|
| Base 3-door van, SWB | $17415 | $15845 |
| Base Grand 4-door van | 20125 | 18270 |
| SE 4-door van, SWB | 21290 | 19255 |
| Grand SE 4-door van | 22285 | 20171 |
| Grand SE 4-door van, AWD | 25650 | 23132 |
| LE 4-door van, SWB | 25030 | 22546 |
| Grand LE 4-door van | 26025 | 23462 |
| Grand LE 4-door van, AWD | 29200 | 29256 |
| Grand ES 4-door van | 26605 | 23972 |
| Grand ES 4-door van, AWD | 29720 | 26714 |
| Destination charge | 580 | 580 |

Sport, ES, and AWD models require option pkg. AWD denotes all-wheel drive. SWB denotes short wheelbase.

## STANDARD EQUIPMENT:

**Base:** 2.4-liter dohc 4-cylinder engine, 3-speed automatic transmission, 3.0-liter V-6 engine (Grand), 4-speed automatic transmission (Grand), driver- and passenger-side air bags, power steering, cloth reclining front bucket seats, 3-passenger rear bench seat (SWB), sliding driver-side door (Grand), 2-passenger middle bench seat (Grand), folding 3-passenger rear bench seat (Grand), cupholders, variable intermittent wipers, variable intermittent rear wiper/washer, coolant-temperature gauge, trip odometer, AM/FM radio, digital clock, front map/reading lights, visor mirrors, front and rear auxiliary power outlets, tinted glass, dual outside mirrors, 205/75R14 tires, wheel covers.

**SE** adds: 3.0-liter V-6 engine, 4-speed automatic transmission, anti-lock brakes, sliding driver-side door, cruise control, tilt steering column, passenger-side underseat storage drawer, rear floor silencer, power mirrors, tachometer, cassette player, 215/65R15 tires. **AWD** model adds: 3.8-liter V-6 engine, 4-wheel disc brakes, load-leveling suspension, air conditioning, power door locks.

**LE and ES** add: 3.3-liter V-6 engine, air conditioning, upgraded cloth upholstery, driver seat lumbar adjustment, heated power mirrors, computer with compass, outside temperature and travel displays, overhead storage console, CD/cassette storage, power windows, power door locks, oil-pressure gauge, voltmeter, windshield wiper de-icer, rear defogger, ignition-switch light, illuminated visor mirrors, remote keyless entry w/headlight-off delay and illuminated entry, deluxe sound insulation, floormats, striping, alloy wheels (ES). **AWD** models add: 3.8-liter V-6 engine, 4-wheel disc brakes, load-leveling suspension.

## OPTIONAL EQUIPMENT:
### Major Packages

| | Retail Price | Dealer Invoice |
|---|---|---|
| Pkg. 22T/24T/28T, Base SWB | $1235 | $1050 |
| *Manufacturer's discount price, w/2.4-liter engine* | NC | NC |
| *w/3.0 or 3.3-liter engine* | 475 | 404 |
| Pkg. 24T/28T, Grand Base | 885 | 752 |
| *Manufacturer's discount price* | 125 | 106 |
| *Air conditioning, underseat storage drawer, rear floor silencer.* | | |
| Pkg. 26B/25B/28B, SE | 1205 | 1024 |
| *Manufacturer's discount price* | 295 | 250 |
| *Air conditioning, 7-passenger seating w/reclining and folding center and back seats, rear defogger, windshield wiper de-icer. NA SE AWD.* | | |
| Pkg. 26D/25D/28D/29D, SE | 2240 | 1904 |
| *Manufacturer's discount price* | 1030 | 875 |
| *Pkg. 26B/25B/28B plus power windows and door locks, power rear quarter vent windows, illuminated visor mirrors, Light Group (interior courtesy lights, illuminated ignition), additional sound insulation, floormats.* | | |
| Pkg. 25C/28C, SE | 2480 | 2108 |
| *Manufacturer's discount price* | 1295 | 1101 |
| *Pkg. 26B/25B/28B plus heavy-duty suspension, front and rear stabilizer bars, leather-wrapped steering wheel, sunscreen glass, fog lights, roof rack, bodyside moldings, 215/65R16 touring tires, sport wheel covers. NA AWD.* | | |

*Prices are accurate at time of publication; subject to manufacturer's change.*

# DODGE

| | Retail Price | Dealer Invoice |
|---|---|---|
| Pkg. 25E/28E, SE | $3515 | $2988 |
| *Manufacturer's discount price* | 2030 | 1726 |

*Pkg. 25C/28C plus power windows and rear quarter vent windows, power door locks, deluxe sound insulation, Light Group (ignition and courtesy lights), illuminated vanity mirrors, floormats. NA AWD.*

| | | |
|---|---|---|
| Pkg. 25K/28K/29K, LE | 1275 | 1084 |
| *Manufacturer's discount price* | 185 | 157 |

*Air conditioning with dual controls, 8-way power driver seat, sunscreen glass, 10-speaker cassette player.*

| | | |
|---|---|---|
| Pkg 29M, ES AWD | 1590 | 1352 |
| *Manufacturer's discount price* | 590 | 502 |

*Air conditioning w/dual controls, AM/FM/cassette/CD changer controls w/ten Infinity speakers, 8-way power driver seat, leather-wrapped steering wheel, automatic headlights, automatic-dim inside mirror and driver-side exterior mirror, sunscreen glass, assist handles, fog lights, 215/65R16 touring tires, alloy wheels.*

| | | |
|---|---|---|
| Pkg. 25M/28M/29M, ES | 1765 | 1500 |
| *Manufacturer's discount price* | 675 | 573 |

*Pkg. 29M (ES AWD) plus heavy-duty suspension, front and rear stabilizer bars, windshield wiper de-icer.*

| | | |
|---|---|---|
| Convenience Group I, Base | 435 | 370 |

*Cruise control, tilt steering column, power mirrors. Requires option pkg.*

| | | |
|---|---|---|
| Convenience Group II, Base | 750 | 638 |
| SE | 315 | 268 |

*Convenience Group I (Base) plus power door locks. Requires option pkg.*

| | | |
|---|---|---|
| Convenience Group III, SE | 685 | 582 |

*Power door locks, power windows and rear quarter vent windows. Requires option pkg. NA AWD.*

| | | |
|---|---|---|
| Convenience Group IV, SE | 235 | 200 |

*Remote keyless entry, illuminated entry, delay-off headlights. SE requires Pkg. 26D/25D/28D/29D or Pkg. 25E/28E.*

| | | |
|---|---|---|
| Convenience Group V, SE | 385 | 327 |
| LE, ES | 150 | 128 |

*Convenience Group IV (SE) plus security alarm. SE requires Pkg. 26D/25D/28D/29D or Pkg. 25E/28E/29E. LE, ES require option pkg.*

| | | |
|---|---|---|
| Climate Group II, Base, SE | 450 | 383 |

*Sunscreen glass. Requires option pkg.*

| | | |
|---|---|---|
| Climate Group III, | | |
| FWD Grand SE w/Pkg. 26B/25B/28B | 1175 | 999 |
| FWD Grand SE w/Pkg. 26D/25D/28D, | | |
| AWD Grand SE | 1065 | 905 |
| Grand SE w/Pkg. 25C/28/C | 660 | 561 |

| | Retail Price | Dealer Invoice |
|---|---|---|
| Grand SE w/Pkg. 25E/28/E | $550 | $468 |
| Grand LE w/option pkg. | 515 | 438 |
| Grand ES | 450 | 383 |

*Rear air conditioning and heater with dual zone controls, overhead console.*

| | | |
|---|---|---|
| Loading & Towing Group II, FWD SE, FWD LE | 180 | 153 |
| FWD LE with Wheel/Handling Group 2, FWD ES | 145 | 123 |

*Full-size spare tire, heavy load/firm ride suspension. Requires option pkg. NA with Pkg. 28C or 28E.*

| | | |
|---|---|---|
| Loading & Towing Group III, Grand SE | 445 | 378 |
| Grand SE, LE (All with Climate Group III) | 380 | 323 |
| ES | 345 | 293 |

*Loading & Towing Group II plus heavy-duty alternator, battery, radiator, brakes, and transmission oil cooler. FWD Grand SE requires Pkg. 26D/25D/28D. Grand Sport Requires Pkg. 26E/28E. FWD LE Requires Pkg. 25K/28K/29K.*

| | | |
|---|---|---|
| Wheel/Handling Group II, FWD LE | 470 | 400 |
| FWD LE w/Loading & Towing Group III | 435 | 370 |

*Front and rear stabilizer bars, heavy-duty suspension, 215/65R16 tires, alloy wheels. Requires Pkg. 25K/28K/29K.*

## Powertrains

| | | |
|---|---|---|
| 3.0-liter V-6 engine, Base SWB | 770 | 655 |

*Requires 3-speed automatic transmission. Base requires option pkg. Not available with base in California, New York, or Massachusetts.*

| | | |
|---|---|---|
| 3.3-liter V-6 engine, Base | 970 | 825 |
| Grand Base, SE FWD | 200 | 170 |

*Requires 4-speed automatic transmission. Base requires option pkg.*

| | | |
|---|---|---|
| 3.8-liter V-6 engine, FWD LE, FWD ES | 335 | 285 |

*Requires option pkg.*

| | | |
|---|---|---|
| 4-speed automatic transmission, Base | 250 | 213 |

*Requires 3.3-liter engine.*

| | | |
|---|---|---|
| Traction control, FWD LE | 175 | 149 |

## Safety Features

| | | |
|---|---|---|
| Anti-lock brakes, Base | 565 | 480 |

## Comfort and Convenience

| | | |
|---|---|---|
| Air conditioning, Base, FWD SE | 860 | 731 |
| Sliding driver-side door, Base SWB | 595 | 506 |

*Requires option pkg.*

| | | |
|---|---|---|
| Rear defogger, Base | 195 | 166 |
| Base w/Climate Group II or Convenience Group I/II, FWD SE | 230 | 196 |

*Includes heated outside mirrors, windshield wiper de-icer.*

# DODGE

| | Retail Price | Dealer Invoice |
|---|---|---|
| Cassette player, Base | $180 | $153 |
| *Requires option pkg.* | | |
| CD player, Base | 325 | 276 |
| *Requires option pkg.* | | |
| AM/FM/cassette/CD w/equalizer, SE | 325 | 276 |
| LE, ES | 310 | 264 |
| *Requires option pkg.* | | |
| 10-speaker Infinity sound system, SE | 395 | 336 |
| *Requires AM/FM/cassette/CD w/amplifier.* | | |
| 7-passenger seating, Base SWB, | 350 | 298 |
| *2-passenger middle bench seat, 3-passenger rear bench seat.* | | |
| 7-passenger seating w/integrated child seat, | | |
| Base Grand | 285 | 242 |
| *2-passenger reclining middle bench seat with headrest and integrated child seats, 3-passenger rear bench seat. Requires option pkg.* | | |
| Deluxe 7-passenger seating w/integrated child seats, | | |
| SE, LE, ES | 225 | 191 |
| *Premium cloth 2-passenger reclining middle bench seat with headrests and integrated child seats, 3-passenger reclining rear bench seat. Requires option pkg.* | | |
| Deluxe 7-passenger seating w/quad bucket seats, | | |
| SE, LE, ES | 670 | 570 |
| *Premium cloth reclining middle bucket seats, 3-passenger reclining rear bench seat with headrests. SE requires Pkg. 26D/25D/29D/28D or Pkg. 25E/28E. LE requires Pkg. 25K/28K.* | | |
| Leather bucket seats, LE, ES | 890 | 757 |
| *Requires option pkg. and deluxe 7-passenger seating w/quad bucket seats.* | | |
| Smoker's Group | 20 | 17 |
| *Cigarette lighter, ashtrays.* | | |

## Appearance and Miscellaneous

| | Retail Price | Dealer Invoice |
|---|---|---|
| Load-leveling suspension, | | |
| FWD Grand SE w/Pkg. 26D/25D/28E, | | |
| FWD LE, FWD ES | 290 | 247 |
| Roof rack | 175 | 149 |
| *Requires option pkg.* | | |
| Engine block heater | 35 | 30 |
| Candy-apple-red metallic paint, SE, LE, ES | 200 | 170 |
| White-pearl paint, ES | 200 | 170 |
| Full-size spare tire | 110 | 94 |
| 16-inch alloy wheels, LE | 410 | 349 |
| Grand SE | 265 | 225 |
| *LE requires Pkg. 25K/28K/29K. Grand SE requires option pkg.* | | |

# DODGE DURANGO

*Dodge Durango*

## SPECIFICATIONS

|  | 4-door wagon |
|---|---|
| Wheelbase, in. | 115.9 |
| Overall length, in. | 193.3 |
| Overall width, in. | 71.5 |
| Overall height, in. | 72.9 |
| Curb weight, lbs. | 4568 |
| Cargo vol., cu. ft. | 88.0 |
| Maximum payload, lbs. | — |
| Fuel capacity, gals. | 25.0 |
| Seating capacity | 8 |
| Front head room, in. | 39.8 |
| Max. front leg room, in. | 41.9 |
| Rear head room, in. | 40.6 |
| Min. rear leg room, in. | 35.4 |

## ENGINES

|  | ohv V-6 | ohv V-8 | ohv V-8 |
|---|---|---|---|
| Size, liters/cu. in. | 3.9/239 | 5.2/318 | 5.9/360 |
| Horsepower @ rpm | 175@ 4800 | 230@ 4400 | 245@ 4000 |
| Torque (lbs./ft.) @ rpm | 225@ 3200 | 300@ 3200 | 335@ 3200 |
| Availability | S | O | O |
| **EPA city/highway mpg** | | | |
| 4-speed OD automatic | NA | 13/17 | 12/16 |

| Dodge Durango | Retail Price | Dealer Invoice |
|---|---|---|
| Base 4-door wagon | $25810 | $23318 |

*Prices are accurate at time of publication; subject to manufacturer's change.*

# DODGE

|  | Retail Price | Dealer Invoice |
|---|---|---|
| Destination charge | $525 | $525 |

Requires a Quick Order Pkg.

## STANDARD EQUIPMENT:

**Base:** 3.9-liter V-6 engine, 4-speed automatic transmission, part-time 4-wheel drive, driver- and passenger-side air bags, air conditioning, power steering, cloth/vinyl front bucket seats w/adjustable lumbar support, 40/20/40 split folding second row seat, cupholders, AM/FM/cassette w/four speakers, visor mirrors, intermittent wipers, trip odometer, tachometer, coolant-temperature gauge, oil-pressure gauge, rear defogger, rear wiper/washer, dual outside mirrors, tinted glass, roof rack, skid plates, 235/75R15 tires, alloy wheels.

## OPTIONAL EQUIPMENT:
### Major Packages

| | Retail | Dealer |
|---|---|---|
| SLT Quick Order Pkg. | 1800 | 1530 |
| *Manufacturer's discount price* | 1100 | 935 |

*Floor console, upgraded door trim, map lights, underhood light, glove box light, auxiliary power outlet, cruise control, tilt steering wheel, power windows and door locks, remote keyless entry, white-letter tires.*

| | | |
|---|---|---|
| SLT Plus Quick Order Pkg. | 3250 | 2763 |
| *Manufacturer's discount price* | 2250 | 1913 |

*SLT Pkg. plus power driver seat, overhead console, trip computer, automatic day/night rearview mirror, illuminated visor mirrors, CD/cassette player, floormats, theft-deterrent system, color-keyed bodyside moldings, fog lights.*

| | | |
|---|---|---|
| Trailer Tow Prep Group | 245 | 208 |

*Includes 7-wire harness, platform hitch. Requires Heavy-Duty Service Group.*

### Powertrains

| | | |
|---|---|---|
| 5.2-liter V-8 engine | 590 | 502 |
| 5.9-liter V-8 engine | 885 | 752 |
| *Requires SLT Plus Pkg.* | | |
| Full-time 4WD | 395 | 336 |
| Limited slip differential | 285 | 242 |
| 3.92 axle ratio | 40 | 34 |

### Safety Features

| | | |
|---|---|---|
| Anti-lock brakes | 565 | 480 |

### Comfort and Convenience

| | | |
|---|---|---|
| Air conditioning | 430 | 366 |
| *Requires Heavy-Duty Service Group.* | | |

|  | Retail Price | Dealer Invoice |
|---|---|---|
| Leather upholstery | $670 | $570 |
| *Requires SLT Plus Pkg.* | | |
| Overhead Console Group | 410 | 349 |
| *Includes illuminated visor mirrors, automatic day/night rearview mirror, compass, trip computer, outside temperature gauge.* | | |
| Power mirrors | 25 | 21 |
| Front split bench seat | NC | NC |
| Third row seat | 550 | 468 |
| Cassette/CD player | 300 | 255 |
| *Includes graphic equalizer.* | | |
| Infinity 8-speaker sound system | 330 | 281 |
| Floormats | 50 | 43 |

## Appearance and Miscellaneous

| | | |
|---|---|---|
| Theft-deterrent system | 150 | 128 |
| Fog lights | 240 | 204 |
| Bodyside moldings | 80 | 68 |
| Engine block heater | 35 | 30 |

## Special Purpose, Wheels and Tires

| | | |
|---|---|---|
| Heavy-Duty Service Group | 245 | 204 |
| *Heavy-duty alternator and battery, maximum engine cooling.* | | |
| Skid Plate Group | 90 | 70 |
| *Fuel tank and transfer case case skid plates.* | | |
| 31x10.5 all-terrain tires | 505 | 429 |
| *Includes body-colored wheel flares.* | | |

# DODGE INTREPID

*Dodge Intrepid ES*

## SPECIFICATIONS

| | 4-door sedan |
|---|---|
| Wheelbase, in. | 113.0 |

*Prices are accurate at time of publication; subject to manufacturer's change.*

# DODGE

| | 4-door sedan |
|---|---|
| Overall length, in. | 203.7 |
| Overall width, in. | 74.7 |
| Overall height, in. | 55.9 |
| Curb weight, lbs. | 3422 |
| Cargo vol., cu. ft. | 18.4 |
| Fuel capacity, gals. | 17.0 |
| Seating capacity | 6 |
| Front head room, in. | 38.3 |
| Max. front leg room, in. | 42.2 |
| Rear head room, in. | 37.5 |
| Min. rear leg room, in. | 39.1 |

## ENGINES

| | dohc V-6 | ohc V-6 |
|---|---|---|
| Size, liters/cu. in. | 2.7/167 | 3.2/197 |
| Horsepower @ rpm | 200@ 5800 | 225@ 6300 |
| Torque (lbs./ft.) @ rpm | 190@ 4850 | 225@ 3800 |
| Availability | S[1] | S[2] |

**EPA city/highway mpg**

| | | |
|---|---|---|
| 4-speed OD automatic | NA | 19/29 |

*1. Base  2. ES.*

| Dodge Intrepid | Retail Price | Dealer Invoice |
|---|---|---|
| Base 4-door sedan | $19545 | $17925 |
| ES 4-door sedan | 22345 | 20399 |
| Destination charge | 550 | 550 |

## STANDARD EQUIPMENT:

**Base:** 2.7-liter dohc V-6 engine, 4-speed automatic transmission, driver- and passenger-side air bags, 4-wheel disc brakes, air conditioning, power steering, tilt steering wheel, cloth front bucket seats, floor console, power mirrors, power windows, power door locks, rear defogger, intermittent wipers, AM/FM/cassette with four speakers, tachometer, power remote decklid release, floormats, 205/70R15 tires, wheel covers.

**ES** adds: 3.2-liter V-6 engine, Autostick 4-speed automatic transmission, anti-lock brakes, 8-way power driver seat, split folding rear seat, leather-wrapped steering wheel, 8-speaker sound system, Headliner Module (illuminated visor mirrors, rear reading lights), remote keyless entry system, fog lights, 225/60R16 tires, alloy wheels.

## OPTIONAL EQUIPMENT:
### Safety Features

| | | |
|---|---|---|
| Anti-lock brakes, Base | 600 | 534 |

| **Major Packages** | Retail Price | Dealer Invoice |
|---|---|---|
| Pkg. 22D, Base............................................... | $1140 | $1015 |

*Leather-wrapped steering wheel, 8-way power driver seat, 8-speaker sound system, remote keyless entry, Headliner Module (illuminated visor mirrors, rear reading lights).*

| | | |
|---|---|---|
| Pkg. 24M, ES................................................. | 1130 | 1006 |

*Traction control, automatic temperature control, overhead trip computer, 8-speaker Infinity sound system, CD changer controls, theft-deterrent system, full-size spare tire.*

| | | |
|---|---|---|
| Comfort and Security Group, ES.................................................................... | 305 | 271 |

*Automatic temperature control, theft-deterrent system.*

## Comfort and Convenience

| | | |
|---|---|---|
| Power moonroof, ES....................................... | 795 | 708 |

*Requires trip computer.*

| | | |
|---|---|---|
| Trip computer, ES.......................................... | 310 | 275 |

*Includes universal garage door opener.*

| | | |
|---|---|---|
| Automatic day/night mirror, ES ...................... | 85 | 76 |

*Requires Pkg. 24M.*

| | | |
|---|---|---|
| 8-speaker sound system, Base ...................... | 290 | 258 |
| CD player, Base............................................. | 435 | 387 |
| Base w/option pkg., ES w/option pkg............... | 145 | 129 |

*Includes eight Infinity speakers, CD changer controls.*

| | | |
|---|---|---|
| CD/cassette player, ES ................................. | 515 | 458 |
| ES w/opt. pkg................................................. | 300 | 267 |

*Includes Infinity speakers.*

| | | |
|---|---|---|
| Cloth front split bench seat............................. | NC | NC |
| Leather upholstery, ES................................... | 1000 | 890 |

*Includes front bucket seats, 8-way power passenger seat. Requires Pkg. 24M.*

| | | |
|---|---|---|
| 8-way power driver seat, Base ....................... | 380 | 338 |
| 8-way power passenger seat, ES.................... | 380 | 338 |

*Requires Pkg. 24M.*

| | | |
|---|---|---|
| Smoker's Group.............................................. | 20 | 18 |

*Includes ashtrays and lighter.*

## Appearance and Miscellaneous

| | | |
|---|---|---|
| Cold Weather Group....................................... | 30 | 27 |

*Includes engine block and battery heater.*

| | | |
|---|---|---|
| Metallic paint ................................................ | 200 | 178 |
| Full-size spare tire......................................... | 125 | 111 |
| Wheel and Tire Group, Base ......................... | 200 | 178 |

*Includes alloy wheels, 225/60R16 tires.*

*Prices are accurate at time of publication; subject to manufacturer's change.*

# DODGE/ PLYMOUTH NEON

*1998 Dodge Neon R/T 2-door*

## SPECIFICATIONS

| | 2-door coupe | 4-door sedan |
|---|---|---|
| Wheelbase, in. | 104.0 | 104.0 |
| Overall length, in. | 171.8 | 171.8 |
| Overall width, in. | 67.4 | 67.2 |
| Overall height, in. | 54.9 | 54.9 |
| Curb weight, lbs. | 2470 | 2507 |
| Cargo vol., cu. ft. | 11.8 | 11.8 |
| Fuel capacity, gals. | 12.5 | 12.5 |
| Seating capacity | 5 | 5 |
| Front head room, in. | 39.6 | 39.6 |
| Max. front leg room, in. | 42.5 | 42.5 |
| Rear head room, in. | 36.5 | 36.5 |
| Min. rear leg room, in. | 35.1 | 35.1 |

## ENGINES

| | ohc I-4 | dohc I-4 |
|---|---|---|
| Size, liters/cu. in. | 2.0/122 | 2.0/122 |
| Horsepower @ rpm | 132@ 6000 | 150@ 6500 |
| Torque (lbs./ft.) @ rpm | 129@ 5000 | 133@ 5500 |
| Availability | S | O |

### EPA city/highway mpg

| | | |
|---|---|---|
| 5-speed OD manual | 29/41 | 29/38 |
| 3-speed automatic | 24/33 | 25/33 |

| Dodge/Plymouth Neon | Retail Price | Dealer Invoice |
|---|---|---|
| Competition 2-door coupe | $10900 | $10313 |

| | Retail Price | Dealer Invoice |
|---|---|---|
| Competition 4-door sedan | $11100 | $10497 |
| Highline 2-door sedan | 11155 | 10325 |
| Highline 4-door sedan | 11355 | 10505 |
| Destination charge | 500 | 500 |

Competition requires Competition Pkg.

## STANDARD EQUIPMENT:

**Competition:** 2.0-liter 4-cylinder engine, 5-speed manual transmission, driver- and passenger-side air bags, power steering, cloth/vinyl reclining bucket seats, storage armrest with cupholders, AM/FM radio with four speakers, trip odometer, variable intermittent wipers, passenger-side visor mirror, tinted glass, dual outside mirrors, 175/70R14 tires, wheel covers.

**Highline** adds: rear defogger, 60/40 split folding rear seat, remote decklid release, trunk light, 185/65R14 touring tires, bodyside moldings.

## OPTIONAL EQUIPMENT:
### Major Packages

| | | |
|---|---|---|
| Competition Pkg., | | |
| Competition 2-door | 2080 | 1914 |
| Competition 4-door | 2060 | 1895 |

*2.0-liter DOHC 4-cylinder engine (2-door), unlimited speed engine controller, 4-wheel disc brakes, Firm Feel power steering, leather-wrapped steering and shift knob, competition suspension, sport bucket seats, tachometer with low-fuel light, power bulge hood, 175/65HR14 tires (4-door), 185/60HR14 tires (2-door), alloy wheels.*

| | | |
|---|---|---|
| Dodge Sport Pkg./Plymouth Expresso Pkg., | | |
| Highline | 1800 | 1602 |
| *Manufacturer's discount price* | 1300 | 1157 |

*2.0-liter DOHC 4-cylinder engine, air conditioning, sport bucket seats, tachometer, interior assist handles, power bulge hood, rear spoiler, fog lamps, sport wheel covers.*

| | | |
|---|---|---|
| R/T Pkg., Dodge Highline | 2140 | 1904 |

*Includes 2.0-liter DOHC 4-cylinder engine, 4-wheel disc brakes, sport suspension, sport bucket seats, leather-wrapped steering wheel, cassette player w/CD controls, tachometer, stripes, rear spoiler, fog lights, 185/65HR14 tires.*

| | | |
|---|---|---|
| Value/Fun Group, Highline | 1435 | 1277 |
| *Manufacturer's discount price* | 835 | 743 |

*Power mirrors, power door locks, power front windows, Premium AM/FM/cassette w/CD changer controls, power sunroof.*

| | | |
|---|---|---|
| Deluxe Convenience Group, Highline | 350 | 312 |
| *Cruise control, tilt steering wheel.* | | |
| Power Convenience Group, Highline 4-door | 300 | 267 |

*Prices are accurate at time of publication; subject to manufacturer's change.*

|  | Retail Price | Dealer Invoice |
|---|---|---|
| Highline 2-door | $260 | $231 |
| *Power door locks, power mirrors.* | | |
| Light Group, Highline | 130 | 116 |
| *Illuminated visor mirrors, courtesy/reading lights, engine compartment light.* | | |

## Powertrains

| | | |
|---|---|---|
| 2.0-liter dohc 4-cylinder engine, | | |
| Competition 2-door, Highline | 150 | 134 |
| *Manufacturer's discount price* | NC | NC |
| 3-speed automatic transmission, Highline | 600 | 534 |

## Safety Features

| | | |
|---|---|---|
| Anti-lock 4-wheel disc brakes, Highline | 565 | 503 |
| Integrated child seat, Highline | 100 | 89 |
| *Includes fixed rear seat back. NA with Sport Pkg., RT Pkg.* | | |

## Comfort and Convenience

| | | |
|---|---|---|
| Air conditioning, Competition, Highline | 1000 | 890 |
| Power moonroof, Highline | 595 | 530 |
| Rear defogger, Competition | 205 | 182 |
| Remote keyless entry, Highline | 155 | 138 |
| *Requires Power Convenience Group.* | | |
| AM/FM/cassette w/eight speakers, Competition | 595 | 530 |
| Highline | 260 | 231 |
| Premium AM/FM/cassette w/eight speakers, Highline | 285 | 254 |
| *Includes CD changer controls.* | | |
| Premium AM/FM/CD player w/eight speakers, | | |
| Highline | 395 | 352 |
| Highline with Value/Fun Group | 110 | 98 |
| Power front door windows, Highline | 265 | 236 |
| *Requires Power Convenience Group.* | | |
| Tachometer with low fuel light, Highline | 100 | 89 |
| Floormats, Highline | 50 | 45 |

## Appearance and Miscellaneous

| | | |
|---|---|---|
| Alloy wheels, Highline | 355 | 316 |

# DODGE STRATUS

## SPECIFICATIONS

|  | 4-door sedan |
|---|---|
| Wheelbase, in. | 108.0 |
| Overall length, in. | 186.0 |

*Dodge Stratus*

|  | 4-door sedan |
|---|---|
| Overall width, in. | 71.7 |
| Overall height, in. | 51.9 |
| Curb weight, lbs. | 2919 |
| Cargo vol., cu. ft. | 15.7 |
| Fuel capacity, gals. | 16.0 |
| Seating capacity | 5 |
| Front head room, in. | 38.1 |
| Max. front leg room, in. | 42.3 |
| Rear head room, in. | 36.8 |
| Min. rear leg room, in. | 37.8 |

## ENGINES

|  | ohc I-4 | dohc I-4 | ohc V-6 |
|---|---|---|---|
| Size, liters/cu. in. | 2.0/122 | 2.4/148 | 2.5/152 |
| Horsepower @ rpm | 132@ 6000 | 150@ 5200 | 168@ 5800 |
| Torque (lbs./ft.) @ rpm | 128@ 5000 | 165@ 4000 | 170@ 4350 |
| Availability | S[1] | S[2] | O[3] |

**EPA city/highway mpg**

| | | | |
|---|---|---|---|
| 5-speed OD manual | 27/37 | | |
| 4-speed OD automatic | | 21/30 | 19/28[4] |

*1. Base. 2. ES; optional Base. 3. ES. 4. 19/29 w/Autostick.*

| Dodge Stratus | Retail Price | Dealer Invoice |
|---|---|---|
| Base 4-door sedan | $14840 | $13638 |
| ES 4-door sedan | 17665 | 16152 |
| Destination charge | 535 | 535 |

## STANDARD EQUIPMENT:

**Base:** 2.0-liter 4-cylinder engine, 5-speed manual transmission, driver- and passenger-side air bags, air conditioning, power steering, cloth reclining front bucket seats, console, folding rear bench seat, AM/FM/cassette w/six speakers, digital clock, trip odometer, oil-pressure and coolant-temperature gauges, tachometer, voltmeter, tilt steering column, rear defogger, intermittent wipers, remote decklid release, visor mirrors, front floormats, tinted glass with solar-control windshield, dual remote mirrors, 195/70R14 tires, wheel covers.

**ES** adds: 2.4-liter dohc 4-cylinder engine, 4-speed automatic transmission, cruise control, variable-assist power steering, leather-wrapped steering wheel and shift knob, 4-way manual driver seat with height and lumbar-support adjusters, power windows, power door locks, heated power mirrors, reading lights, illuminated visor mirrors, rear floormats, assist handles, cruise control, touring suspension, fog lights, 195/65HR15 touring tires, alloy wheels.

## OPTIONAL EQUIPMENT:

| | Retail Price | Dealer Invoice |
|---|---|---|
| **Major Packages** | | |
| Pkg. 21B/24B, Base | $760 | $676 |
| *Manufacturer's discount price* | 685 | 609 |
| *Power windows and door locks, heated power mirrors, 4-way manual driver seat with height adjuster, rear floormats. Pkg. 24B requires 2.4-liter DOHC 4-cylinder engine and 4-speed automatic transmission.* | | |
| Pkg. 26R, ES | 715 | 636 |
| *Manufacturer's discount price* | 345 | 307 |
| *Anti-lock brakes, autostick transmission. Requires 2.5-liter engine.* | | |
| Pkg. 26S, ES | 1995 | 1776 |
| *Manufacturer's discount price* | 995 | 886 |
| *Pkg. 26R plus leather upholstery, 8-way power driver seat, remote keyless entry, illuminated entry, cargo net. Requires 2.5-liter engine.* | | |
| Remote/Illuminated Entry Group | 170 | 151 |
| *Remote keyless entry, illuminated entry. Base requires Pkg. 21B/24B.* | | |
| **Powertrains** | | |
| 2.4-liter dohc 4-cylinder engine, Base | 450 | 401 |
| *Requires 4-speed automatic transmission.* | | |
| 2.5-liter V-6 engine, ES | 800 | 712 |
| *Requires option pkg.* | | |
| 4-speed automatic transmission, Base | 1050 | 935 |
| *Includes cruise control. Requires 2.4-liter engine.* | | |
| **Safety Features** | | |
| Anti-lock brakes, Base | 565 | 503 |
| Integrated child safety seat, Base | 100 | 89 |
| *Includes fixed rear seatback.* | | |
| **Comfort and Convenience** | | |
| Power sunroof, Base | $695 | $619 |
| ES | 580 | 519 |
| *Includes assist handles, map lights, illuminated visor mirrors (Base). Base requires option pkg. NA with integrated child seat.* | | |

| | Retail Price | Dealer Invoice |
|---|---|---|
| Premium cassette player........................................... | $340 | $303 |
| *Includes eight speakers, power amplifier, CD controls.* | | |
| CD player, Base.......................................................... | 200 | 178 |
| 6-disc CD changer and premium cassette player .......... | 550 | 490 |

### Appearance and Miscellaneous

| | | |
|---|---|---|
| Security alarm, ES...................................................... | 150 | 134 |
| *Requires Remote/Illuminated Entry Group.* | | |
| Candy apple red metallic paint .................................... | 200 | 178 |
| Full-size spare tire....................................................... | 125 | 111 |

# EAGLE TALON

*Eagle Talon TSi*

## SPECIFICATIONS

| | 2-door hatchback |
|---|---|
| Wheelbase, in. ................................................................ | 98.8 |
| Overall length, in. ........................................................... | 174.8 |
| Overall width, in. ............................................................ | 69.9 |
| Overall height, in. ........................................................... | 51.6 |
| Curb weight, lbs. ............................................................ | 2729 |
| Cargo vol., cu. ft. ........................................................... | 16.6 |
| Fuel capacity, gals. ........................................................ | 16.9 |
| Seating capacity ............................................................. | 4 |
| Front head room, in. ....................................................... | 37.9 |
| Max. front leg room, in. .................................................. | 43.3 |
| Rear head room, in. ........................................................ | 34.1 |
| Min. rear leg room, in. .................................................... | 28.4 |

## ENGINES

| | dohc I-4 | Turbo dohc I-4 |
|---|---|---|
| Size, liters/cu. in. ........................................... | 2.0/122 | 2.0/122 |
| Horsepower @ rpm .......................................... | 140@ 6000 | 210@ 6000 |

*Prices are accurate at time of publication; subject to manufacturer's change.*

| | dohc I-4 | Turbo dohc I-4 |
|---|---|---|
| Torque (lbs./ft.) @ rpm | 130@ 4800 | 214@ 3000 |
| Availability | S[1] | S[2] |
| **EPA city/highway mpg** | | |
| 5-speed OD manual | 23/33 | 23/31 |
| 4-speed OD automatic | 21/30 | 21/28 |

1. Base and ESi. 2. TSi and TSi AWD.

| Eagle Talon | Retail Price | Dealer Invoice |
|---|---|---|
| Base 2-door hatchback | $14505 | $13435 |
| ESi 2-door hatchback | 15275 | 14173 |
| TSi 2-door hatchback | 18460 | 17069 |
| TSi AWD 2-door hatchback | 20715 | 19119 |
| Destination charge | 535 | 535 |

AWD denotes all-wheel drive.

## STANDARD EQUIPMENT:

**Base** 2.0-liter dohc 4-cylinder engine, 5-speed manual transmission, driver- and passenger-side air bags, variable-assist power steering, cloth reclining front bucket seats, folding rear seat, front console with storage and armrest, tinted glass, tachometer, coolant temperature gauge, trip odometer, map lights, dual remote mirrors, visor mirrors, digital clock, remote fuel-door and hatch releases, tilt steering column, intermittent wipers, 195/70R14 tires, wheel covers.

**ESi** adds: AM/FM radio, variable intermittent wipers, color-keyed bodyside moldings, rear spoiler.

**TSi** adds: turbocharged engine, sport-tuned exhaust system, 4-wheel disc brakes, fog lamps, driver-seat lumbar support adjustment, split folding rear seat, leather-wrapped steering wheel and manual gearshift handle, power mirrors, turbo-boost and oil-pressure gauges, cassette player, rear wiper/washer, illuminated visor mirrors, rear defogger, cargo-area cover, cargo net, upgraded suspension, 205/55R16 tires, painted alloy wheels.

**TSi AWD** adds: permanent 4-wheel drive, cruise control, power door locks and windows, 215/50VR17 tires, alloy wheels.

## OPTIONAL EQUIPMENT:

### Powertrains

| | | |
|---|---|---|
| 4-speed automatic transmission, Base, ESi | 745 | 633 |
| TSi, TSi AWD | 890 | 757 |
| Limited-slip differential, | | |
| TSi AWD w/option pkg. | 265 | 225 |

## Major Packages

| | Retail Price | Dealer Invoice |
|---|---|---|
| Pkg. 21B/22B, ESi | $1695 | $1441 |

*Air conditioning, cruise control, rear defogger, power mirrors, cassette player, cargo area cover, front floormats.*

| | | |
|---|---|---|
| Pkg. 21C/22C, ESi | 2740 | 2329 |

*Pkg. 21B/22B plus power windows and door locks, cargo net, upgraded interior trim, 205/55HR16 tires, alloy wheels.*

| | | |
|---|---|---|
| Pkg. 23P/24P, TSi | 2005 | 1704 |

*Air conditioning, CD/cassette player, cruise control, power windows and door locks, front floormats.*

| | | |
|---|---|---|
| Pkg. 25S/26S, TSi AWD | 1225 | 1041 |

*Air conditioning, remote keyless entry with security alarm, front floormats.*

| | | |
|---|---|---|
| Pkg. 25L/26L, TSi AWD | 4195 | 3566 |

*Pkg. 25S/26S plus anti-lock brakes, power driver seat, leather/vinyl front upholstery, CD/cassette player with graphic equalizer and eight Infinity speakers, power sunroof.*

## Safety Features

| | | |
|---|---|---|
| Anti-lock brakes | 650 | 553 |

*Requires option pkg. NA base.*

## Comfort and Convenience

| | | |
|---|---|---|
| Rear defogger, Base, ESi | 165 | 140 |
| AM/FM radio, Base | 235 | 200 |
| Power sunroof | 730 | 621 |

*ESi requires Pkg. 21C/22C. TSi, TSi AWD requires option pkg. NA Base.*

| | | |
|---|---|---|
| Power driver seat, TSi, TSi AWD | 335 | 285 |

*Requires option pkg.*

| | | |
|---|---|---|
| Air conditioning | 860 | 731 |
| Remote keyless entry with security alarm, ESi w/Pkg. 21C/22C, TSi w/option pkg. | 335 | 285 |
| AM/FM/cassette, Base | 500 | 425 |
| CD player, ESi | 150 | 128 |
| Cassette/CD player, ESi, TSi, TSi AWD | 390 | 332 |

*Includes graphic equalizer, CD changer controls. ESi requires Pkg. 21C/22C. TSi AWD requires pkg. 25S/26S.*

| | | |
|---|---|---|
| Cassette/CD player w/graphic equalizer, TSi AWD | 795 | 676 |
| TSi w/option pkg. | 405 | 344 |

*Includes eight Infinity speakers. TSi requires Pkg. 25S/26S.*

## Appearance and Miscellaneous

| | | |
|---|---|---|
| Alloy wheels, ESi | 510 | 434 |

*Includes 205/55HR16 tires.*

# FORD CONTOUR

*Ford Contour LX*

## SPECIFICATIONS

| | 4-door sedan |
|---|---|
| Wheelbase, in. | 106.5 |
| Overall length, in. | 184.7 |
| Overall width, in. | 69.1 |
| Overall height, in. | 54.5 |
| Curb weight, lbs. | 2772 |
| Cargo vol., cu. ft. | 13.9 |
| Fuel capacity, gals. | 14.5 |
| Seating capacity | 5 |
| Front head room, in. | 39.0 |
| Max. front leg room, in. | 42.4 |
| Rear head room, in. | 36.7 |
| Min. rear leg room, in. | 34.4 |

## ENGINES

| | dohc I-4 | dohc V-6 | dohc V-6 |
|---|---|---|---|
| Size, liters/cu. in. | 2.0/121 | 2.5/155 | 2.5/155 |
| Horsepower @ rpm | 125@ 5500 | 170@ 6250 | 195@ 6625 |
| Torque (lbs./ft.) @ rpm | 130@ 4000 | 165@ 4250 | 165@ 5625 |
| Availability | S[1] | S[2] | S[3] |
| **EPA city/highway mpg** | | | |
| 5-speed OD manual | 24/35 | 21/30 | 20/29 |
| 4-speed OD automatic | 24/32 | 20/29 | |

1. Base, GL, and LX. 2. SE; optional on GL and LX. 3. SVT.

| Ford Contour | Retail Price | Dealer Invoice |
|---|---|---|
| LX 4-door sedan | $14460 | $13544 |
| SE 4-door sedan | 15785 | 14434 |

| | Retail Price | Dealer Invoice |
|---|---|---|
| SVT 4-door sedan | $22365 | $20270 |
| Destination charge | 535 | 535 |

Pricing and contents may vary in some regions.

## STANDARD EQUIPMENT:

**LX:** 2.0-liter dohc 4-cylinder engine, 5-speed manual transmission, driver- and passenger-side air bags, air conditioning, power steering, cloth reclining front bucket seats, cloth door-trim panel, power mirrors, tilt steering wheel, console w/cupholder, AM/FM radio, digital clock, trip odometer, coolant temperature gauge, rear passenger grab handles, intermittent wipers, visor mirrors, remote decklid release, interior air filter, solar-control tinted glass, 185/70R14 tires, wheel covers.

**SE** adds: power windows, power door locks, cruise control, cassette player, rear defogger.

**SVT** adds: 2.5-liter 195-horsepower dohc V-6 engine, 4-wheel disc anti-lock brakes, 10-way power driver's seat, leather upholstery, split folding rear seat, tachometer, AM/FM/cassette player with Premium Sound, power antenna, remote keyless entry, floormats, fog lamps, sport suspension, 205/55ZR16 tires, 5-spoke alloy wheels.

## OPTIONAL EQUIPMENT:
### Major Packages

| | | |
|---|---|---|
| Comfort Group, SE | 795 | 708 |

    *Leather-wrapped steering wheel, 10-way power driver seat, variable intermittent wipers, illuminated visor mirrors, power antenna, fog lights, 8-spoke alloy wheels. NA with Sport Group.*

| | | |
|---|---|---|
| Sport Group, SE | 1000 | 890 |

    *2.5-liter V-6 170-horsepower engine, tachometer, cloth sport bucket seats, leather-wrapped steering wheel, illuminated visor mirrors, sport floormats, variable intermittent wipers, rear spoiler, body cladding, badging, fog lights, 4-wheel disc brakes (w/manual transmission), performance suspension, 12-spoke alloy wheels, 205/60TR15 tires. NA with Comfort Group.*

### Powertrains

| | | |
|---|---|---|
| 2.5-liter dohc V-6 170-horsepower engine, LX, SE | 495 | 441 |

    *Includes performance suspension, 4-wheel disc brakes (w/manual transmission), 195/65R14 tires, tachometer.*

| | | |
|---|---|---|
| 4-speed automatic transmission, LX, SE | 815 | 725 |

### Safety Features

| | | |
|---|---|---|
| Anti-lock brakes, LX, SE | 500 | 445 |
| Integrated child seat, SE | 135 | 120 |

    *NA with leather upholstery.*

*Prices are accurate at time of publication; subject to manufacturer's change.*

## Comfort and Convenience

| | Retail Price | Dealer Invoice |
|---|---|---|
| Leather upholstery, SE | $895 | $797 |
| *Requires split folding rear seat.* | | |
| 10-way power driver's seat, SE | 350 | 312 |
| Split folding rear seat, SE | 205 | 182 |
| Cassette player with Premium Sound, SE | 135 | 120 |
| *Includes amplifier.* | | |
| CD player with Premium Sound, SE | 270 | 240 |
| SVT | 140 | 124 |
| Power antenna, SE | 95 | 85 |
| Remote keyless entry, SE | 190 | 169 |
| *Includes illuminated entry.* | | |
| Power moonroof, SE, SVT | 595 | 530 |
| Rear defogger, LX | 190 | 169 |
| Smoker's Pkg. | 15 | 13 |
| *Ashtray, cigarette lighter.* | | |
| Floormats, LX, SE | 55 | 49 |

## Appearance and Miscellaneous

| | | |
|---|---|---|
| Engine block heater | 20 | 18 |
| Special wheel covers, SE | 135 | 120 |
| *Includes 205/60TR15 tires.* | | |
| 8-spoke alloy wheels, SE | 425 | 379 |
| *Includes 205/60TR15 tires.* | | |

# FORD CROWN VICTORIA

*Ford Crown Victoria LX*

## SPECIFICATIONS

| | 4-door sedan |
|---|---|
| Wheelbase, in. | 114.4 |
| Overall length, in. | 212.0 |

| | 4-door sedan |
|---|---|
| Overall width, in. | 78.2 |
| Overall height, in. | 56.8 |
| Curb weight, lbs. | 3917 |
| Cargo vol., cu. ft. | 20.6 |
| Fuel capacity, gals. | 19.0 |
| Seating capacity | 6 |
| Front head room, in. | 39.4 |
| Max. front leg room, in. | 42.5 |
| Rear head room, in. | 38.0 |
| Min. rear leg room, in. | 39.6 |

## ENGINES

| | ohc V-8 | ohc V-8 |
|---|---|---|
| Size, liters/cu. in. | 4.6/281 | 4.6/281 |
| Horsepower @ rpm | 200@ 4250 | 215@ 4500 |
| Torque (lbs./ft.) @ rpm | 265@ 3000 | 275@ 3000 |
| Availability | S | O |

**EPA city/highway mpg**

| | | |
|---|---|---|
| 4-speed OD automatic | 17/25 | 17/25 |

| Ford Crown Victoria | Retail Price | Dealer Invoice |
|---|---|---|
| Base 4-door notchback | $20935 | $19566 |
| LX 4-door notchback | 23135 | 21568 |
| Destination charge | 605 | 605 |

## STANDARD EQUIPMENT:

**Base:** 4.6-liter V-8 190-horsepower engine, 4-speed automatic transmission, driver- and passenger-side air bags, 4-wheel disc brakes, air conditioning, variable-assist power steering, tilt steering wheel, cruise control, cloth reclining split bench seat, cupholders, AM/FM radio with four speakers, digital clock, power mirrors, power windows, power door locks, power decklid release, voltmeter, oil-pressure and coolant-temperature gauges, trip odometer, rear defogger, intermittent wipers, automatic headlights, rear heat ducts, theft-deterrent system, 225/60SR16 all-season tires, wheel covers.

**LX** adds: upgraded interior trim, power driver seat with power recliner and power lumbar support, cassette player, Light/Decor Group (illuminated visor mirrors, map lights, body striping), remote keyless entry, carpeted spare tire cover.

## OPTIONAL EQUIPMENT:
### Safety Features

| | | |
|---|---|---|
| Anti-lock brakes with Traction Assist | 775 | 690 |

*Prices are accurate at time of publication; subject to manufacturer's change.*

## Major Packages

| | Retail Price | Dealer Invoice |
|---|---|---|
| Comfort Group, LX .............................................. | $900 | $801 |

*Automatic temperature control, power passenger seat with power lumbar support, leather-wrapped steering wheel, automatic day/night mirror with compass, alloy wheels.*

| | | |
|---|---|---|
| Comfort Plus Group, LX .................................... | 2200 | 1958 |

*Comfort Group plus anti-lock brakes, traction control, trip computer, digital instrumentation, Premium Audio System.*

| | | |
|---|---|---|
| Handling and Performance Pkg., Base.......................... | 935 | 832 |
| LX............................................................ | 740 | 658 |
| LX w/Comfort Group or Comfort Plus Group ............. | 615 | 547 |

*Includes 215-horsepower engine, dual exhaust, performance springs, shocks and stabilizer bars, rear air suspension, 3.27 axle ratio, 225/60TR16 touring tires, alloy wheels.*

## Comfort and Convenience

| | | |
|---|---|---|
| Remote keyless entry, Base ........................................... | 240 | 213 |
| Leather upholstery, LX.................................................. | 735 | 654 |
| *Requires Comfort Group.* | | |
| 6-way power driver seat, Base ...................................... | 360 | 321 |
| Cassette player, Base.................................................... | 185 | 165 |
| Premium Audio System, LX............................................ | 360 | 321 |
| *Upgraded amplifier and six speakers. Requires Comfort Group.* | | |
| Universal garage door opener, LX.................................. | 115 | 102 |
| Floormats............................................................ | 55 | 50 |

## Appearance and Miscellaneous

| | | |
|---|---|---|
| Engine block heater................................................ | 25 | 23 |
| 225/60SR16 whitewall tires........................................... | 80 | 71 |
| Full-size spare tire........................................................ | 120 | 107 |

# FORD ESCORT/ZX2

| SPECIFICATIONS | 4-door sedan | 4-door wagon | 2-door coupe |
|---|---|---|---|
| Wheelbase, in. ..................... | 98.4 | 98.4 | 98.4 |
| Overall length, in. ................ | 174.7 | 172.7 | 175.2 |
| Overall width, in. .................. | 67.0 | 67.0 | 67.4 |
| Overall height, in. ................ | 53.3 | 53.9 | 52.3 |
| Curb weight, lbs. .................. | 2468 | 2531 | 2478 |
| Cargo vol., cu. ft. ................. | 12.8 | 63.4 | 11.8 |
| Fuel capacity, gals. .............. | 12.8 | 12.8 | 12.8 |
| Seating capacity ................... | 5 | 5 | 4 |
| Front head room, in. ............. | 39.0 | 38.7 | 38.0 |

*Ford Escort LX sedan*

|  | 4-door sedan | 4-door wagon | 2-door coupe |
|---|---|---|---|
| Max. front leg room, in. | 42.5 | 42.5 | 42.5 |
| Rear head room, in. | 36.7 | 39.1 | 35.1 |
| Min. rear leg room, in. | 34.0 | 34.0 | 33.4 |

## ENGINES

|  | ohc I-4 | dohc I-4 |
|---|---|---|
| Size, liters/cu. in. | 2.0/121 | 2.0/121 |
| Horsepower @ rpm | 110@ 5000 | 130@ 5750 |
| Torque (lbs./ft.) @ rpm | 125@ 3750 | 127@ 4250 |
| Availability | S[1] | S[2] |

**EPA city/highway mpg**

|  | | |
|---|---|---|
| 5-speed OD manual | 28/38 | 26/33 |
| 4-speed OD automatic | 25/34 | 25/33 |

1. Sedan and Wagon. 2. Escort ZX2.

| Ford Escort/Escort ZX2 | Retail Price | Dealer Invoice |
|---|---|---|
| LX 4-door sedan | $11280 | $10584 |
| SE 4-door sedan | 12580 | 11767 |
| SE 4-door wagon | 13780 | 12859 |
| ZX2 Cool 2-door notchback | 12580 | 11762 |
| ZX2 Hot 2-door notchback | 13895 | 12965 |
| Destination charge | 415 | 415 |

## STANDARD EQUIPMENT:

**LX:** 2.0-liter 4-cylinder engine, 5-speed manual transmission, driver- and passenger-side air bags, power steering, cloth and vinyl reclining bucket seats, center console with cupholders, split folding rear seat, passenger-side visor mirror, coolant temperature gauge, trip odometer, AM/FM radio, digital clock, variable intermittent wipers, door pockets, tinted glass, dual outside mirrors, 185/65R14 tires, wheel covers.

*Prices are accurate at time of publication; subject to manufacturer's change.*

# FORD

**ZX2 Cool** adds to LX: tachometer, driver seat memory recline.

**SE** adds to LX: upgraded upholstery, air conditioning, rear defogger, power mirrors, driver door remote keyless entry system, bodyside moldings, deletes tachometer, driver seat memory recline.

**ZX2 Hot** adds to SE: tachometer, driver seat memory recline.

## OPTIONAL EQUIPMENT:

| | Retail Price | Dealer Invoice |
|---|---|---|
| **Major Packages** | | |
| Sport Group, ZX2 Hot | $595 | $530 |
| SE sedan | 495 | 441 |
| *Sport seats w/rear integrated headrests, passenger-side, rear map pocket, rear spoiler, bright exhaust outlets, fog lights (ZX2 Hot), alloy wheels, 185/60HR15 tires (ZX2 Hot). NA with Appearance Pkg.* | | |
| Appearance Pkg., SE sedan, ZX2 Hot | 155 | 138 |
| SE wagon | 120 | 107 |
| *Leather-wrapped steering wheel, bright exhaust outlets (SE sedan, ZX2 Hot), chrome wheel covers.* | | |
| Power Group, SE, ZX2 Hot | 395 | 352 |
| *Power windows, power door locks, all-door remote keyless entry.* | | |
| Comfort Group, SE, ZX2 Hot | 345 | 307 |
| *Cruise control, tilt steering wheel, map lights, driver-side visor mirror.* | | |
| Wagon Group, SE Wagon | 295 | 263 |
| *Cargo cover, rear wiper/washer, roof rack.* | | |
| **Powertrains** | | |
| 4-speed automatic transmission | 815 | 725 |
| **Safety Features** | | |
| Anti-lock brakes | 400 | 356 |
| Integrated child seat, SE wagon | 135 | 120 |
| *Downgrades split folding rear seat to folding rear seat. NA with Sport Group.* | | |
| **Comfort and Convenience** | | |
| Air conditioning, LX, ZX2 Cool | 795 | 708 |
| Rear defogger, LX, ZX2 Cool | 190 | 169 |
| AM/FM/cassette | 185 | 165 |
| *LX, ZX2 Cool require rear defogger or air conditioning.* | | |
| Premium AM/FM/cassette, SE, ZX2 Hot | 255 | 221 |
| AM/FM/cassette w/6-disc CD changer, | | |
| SE, ZX2 Hot | 515 | 458 |
| *Includes premium sound system.* | | |
| Remote keyless entry, LX, ZX2 Cool | 135 | 120 |
| *Driver door only.* | | |
| Power moonroof, ZX2 Hot | 595 | 530 |

| | Retail Price | Dealer Invoice |
|---|---|---|
| Smoker's Pkg. | $15 | $13 |
| *Includes ashtray, lighter.* | | |
| Floormats | 55 | 49 |

## Appearance and Miscellaneous

| | | |
|---|---|---|
| Engine block heater | 20 | 18 |
| Alloy wheels, SE, ZX2 Hot | 265 | 236 |

# FORD EXPEDITION

*Ford Expedition*

## SPECIFICATIONS

| | 4-door wagon |
|---|---|
| Wheelbase, in. | 119.1 |
| Overall length, in. | 204.6 |
| Overall width, in. | 78.6 |
| Overall height, in. | 76.6 |
| Curb weight, lbs. | 4850 |
| Cargo vol., cu. ft. | 118.3 |
| Fuel capacity, gals. | 26.0 |
| Seating capacity | 9 |
| Front head room, in. | 39.8 |
| Max. front leg room, in. | 40.9 |
| Rear head room, in. | 39.8 |
| Min. rear leg room, in. | 38.9 |

## ENGINES

| | ohc V-8 | ohc V-8 |
|---|---|---|
| Size, liters/cu. in. | 4.6/281 | 5.4/330 |
| Horsepower @ rpm | 215@ 4400 | 230@ 4250 |
| Torque (lbs./ft.) @ rpm | 290@ 3250 | 325@ 3000 |

*Prices are accurate at time of publication; subject to manufacturer's change.*

# FORD

| | ohc V-8 | ohc V-8 |
|---|---|---|
| Availability ................................................ | S | O |
| **EPA city/highway mpg** | | |
| 4-speed OD automatic................................... | 14/19[1] | 13/18[2] |

*1. 13/18 w/4WD. 2. 12/16 w/4WD.*

| Ford Expedition | Retail Price | Dealer Invoice |
|---|---|---|
| XLT 4-door wagon, 2WD ............................... | $27985 | $24533 |
| XLT 4-door wagon, 4WD ............................... | 30585 | 26743 |
| Eddie Bauer 4-door wagon, 2WD ................ | 31955 | 27908 |
| Eddie Bauer 4-door wagon, 4WD ................ | 34590 | 30148 |
| Destination charge ...................................... | 640 | 640 |

## STANDARD EQUIPMENT:

**XLT:** 4.6-liter V-8 engine, 4-speed automatic transmission, driver- and pas-senger-side air bags, anti-lock 4-wheel disc brakes, front cloth 40/60 split bench seat with manual driver-side lumbar support, variable-assist power steering, second-row cloth 60/40 split-folding-reclining bench seat, tilt steering wheel, front and rear cupholders, tinted glass, power mirrors, power windows, power door locks, AM/FM/cassette player, tachometer, voltmeter, coolant-temperature and oil-pressure gauge, remote keyless entry, front map lights, passenger-side illuminated visor mirror, rear defog-ger, speed-sensitive intermittent wipers, rear wiper/washer, front auxiliary power outlet, rear heat ducts, rear lift gate with flip-up glass, floormats, bright grille, 255/70R16 tires, full-size spare tire, styled steel wheels, 4WD adds: Control-Trac part-time 4WD, 2-speed transfer case, front tow hooks, 30-gallon fuel tank.

**Eddie Bauer** adds: cruise control, leather upholstery, front captain's chairs with lumbar support and 6-way power driver seat, front storage console (rear radio controls, auxiliary rear power outlet, headphone jacks), over-head storage console with trip computer, leather-wrapped steering wheel, dual illuminated visor mirrors, rear map lights, power rear quarter windows, rear privacy glass, automatic headlights, roof rack, wheel-lip and rocker moldings, color-keyed grille and mirrors, fog lights, 255/70R16 all-terrain outline-white-letter tires, alloy wheels, 4WD adds: Control-Trac part-time 4WD, 2-speed transfer case, front tow hooks, 30-gallon fuel tank.

## OPTIONAL EQUIPMENT:
### Major Packages

| | | |
|---|---|---|
| Preferred Equipment Pkg. 685A, XLT ............... | 1770 | 1505 |
| *Manufacturer's discount price.........................* | 1050 | 893 |

Front captain's chairs with lumbar support and 6-way power driver seat, front storage console (rear radio controls, auxiliary rear power outlet, headphone jacks), cruise control, rear privacy glass, dual illuminated visor mirrors, roof rack, alloy wheels.

| | Retail Price | Dealer Invoice |
|---|---|---|
| Preferred Equipment Pkg. 687A, Eddie Bauer 2WD ..... | $1605 | $1364 |
| Manufacturer's discount price ......................... | 1030 | 876 |

    *5.4-liter V-8 engine, engine-oil cooler, super engine cooling, Mach audio system with seven premium speakers, power signal mirrors, illuminated running boards, 265/70R17 all-terrain outline-white-letter tires (4WD), cast alloy wheels (4WD).*

| | Retail Price | Dealer Invoice |
|---|---|---|
| Preferred Equipment Pkg. 687A, Eddie Bauer 4WD ..... | 2255 | 1917 |
| Manufacturer's discount price ......................... | 1505 | 1279 |

    *5.4-liter V-8 engine, engine-oil cooler, super engine cooling, Mach audio system with seven premium speakers, power signal mirrors, illuminated running boards, 265/70R17 all-terrain outline-white-letter tires (4WD), cast alloy wheels (4WD).*

| | | |
|---|---|---|
| Extreme Weather Group, XLT ............................. | 190 | 162 |
|    Eddie Bauer ....................................... | 80 | 68 |
| Class III Trailer Tow Group, 2WD w/4.6-liter engine....... | 880 | 748 |
|    4WD w/4.6-liter engine................................. | 390 | 332 |
|    2WD w/5.4-liter engine................................. | 940 | 799 |
|    4WD w/5.4-liter engine................................. | 450 | 383 |

    *7-pin trailer wiring harness, frame-mounted hitch, auxiliary transmission-oil cooler, super engine cooling, heavy-duty battery. 2WD models include rear load-leveling suspension and 30-gallon fuel tank. Includes engine-oil cooler when ordered with 5.4-liter engine.*

## Powertrains

| | | |
|---|---|---|
| 5.4-liter V-8 engine................................. | 665 | 565 |
| Limited-slip rear axle, ordered with 4.6-liter engine........ | 255 | 217 |
|    ordered with 5.4-liter engine.............................. | 315 | 267 |

    *Includes engine-oil cooler when ordered with 5.4-liter engine.*

## Comfort and Convenience

| | | |
|---|---|---|
| High-capacity front and rear air conditioning, XLT......... | 755 | 642 |
|    Eddie Bauer ....................................... | 705 | 599 |

    *XLT includes overhead console. NA with power moonroof.*

| | | |
|---|---|---|
| Power signal mirrors, Eddie Bauer.............................. | 150 | 128 |
| Power moonroof, Eddie Bauer .............................. | 800 | 680 |
| Cruise control, XLT .............................. | 235 | 200 |
| Leather captain's chairs, XLT w/Pkg. 685A ............ | 1300 | 1105 |
| Cloth folding third-row seat, XLT.............................. | 600 | 510 |

    *NA with leather captain's chairs.*

| | | |
|---|---|---|
| Leather folding third-row seat.............................. | 855 | 727 |

    *XLT requires leather captain's chairs.*

| | | |
|---|---|---|
| Mach audio system, Eddie Bauer.............................. | 355 | 302 |

    *Includes seven premium speakers.*

| | | |
|---|---|---|
| 6-disc CD changer.............................. | 475 | 404 |

    *XLT requires Pkg. 685A.*

## Appearance and Miscellaneous

| | Retail Price | Dealer Invoice |
|---|---|---|
| Illuminated running boards | $435 | $370 |
| Engine-block heater | 35 | 30 |

NA XLT w/Pkg. 685A. Eddie Bauer requires Pkg. 687A.

## Special Purpose, Wheels and Tires

| | | |
|---|---|---|
| Load-leveling suspension, 4WD | 815 | 692 |
| XLT requires Pkg. 685A. | | |
| Rear load-leveling suspension, 2WD | 490 | 417 |
| Includes 30-gallon fuel tank. XLT requires 685A. | | |
| Front tow hooks, XLT 4WD | 40 | 34 |
| Skid plates, 4WD | 105 | 89 |
| 255/70R16 all-terrain outline-white-letter tires, XLT with Pkg. 685A | 230 | 196 |
| 265/70R17 all-terrain outline-white-letter tires, XLT 4WD | 380 | 323 |
| Eddie Bauer 4WD | 150 | 128 |
| Requires cast alloy wheels. XLT requires Pkg. 685A. | | |
| 17-inch alloy wheels, 4WD | 185 | 158 |
| Requires 265/70R17 all-terrain outline-white-letter tires. XLT requires Pkg. 685A. | | |
| Chrome steel wheels, 2WD | NC | NC |
| XLT requires Pkg. 685A. | | |

# FORD EXPLORER

*Ford Explorer Sport 2-door*

## SPECIFICATIONS

| | 2-door wagon | 4-door wagon |
|---|---|---|
| Wheelbase, in. | 101.7 | 111.5 |
| Overall length, in. | 178.6 | 188.5 |
| Overall width, in. | 70.2 | 70.2 |

| | 2-door wagon | 4-door wagon |
|---|---|---|
| Overall height, in. | 67.9 | 67.7 |
| Curb weight, lbs. | 3692 | 3911 |
| Cargo vol., cu. ft. | 69.4 | 81.6 |
| Fuel capacity, gals. | 17.5 | 21.0 |
| Seating capacity | 4 | 6 |
| Front head room, in. | 39.9 | 39.9 |
| Max. front leg room, in. | 42.4 | 42.4 |
| Rear head room, in. | 39.1 | 39.3 |
| Min. rear leg room, in. | 36.5 | 37.7 |

## ENGINES

| | ohv V-6 | ohc V-6 | ohv V-8 |
|---|---|---|---|
| Size, liters/cu. in. | 4.0/245 | 4.0/245 | 5.0/302 |
| Horsepower @ rpm | 160@ 4200 | 205@ 5000 | 215@ 4200 |
| Torque (lbs./ft.) @ rpm | 225@ 2800 | 250@ 3000 | 288@ 3300 |
| Availability | S[1] | S[2] | O[3] |

**EPA city/highway mpg**

| | ohv V-6 | ohc V-6 | ohv V-8 |
|---|---|---|---|
| 5-speed OD manual | 17/21[4] | | |
| 4-speed OD automatic | | | 14/19[6] |
| 5-speed OD automatic | | 15/20[5] | |

1. XL, Sport, and XLT. 2. Eddie Bauer and Limited; optional Sport and XLT. 3. XLT, Eddie Bauer, and Limited. 4. 16/20 w/4WD. 5. 15/19 w/4WD. 6. 14/18 w/AWD.

| Ford Explorer | Retail Price | Dealer Invoice |
|---|---|---|
| XL 4-door wagon, 2WD | $21485 | $19532 |
| XL 4-door wagon, 4WD | 23405 | 21221 |
| Sport 2-door wagon, 2WD | 19880 | 18119 |
| Sport 2-door wagon, 4WD | 22650 | 20558 |
| XLT 4-door wagon, 2WD | 24615 | 22286 |
| XLT 4-door wagon, 4WD | 26620 | 24051 |
| XLT 4-door wagon, AWD | 26620 | 24051 |
| Eddie Bauer 4-door wagon, 2WD | 28785 | 25956 |
| Eddie Bauer 4-door wagon, 4WD | 30790 | 27721 |
| Eddie Bauer 4-door wagon, AWD | 30340 | 27324 |
| Limited 4-door wagon, 2WD | 31590 | 28425 |
| Limited 4-door wagon, 4WD | 33595 | 30189 |
| Limited 4-door wagon, AWD | 33145 | 29792 |
| Destination charge | 525 | 525 |

Sport, XLT, and Eddie Bauer require a Preferred Equipment Pkg. AWD denotes all-wheel drive. AWD models require 5.0-liter V-8 engine.

## STANDARD EQUIPMENT:

**XL:** 4.0-liter V-6 engine, 5-speed manual transmission, 3.27 ratio axle,

# FORD

anti-lock 4-wheel disc brakes, driver- and passenger-side air bags, power steering, air conditioning, vinyl front bucket seats, split folding rear bench seat with headrests, solar-control tinted windshield, intermittent wipers, auxiliary power outlet, illuminated entry, trip odometer, tachometer, AM/FM/cassette with digital clock, map light, cargo hooks, passenger-side visor mirror, chrome bumpers, 225/70R15 tires, full-size spare tire, 4WD adds: Control Trac part-time 4WD, transfer-case skid plate.

**Sport and XLT** add: cloth front captain's chairs (XLT), console (XLT), Power Equipment Group (power window, door and liftgate locks, power mirrors, upgraded door-panel trim, delayed-off accessory power), speed-sensitive intermittent wipers, rear privacy glass, rear wiper/washer and defogger, power rear-liftgate lock, leather-wrapped steering wheel, cruise control (XLT), tilt steering wheel (XLT), cargo cover (Sport), illuminated visor mirrors, color-keyed grille (Sport), color-keyed bodyside moldings, black painted bumpers (Sport), striping (XLT), alloy wheels, 4WD models add: Control Trac part-time 4WD, transfer-case skid plate, AWD adds: permanent 4-wheel drive.

**Eddie Bauer** adds: 4.0-liter OHC V-6 engine, 5-speed automatic transmission, 4.10 ratio axle, 6-way power sport cloth front bucket seats with power lumbar adjusters, roof rack, CD player, cargo cover, floormats, 2-tone paint, 255/70R16 white-letter all-terrain tires, chrome wheels, deletes full-size spare tire, 4WD adds: Control Trac part-time 4WD, transfer-case skid plate, AWD adds: permanent 4-wheel drive.

**Limited** adds: automatic air conditioning, leather upholstery and door trim, Mach Audio System with CD/cassette player, power antenna, console with rear climate and radio controls, systems message center, overhead console with electronic compass and outside temperature indicator, Electronics Group (remote keyless entry, theft-deterrent system, automatic door locks, door keypad), heated power mirrors, automatic day/night rearview mirror, automatic headlights, fog lights, running boards, color-keyed grille and bumpers, full-size spare tire, 235/75R15 outline-white-letter all-terrain tires, deletes 2-tone paint, 4WD adds: Control Trac part-time 4WD, transfer-case skid plate, AWD adds: permanent 4-wheel drive.

# OPTIONAL EQUIPMENT:

## Major Packages

| | Retail Price | Dealer Invoice |
|---|---|---|
| Convenience Group, XL, Sport.......................................... | $665 | $565 |
| *Cruise control, leather-wrapped steering wheel, defogger, rear wiper/washer.* | | |
| Electronics Group, Eddie Bauer ....................................... | 415 | 357 |
| *Remote keyless entry, anti-theft system, puddle lights, automatic door locks, door keypad.* | | |
| Preferred Equipment Pkg. 931A, Sport........................... | 650 | 553 |
| *Manufacturer's discount price..........................................* | 75 | 64 |
| *Cloth front captain's chairs, 235/75R15 all-terrain white-letter tires.* | | |

|  | Retail Price | Dealer Invoice |
|---|---|---|
| Preferred Equipment Pkg. 934A, Sport............................ | $3620 | $3086 |
| *Manufacturer's discount price.........................................* | 2290 | 1947 |

5-speed automatic transmission, 6-way power sport cloth bucket seats with power lumbar adjusters, Luxury Group (floor console with rear climate and radio controls, overhead console with electronic compass and outside-temperature indicator, Electronics Group [remote keyless entry, anti-theft system, automatic door locks, door keypad, puddle lights], fog lights), roof rack, cargo cover, floormats, 235/75R15 all-terrain white-letter tires.

|  |  |  |
|---|---|---|
| Preferred Equipment Pkg. 941A, XLT............................. | 290 | 247 |
| *Manufacturer's discount price.........................................* | NC | NC |

Roof rack, CD player.

|  |  |  |
|---|---|---|
| Preferred Equipment Pkg. 945A, XLT............................. | 3255 | 2767 |
| *Manufacturer's discount price.........................................* | 1900 | 1615 |

Pkg. 941A plus 5-speed automatic transmission, 6-way power sport cloth bucket seats with power lumbar adjusters, Luxury Group, cargo cover, floormats.

|  |  |  |
|---|---|---|
| Preferred Equipment Pkg. 942A, Eddie Bauer............... | 1050 | 893 |
| *Manufacturer's discount price.........................................* | NC | NC |

6-way power leather bucket seats with power lumbar adjusters, running boards.

|  |  |  |
|---|---|---|
| Preferred Equipment Pkg. 946A, Eddie Bauer............... | 3375 | 2869 |
| *Manufacturer's discount price.........................................* | 1805 | 1535 |

Pkg. 942A plus Mach Audio System, automatic temperature control, systems message center, Luxury Group.

|  |  |  |
|---|---|---|
| Premium Sport Pkg., Sport ............................................. | 2000 | 1700 |
| *Manufacturer's discount price.........................................* | 1000 | 850 |

Includes 4.0-liter OHC V-6 engine, 5-speed automatic transmission, 4.10 ratio axle (4WD), 3.73 ratio axle (2WD), medium-graphite bumpers, moldings, and side-step bar, roof rack, rear tow hook, chrome wheels (2WD), alloy wheels (4WD), 235/75R15 white-letter tires (2WD), 255/70R16 all-terrain white-letter tires (4WD).

## Powertrains

|  |  |  |
|---|---|---|
| 4.0-liter OHC V-6 engine, XLT, Sport............................... | 540 | 459 |

*Requires 5-speed automatic transmission.*

|  |  |  |
|---|---|---|
| 5.0-liter V-8 engine, XLT w/Pkg. 941A............................. | 1125 | 956 |
| XLT w/Pkg. 945A | 1005 | 854 |
| Eddie Bauer 2WD, Limited 2WD............................... | 430 | 366 |
| Eddie Bauer AWD, Limited AWD................................. | 895 | 761 |

*NA 4WD. Requires 4-speed automatic transmission. Includes limited-slip 3.73 ratio axle with Trailer Towing Pkg., 235/75R15 all-terrain white-letter tires (includes full-size spare on XLT 2WD only).*

|  |  |  |
|---|---|---|
| 4-speed automatic transmission, XLT w/Pkg. 941A....... | 945 | 803 |

*NA 4WD. Requires 5.0-liter V-8 engine.*

# FORD

|  | Retail Price | Dealer Invoice |
|---|---|---|
| 5-speed automatic transmission, XL, XLT, Sport............ | $1065 | $905 |
| *NA with 5.0-liter engine.* | | |
| Limited-slip axle (3.73 ratio) and Trailer Tow Pkg., | | |
| 4.0-liter manual ................................................................ | 355 | 302 |
| *NA Eddie Bauer or with Premium Sport Pkg.* | | |
| Limited-slip axle (4.10 ratio) and Trailer Tow Pkg., | | |
| Sport w/Pkg. 934B, Eddie Bauer................................. | 310 | 263 |
| *Std. with AWD.* | | |

## Safety Features

|  | | |
|---|---|---|
| Integrated rear child seat, 4-door...................................... | 200 | 170 |
| *XL requires captain's chairs.* | | |

## Comfort and Convenience

|  | | |
|---|---|---|
| Cloth captain's chairs, XL................................................. | 280 | 238 |
| *Includes console.* | | |
| Cloth 60/40 bench seat, XLT w/Pkg. 941A .................. | 10 | 8 |
| *Includes storage consolette. Requires automatic transmission.* | | |
| 6-way power cloth bucket seats, Sport ........................... | 1020 | 867 |
| XLT w/Pkg. 941A............................................................. | 650 | 553 |
| *Includes power lumbar adjusters and console. Requires Premium Sound stereo.* | | |
| 6-way power leather bucket seats, | | |
| Sport w/Pkg. 934B, XLT w/Pkg. 945B........................ | 655 | 557 |
| *Includes floor console (XLT).* | | |
| 6-way power cloth bucket seats, Eddie Bauer, (credit).. | (655) | (557) |
| High Series floor console, Eddie Bauer .......................... | 380 | 323 |
| *Includes rear climate and radio controls. Requires Electronics Group.* | | |
| Automatic day/night mirror, | | |
| Sport w/Pkg. 934B, XLT w/Pkg. 945A, | | |
| Eddie Bauer w/Pkg. 946A............................................ | 185 | 158 |
| *Includes automatic headlights.* | | |
| Power moonroof, | | |
| Sport w/Pkg. 934A, XLT w/Pkg. 945B, | | |
| Eddie Bauer w/Pkg. 946A, Limited.............................. | 800 | 680 |
| *Includes front overhead console with rear reading lamps. Sport requires roof rack.* | | |
| CD player, XL.................................................................... | 150 | 128 |
| *Requires Convenience Pkg.* | | |
| CD/cassette player, Sport................................................ | 325 | 277 |
| Sport w/Prem. Sport Pkg., Eddie Bauer ..................... | 175 | 149 |
| Mach Audio System, | | |
| Sport w/Pkg. 934A, XLT w/Pkg. 945A, Eddie Bauer.. | 650 | 553 |
| *Includes subwoofer and power antenna. Eddie Bauer and XLT require console with rear climate and radio controls, Electronics Group.* | | |

| | Retail Price | Dealer Invoice |
|---|---|---|
| CD changer, Sport w/Pkg. 934A, XLT w/Pkg. 945A, Eddie Bauer, Limited | $370 | $314 |
| *Eddie Bauer requires high series floor console.* | | |
| Cellular telephone, Eddie Bauer w/Pkg. 946A, Limited | 690 | 587 |
| Floormats/Cargo Cover Group, XLT | 165 | 140 |
| Sport | 85 | 73 |
| *XLT includes cargo mat.* | | |

## Appearance and Miscellaneous

| | | |
|---|---|---|
| Side-step bar, Sport | 295 | 251 |
| Running boards, XLT, Eddie Bauer | 395 | 336 |
| 2-tone paint, XLT | 120 | 102 |
| Engine-block heater | 35 | 30 |

## Special Purpose, Wheels and Tires

| | | |
|---|---|---|
| Automatic Ride Control, Eddie Bauer w/Pkg. 946A, Limited | 650 | 553 |
| *NA 2WD.* | | |
| Deep-dish alloy wheels, XLT | NC | NC |
| 235/75R15 all-terrain white-letter tires, XLT | 230 | 196 |
| *Includes full-size spare tire on 2WD only.* | | |

# FORD MUSTANG

*Ford Mustang GT convertible*

## SPECIFICATIONS

| | 2-door coupe | 2-door conv. |
|---|---|---|
| Wheelbase, in. | 101.3 | 101.3 |
| Overall length, in. | 181.5 | 181.5 |
| Overall width, in. | 71.8 | 71.8 |
| Overall height, in. | 53.4 | 53.3 |

*Prices are accurate at time of publication; subject to manufacturer's change.*

# FORD

| | 2-door coupe | 2-door conv. |
|---|---|---|
| Curb weight, lbs. | 3393 | 3565 |
| Cargo vol., cu. ft. | 10.9 | 7.7 |
| Fuel capacity, gals. | 15.4 | 15.4 |
| Seating capacity | 4 | 4 |
| Front head room, in. | 38.2 | 38.1 |
| Max. front leg room, in. | 41.9 | 41.9 |
| Rear head room, in. | 35.9 | 35.7 |
| Min. rear leg room, in. | 30.3 | 30.3 |

## ENGINES

| | ohv V-6 | ohc V-8 | dohc V-8 |
|---|---|---|---|
| Size, liters/cu. in. | 3.8/232 | 4.6/282 | 4.6/282 |
| Horsepower @ rpm | 150@ 4000 | 225@ 4750 | 305@ 5800 |
| Torque (lbs./ft.) @ rpm | 215@ 2750 | 290@ 3500 | 300@ 4800 |
| Availability | S[1] | S[2] | S[3] |

### EPA city/highway mpg

| | | | |
|---|---|---|---|
| 5-speed OD manual | 20/29 | 17/26 | 17/25 |
| 4-speed OD automatic | 19/28 | 17/24 | |

1. Base. 2. GT. 3. Cobra.

| Ford Mustang | Retail Price | Dealer Invoice |
|---|---|---|
| Base 2-door coupe | $15970 | $14658 |
| Base 2-door convertible | 20470 | 18663 |
| GT 2-door coupe | 19970 | 18218 |
| GT 2-door convertible | 23970 | 21778 |
| Cobra 2-door coupe | 25630 | 23256 |
| Cobra 2-door convertible | 28430 | 25748 |
| Destination charge | 525 | 525 |

## STANDARD EQUIPMENT:

**Base coupe:** 3.8-liter V-6 engine, 5-speed manual transmission, driver- and passenger-side air bags, 4-wheel disc brakes, power steering, tilt steering wheel, air conditioning, reclining cloth bucket seats, split folding rear seat (coupes), storage console with armrest and cupholder, power mirrors, power windows, power door locks, remote keyless entry, AM/FM/CD/cassette, digital clock, tachometer, trip odometer, coolant-temperature and oil-pressure gauges, voltmeter, dual visor mirrors, intermittent wipers, auxiliary power outlet, power remote decklid release, theft-deterrent system, tinted glass, 205/65R15 all-season tires, alloy wheels.

**Base convertible** adds: power convertible top, illuminated visor mirrors.

**GT coupe** adds to base coupe: 4.6-liter ohc V-8 engine, traction control, dual exhaust, GT bucket seats, power driver seat, leather-wrapped steering wheel, fog lamps, GT Suspension Pkg., 225/55ZR16 all-season tires.

**GT convertible** adds to GT coupe: power convertible top, illuminated visor mirrors, rear decklid spoiler.

**Cobra coupe** adds: 4.6-liter dohc V-8 engine, limited slip differential, anti-lock 4-wheel disc brakes, sport bucket seats, cruise control, illuminated visor mirrors, rear defogger, front floormats, performance suspension, 245/45ZR17 tires.

**Cobra convertible** adds: power convertible top.

## OPTIONAL EQUIPMENT:

| | Retail Price | Dealer Invoice |
|---|---|---|
| **Major Packages** | | |
| Convenience Group, Base | $495 | $441 |
|    GT | 295 | 263 |
|    *Cruise control, power driver seat (Base), rear defogger, floormats.* | | |
| Electronics and Leather Group, Cobra convertible | 1040 | 926 |
|    Cobra coupe | NC | NC |
|    *Leather upholstery, front sport bucket seats w/power lumbar adjustment, Mach 460 sound system, theft-deterrent system w/alarm.* | | |
| **Powertrains** | | |
| 4-speed automatic transmission, Base, GT | 815 | 725 |
| Optional axle ratio, GT | 200 | 178 |
| **Safety Features** | | |
| Anti-lock brakes, Base, GT | 500 | 445 |
| **Comfort and Convenience** | | |
| Leather upholstery, Base, GT | 500 | 445 |
| Mach 460 sound system, Base, GT | 395 | 352 |
|    *Includes 460 watts peak power, AM/FM stereo, 60-watt equalizer, CD-changer compatibility, soft-touch tape controls, ten speakers.* | | |
| Rear defogger, Base, GT | 190 | 169 |
| Illuminated visor mirrors, Base coupe, GT coupe | 95 | 85 |
| **Appearance and Miscellaneous** | | |
| Theft-deterrent system w/alarm, Base, GT | 145 | 129 |
| Rear decklid spoiler, Base, GT coupe, Cobra | 195 | 174 |
| 17-inch alloy wheels, GT | 500 | 445 |
|    *Includes 245/45ZR17 tires* | | |

# FORD TAURUS

## SPECIFICATIONS

| | 4-door sedan | 4-door wagon |
|---|---|---|
| Wheelbase, in. | 108.5 | 108.5 |

*Prices are accurate at time of publication; subject to manufacturer's change.*

*Ford Taurus LX sedan*

|  | 4-door sedan | 4-door wagon |
|---|---|---|
| Overall length, in. | 197.5 | 199.6 |
| Overall width, in. | 73.0 | 73.0 |
| Overall height, in. | 55.1 | 57.6 |
| Curb weight, lbs. | 3329 | 3480 |
| Cargo vol., cu. ft. | 15.8 | 81.3 |
| Fuel capacity, gals. | 16.0 | 16.0 |
| Seating capacity | 6 | 8 |
| Front head room, in. | 39.2 | 39.3 |
| Max. front leg room, in. | 42.2 | 42.2 |
| Rear head room, in. | 36.2 | 38.9 |
| Min. rear leg room, in. | 38.9 | 38.5 |

## ENGINES

|  | ohv V-6 | dohc V-6 | dohc V-8 |
|---|---|---|---|
| Size, liters/cu. in. | 3.0/182 | 3.0/181 | 3.4/207 |
| Horsepower @ rpm | 145@ 5250 | 200@ 5750 | 235@ 6100 |
| Torque (lbs./ft.) @ rpm | 170@ 3250 | 200@ 4500 | 230@ 4800 |
| Availability | S[1] | O[1] | S[2] |

**EPA city/highway mpg**

|  | | | |
|---|---|---|---|
| 4-speed OD automatic | 19/28 | 18/27 | 17/25 |

*1. LX and SE. 2. SHO.*

| Ford Taurus | Retail Price | Dealer Invoice |
|---|---|---|
| LX 4-door sedan | $18245 | $16875 |
| SE 4-door sedan | 19445 | 17761 |
| SE 4-door wagon | 21105 | 19239 |
| SE Comfort 4-door sedan | 19445 | 17761 |
| SE Comfort 4-door wagon | 21105 | 19239 |
| SHO 4-door sedan | 28920 | 26194 |
| Destination charge | 550 | 550 |

SE Comfort requires SE Comfort Group.

## STANDARD EQUIPMENT:

**LX:** 3.0-liter V-6 engine, 4-speed automatic transmission, driver- and passenger-side air bags, air conditioning, variable-assist power steering, tilt steering wheel, 6-passenger seating with dual recliners, front center seating console and cupholders, power windows, power mirrors, visor mirrors, intermittent wipers, rear defogger, AM/FM radio, digital clock, tachometer, coolant-temperature gauge, trip odometer, remote decklid release, tinted glass, 205/65R15 tires, wheel covers.

**SE** adds: cassette player with six speakers, power antenna (wagon), power door locks, remote keyless entry, 60/40 split-folding rear seat, cruise control, interior air filter, rear wiper/washer (wagon), 4-wheel disc brakes (wagon), luggage rack (wagon).

**SHO** adds: 3.4-liter dohc V-8 engine, anti-lock 4-wheel disc brakes, automatic air conditioning, heated power mirrors, leather upholstery, 5-passenger seating with reclining front bucket seats and floor console, 6-way power front seats with driver-side power lumbar support, map pockets, floor shifter, rear air conditioning ducts, illuminated visor mirrors, low fuel warning light, Mach audio system, 6-disc CD changer, power antenna, power moonroof, leather-wrapped steering wheel, Light Group (map lights, courtesy lights), grab handles, automatic headlights, floormats, bodyside cladding, dual exhaust outlets, aerodynamic wipers, theft-deterrent system, rear spoiler, semi-active handling suspension, sport variable-assist power steering, overdrive lock-out switch, 225/55ZR16 tires, chrome alloy wheels.

## OPTIONAL EQUIPMENT:

| | Retail Price | Dealer Invoice |
|---|---|---|
| **Major Packages** | | |
| SE Sport Group, SE sedan | $695 | $619 |
| *Includes 3.0-liter DOHC V-6 engine, 5-passenger seating w/center console and floor shifter, rear spoiler, chrome wheel covers.* | | |
| SE Comfort Group, SE Comfort sedan | 1450 | 1291 |
| SE Comfort wagon | 1285 | 1144 |
| *Includes 3.0-liter DOHC V-6 engine, 5-passenger seating w/center console and floor shifter, power driver seat w/power lumbar support, leather-wrapped steering wheel, automatic air conditioning, power antenna, Light Group (map and courtesy lights), delay-off headlight control, theft-deterrent system, illuminated visor mirrors, alloy wheels.* | | |
| SE Comfort and Sport Group, | | |
| SE Comfort sedan | 2000 | 1780 |
| *SE Comfort Group plus, rear spoiler and chrome alloy wheels.* | | |
| **Powertrains** | | |
| 3.0-liter dohc engine, LX, SE | 495 | 441 |

*Prices are accurate at time of publication; subject to manufacturer's change.*

## Safety Feature

| | Retail Price | Dealer Invoice |
|---|---|---|
| Anti-lock 4-wheel disc brakes, LX, SE, SE Comfort | $600 | $534 |
| Integrated child seat, wagon | 135 | 120 |
| *NA with leather upholstery.* | | |
| Daytime running lights | 40 | 35 |
| *Includes heavy-duty battery.* | | |

## Comfort and Convenience

| | | |
|---|---|---|
| Power door locks, LX | 275 | 245 |
| Heated mirrors, SE, SE Comfort | 55 | 49 |
| Leather upholstery, SE, SE Comfort | 895 | 797 |
| 6-passenger seating, SE Comfort | NC | NC |
| 6-way power driver seat, SE | 350 | 312 |
| 6-way power passenger seat, SE Comfort | 350 | 312 |
| Rear-facing third seat, wagon | 200 | 178 |
| Cassette player, LX | 185 | 165 |
| Mach Audio System, SE, SE Comfort | 400 | 356 |
| *Includes power antenna.* | | |
| 6-disc CD changer, SE, SE Comfort | 350 | 312 |
| Remote keyless entry, LX | 190 | 169 |
| Power moonroof, SE, SE Comfort | 740 | 658 |
| *Includes overhead map lights.* | | |
| Light Group, SE | 45 | 40 |
| *Map and courtesy lights.* | | |
| Wagon Group, wagon | 140 | 124 |
| *Cargo area cover and net.* | | |
| Floormats, LX, SE, SE Comfort | 55 | 49 |

## Appearance and Miscellaneous

| | | |
|---|---|---|
| Engine block heater | 35 | 31 |
| Heavy-duty suspension, wagon | 25 | 23 |
| Full-size spare tire, SE, SE Comfort | 125 | 112 |
| *NA on wagon.* | | |
| Alloy wheels, LX, SE | 315 | 280 |
| Chrome alloy wheels, SE | 725 | 646 |
| SE Comfort | 495 | 441 |

# FORD WINDSTAR

## SPECIFICATIONS

| | 3-door van |
|---|---|
| Wheelbase, in. | 120.7 |
| Overall length, in. | 201.2 |
| Overall width, in. | 75.4 |

*Ford Windstar GL*

|  | 3-door van |
| --- | --- |
| Overall height, in. | 68.0 |
| Curb weight, lbs. | 3762 |
| Cargo vol., cu. ft. | 144.0 |
| Fuel capacity, gals. | 20.0 |
| Seating capacity | 7 |
| Front head room, in. | 39.3 |
| Max. front leg room, in. | 40.7 |
| Rear head room, in. | 38.9 |
| Min. rear leg room, in. | 39.2 |

## ENGINES

|  | ohv V-6 | ohv V-6 |
| --- | --- | --- |
| Size, liters/cu. in. | 3.0/182 | 3.8/232 |
| Horsepower @ rpm | 150@ 5000 | 200@ 5000 |
| Torque (lbs./ft.) @ rpm | 172@ 3300 | 225@ 3000 |
| Availability | S[1] | S[2] |

**EPA city/highway mpg**

|  | ohv V-6 | ohv V-6 |
| --- | --- | --- |
| 4-speed OD automatic | 18/25 | 17/24 |

*1. Base, GL. 2. LX, Limited; optional, GL.*

| Ford Windstar | Retail Price | Dealer Invoice |
| --- | --- | --- |
| Cargo 3-door van | $18010 | $16384 |
| Base 3-door van | 19380 | 17977 |
| GL 3-door van | 20960 | 18980 |
| LX 3-door van | 26205 | 23595 |
| Limited 3-door van | 29505 | 26499 |
| Destination charge | 580 | 580 |

Base, GL, LX, and Limited require a Preferred Pkg.

*Prices are accurate at time of publication; subject to manufacturer's change.*

# FORD

## STANDARD EQUIPMENT:

**Cargo:** 3.0-liter V-6 engine, 4-speed automatic transmission, driver- and passenger-side air bags, anti-lock brakes, power steering, 2-passenger seating (vinyl high-back front buckets), front passenger area carpeting and cloth headliner, solar-tinted windshield and front door glass, AM/FM radio, intermittent wipers, rear wiper/washer, cupholders, coolant-temperature gauge, front-door map pockets, storage bins, visor mirrors, dual outside mirrors, 20 gallon fuel tank, 215/70R15 tires, full wheel covers.

**Base** adds: 7-passenger seating (cloth high-back bucket seats, 2-place middle seat and 3-place bench seats), rear passenger area carpeting and cloth headliner, 205/70R15 tires.

**GL** adds: reclining middle bench seat, adjustable rear-seat track.

**LX** adds: Power Convenience Group (power windows, door locks, and mirrors), Light Group (front map/dome light and glovebox, instrument-panel and engine-compartment lights), 3.8-liter V-6 engine, front air conditioning, low-back front bucket seats with power lumbar adjustment, 6-way power tip-slide driver seat, AM/FM/cassette, tilt steering wheel, cruise control, tachometer, illuminated entry, illuminated visor vanity mirrors, closed cargo bins, map pockets on front seatbacks, cargo net, bodyside molding, 25-gallon fuel tank, 215/70R15 tires, alloy wheels.

**Limited** adds: rear air conditioning, rear defogger, quad bucket seats, leather upholstery, premium AM/FM/cassette, automatic headlights, remote entry system, electrochromatic rearview mirror, overhead console (includes rear seat radio controls, compass, thermometer, conversation mirror, coin holder, and garage door opener/sunglasses holder), storage drawer under front passenger seat, fog lights, 225/60R16 tires, polished alloy wheels.

## OPTIONAL EQUIPMENT:
### Major Packages

| | Retail Price | Dealer Invoice |
|---|---|---|
| Gold Appearance Pkg., LX | $235 | $200 |
| *Manufacturer's discount price* | NC | NC |
| *Gold-tone badging, gold-tone grille surround and bodyside molding inserts, two-tone paint delete, alloy wheels with gold accents. Requires Pkg. 477B.* | | |
| Light Group, Base, GL | 75 | 63 |
| *Front map/dome light and glovebox light.* | | |
| Premium Light Group, LX | 295 | 251 |
| *Includes fog lamps, automatic headlamps, electrochromatic mirror.* | | |
| Interior Convenience Group, GL | 50 | 43 |
| *Left rear storage bin, covered center bin, cargo net.* | | |
| Power Convenience Group, Cargo | 680 | 578 |
| *Power window and power door locks, power mirrors.* | | |

| | Retail Price | Dealer Invoice |
|---|---|---|
| Power Convenience Group delete, Base, GL (credit).... | ($680) | ($578) |
| Preferred Pkg. 481B, Cargo................................ | 2730 | 2320 |
| *Manufacturer's discount price*............................ | 1880 | 1597 |

*Front air conditioning, cloth reclining high-back bucket seats w/under-seat storage drawer, cruise control, tilt steering wheel, Power Convenience Group (power windows and door locks, power mirrors), AM/FM/cassette, rear defogger.*

| | | |
|---|---|---|
| Preferred Pkg. 470B, Base .............................. | 1535 | 1305 |
| *Manufacturer's discount price*............................ | 1010 | 859 |

*Front air conditioning, Power Convenience Group (power windows, door locks, and mirrors).*

| | | |
|---|---|---|
| Preferred Pkg. 472B, GL.................................. | 2480 | 2108 |
| *Manufacturer's discount price*............................ | 1800 | 1530 |

*Front air conditioning, tip-slide driver seat, cassette player, cruise control, tilt steering wheel, tachometer, Power Convenience Group (power windows and door locks, power mirrors), rear defogger, bodyside moldings.*

| | | |
|---|---|---|
| Preferred Pkg. 473B, GL.................................. | 4405 | 3745 |
| *Manufacturer's discount price*............................ | 3075 | 2614 |

*Pkg. 472B plus 3.8-liter V-6 engine, rear air conditioning, Light Group (front map/dome light, glovebox light), overhead console, privacy glass, luggage rack.*

| | | |
|---|---|---|
| Preferred Pkg. 477B, LX ................................. | 2545 | 2161 |
| *Manufacturer's discount price*............................ | 1580 | 1340 |

*Rear air conditioning, rear defogger, quad bucket seats, overhead console, privacy glass, front and rear floormats, luggage rack, 2-tone paint, remote entry system.*

| | | |
|---|---|---|
| Preferred Pkg. 479B, Limited............................ | 680 | 578 |
| *Manufacturer's discount price*............................ | NC | NC |

*Privacy glass, roof rack, floormats.*

| | | |
|---|---|---|
| Northwoods Appearance Pkg., GL..................... | 795 | 676 |
| LX.......................................................... | 285 | 243 |

*Tan roof rack, green grille and door handles, badging and graphics, special floormats, alloy wheels with tan accents.*

| | | |
|---|---|---|
| Trailer Towing Pkg., GL, LX ............................. | 435 | 370 |
| GL or LX with front and rear air conditioning, Limited | 410 | 347 |

*Includes heavy-duty battery, engine-oil and power-steering coolers, auxiliary transmission-oil cooler, trailer wiring-harness, full-size spare tire. NA base.*

| | | |
|---|---|---|
| Security Group, LX, Limited............................. | 200 | 171 |

*Includes programmable garage door opener, theft-deterrent system.*

| | | |
|---|---|---|
| Family Security Pkg., GL................................ | 1050 | 893 |
| *Manufacturer's discount price*............................ | 655 | 557 |

*Security Group plus remote keyless entry, self-sealing tires, sport wheel covers.*

*Prices are accurate at time of publication; subject to manufacturer's change.*

# FORD

|  | Retail Price | Dealer Invoice |
|---|---|---|
| Family Security Pkg., LX | $875 | $744 |
| *Manufacturer's discount price* | 480 | 408 |

*Security Group plus remote keyless entry, self-sealing tires, sport wheel covers.*

## Powertrains

| | | |
|---|---|---|
| 3.8-liter V-6 engine, Cargo, GL | 685 | 583 |
| *Includes tachometer.* | | |
| Traction Control, GL, LX, Limited | 395 | 336 |

## Safety Features

| | | |
|---|---|---|
| Integrated child seats (two), Base | 285 | 242 |
| GL | 225 | 191 |
| LX, replacing quad bucket seats (credit) | (285) | (242) |

## Comfort and Convenience

| | | |
|---|---|---|
| Front air conditioning, Cargo | 855 | 727 |
| Front air conditioning delete, Base, GL (credit) | (855) | (727) |
| Rear air conditioning, GL | 475 | 404 |
| *Includes rear heater. Requires Light Group.* | | |
| Rear defogger, Cargo, Base | 170 | 144 |
| Cruise control/tilt steering wheel, Base | 375 | 319 |
| Floor console, GL, LX, Limited | 155 | 132 |
| *Includes cupholders and covered storage bin. Requires rear air conditioning. GL requires Pkg. 473B.* | | |
| Overhead console, GL | 100 | 85 |
| *Includes rear seat radio controls, conversation mirror, coin holder, and garage door opener/sunglasses holder. Requires Light Group.* | | |
| Remote keyless entry, GL | 175 | 149 |
| *Remote entry system and illuminated entry. Requires Power Convenience Group.* | | |
| Cassette player, Cargo, Base | 170 | 144 |
| Premium AM/FM/cassette, LX | 155 | 132 |
| Premium AM/FM/CD player, GL, LX | 325 | 276 |
| Limited | 170 | 144 |
| *Requires cruise control/tilt steering wheel, Light Group.* | | |
| JBL Audio System, LX | 665 | 565 |
| Limited | 510 | 433 |
| *LX requires Premium radio.* | | |
| Cloth high back bucket seats, GL | 615 | 522 |
| *Includes tip-slide driver seat, rear seat bed.* | | |
| Cloth reclining high back bucket seats, Cargo | 490 | 417 |
| *Includes underseat storage drawer.* | | |
| Low-back bucket seats, GL | 550 | 468 |
| *Includes two integrated child seats.* | | |

| | Retail Price | Dealer Invoice |
|---|---|---|
| Quad bucket seats, GL | $745 | $633 |
| Quad bucket seats delete, LX (credit) | (625) | (532) |
| *Quad buckets seats included in Pkg. 477B.* | | |
| Low-back quad bucket seats, GL | 1040 | 884 |
| *Includes power driver seat. Requires Pkg. 473B* | | |
| Power driver seat, GL | 325 | 277 |
| *Requires Pkg. 473B.* | | |
| Tip-slide driver seat, Base | 150 | 128 |
| Leather upholstery, LX | 865 | 735 |
| *Requires quad bucket seats.* | | |
| Floormats, Base, GL | 90 | 77 |

## Appearance and Miscellaneous

| | | |
|---|---|---|
| Luggage rack, GL | 175 | 149 |
| Load-leveling air suspension, LX, Limited | 290 | 247 |
| *Requires Power Convenience Group.* | | |
| Privacy glass, Cargo, Base, GL | 415 | 352 |
| *Cargo requires Preferred Pkg. 481A.* | | |
| Bodyside molding, GL | 80 | 68 |
| 25-gallon fuel tank, Cargo, GL | 30 | 26 |
| Engine block heater | 35 | 30 |
| Alloy wheels, GL | 415 | 352 |
| *Includes 215/70R15 tires.* | | |
| 215/70R15 self-sealing tires, GL, LX | 280 | 238 |
| *GL requires alloy wheels.* | | |
| Full-size spare tire | 110 | 93 |

# HONDA ACCORD

| SPECIFICATIONS | 2-door coupe | 4-door sedan |
|---|---|---|
| Wheelbase, in. | 105.1 | 106.9 |
| Overall length, in. | 186.8 | 188.8 |
| Overall width, in. | 70.3 | 70.3 |
| Overall height, in. | 55.1 | 56.9 |
| Curb weight, lbs. | 2943 | 2888 |
| Cargo vol., cu. ft. | 13.6 | 14.1 |
| Fuel capacity, gals. | 17.1 | 17.1 |
| Seating capacity | 5 | 5 |
| Front head room, in. | 39.7 | 40.0 |
| Max. front leg room, in. | 42.6 | 42.1 |
| Rear head room, in. | 36.5 | 37.6 |
| Min. rear leg room, in. | 32.4 | 37.9 |

*Prices are accurate at time of publication; subject to manufacturer's change.*

# HONDA

*Honda Accord LX V-6 sedan*

## ENGINES

| | ohc I-4 | ohc I-4 | ohc V-6 |
|---|---|---|---|
| Size, liters/cu. in. | 2.3/137 | 2.3/137 | 3.0/183 |
| Horsepower @ rpm | 135@ 5400 | 150@ 5700 | 200@ 5500 |
| Torque (lbs./ft.) @ rpm | 145@ 4700 | 152@ 4900 | 195@ 4700 |
| Availability | S[1] | S[2] | S[3] |
| **EPA city/highway mpg** | | | |
| 5-speed OD manual | 24/31 | 25/31 | |
| 4-speed OD automatic | 22/29 | 23/30 | 20/28 |

1. DX models.  2. LX, EX models.  3. V-6 models.

| Honda Accord | Retail Price | Dealer Invoice |
|---|---|---|
| DX 4-door sedan, 5-speed | $15100 | $13343 |
| DX 4-door sedan, automatic | 15900 | 14050 |
| LX 2-door notchback, 5-speed | 18290 | 16162 |
| LX 2-door notchback, automatic | 19090 | 16869 |
| LX 4-door sedan, 5-speed | 18290 | 16162 |
| LX 4-door sedan, automatic | 19090 | 16869 |
| LX 4-door sedan w/ABS, automatic | 19690 | 17399 |
| LX V-6 2-door notchback, automatic | 21550 | 19042 |
| LX V-6 4-door sedan, automatic | 21550 | 19042 |
| EX 2-door notchback, 5-speed | 20800 | 18380 |
| EX 2-door notchback, automatic | 21600 | 19086 |
| EX 2-door notchback w/leather, 5-speed | 21950 | 19396 |
| EX 2-door notchback w/leather, automatic | 22750 | 20103 |
| EX 4-door sedan, 5-speed | 20800 | 18380 |
| EX 4-door sedan, automatic | 21600 | 19086 |
| EX 4-door sedan w/leather, 5-speed | 21950 | 19396 |
| EX 4-door sedan w/leather, automatic | 22750 | 20103 |
| EX V-6 2-door notchback, automatic | 24150 | 21340 |
| EX V-6 4-door sedan, automatic | 24150 | 21340 |
| Destination charge | 395 | 395 |

ABS denotes anti-lock 4-wheel disc brakes.

## STANDARD EQUIPMENT:

**DX:** 2.3-liter 4-cylinder 135-horsepower engine, 5-speed manual or 4-speed automatic transmission, driver- and passenger-side air bags, variable-assist power steering, cloth reclining front bucket seats, folding rear seat, storage console with armrest, tachometer, coolant-temperature gauge, trip odometer, maintenance interval indicator, AM/FM/cassette w/two speakers, integrated antenna, digital clock, tilt steering column, cupholder, intermittent wipers, rear defogger, remote fuel-door and decklid releases, visor mirrors, rear heat ducts, tinted glass, dual remote outside mirrors, 195/70R14 tires, wheel covers.

**LX** adds: 2.3-liter 4-cylinder VTEC 150-horsepower engine, cruise control, air conditioning, power windows, power door locks, power mirrors, illuminated visor mirrors, driver seat manual height adjustment, map lights, rear armrest w/trunk pass-through (4-door), split folding rear seat (2-door), variable intermittent wipers, 4-speaker sound system, 195/65HR15 tires.

**LX V-6** adds: 3.0-liter V-6 engine, 4-speed automatic transmission, anti-lock 4-wheel disc brakes, 6-way power driver seat, 205/65R15 tires.

**EX** adds to LX: anti-lock 4-wheel disc brakes, power sunroof, driver seat power height adjustment, driver seat adjustable lumbar support, CD player w/six speakers, automatic-off headlights, power decklid release, alloy wheels.

**EX w/leather** adds: leather upholstery, leather-wrapped steering wheel, 8-way power driver seat.

**EX V-6** adds: 3.0-liter V-6-cylinder engine, 4-speed automatic transmission, automatic temperature control, Homelink universal garage door opener, 205/65R15 tires (4-door), 205/60R16 tires (2-door).

**Options** are available as dealer-installed accessories.

# HONDA CIVIC

| SPECIFICATIONS | 2-door coupe | 2-door hatchback | 4-door sedan |
|---|---|---|---|
| Wheelbase, in. | 103.2 | 103.2 | 103.2 |
| Overall length, in. | 175.1 | 175.1 | 175.1 |
| Overall width, in. | 67.1 | 67.1 | 67.1 |
| Overall height, in. | 54.1 | 54.1 | 54.1 |
| Curb weight, lbs. | 2262 | 2222 | 2319 |
| Cargo vol., cu. ft. | 11.9 | 13.4 | 11.9 |
| Fuel capacity, gals. | 11.9 | 11.9 | 11.9 |
| Seating capacity | 5 | 5 | 5 |
| Front head room, in. | 38.8 | 38.8 | 39.8 |
| Max. front leg room, in. | 42.7 | 42.7 | 42.7 |
| Rear head room, in. | 36.2 | 37.2 | 37.6 |
| Min. rear leg room, in. | 34.1 | 34.1 | 34.1 |

*Prices are accurate at time of publication; subject to manufacturer's change.*

# HONDA

*Honda Civic EX sedan*

## ENGINES

| | ohc I-4 | ohc I-4 | ohc I-4 |
|---|---|---|---|
| Size, liters/cu. in. | 1.6/97 | 1.6/97 | 1.6/97 |
| Horsepower @ rpm | 106@ 6200 | 115@ 6300 | 127@ 6600 |
| Torque (lbs./ft.) @ rpm | 103@ 4600 | 104@ 5400 | 107@ 5500 |
| Availability | S[1] | S[2] | S[3] |
| **EPA city/highway mpg** | | | |
| 5-speed OD manual | 32/37 | 36/44 | 30/35 |
| 4-speed OD automatic | 29/36 | | 28/35 |

*1. CX, DX, LX.  2. HX.  3. EX.*

| Honda Civic | Retail Price | Dealer Invoice |
|---|---|---|
| CX 2-door hatchback, 5-speed | $10650 | $9990 |
| CX 2-door hatchback, automatic | 11650 | 10928 |
| DX 2-door hatchback, 5-speed | 12100 | 10856 |
| DX 2-door hatchback, automatic | 12900 | 11574 |
| DX 2-door notchback, 5-speed | 12580 | 11287 |
| DX 2-door notchback, automatic | 13380 | 12005 |
| DX 4-door sedan, 5-speed | 12735 | 11426 |
| DX 4-door sedan, automatic | 13535 | 12144 |
| HX 2-door notchback, 5-speed | 13400 | 12022 |
| HX 2-door notchback, CVT | 14400 | 12920 |
| LX 4-door sedan, 5-speed | 14750 | 12988 |
| LX 4-door sedan, automatic | 15550 | 13706 |
| EX 2-door notchback, 5-speed | 15250 | 13682 |
| EX 2-door notchback, automatic | 16050 | 14400 |
| EX 2-door notchback w/ABS, automatic | 16650 | 14938 |
| EX 4-door sedan, 5-speed | 16480 | 14786 |
| EX 4-door sedan, automatic | 17280 | 15504 |
| Destination charge | 395 | 395 |

ABS denotes anti-lock brakes.

## STANDARD EQUIPMENT:

**CX:** 1.6-liter 4-cylinder 106-horsepower engine, 5-speed manual or 4-speed automatic transmission, driver- and passenger-side air bags, power steering (requires automatic transmission), reclining cloth front bucket seats, 50/50 split folding rear seats, remote fuel-door and hatch releases, rear defogger, dual remote outside mirrors, cupholder, intermittent wipers, visor mirrors, tinted glass, 185/65R14 tires.

**DX hatchback** adds: rear wiper/washer, AM/FM stereo w/clock, rear map pocket, cargo cover, wheel covers.

**DX sedan/notchback** adds to CX: power steering (2-door requires automatic transmission), lockable 60/40 fold-down rear seat, AM/FM stereo w/clock, tilt steering column, rear heat ducts, remote trunk release, rear map pocket, full wheel covers.

**HX** adds to DX sedan/notchback: 1.6-liter 4-cylinder VTEC 115-horsepower engine, 5-speed manual or Continuously Variable Transmission (CVT), power steering, power windows, power mirrors, power door locks, console, tachometer, cargo-area light, alloy wheel covers.

**LX** adds to DX sedan/notchback: air conditioning, power steering, power mirrors, power windows, cruise control, power door locks, tachometer, front storage console with armrest, cargo-area light.

**EX** adds to LX: 1.6-liter 4-cylinder VTEC 127-horsepower engine, anti-lock brakes (4-door), power moonroof, six-speakers (2-door), remote keyless entry, color-keyed bodyside molding.

**Options** are available as dealer-installed accessories.

# HONDA CR-V

## SPECIFICATIONS

| | 4-door wagon |
|---|---|
| Wheelbase, in. | 103.2 |
| Overall length, in. | 177.6 |
| Overall width, in. | 68.9 |
| Overall height, in. | 65.9 |
| Curb weight, lbs. | 3150 |
| Cargo vol., cu. ft. | 67.2 |
| Fuel capacity, gals. | 15.3 |
| Seating capacity | 5 |
| Front head room, in. | 40.5 |
| Max. front leg room, in. | 41.5 |
| Rear head room, in. | 39.2 |
| Min. rear leg room, in. | 36.7 |

## ENGINES

| | dohc I-4 |
|---|---|
| Size, liters/cu. in. | 2.0/122 |

*Prices are accurate at time of publication; subject to manufacturer's change.*

# HONDA

*Honda CR-V EX*

|  | dohc I-4 |
|---|---|
| Horsepower @ rpm | 126@ 5400 |
| Torque (lbs./ft.) @ rpm | 133@ 4300 |
| Availability | S |
| **EPA city/highway mpg** | |
| 4-speed OD automatic | 22/25 |

| Honda CR-V | Retail Price | Dealer Invoice |
|---|---|---|
| 1997 4-door wagon | $19400 | $17604 |
| 1997 4-door wagon w/ABS | 20400 | 18511 |
| Destination charge | 395 | 395 |

## STANDARD EQUIPMENT:

2.0-liter dohc 4-cylinder engine, 4-speed automatic transmission, variable-assist power steering, Real-Time 4-wheel drive, air conditioning, driver- and passenger-side air bags, cruise control, reclining front bucket seats w/driver-seat height adjustment, split folding and reclining 50/50 rear bench seat, cupholders, power windows, power door locks, power mirrors, tilt steering column, tachometer, solar-control tinted glass, AM/FM radio w/clock, rear defogger, intermittent rear wiper/washer, rear heat ducts, visor mirrors, interior air filter, map lights, remote hatch release, lift-out folding picnic table, auxiliary power outlet, rear mud guards, outside spare-tire carrier w/cover, 205/70R15 tires.

**ABS** adds: 4-wheel anti-lock brakes, alloy wheels.

**Options** are available as dealer-installed accessories.

# HONDA ODYSSEY

*Honda Odyssey EX*

## SPECIFICATIONS

| | 4-door van |
|---|---|
| Wheelbase, in. | 111.4 |
| Overall length, in. | 187.2 |
| Overall width, in. | 70.6 |
| Overall height, in. | 64.6 |
| Curb weight, lbs. | 3450 |
| Cargo vol., cu. ft. | 102.5 |
| Fuel capacity, gals. | 17.2 |
| Seating capacity | 7/8 |
| Front head room, in. | 40.1 |
| Max. front leg room, in. | 40.7 |
| Rear head room, in. | 39/37 |
| Min. rear leg room, in. | 40/34 |

## ENGINES

| | dohc I-4 |
|---|---|
| Size, liters/cu. in. | 2.3/140 |
| Horsepower @ rpm | 150@ 5700 |
| Torque (lbs./ft.) @ rpm | 152@ 4900 |
| Availability | S |

**EPA city/highway mpg**

| | |
|---|---|
| 4-speed OD automatic | 21/26 |

| Honda Odyssey | Retail Price | Dealer Invoice |
|---|---|---|
| LX 4-door van, 7-passenger | $23810 | $21039 |
| LX 4-door van, 6-passenger | 24220 | 21401 |
| EX 4-door van | 25800 | 22798 |

*Prices are accurate at time of publication; subject to manufacturer's change.*

# HONDA

|  | Retail Price | Dealer Invoice |
|---|---|---|
| Destination charge ......................................................... | $395 | $395 |

## STANDARD EQUIPMENT:

**LX:** 2.3-liter 4-cylinder engine, 4-speed automatic transmission, driver- and passenger-side air bags, anti-lock 4-wheel disc brakes, front and rear air conditioning, variable-assist power steering, tilt steering column, cruise control, cloth front bucket seats, split folding middle bench seat (7-passenger seating) or removable captain's chairs (6-passenger seating), folding third bench seat, AM/FM/cassette, digital clock, power mirrors, power windows, power door locks, remote fuel-door release, tachometer, intermittent wipers, rear defogger, rear wiper/washer, illuminated visor mirrors, cupholders, theft-deterrent system, bodyside moldings, 205/65R15 tires.

**EX** adds: power sunroof, 6-passenger seating, driver's seat with power height adjustment, remote keyless entry system, 6-speaker sound system, map lights, color-keyed bodyside moldings, alloy wheels.

**Options** are available as dealer-installed accessories.

# HONDA PASSPORT

*Honda Passport EX*

## SPECIFICATIONS

|  | 4-door wagon |
|---|---|
| Wheelbase, in. ........................................................ | 106.4 |
| Overall length, in. ................................................... | 177.4 |
| Overall width, in. .................................................... | 70.4 |
| Overall height, in. ................................................... | 67.9 |
| Curb weight, lbs. .................................................... | 3589 |
| Cargo vol., cu. ft. ................................................... | 81.1 |
| Fuel capacity, gals. ................................................ | 21.1 |
| Seating capacity .................................................... | 5 |
| Front head room, in. ............................................... | 38.9 |
| Max. front leg room, in. ........................................... | 42.1 |

|  | 4-door wagon |
|---|---|
| Rear head room, in. | 38.3 |
| Min. rear leg room, in. | 35.0 |

## ENGINES

|  | dohc V-6 |
|---|---|
| Size, liters/cu. in. | 3.2/193 |
| Horsepower @ rpm | 205@ 5400 |
| Torque (lbs./ft.) @ rpm | 214@ 3000 |
| Availability | S |

### EPA city/highway mpg

|  |  |
|---|---|
| 5-speed OD manual | 18/20 |
| 4-speed OD automatic | 16/20 |

| Honda Passport | Retail Price | Dealer Invoice |
|---|---|---|
| LX 2WD 4-door wagon, 5-speed | $22700 | $20135 |
| LX 2WD 4-door wagon, automatic | 23850 | 21155 |
| LX 4WD 4-door wagon, 5-speed | 25450 | 22574 |
| LX 4WD 4-door wagon with 16-inch Wheel Pkg., 5-speed | 25850 | 22929 |
| LX 4WD 4-door wagon, automatic | 26600 | 23594 |
| LX 4WD 4-door wagon with 16-inch Wheel Pkg., automatic | 27000 | 23949 |
| EX 2WD 4-door wagon, automatic | 26500 | 23506 |
| EX 2WD 4-door wagon w/leather, automatic | 27500 | 24393 |
| EX 4WD 4-door wagon, automatic | 28950 | 25679 |
| EX 4WD 4-door wagon w/leather, automatic | 29950 | 26566 |
| Destination charge | 395 | 395 |

## STANDARD EQUIPMENT:

**LX 2WD:** 3.2-liter V-6 engine, 5-speed manual or 4-speed automatic transmission, driver- and passenger-side air bags, anti-lock brakes, variable-assist power steering, tilt steering column, cruise control, reclining front bucket seats, center storage console, cupholders, 60/40 split folding rear bench seat, power windows, power door locks, tachometer, rear defogger, AM/FM/cassette, visor mirrors, remote tailgate release, tinted glass, dual outside mirrors, skid plates, full-size spare tire, 225/75R16 mud and snow tires.

**LX 4WD** adds: part-time 4-wheel drive, automatic locking front hubs, 2-speed transfer case, 4-wheel disc brakes, air conditioning, transfer case skid plate, alloy wheels.

**LX 4WD w/16-inch Wheel Pkg.** adds to LX 4WD: flared wheel opening moldings, splash guards, 245/70R16 tires, 16-inch alloy wheels.

*Prices are accurate at time of publication; subject to manufacturer's change.*

## HONDA

**EX 2WD** adds to LX 2WD: removable tilt-up moonroof, air conditioning, leather upholstery (w/leather models), heated power mirrors, rear wiper/washer, leather-wrapped steering wheel, intermittent wipers, cargo net, map lights, chrome bumpers, rear privacy glass, 16-inch Wheel Pkg. (16-inch alloy wheels, 245/70R16 tires, flared wheel openings, splash guards).

**EX 4WD** adds: part-time 4-wheel drive, limited-slip differential, automatic locking front hubs, 2-speed transfer case, 4-wheel disc brakes, transfer-case skid plate.

**Options** are available as dealer-installed accessories.

# HONDA PRELUDE

*Honda Prelude SE*

## SPECIFICATIONS

|  | 2-door coupe |
| --- | --- |
| Wheelbase, in. | 101.8 |
| Overall length, in. | 178.0 |
| Overall width, in. | 69.0 |
| Overall height, in. | 51.8 |
| Curb weight, lbs. | 2954 |
| Cargo vol., cu. ft. | 8.7 |
| Fuel capacity, gals. | 15.9 |
| Seating capacity | 5 |
| Front head room, in. | 37.9 |
| Max. front leg room, in. | 43.0 |
| Rear head room, in. | 35.3 |
| Min. rear leg room, in. | 28.1 |

## ENGINES

|  | dohc I-4 |
| --- | --- |
| Size, liters/cu. in. | 2.2/132 |
| Horsepower @ rpm | 195@ 7000 |
| Torque (lbs./ft.) @ rpm | 156@ 5250 |
| Availability | S |

**EPA city/highway mpg**
5-speed OD manual.................................................................. 23/27
4-speed OD automatic............................................................. 21/27

| Honda Prelude | Retail Price | Dealer Invoice |
|---|---|---|
| Base 2-door coupe, 5-speed | $23300 | $20667 |
| Base 2-door coupe, automatic | 24300 | 21554 |
| SH 2-door coupe, 5-speed | 25800 | 22885 |
| Destination charge | 395 | 395 |

## STANDARD EQUIPMENT:

**Base:** 2.2-liter 4-cylinder VTEC engine, 5-speed manual or 4-speed Sequential SportShift automatic transmission, driver- and passenger-side air bags, anti-lock 4-wheel disc brakes, air conditioning, variable-assist power steering, tilt steering wheel, leather-wrapped steering wheel, cruise control, cloth upholstery, reclining front bucket seats w/driver-seat height adjustment, folding rear seat, storage console w/armrest, front and rear cupholders, power windows, power door locks, power outside mirrors, power moonroof, AM/FM/CD player w/Acoustic Feedback Control, integrated rear-window antenna, digital clock, tachometer, visor mirrors, map lights, rear defogger, remote fuel-door and decklid release, variable intermittent wipers, auxiliary power outlet, dual exhaust outlets, theft-deterrent system, 205/50R16 tires, alloy wheels.

**SH adds:** 5-speed manual transmission, Active Torque Steer System, leather-wrapped shifter, rear spoiler.

**Options** are available as dealer-installed accessories.

# HYUNDAI ACCENT

| SPECIFICATIONS | 2-door hatchback | 4-door sedan |
|---|---|---|
| Wheelbase, in. | 94.5 | 94.5 |
| Overall length, in. | 161.5 | 162.1 |
| Overall width, in. | 63.8 | 63.8 |
| Overall height, in. | 54.9 | 54.9 |
| Curb weight, lbs. | 2101 | 2105 |
| Cargo vol., cu. ft. | 16.1 | 10.7 |
| Fuel capacity, gals. | 11.9 | 11.9 |
| Seating capacity | 5 | 5 |
| Front head room, in. | 38.7 | 38.7 |
| Max. front leg room, in. | 42.6 | 42.6 |
| Rear head room, in. | 37.8 | 38.0 |
| Min. rear leg room, in. | 32.7 | 32.7 |

*Prices are accurate at time of publication; subject to manufacturer's change.*

*Hyundai Accent GSi hatchback*

## ENGINES

|  | ohc I-4 |
|---|---|
| Size, liters/cu. in. | 1.5/91 |
| Horsepower @ rpm | 92 @ 5500 |
| Torque (lbs./ft.) @ rpm | 97 @ 4000 |
| Availability | S |

**EPA city/highway mpg**

|  |  |
|---|---|
| 5-speed OD manual | 28/36 |
| 4-speed OD automatic | 27/35 |

| Hyundai Accent | Retail Price | Dealer Invoice |
|---|---|---|
| L 2-door hatchback, 5-speed | $9099 | $8622 |
| GS 2-door hatchback, 5-speed | 9899 | 9176 |
| GS 2-door hatchback, automatic | 10654 | 9860 |
| GL 4-door sedan, 5-speed | 10299 | 9547 |
| GL 4-door sedan, automatic | 11054 | 10231 |
| GSi 2-door hatchback, 5-speed | 10699 | 9918 |
| GSi 2-door hatchback, automatic | 11454 | 10602 |
| Destination charge | 435 | 435 |

## STANDARD EQUIPMENT:

**L:** 1.5-liter 4-cylinder engine, 5-speed manual transmission, driver- and passenger-side air bags, cloth reclining front bucket seats, folding rear seat, front and rear center consoles, AM/FM/cassette, coolant-temperature gauge, trip odometer, rear defogger, remote fuel-door release, passenger-side visor mirror, intermittent wipers, cargo-area cover, remote outside mirrors, 155/80R13 tires.

**GS and GL** add: 5-speed manual or 4-speed automatic transmission, power steering, 5-way adjustable driver seat w/lumbar support, 60/40 split folding rear seat (GS), fixed rear seat (GL), tachometer, digital clock, remote hatch/decklid release, rear wiper/washer (GS), cargo-area cover (GS), tinted glass, bodyside moldings, 175/70R13 tires, wheel covers.

**GSi** adds to GS: power mirrors, power windows, passenger-side walk-in seat, leather-wrapped steering wheel and shifter, sports-tuned suspension, rear spoiler, lower bodyside cladding, fog lights, 175/65R14 performance tires, alloy wheels.

## OPTIONAL EQUIPMENT:

### Major Packages

| | Retail Price | Dealer Invoice |
|---|---|---|
| Option Pkg. 4, GS, GL | $994 | $855 |
| *Air conditioning.* | | |
| Option Pkg. 5, GS, GL | 1605 | 1422 |
| *Anti-lock brakes, air conditioning. Requires automatic transmission.* | | |
| Option Pkg. 15, GSi | 1439 | 1222 |
| *Air conditioning, pop-up sunroof.* | | |
| Option Pkg. 17, GSi | 2133 | 1854 |
| *Anti-lock brakes air conditioning, CD player, pop-up sunroof. Requires automatic transmission.* | | |

### Comfort and Convenience

| | | |
|---|---|---|
| Remote keyless entry | 349 | 215 |
| *Includes theft-deterrent system.* | | |

### Appearance and Miscellaneous

| | | |
|---|---|---|
| Theft-deterrent system | 249 | 155 |
| Rear spoiler, L, GS, GL | 395 | 261 |

Other options are available as port installed items.

# HYUNDAI ELANTRA

| SPECIFICATIONS | 4-door sedan | 4-door wagon |
|---|---|---|
| Wheelbase, in. | 100.4 | 100.4 |
| Overall length, in. | 174.0 | 175.2 |
| Overall width, in. | 66.9 | 66.9 |
| Overall height, in. | 54.9 | 58.8 |
| Curb weight, lbs. | 2458 | 2619 |
| Cargo vol., cu. ft. | 11.4 | 32.3 |
| Fuel capacity, gals. | 14.5 | 14.5 |
| Seating capacity | 5 | 5 |
| Front head room, in. | 38.6 | 38.6 |

*Prices are accurate at time of publication; subject to manufacturer's change.*

*Hyundai Elantra GLS sedan*

| | 4-door sedan | 4-door wagon |
|---|---|---|
| Max. front leg room, in. | 43.2 | 43.2 |
| Rear head room, in. | 37.6 | 38.9 |
| Min. rear leg room, in. | 34.6 | 34.8 |

## ENGINES

| | dohc I-4 |
|---|---|
| Size, liters/cu. in. | 1.8/110 |
| Horsepower @ rpm | 130@ 6000 |
| Torque (lbs./ft.) @ rpm | 122@ 5000 |
| Availability | S |

**EPA city/highway mpg**

| | |
|---|---|
| 5-speed OD manual | 24/32 |
| 4-speed OD automatic | 22/30 |

| Hyundai Elantra | Retail Price | Dealer Invoice |
|---|---|---|
| Base 4-door sedan, 5-speed | $11499 | $10541 |
| Base 4-door sedan, automatic | 12299 | 11266 |
| Base 4-door wagon, 5-speed | 12399 | 11366 |
| Base 4-door wagon, automatic | 13199 | 12091 |
| GLS 4-door sedan, 5-speed | 12549 | 11245 |
| GLS 4-door sedan, automatic | 13349 | 11970 |
| GLS 4-door wagon, automatic | 13999 | 12545 |
| Destination charge | 435 | 435 |

## STANDARD EQUIPMENT:

**Base:** 1.8-liter dohc 4-cylinder engine, 5-speed manual or 4-speed automatic transmission, driver- and passenger-side air bags, variable-assist power steering, tilt steering column, cloth reclining front bucket seats, 60/40 split folding rear seat (wagon), front storage console, tachometer, AM/FM/cassette, digital clock, trip odometer, coolant-temperature gauge, passenger-side visor mirror, variable intermittent wipers, rear defogger, remote fuel-door and decklid release, rear heat ducts, remote outside mirrors, tinted glass, roof rack (wagon), 175/65R14 tires, wheel covers.

**GLS** adds: 4-wheel disc brakes, upgraded cloth upholstery, 6-way adjustable driver seat, deluxe front storage console w/armrest, 60/40 split folding rear seat, power mirrors, power windows, power door locks, full cargo-area trim, cargo-area cover (wagon), driver-side visor mirror, map lights, rear wiper/washer (wagon), 195/60HR14 tires, deluxe wheel covers.

## OPTIONAL EQUIPMENT:
### Major Packages

| | Retail Price | Dealer Invoice |
|---|---|---|
| Option Pkg. 2, Base.................................................. | $994 | $819 |
| Air conditioning. | | |
| Option Pkg. 3, Base.................................................. | 1239 | 1021 |
| Air conditioning, cruise control. | | |
| Option Pkg. 10, GLS ............................................... | 1239 | 1021 |
| Air conditioning, cruise control. | | |
| Option Pkg. 11, GLS ............................................... | 2100 | 1819 |
| Air conditioning, cruise control, anti-lock brakes. | | |
| Option Pkg. 12, GLS ............................................... | 1773 | 1452 |
| Air conditioning, cruise control, rear spoiler, alloy wheels. | | |
| Option Pkg. 13, GLS ............................................... | 1767 | 1449 |
| Air conditioning, cruise control, AM/FM/CD player, alloy wheels. | | |
| Option Pkg. 14, GLS ............................................... | 2045 | 1678 |
| Air conditioning, cruise control, power moonroof, AM/FM/CD player. | | |
| Option Pkg. 15, GLS ............................................... | 2579 | 2109 |
| Air conditioning, cruise control, AM/FM/CD player, power moonroof, rear spoiler, alloy wheels. | | |

### Comfort and Convenience

| | | |
|---|---|---|
| Remote keyless entry, GLS ..................................... | 365 | 230 |
| Includes theft-deterrent system. | | |

### Appearance and Miscellaneous

| | | |
|---|---|---|
| Theft-deterrent system ........................................... | 260 | 160 |
| Rear spoiler............................................................. | 395 | 261 |
| NA wagon. | | |

Other options are available as port installed items.

# HYUNDAI SONATA

## SPECIFICATIONS

| | 4-door sedan |
|---|---|
| Wheelbase, in. ....................................................... | 106.3 |
| Overall length, in. .................................................. | 185.0 |

*Prices are accurate at time of publication; subject to manufacturer's change.*

*Hyundai Sonata GLS*

|  | 4-door sedan |
|---|---|
| Overall width, in. | 69.7 |
| Overall height, in. | 55.3 |
| Curb weight, lbs. | 2935 |
| Cargo vol., cu. ft. | 13.2 |
| Fuel capacity, gals. | 17.2 |
| Seating capacity | 5 |
| Front head room, in. | 38.5 |
| Max. front leg room, in. | 43.3 |
| Rear head room, in. | 37.7 |
| Min. rear leg room, in. | 36.6 |

## ENGINES

|  | dohc I-4 | ohc V-6 |
|---|---|---|
| Size, liters/cu. in. | 2.0/122 | 3.0/181 |
| Horsepower @ rpm | 137@ 6000 | 142@ 5000 |
| Torque (lbs./ft.) @ rpm | 129@ 4000 | 168@ 2400 |
| Availability | S[1] | S[2] |

**EPA city/highway mpg**

|  | | |
|---|---|---|
| 5-speed OD manual | 21/28 | |
| 4-speed OD automatic | 20/27 | 17/24 |

*1. Base model, GL. 2. GLS; optional, GL.*

| Hyundai Sonata | Retail Price | Dealer Invoice |
|---|---|---|
| Base 4-door sedan, 5-speed | $14749 | $13444 |
| Base 4-door sedan, automatic | 15549 | 14235 |
| GL 4-door sedan, automatic | 16349 | 14735 |
| GL 4-door sedan, V-6 automatic | 17349 | 15636 |
| GLS 4-door sedan, V-6 automatic | 18549 | 16335 |
| Destination charge | 435 | 435 |

## STANDARD EQUIPMENT:

**Base:** 2.0-liter dohc 4-cylinder engine, 5-speed manual or 4-speed automatic transmission, driver- and passenger-side air bags, air conditioning, power steering, tilt steering wheel, cloth reclining front bucket seats w/4-way adjustable driver seat, front storage console, 60/40 split-folding rear seat, cupholders, tachometer, coolant-temperature gauge, trip odometer, AM/FM/cassette w/6-speakers, steering wheel radio controls, digital clock, visor mirrors, remote fuel-door and deck-lid releases, rear defogger, rear heat ducts, variable intermittent wipers, remote outside mirrors, tinted glass, 195/70R14 tires, wheel covers.

**GL** adds: 2.0-liter dohc 4-cylinder or 3.0-liter V-6 engine, 4-speed automatic transmission, power mirrors, power windows, power door locks, deluxe wheel covers.

**GLS** adds to GL: 3.0-liter V-6 engine, 4-wheel disc brakes, cruise control, upgraded cloth upholstery, manual 6-way adjustable driver seat, console armrest, rear armrest, AM/FM/cassette/CD player w/6-speakers, power antenna, illuminated passenger-side visor mirror, seatback pockets, map lights, 205/60HR15 tires, alloy wheels.

## OPTIONAL EQUIPMENT:
### Major Packages

| | Retail Price | Dealer Invoice |
|---|---|---|
| Option Pkg. 2, GL | $256 | $211 |
| *Cruise control.* | | |
| Option Pkg. 3, GL | 923 | 760 |
| *Cruise control, power moonroof, map lights.* | | |
| Option Pkg. 4, GL | 1234 | 1138 |
| *Anti-lock 4-wheel disc brakes, cruise control, moonroof, map lights.* | | |
| Option Pkg. 10, GLS | 667 | 549 |
| *Power moonroof, map lights.* | | |
| Option Pkg. 11, GLS | 1500 | 1236 |
| *Power moonroof, AM/FM/cassette/CD player, leather-wrapped steering wheel.* | | |
| Option Pkg. 12, GLS | 1561 | 1236 |
| *AM/FM/cassette/CD player, Leather Pkg. (leather upholstery, leather-wrapped steering wheel).* | | |
| Option Pkg. 13, GLS | 2228 | 1880 |
| *Power moonroof, AM/FM/cassette/CD player, Leather Pkg. (leather upholstery, leather-wrapped steering wheel), map lights.* | | |
| Option Pkg. 14, GLS | 3206 | 2807 |
| *Anti-lock brakes, power moonroof, AM/FM/cassette/CD player, Leather Pkg. (leather upholstery, leather-wrapped steering wheel), map lights.* | | |
| Luxury Pkg., GL, GLS | — | — |
| *Wood dashboard trim, sill plates, theft-deterrent system.* | | |

*Prices are accurate at time of publication; subject to manufacturer's change.*

| **Comfort and Convenience** | Retail Price | Dealer Invoice |
|---|---|---|
| Wood dashboard trim | $425 | $270 |

**Appearance and Miscellaneous**

| | | |
|---|---|---|
| Theft-deterrent system | 365 | 225 |
| *Includes remote keyless entry.* | | |
| Rear spoiler | 415 | 275 |

Other options are available as port installed items.

# HYUNDAI TIBURON

*Hyundai Tiburon FX*

| **SPECIFICATIONS** | 2-door hatchback |
|---|---|
| Wheelbase, in. | 97.4 |
| Overall length, in. | 170.9 |
| Overall width, in. | 68.1 |
| Overall height, in. | 51.7 |
| Curb weight, lbs. | 2570 |
| Cargo vol., cu. ft. | 12.8 |
| Fuel capacity, gals. | 14.5 |
| Seating capacity | 4 |
| Front head room, in. | 38.0 |
| Max. front leg room, in. | 43.1 |
| Rear head room, in. | 34.4 |
| Min. rear leg room, in. | 29.9 |

| **ENGINES** | dohc I-4 |
|---|---|
| Size, liters/cu. in. | 2.0/122 |
| Horsepower @ rpm | 140@ 6000 |
| Torque (lbs./ft.) @ rpm | 133@ 4800 |

| | dohc I-4 |
|---|---|
| Availability ................................................................................ | S |

**EPA city/highway mpg**

| | |
|---|---|
| 5-speed OD manual................................................................. | 22/31 |
| 4-speed OD automatic.............................................................. | 22/29 |

| Hyundai Tiburon | Retail Price | Dealer Invoice |
|---|---|---|
| Base 2-door hatchback, 5-speed ...................................... | $13599 | $12326 |
| Base 2-door hatchback, automatic ..................................... | 14399 | 13051 |
| FX 2-door hatchback, 5-speed ........................................... | 14899 | 13198 |
| FX 2-door hatchback, automatic ......................................... | 15699 | 13923 |
| Destination charge ............................................................. | 435 | 435 |

## STANDARD EQUIPMENT:

**Base:** 2.0-liter dohc 4-cylinder engine, 5-speed manual or 4-speed automatic transmission, driver- and passenger-side air bags, power steering, tilt steering column, cloth reclining front bucket seats, front storage console, split-folding rear seat, cupholders, power windows, coolant-temperature gauge, tachometer, trip odometer, AM/FM/cassette, digital clock, rear defogger, remote hatch and fuel-door releases, variable intermittent wipers, map lights, rear heat ducts, cargo-area cover, remote outside mirrors, tinted glass, bright exhaust outlets, 195/60R14 performance tires, wheel covers.

**FX adds:** 4-wheel disc brakes, upgraded seat trim, 6-way adjustable driver seat, deluxe front storage console w/armrest, power door locks, power mirrors, passenger-side visor mirror, rear wiper/washer, fog lights, rear spoiler, alloy wheels.

## OPTIONAL EQUIPMENT:
### Major Packages

| | | |
|---|---|---|
| Option Pkg. 1, Base............................................................. | 333 | 275 |
| *Upgraded AM/FM/cassette.* | | |
| Option Pkg. 2, Base............................................................. | 1383 | 1140 |
| *Air conditioning, upgraded AM/FM/cassette and speakers.* | | |
| Option Pkg. 3, Base............................................................. | 2378 | 1916 |
| *Air conditioning, upgraded AM/FM/cassette and speakers, rear spoiler, fog lights, alloy wheels.* | | |
| Option Pkg. 11, FX.............................................................. | 1583 | 1305 |
| *Air conditioning, cruise control, upgraded AM/FM/cassette.* | | |
| Option Pkg. 12, FX .............................................................. | 2277 | 1877 |
| *Air conditioning, cruise control, power sunroof, upgraded AM/FM/cassette.* | | |
| Option Pkg. 13, FX .............................................................. | 2694 | 2220 |
| *Air conditioning, cruise control, power sunroof, premium AM/FM/cassette/CD player.* | | |

*Prices are accurate at time of publication; subject to manufacturer's change.*

|  | Retail Price | Dealer Invoice |
|---|---|---|
| Option Pkg. 14, FX | $3472 | $2941 |

*Anti-lock brakes, air conditioning, cruise control, power sunroof, premium AM/FM/cassette/CD player.*

| Option Pkg. 15, FX | 3472 | 2941 |
|---|---|---|

*Air conditioning, cruise control, leather upholstery, leather-wrapped steering wheel, power sunroof, premium AM/FM/cassette/CD player.*

| Option Pkg. 16, FX | 4250 | 3662 |
|---|---|---|

*Anti-lock brakes, air conditioning, cruise control, leather upholstery, leather-wrapped steering wheel, power sunroof, premium AM/FM/cassette/CD player.*

## Comfort and Convenience

| Remote keyless entry | 375 | 240 |
|---|---|---|

*Includes theft-deterrent system.*

## Appearance and Miscellaneous

| Theft-deterrent system | 285 | 175 |
|---|---|---|
| Rear spoiler, Base | 450 | 290 |

Other options are available as port installed items.

# INFINITI I30

*Infiniti I30t*

## SPECIFICATIONS

|  | 4-door sedan |
|---|---|
| Wheelbase, in. | 106.3 |
| Overall length, in. | 189.6 |
| Overall width, in. | 69.7 |
| Overall height, in. | 55.7 |
| Curb weight, lbs. | 3090 |
| Cargo vol., cu. ft. | 14.1 |

| | 4-door sedan |
|---|---|
| Fuel capacity, gals. | 18.5 |
| Seating capacity | 5 |
| Front head room, in. | 40.1 |
| Max. front leg room, in. | 43.9 |
| Rear head room, in. | 37.4 |
| Min. rear leg room, in. | 34.3 |

## ENGINES

| | dohc V-6 |
|---|---|
| Size, liters/cu. in. | 3.0/181 |
| Horsepower @ rpm | 190@ 5600 |
| Torque (lbs./ft.) @ rpm | 205@ 4000 |
| Availability | S |

### EPA city/highway mpg

| | |
|---|---|
| 5-speed OD manual | 21/26 |
| 4-speed OD automatic | 21/28 |

| Infiniti I30 | Retail Price | Dealer Invoice |
|---|---|---|
| I30 4-door sedan | $28900 | $25683 |
| I30t Touring 4-door sedan, 5-speed | 31500 | 27676 |
| I30t Touring 4-door sedan, automatic | 32500 | 28555 |
| Destination charge | 495 | 495 |

## STANDARD EQUIPMENT:

**I30:** 3.0-liter dohc V-6 engine, 4-speed automatic transmission, anti-lock 4-wheel disc brakes, driver- and passenger-side air bags, automatic climate control, air conditioning, variable-assist power steering, tilt steering column, leather-wrapped steering wheel, shifter knob and parking brake handle, illuminated remote keyless entry, cruise control, power cloth front bucket seats, console with armrest, AM/FM/cassette and CD player with six speakers, power antenna, power windows, power door locks, power mirrors, rear defogger, remote fuel-door and decklid releases, intermittent wipers, tachometer, coolant-temperature gauge, trip odometer, digital clock, rear folding armrest, illuminated visor mirrors, map lights, cargo net, floormats, tinted glass, anti-theft alarm, fog lights, 205/65R15 tires, cast alloy wheels.

**I30t** adds: 5-speed manual or 4-speed automatic transmission, limited-slip differential, Leather and Convenience Pkg. (leather upholstery, power sunroof, Homelink universal garage door opener, automatic day/night inside mirror), Heated Seat Pkg. (heated front seats, heated mirrors, low-windshield-washer-fluid warning light, heavy-duty battery), sport suspension, decklid spoiler, 215/60HR15 touring tires, forged alloy wheels.

## OPTIONAL EQUIPMENT:

| | Retail Price | Dealer Invoice |
|---|---|---|

### Major Packages

Leather and Convenience Pkg., I30 ............................... $1300    $985
   *Leather upholstery, power sunroof, automatic day/night inside mirror, Homelink universal garage door opener.*

Heated Seat Pkg., I30 ..................................................... 400    351
   *Heated front seats and mirrors, low-windshield-washer-fluid warning light, heavy-duty battery. Requires Leather and Convenience Pkg.*

Traction Enhancement Pkg., I30 ..................................... 830    729
   *Heated Seat Pkg. plus limited slip differential. Requires Leather and Convenience Pkg.*

Safe and Sound Pkg. ......................................................... 990    732
   *6-disc CD changer, mud guards, wheel locks, trunk mat.*

### Comfort and Convenience

Power sunroof, I30 ............................................................ 950    835
6-disc CD changer ............................................................ 680    489

# INFINITI Q45

*Infiniti Q45*

## SPECIFICATIONS

| | 4-door sedan |
|---|---|
| Wheelbase, in. | 111.4 |
| Overall length, in. | 199.2 |
| Overall width, in. | 71.7 |
| Overall height, in. | 56.9 |
| Curb weight, lbs. | 3879 |
| Cargo vol., cu. ft. | 12.6 |
| Fuel capacity, gals. | 21.1 |
| Seating capacity | 5 |
| Front head room, in. | 37.6 |
| Max. front leg room, in. | 43.6 |
| Rear head room, in. | 36.9 |
| Min. rear leg room, in. | 35.9 |

## ENGINES

|  | dohc V-8 |
| --- | --- |
| Size, liters/cu. in. | 4.1/252 |
| Horsepower @ rpm | 266@ 5600 |
| Torque (lbs./ft.) @ rpm | 278@ 4000 |
| Availability | S |

**EPA city/highway mpg**

|  |  |
| --- | --- |
| 4-speed OD automatic | 18/23 |

| Infiniti Q45 | Retail Price | Dealer Invoice |
| --- | --- | --- |
| Q45 4-door sedan | $47900 | $42569 |
| Q45t 4-door sedan | 49900 | 44346 |
| Destination charge | 495 | 495 |

## STANDARD EQUIPMENT:

**Q45:** 4.1-liter dohc V-8 engine, 4-speed automatic transmission, traction control system, limited-slip differential, driver- and passenger-side air bags, front side-impact air bags, anti-lock 4-wheel disc brakes, air conditioning w/automatic climate control, interior air filter, rear air ducts, variable-assist power steering, tilt/telescopic steering wheel w/memory, leather-wrapped steering wheel and shifter, cruise control, leather upholstery, 10-way power front bucket seats, memory driver seat, folding rear seat with armrest, front storage console with auxiliary power outlet, cupholders, Nissan/Bose AM/FM/CD/cassette player, power antenna, integrated diversity antenna, power sunroof, power windows, power door locks, remote keyless entry, heated power mirrors, tachometer, coolant-temperature gauge, digital clock, outside temperature indicator, automatic day/night inside mirror, rear defogger, remote fuel-door and decklid releases, illuminated visor mirrors, map lights, variable intermittent wipers, automatic headlamps, Homelink universal garage-door opener, floormats, cargo net, theft-deterrent system, green tinted glass, fog lights, 215/60R16 tires, alloy wheels.

**Q45t adds:** heated front seats, leather-wrapped sport steering wheel, 6-disc CD changer, sport-tuned suspension, rear spoiler, performance alloy wheels.

## OPTIONAL EQUIPMENT:
### Major Packages

| | | |
| --- | --- | --- |
| Safe and Sound Pkg., Q45 | 880 | 627 |

*Trunk mat, 6-disc CD changer, mud guards, wheel locks.*

### Comfort and Convenience

| | | |
| --- | --- | --- |
| Heated front seats, Q45 | 400 | 355 |
| 6-disc CD changer, Q45 | 680 | 486 |

### Appearance and Miscellaneous

| | Retail Price | Dealer Invoice |
|---|---|---|
| Mud guards | $120 | $82 |

# INFINITI QX4

*Infiniti QX4*

## SPECIFICATIONS

| | 4-door wagon |
|---|---|
| Wheelbase, in. | 106.3 |
| Overall length, in. | 178.3 |
| Overall width, in. | 68.7 |
| Overall height, in. | 67.1 |
| Curb weight, lbs. | 4275 |
| Cargo vol., cu. ft. | 85.0 |
| Fuel capacity, gals. | 21.1 |
| Seating capacity | 5 |
| Front head room, in. | 39.5 |
| Max. front leg room, in. | 41.7 |
| Rear head room, in. | 37.5 |
| Min. rear leg room, in. | 31.8 |

## ENGINES

| | ohc V-6 |
|---|---|
| Size, liters/cu. in. | 3.3/201 |
| Horsepower @ rpm | 168@ 4800 |
| Torque (lbs./ft.) @ rpm | 196@ 2800 |
| Availability | S |

**EPA city/highway mpg**

| | |
|---|---|
| 4-speed OD automatic | 15/19 |

## Infiniti QX4

|  | Retail Price | Dealer Invoice |
|---|---|---|
| 4-door wagon | $35550 | $31666 |
| Destination charge | 495 | 495 |

## STANDARD EQUIPMENT:

**Base:** 3.3-liter V-6 engine, 4-speed automatic transmission, All-Mode 4-wheel drive, driver- and passenger-side air bags, anti-lock brakes, air conditioning w/automatic climate control, variable-assist power steering, tilt steering column, leather-wrapped steering wheel and shifter, cruise control, leather upholstery, power front bucket seats, reclining 60/40 split-folding rear seat, rear armrest, center storage console w/armrest, overhead storage console (includes outside-temperature indicator, compass, map lights), cupholders, heated power mirrors, power windows, power door locks, remote keyless entry, tachometer, trip odometer, 6-speaker Bose audio system with AM/FM/cassette/CD player, integrated diversity antenna, variable intermittent wipers, intermittent rear wiper, rear defogger, remote fuel-door and hatch releases, auxiliary power outlet, illuminated visor mirrors, wood interior trim, cargo net and cover, rear storage bin, floormats, fog lights, theft-deterrent system, tinted glass, step rail, roof rack, mud guards, fuel-tank skid plates, 245/70R16 tires, alloy wheels.

## OPTIONAL EQUIPMENT:
### Major Packages

| | | |
|---|---|---|
| Premium Sport Pkg. | 700 | 622 |

*Limited-slip rear differential, heated front seats. Requires Sunroof Pkg.*

| | | |
|---|---|---|
| Sunroof Preferred Pkg. | 1250 | 1112 |

*Sunroof, 6-disc CD changer, rear window wind deflector.*

### Comfort and Convenience

| | | |
|---|---|---|
| Heated front seats | 400 | 355 |

*Requires sunroof.*

| | | |
|---|---|---|
| Power sunroof | 950 | 845 |

### Special Purpose, Wheels and Tires

| | | |
|---|---|---|
| Tow hitch | 390 | 289 |

# ISUZU OASIS

| SPECIFICATIONS | 4-door van |
|---|---|
| Wheelbase, in. | 111.4 |
| Overall length, in. | 187.2 |
| Overall width, in. | 70.6 |
| Overall height, in. | 64.6 |

*Prices are accurate at time of publication; subject to manufacturer's change.*

*Isuzu Oasis*

## SPECIFICATIONS

| | 4-door van |
| --- | --- |
| Curb weight, lbs. | 3473 |
| Cargo vol., cu. ft. | 102.5 |
| Fuel capacity, gals. | 17.2 |
| Seating capacity | 7 |
| Front head room, in. | 40.1 |
| Max. front leg room, in. | 40.7 |
| Rear head room, in. | 39.3 |
| Min. rear leg room, in. | 40.2 |

## ENGINES

| | dohc I-4 |
| --- | --- |
| Size, liters/cu. in. | 2.3/137 |
| Horsepower @ rpm | 150@ 5600 |
| Torque (lbs./ft.) @ rpm | 152@ 4700 |
| Availability | S |

**EPA city/highway mpg**

| | |
| --- | --- |
| 4-speed OD automatic | 21/26 |

| Isuzu Oasis | Retail Price | Dealer Invoice |
| --- | --- | --- |
| S 4-door van | $23532 | $21649 |
| LS 4-door van | 25802 | 23738 |
| Destination charge | 445 | 445 |

## STANDARD EQUIPMENT:

**S:** 2.3-liter 4-cylinder engine, 4-speed automatic transmission, driver- and passenger-side air bags, anti-lock 4-wheel disc brakes, variable assist power steering, dual air conditioning, power steering, tilt steering column, cruise control, power mirrors, power windows, power door locks, 4-speaker AM/FM/cassette player, digital clock, rear defogger, rear wiper/washer, intermittent wipers, dual visor mirrors with passenger-side illumination, reclining cloth front bucket seats, 3-passenger center bench seat, folding retractable rear bench seat, front and center storage console w/cupholders, door pockets, remote fuel door and tailgate releases, rear-seat heat ducts, coolant-temperature gauge, trip odometer, tachometer, theft-deterrent system, tinted glass, dual exhaust, tool kit, bodyside molding, mud guards, 205/65R15 tires, wheel covers.

**LS** adds: power driver's seat height adjustment, center captain's chairs, power sunroof, remote keyless entry, 6-speaker sound system, map lights, roof rack, alloy wheels.

## OPTIONAL EQUIPMENT:
### Comfort and Convenience

| | Retail Price | Dealer Invoice |
|---|---|---|
| CD player | $470 | $369 |
| CD changer | 565 | 447 |
| Rear underseat storage tray, LS | 70 | 55 |

### Appearance and Miscellaneous

| | Retail Price | Dealer Invoice |
|---|---|---|
| Roof rack, S | 230 | 181 |

# ISUZU RODEO

*Isuzu Rodeo LS V-6*

## SPECIFICATIONS

| | 4-door wagon |
|---|---|
| Wheelbase, in. | 106.4 |
| Overall length, in. | 176.7 |
| Overall width, in. | 70.4 |
| Overall height, in. | 68.8 |
| Curb weight, lbs. | 3260 |
| Cargo vol., cu. ft. | 81.1 |
| Fuel capacity, gals. | 21.9 |

*Prices are accurate at time of publication; subject to manufacturer's change.*

| | 4-door wagon |
|---|---|
| Seating capacity | 5 |
| Front head room, in. | 38.9 |
| Max. front leg room, in. | 42.1 |
| Rear head room, in. | 38.3 |
| Min. rear leg room, in. | 35.0 |

## ENGINES

| | dohc I-4 | dohc V-6 |
|---|---|---|
| Size, liters/cu. in. | 2.2/134 | 3.2/193 |
| Horsepower @ rpm | 129@ 5200 | 205@ 5400 |
| Torque (lbs./ft.) @ rpm | 144@ 4000 | 214@ 3000 |
| Availability | S[1] | S[2] |
| **EPA city/highway mpg** | | |
| 5-speed OD manual | 21/24 | 16/20 |
| 4-speed OD automatic | | 18/20 |

1. 2WD S. 2. S V-6, LS.

## Isuzu Rodeo

| | Retail Price | Dealer Invoice |
|---|---|---|
| S 4-cylinder 2WD 4-door wagon, 5-speed | $17995 | $16916 |
| S V-6 2WD 4-door wagon, 5-speed | 20950 | 18750 |
| S V-6 2WD 4-door wagon, automatic | 21950 | 19645 |
| S V-6 4WD 4-door wagon, 5-speed | 23240 | 20684 |
| S V-6 4WD 4-door wagon, automatic | 24240 | 21574 |
| LS V-6 2WD 4-door wagon, automatic | 26390 | 23488 |
| LS V-6 4WD 4-door wagon, 5-speed | 27910 | 24700 |
| LS V-6 4WD 4-door wagon, automatic | 28910 | 25585 |
| Destination charge | 445 | 445 |

## STANDARD EQUIPMENT:

**S:** 2.2-liter 4-cylinder engine, 5-speed manual transmission, driver- and passenger-side air bags, anti-lock brakes, variable-assist power steering, cloth reclining front bucket seats with folding armrest, folding rear seat, center storage console, 4-speaker AM/FM/cassette, rear defogger, coolant-temperature gauge, trip odometer, visor mirrors, cargo rope hooks, rear wiper/washer, dual outside mirrors, tinted glass, fuel-tank skid plate, full-size spare tire, 225/75R16 all-season tires, alloy wheels.

**S V-6** adds: 3.2-liter V-6 engine, 5-speed manual or 4-speed automatic transmission, 4-wheel disc brakes, tachometer, voltmeter, oil-pressure gauge, radiator skid plate, floormats, outside spare-tire carrier, 4WD adds: part-time 4WD, automatic locking hubs, tow hooks, transfer-case skid plate.

**LS** adds: air conditioning, moquette upholstery, tilt steering wheel, leather-wrapped steering wheel, cruise control, split folding rear seat, power windows, power door locks, remote keyless entry, heated power mirrors, 6-speaker premium audio system, illuminated visor mirrors, intermittent front wipers, power hatchgate release, front-door map pockets, map and courtesy lights, cargo net and cover, theft-deterrent system, fog lamps, roof rack, privacy rear quarter and rear side glass, bright exterior trim, dual note horn, mud guards, 245/70R16 tires. 4WD adds: part-time 4WD, automatic locking hubs, tow hooks, transfer-case skid plate.

## OPTIONAL EQUIPMENT:

|  | Retail Price | Dealer Invoice |
|---|---|---|
| **Major Packages** | | |
| Preferred Equipment Pkg. 1, S, S V-6 | $1010 | $899 |
| *Air conditioning, cargo net and cover.* | | |
| Preferred Equipment Pkg. 2, S V-6 | 2350 | 2092 |
| *Preferred Equipment Pkg. 1 plus tilt steering wheel, cruise control, heated power mirrors, power windows, power door locks, remote keyless entry, power tailgate release, center armrest pad, 6-speaker sound system, theft-deterrent system.* | | |
| Sport Pkg., S V-6 2WD | 520 | 256 |
| *Fog lights, 235/75R15 tires, wheel locks.* | | |
| SP2 Sport Pkg., S V-6 4WD | 770 | 686 |
| *Fog lights, limited-slip differential, 235/75R16 tires, wheel locks.* | | |
| SP3 Sport Pkg., S V-6 4WD | 970 | 864 |
| *SP2 Sport Pkg. plus 245/75R16 tires.* | | |
| **Powertrains** | | |
| Limited-slip differential, LS 4WD | 250 | 224 |
| **Comfort and Convenience** | | |
| Air conditioning, S | 950 | 845 |
| Leather upholstery, LS | 995 | 886 |
| Power sunroof, S V-6, LS | 700 | 623 |
| CD player, S V-6, LS | 550 | 434 |
| *S V-6 requires Preferred Equipment Pkg. 2.* | | |
| 6-disc CD changer, S V-6, LS | 650 | 513 |
| *S V-6 requires Preferred Equipment Pkg. 2.* | | |
| **Appearance and Miscellaneous** | | |
| Color-keyed bumpers, S V-6 | 100 | 89 |
| Running boards | 360 | 283 |
| Side steps | 355 | 281 |
| **Special Purpose, Wheels and Tires** | | |
| Trailer hitch | 253 | 200 |

*Prices are accurate at time of publication; subject to manufacturer's change.*

# ISUZU TROOPER

*Isuzu Trooper S*

## SPECIFICATIONS

|  | 4-door wagon |
|---|---|
| Wheelbase, in. | 108.7 |
| Overall length, in. | 185.5 |
| Overall width, in. | 72.2 |
| Overall height, in. | 72.2 |
| Curb weight, lbs. | 4530 |
| Cargo vol., cu. ft. | 90.2 |
| Fuel capacity, gals. | 22.5 |
| Seating capacity | 5 |
| Front head room, in. | 39.8 |
| Max. front leg room, in. | 40.8 |
| Rear head room, in. | 39.8 |
| Min. rear leg room, in. | 39.1 |

## ENGINES

|  | dohc V-6 |
|---|---|
| Size, liters/cu. in. | 3.5/213 |
| Horsepower @ rpm | 215@ 5400 |
| Torque (lbs./ft.) @ rpm | 230@ 3000 |
| Availability | S |

**EPA city/highway mpg**

| | |
|---|---|
| 5-speed OD manual | 16/19 |
| 4-speed OD automatic | 15/19 |

| Isuzu Trooper | Retail Price | Dealer Invoice |
|---|---|---|
| S 4-door 4WD wagon, 5-speed | $26550 | $23630 |
| S 4-door 4WD wagon, automatic | 27800 | 24742 |

| | Retail Price | Dealer Invoice |
|---|---|---|
| Destination charge .............................................................. | $445 | $445 |

## STANDARD EQUIPMENT:

**S:** 3.5-liter dohc V-6 engine, 5-speed manual or 4-speed automatic transmission, part-time 4WD system with automatic locking front hubs, skid plates, driver- and passenger-side air bags, anti-lock 4-wheel disc brakes, air conditioning, variable-assist power steering, tilt steering wheel, cruise control, cloth reclining front bucket seats, front and center storage console, split folding and reclining rear seat, full door trim, AM/FM/cassette w/six speakers, heated power mirrors, power windows, power door locks, rear defogger, rear wiper/washer, remote fuel door release, intermittent wipers, tachometer, voltmeter, coolant-temperature and oil-pressure gauges, trip odometer, illuminated visor mirrors, door map pockets, cargo tie down hooks, cargo cover and net, cornering lights, theft-deterrent system, tinted glass, fender flares, rear step bumper, rear air deflector, front and rear tow hooks, full-size spare tire, 245/70R16 tires, alloy wheels.

## OPTIONAL EQUIPMENT:

### Major Packages

| | | |
|---|---|---|
| Performance Pkg., w/automatic transmission................. | 2180 | 1744 |

*Torque-On-Demand System, limited-slip differential, leather-wrapped steering wheel, map lights, cargo area floor rails, variable-intermittent wipers, privacy glass, integrated antenna, bodyside moldings. Deletes standard oil-pressure and voltmeter gauges.*

| | | |
|---|---|---|
| Luxury Pkg., w/automatic transmission.......................... | 4000 | 3360 |

*Leather upholstery, heated front bucket seats w/6-way power adjustment, 6-disc CD player, multi-meter, power moonroof, fog lights, two-tone paint. Requires Performance Pkg.*

### Powertrains

| | | |
|---|---|---|
| Limited-slip differential ................................................ | 290 | 258 |

### Comfort and Convenience

| | | |
|---|---|---|
| Power moonroof, w/automatic transmission ................... | 1100 | 979 |
| *Requires Performance Pkg.* | | |
| Leather power/heated front seats, w/automatic transmission..................................... | 2250 | 2002 |
| *Requires Performance Pkg.* | | |
| CD player ...................................................................... | 550 | 434 |
| 12-disc CD changer....................................................... | 650 | 513 |
| Multi-meter gauge, w/automatic transmission ................ | 200 | 178 |
| *Requires Performance Pkg.* | | |

### Appearance and Miscellaneous

| | | |
|---|---|---|
| Running boards............................................................... | 340 | 269 |

*Prices are accurate at time of publication; subject to manufacturer's change.*

| | Retail Price | Dealer Invoice |
|---|---|---|
| Side steps | $340 | $269 |
| Ski rack | 293 | 231 |

# JAGUAR XJ SEDAN

Jaguar XJ8

## SPECIFICATIONS

| | 4-door sedan | 4-door sedan |
|---|---|---|
| Wheelbase, in. | 113.0 | 117.9 |
| Overall length, in. | 197.8 | 202.7 |
| Overall width, in. | 70.8 | 70.8 |
| Overall height, in. | 52.7 | 53.2 |
| Curb weight, lbs. | 3996 | 4048 |
| Cargo vol., cu. ft. | 12.7 | 12.7 |
| Fuel capacity, gals. | 21.4 | 21.4 |
| Seating capacity | 5 | 5 |
| Front head room, in. | 37.2 | 37.8 |
| Max. front leg room, in. | 41.2 | 41.2 |
| Rear head room, in. | 36.3 | 37.0 |
| Min. rear leg room, in. | 34.3 | 39.2 |

## ENGINES

| | dohc V-8 | Super dohc V-8 |
|---|---|---|
| Size, liters/cu. in. | 4.0/244 | 4.0/244 |
| Horsepower @ rpm | 290@ 6100 | 370@ 6150 |
| Torque (lbs./ft.) @ rpm | 290@ 4250 | 387@ 3600 |
| Availability | S[1] | S[2] |

**EPA city/highway mpg**

| | | |
|---|---|---|
| 4-speed OD automatic | 17/24 | 16/21 |

1. XJ8. 2. XJR.

CONSUMER GUIDE™

| Jaguar XJ Sedan | Retail Price | Dealer Invoice |
|---|---|---|
| XJ8 4-door sedan | $54750 | $47830 |
| XJ8L 4-door sedan | 59750 | 52198 |
| Vanden Plas 4-door sedan | 63800 | 55736 |
| XJR 4-door sedan | 67400 | 55881 |
| Destination charge | 580 | 580 |

XJR retail price includes $2100 Gas Guzzler tax.

## STANDARD EQUIPMENT:

**XJ8:** 4.0-liter dohc V-8 engine, 5-speed automatic transmission, traction control, driver- and passenger-side side air bags, front side-impact air bags, anti-lock 4-wheel disc brakes, variable-assist power steering, power tilt/telescopic steering wheel, cruise control, air conditioning w/automatic climate control, leather upholstery, walnut interior trim, 12-way power front bucket seats with power lumbar adjusters, contoured rear bench seat, front storage console, overhead console, cupholders, driver memory system (seat, steering wheel, outside mirrors), automatic headlights, power sunroof, power heated mirrors w/memory feature, power windows, automatic power door locks, remote keyless entry, trip computer, outside-temperature indicator, automatic day/night inside mirror, AM/FM/cassette, rear defogger, remote fuel-door and decklid releases, illuminated visor mirrors, universal garage-door opener, map lights, variable intermittent wipers, carpeted floormats, theft-deterrent system, chrome hood ornament, front and rear fog lamps, 225/60ZR16 tires, full-size spare tire, alloy wheels.

**XJ8L** adds: 5-inch longer wheelbase.

**Vanden Plas** adds: wood and leather-wrapped steering wheel, wood shift knob, walnut picnic trays on front seatbacks, upgraded leather upholstery and wood interior trim, lambswool floormats.

**XJR** adds to XJ8: supercharged 4.0-liter dohc V-8 engine, full traction control, limited-slip differential, Harmon-Kardon audio system w/CD changer, heated front and rear seats, wood and leather-wrapped steering wheel, maple interior trim and shifter, sport suspension, 255/45ZR17 tires.

## OPTIONAL EQUIPMENT:
### Major Packages

| | | |
|---|---|---|
| All-Weather Pkg., XJ8, XJ8L, Vanden Plas | 2000 | 1680 |
| *Full traction control, heated front and rear seats.* | | |

### Comfort and Convenience

| | | |
|---|---|---|
| 6-disc CD changer | 800 | 672 |
| Harmon-Kardon audio system w/CD changer, XJ8, XJ8L, Vanden Plas | 1800 | 1512 |

### Appearance and Miscellaneous

| | | |
|---|---|---|
| Extra-cost paint | 1000 | 840 |

*Prices are accurate at time of publication; subject to manufacturer's change.*

# JAGUAR XK8

*Jaguar XK8 convertible*

## SPECIFICATIONS

| | 2-door coupe | 2-door conv. |
|---|---|---|
| Wheelbase, in. | 101.9 | 101.9 |
| Overall length, in. | 187.4 | 187.4 |
| Overall width, in. | 72.0 | 72.0 |
| Overall height, in. | 51.0 | 51.4 |
| Curb weight, lbs. | 3673 | 3867 |
| Cargo vol., cu. ft. | 11.1 | 9.5 |
| Fuel capacity, gals. | 19.9 | 19.9 |
| Seating capacity | 4 | 4 |
| Front head room, in. | 37.4 | 37.0 |
| Max. front leg room, in. | 43.0 | 43.0 |
| Rear head room, in. | 33.3 | 33.1 |
| Min. rear leg room, in. | NA | NA |

## ENGINES

| | dohc V-8 |
|---|---|
| Size, liters/cu. in. | 4.0/244 |
| Horsepower @ rpm | 290@ 6100 |
| Torque (lbs./ft.) @ rpm | 290@ 4200 |
| Availability | S |

**EPA city/highway mpg**

| | |
|---|---|
| 5-speed OD automatic | 17/24 |

| Jaguar XK8 | Retail Price | Dealer Invoice |
|---|---|---|
| 2-door notchback | $64900 | $57104 |
| 2-door convertible | 69900 | 61472 |
| Destination charge | 580 | 580 |

## STANDARD EQUIPMENT:

**Base:** 4.0-liter dohc V-8 engine, 5-speed automatic transmission, traction control, driver- and passenger-side air bags, anti-lock 4-wheel disc brakes, air conditioning w/automatic climate control, variable-assist power steering, power tilt/telescopic steering wheel, leather-wrapped steering wheel, cruise control, power top (convertible), leather upholstery, 4-way power front bucket seats w/power lumbar support, memory driver seat, cupholders, walnut interior trim and shifter, tachometer, voltmeter, oil-pressure gauge, trip computer, outside-temperature indicator, automatic headlights, AM/FM/cassette, heated power mirrors w/memory feature, power windows, automatic power door locks, remote keyless entry, universal garage-door opener, illuminated visor mirrors, automatic day/night rearview mirror, rear defogger, remote fuel-door and decklid release, variable intermittent windshield wipers, map lights, theft-deterrent system, front and rear fog lights, full-size spare tire, 245/50ZR17 tires, alloy wheels.

## OPTIONAL EQUIPMENT:

| | Retail Price | Dealer Invoice |
|---|---|---|
| **Major Packages** | | |
| All-Weather Pkg. | $2000 | $1680 |
| *Full traction control, heated front seats, headlamp washers.* | | |
| **Comfort and Convenience** | | |
| 6-disc CD changer | 800 | 672 |
| Harmon-Kardon sound system w/CD changer | 1800 | 1512 |
| **Appearance and Miscellaneous** | | |
| Extra-cost paint | 1000 | 840 |
| Chrome wheels | 1000 | 840 |

# JEEP CHEROKEE

## SPECIFICATIONS

| | 2-door wagon | 4-door wagon |
|---|---|---|
| Wheelbase, in. | 101.4 | 101.4 |
| Overall length, in. | 167.5 | 167.5 |
| Overall width, in. | 69.4 | 69.4 |
| Overall height, in. | 64.0 | 64.0 |
| Curb weight, lbs. | 2979 | 3032 |
| Cargo vol., cu. ft. | 69.0 | 69.0 |
| Fuel capacity, gals. | 20.0 | 20.0 |
| Seating capacity | 5 | 5 |
| Front head room, in. | 37.8 | 37.8 |
| Max. front leg room, in. | 41.4 | 41.4 |
| Rear head room, in. | 37.8 | 38.0 |
| Min. rear leg room, in. | 41.4 | 35.0 |

*Prices are accurate at time of publication; subject to manufacturer's change.*

*Jeep Cherokee Classic 4-door*

## ENGINES

| | ohv I-4 | ohv I-6 |
|---|---|---|
| Size, liters/cu. in. | 2.5/150 | 4.0/242 |
| Horsepower @ rpm | 125@ 5400 | 190@ 4600 |
| Torque (lbs./ft.) @ rpm | 150@ 3250 | 225@ 3000 |
| Availability | S[1] | S[2] |
| **EPA city/highway mpg** | | |
| 5-speed OD manual | 21/25[3] | 18/22[4] |
| 3-speed automatic | 18/22 | |
| 4-speed OD automatic | | 16/21[5] |

1. SE. 2. Optional, SE. 3. 18/20 w/4WD. 4. 17/20 w/4WD. 5. 15/21.

| Jeep Cherokee | Retail Price | Dealer Invoice |
|---|---|---|
| SE 2-door wagon 2WD | $15440 | $14510 |
| SE 2-door wagon 4WD | 16955 | 15909 |
| SE 4-door wagon 2WD | 16480 | 15477 |
| SE 4-door wagon 4WD | 17990 | 16871 |
| Sport 2-door wagon 2WD | 18055 | 16348 |
| Sport 2-door wagon 4WD | 19565 | 17697 |
| Sport 4-door wagon 2WD | 19090 | 17279 |
| Sport 4-door wagon 4WD | 20600 | 18628 |
| Classic 4-door wagon 2WD | 20480 | 18502 |
| Classic 4-door wagon 4WD | 21995 | 19856 |
| Destination charge | 525 | 525 |

## STANDARD EQUIPMENT:

**SE:** 2.5-liter 4-cylinder engine, 5-speed manual transmission, driver- and passenger-side air bags, power steering, vinyl upholstery, front bucket seats, folding rear seat, floor console, AM/FM radio w/two speakers, intermittent wipers, remote outside mirrors, tinted glass, 215/75R15 tires, 4WD adds: Command-Trac part-time 4-wheel drive.

**Sport** adds: 4.0-liter 6-cylinder engine, cloth/vinyl upholstery, tachometer, cassette player w/four speakers, Sport Decor Group, lower bodyside molding, spare-tire cover, 225/75R15 outline-white-letter all-terrain tires, 4WD adds: Command-Trac part-time 4-wheel drive.

**Classic** adds: 4-speed automatic transmission, upgraded cloth upholstery, tilt steering wheel, leather-wrapped steering wheel, power mirrors, courtesy lights, map/dome lights, cargo-area light, intermittent rear wiper/washer, cloth door trim and map pockets, floormats, striping, roof rack, 225/70R15 outline-white-letter tires, alloy wheels, 4WD adds: Command-Trac part-time 4-wheel drive.

## OPTIONAL EQUIPMENT:
## Major Packages

| | Retail Price | Dealer Invoice |
|---|---|---|
| Quick Order Pkg. 22B/23B/25B/26B, SE | $1275 | $1084 |
| *Manufacturer's discount price* | NC | NC |

Air conditioning, cloth and vinyl high-back bucket seats, power mirrors, intermittent rear wiper/washer.

| | | |
|---|---|---|
| Quick Order Pkg. 25J/26J, | | |
| Sport 2-door | 2170 | 1845 |
| Sport 4-door | 2345 | 1993 |
| *Manufacturer's discount price* | NC | NC |

Air conditioning, Light Group (On Time Delay headlights, illuminated visor mirrors, map lights, underhood light), Power Equipment Group (power windows and door locks, remote keyless entry, power mirrors), intermittent rear wiper/washer, leather-wrapped tilt steering wheel, floormats, roof rack.

| | | |
|---|---|---|
| Quick Order Pkg. 26S, Classic | 1825 | 1551 |
| *Manufacturer's discount price* | NC | NC |

Air conditioning, Light Group (On Time Delay headlights, illuminated visor mirrors, map lights, underhood light), Power Equipment Group (power windows and door locks, remote keyless entry), tilt steering wheel.

| | | |
|---|---|---|
| Limited Quick Order Pkg. 26H, Classic 4WD | 4345 | 3693 |
| *Manufacturer's discount price* | 2365 | 2010 |

Quick Order Group 26S plus Limited Group (rear defogger, leather upholstery, front low-back bucket seats, overhead console, cruise control, deep-tinted glass, body striping, Selec-Trac transfer case full-time 4WD (4WD), 225/70R15 white letter tires), 6-way power driver seat.

| | | |
|---|---|---|
| Limited Quick Order Pkg. 26H, Classic 2WD | 3950 | 3358 |
| *Manufacturer's discount price* | 1970 | 1675 |

Quick Order Group 26S plus Limited Group (rear defogger, leather upholstery, front low-back bucket seats, overhead console, cruise control, deep-tinted glass, body striping, Selec-Trac transfer case full-time 4WD (4WD), 225/70R15 white-letter tires), 6-way power driver seat.

| | | |
|---|---|---|
| Power Equipment Group, Sport 2-door | 630 | 536 |

# JEEP

| | Retail Price | Dealer Invoice |
|---|---|---|
| Sport 4-door | $805 | $684 |
| Light Group, SE, Sport | 160 | 136 |

*On Time Delay headlights, illuminated visor mirrors, underhood light, courtesy lights, map/dome lights, cargo-area light.*

| | | |
|---|---|---|
| Trailer Tow Group | 365 | 310 |
| 4WD w/Up Country Suspension Group | 245 | 208 |

*Equalizer hitch, 7-wire receptacle, 4-wire trailer adapter, maximum engine cooling. SE and Sport require automatic transmission and full-size spare tire. Classic requires full-size spare tire.*

Up Country Suspension Group,

| | | |
|---|---|---|
| SE 4WD w/4.0-liter engine | 1070 | 910 |
| SE 4WD w/2.5-liter engine | 1030 | 876 |
| Sport 4WD w/alloy wheels, automatic, Classic | 845 | 718 |
| Sport 4WD w/alloy wheels, manual | 805 | 684 |
| Sport 4WD w/automatic | 780 | 663 |
| Sport 4WD w/manual | 740 | 629 |
| Classic w/Limited Pkg. | 760 | 646 |

*Trac-Lok rear differential, maximum engine cooling, off-road suspension, tow hooks, Skid Plate Group, rear stabilizer bar delete, 225/75R15 outline-white-letter all-terrain tires, full-size spare tire.*

## Powertrains

| | | |
|---|---|---|
| 4.0-liter 6-cylinder engine, SE | 995 | 846 |
| 3-speed automatic transmission, SE 2WD | 665 | 565 |

*Requires 2.5-liter engine.*

| | | |
|---|---|---|
| 4-speed automatic transmission, SE, Sport | 945 | 803 |

*SE requires 4.0-liter 6-cylinder engine.*

Selec-Trac full-time 4-wheel drive,

| | | |
|---|---|---|
| Sport 4WD, Classic 4WD | 395 | 336 |

*Sport requires automatic transmission.*

| | | |
|---|---|---|
| Trac-Lok rear differential | 285 | 242 |

*Requires full-size spare tire.*

## Safety Features

| | | |
|---|---|---|
| Anti-lock brakes | 600 | 510 |

*SE requires 4.0-liter 6-cylinder engine.*

## Comfort and Convenience

| | | |
|---|---|---|
| Air conditioning | 850 | 723 |
| Cloth upholstery, SE | 145 | 123 |
| 6-way power driver seat, Sport, Classic | 300 | 255 |

*Sport requires Power Equipment Group.*

| | | |
|---|---|---|
| Overhead console, Sport, Classic | 235 | 200 |

*Sport requires Power Equipment Group, Light Group, rear wiper/washer.*

| | Retail Price | Dealer Invoice |
|---|---|---|
| Tilt steering column | $140 | $119 |
| Leather-wrapped steering wheel, SE, Sport | 50 | 43 |
| Cruise control | 250 | 213 |
| *SE and Sport require leather-wrapped steering wheel.* | | |
| Power mirrors, SE, Sport | 130 | 111 |
| Heated power mirrors, SE | 175 | 149 |
| SE/Sport w/Quick Order Pkg., Classic | 45 | 38 |
| *Requires rear defogger.* | | |
| Cassette player, SE | 300 | 255 |
| *Includes four speakers.* | | |
| Cassette/CD player, SE | 710 | 604 |
| Sport, Classic | 410 | 349 |
| *SE includes four speakers.* | | |
| Infinity speakers | 350 | 298 |
| *Includes power amplifier, eight speakers, cargo-area light. Requires cassette/CD player.* | | |
| Rear defogger | 165 | 140 |
| *SE and Sport require rear wiper/washer.* | | |
| Intermittent rear wiper/washer, SE, Sport | 150 | 128 |
| Cargo-area cover | 75 | 64 |

## Appearance and Miscellaneous

| | | |
|---|---|---|
| Sunscreen glass, Sport 2-door | 375 | 319 |
| Sport 4-door, Classic | 270 | 230 |
| *Requires rear defogger.* | | |
| Fog lights, Sport, Classic | 110 | 94 |
| *Sport requires rear defogger and rear wiper/washer.* | | |
| Spare-tire cover, SE | 50 | 43 |
| Roof rack, SE, Sport | 140 | 119 |
| Engine-block heater | 40 | 34 |

## Special Purpose, Wheels and Tires

| | | |
|---|---|---|
| Alloy wheels, SE | 440 | 374 |
| *Requires full-size spare tire.* | | |
| 225/75R15 white-letter tires, SE | 315 | 268 |
| *Requires full-size spare tire.* | | |
| Full-size spare tire, SE w/std. 215/75R15 tires | 75 | 64 |
| SE w/225/75R16 tires | 120 | 102 |
| Sport w/alloy wheels | 210 | 179 |
| Classic | 280 | 238 |
| *Includes spare wheel.* | | |
| Skid Plate Group, 4WD | 145 | 123 |
| *Fuel-tank, transfer-case, and front-suspension skid plates.* | | |
| Maximum engine cooling, SE, Sport | 120 | 102 |
| *Requires Quick Order Pkg.* | | |

*Prices are accurate at time of publication; subject to manufacturer's change.*

| | Retail Price | Dealer Invoice |
|---|---|---|
| Alloy wheels, Sport .......................................... | $245 | $208 |
| *Requires full-size spare tire.* | | |
| Full-size spare tire, Sport................................. | 145 | 123 |
| *Includes spare wheel.* | | |

# JEEP GRAND CHEROKEE

*Jeep Grand Cherokee Limited Plus*

## SPECIFICATIONS

| | 4-door wagon |
|---|---|
| Wheelbase, in. ........................................... | 105.9 |
| Overall length, in. ....................................... | 177.2 |
| Overall width, in. ........................................ | 70.7 |
| Overall height, in. ....................................... | 64.9 |
| Curb weight, lbs. ........................................ | 3800 |
| Cargo vol., cu. ft. ....................................... | 79.3 |
| Fuel capacity, gals. ..................................... | 23.0 |
| Seating capacity ........................................ | 5 |
| Front head room, in. .................................... | 38.9 |
| Max. front leg room, in. ................................ | 40.9 |
| Rear head room, in. ..................................... | 39.1 |
| Min. rear leg room, in. .................................. | 35.7 |

## ENGINES

| | ohv I-6 | ohv V-8 | ohv V-8 |
|---|---|---|---|
| Size, liters/cu. in. ................ | 4.0/242 | 5.2/318 | 5.9/360 |
| Horsepower @ rpm .............. | 185@ 4600 | 220@ 4400 | 245@ 4000 |
| Torque (lbs./ft.) @ rpm ......... | 220@ 2400 | 300@ 2800 | 345@ 3200 |
| Availability .......................... | S | O[1] | S[2] |

**EPA city/highway mpg**
4-speed OD automatic..................... 16/21[3]    14/18    13/17
1. Laredo, TSi, Limited. 2. 5.9 Limited. 3. 15/21 w/4WD.

| Jeep Grand Cherokee | Retail Price | Dealer Invoice |
|---|---|---|
| Laredo 4-door wagon 2WD ............................ | $25845 | $23419 |
| Laredo 4-door wagon 4WD ............................ | 27815 | 25187 |
| TSi 4-door wagon 2WD ................................. | 27995 | 25311 |
| TSi 4-door wagon 4WD ................................. | 29965 | 27079 |
| Limited 4-door wagon 2WD ......................... | 31360 | 28272 |
| Limited 4-door wagon 4WD ......................... | 33790 | 30445 |
| 5.9 Limited 4-door wagon 4WD ..................... | 38175 | 34304 |
| Destination charge ...................................... | 525 | 525 |

TSi requires Pkg. 26S/28S.

## STANDARD EQUIPMENT:

**Laredo:** 4.0-liter 6-cylinder engine, 4-speed automatic transmission, driver- and passenger-side air bags, anti-lock 4-wheel disc brakes, power steering, leather-wrapped tilt steering wheel, cruise control, cloth reclining front bucket seats, split folding rear seat, air conditioning, power mirrors, power windows, power door locks, remote keyless entry, tachometer, voltage and temperature gauges, trip odometer, illuminated entry system, storage console with armrest and cupholders, AM/FM/cassette w/four speakers, rear defogger, intermittent front and rear wiper/washer, illuminated visor mirrors, floormats, cargo cover, net and tiedown hooks, tinted glass, roof rack, 215/75R15 tires, alloy wheels, 4WD adds: Selec-Trac full-time 4WD.

**TSi adds:** eight Infinity speakers, leather reclining front bucket seats, cruise control, steering wheel with radio controls and cruise control buttons, body-color grille, 4WD adds: Quadra-Trac permanent 4WD.

**Limited adds:** automatic temperature control, Luxury Group (power front seats w/memory, automatic day/night mirror, automatic headlights, vehicle information system), remote keyless entry w/memory feature, heated memory outside mirrors, universal garage-door opener, overhead console (compass, trip computer, map/reading lights), Infinity Gold speakers, fog lights, deep-tinted side and rear glass, theft-deterrent system, gold or silver badging and graphics, 225/70R16 outline white-letter tires, gold- or silver-accented alloy wheels, 4WD adds: Quadra-Trac permanent 4WD.

**5.9 Limited adds:** 5.9-liter V-8 engine, Quadra-Trac permanent 4WD, heated front seats, CD/cassette player, ten Infinity speakers, power sunroof.

## OPTIONAL EQUIPMENT:
### Major Packages
Pkg. 26X/28X, Laredo ..................................... 755    642

*Prices are accurate at time of publication; subject to manufacturer's change.*

# JEEP

|  | Retail Price | Dealer Invoice |
|---|---|---|
| *Manufacturer's discount price* ........................................ | $55 | $47 |
| Deep-tinted glass, overhead console (except w/sunroof), 225/75R15 tires. | | |
| Pkg. 26Y/28Y, Laredo ................................................. | 2645 | 2248 |
| *Manufacturer's discount price* ........................................ | 1495 | 1270 |
| Pkg. 26X/28X plus 8-speaker Infinity sound system, Luxury Group (automatic headlights, automatic day/night rearview mirror, power driver seat w/memory, leather-wrapped steering wheel w/radio controls, driver's information center), heated power mirrors, theft-deterrent system, fog lights. | | |
| Pkg. 26Z/28Z, Laredo ................................................. | 3100 | 2635 |
| *Manufacturer's discount price* ........................................ | 1700 | 1445 |
| Pkg. 26Y/28Y plus monotone exterior, body-colored fascias, chrome grille, alloy wheels. | | |
| Pkg. 26S/28S, 2WD TSi ............................................... | 2700 | 2295 |
| *Manufacturer's discount price* ........................................ | 1300 | 1105 |
| Overhead console, fog lights, deep tinted glass, Luxury Group (power driver seat w/memory, leather-wrapped steering wheel w/radio controls, automatic day/night rearview mirror, automatic headlights, vehicle information system), heated mirrors, Infinity Gold speakers, theft-deterrent system, Quadra-Trac transfer case (4WD), full-size spare tire (4WD), P225/70R16 white-letter tires. | | |
| Pkg. 26S/28S, 4WD TSi ............................................... | 3305 | 2809 |
| *Manufacturer's discount price* ........................................ | 1905 | 1619 |
| Overhead console, fog lights, deep-tinted glass, Luxury Group (power driver seat w/memory, leather-wrapped steering wheel w/radio controls, automatic day/night rearview mirror, automatic headlights, vehicle information system), heated mirrors, Infinity Gold speakers, theft-deterrent system, Quadra-Trac transfer case (4WD), full-size spare tire (4WD), P225/70R16 white letter tires. | | |
| Pkg. 26K/28K, Limited ................................................ | 1290 | 1097 |
| *Manufacturer's discount price* ........................................ | 790 | 672 |
| Power sunroof, mini overhead console, heated front seats, CD/cassette player. | | |
| Trailer Tow Prep Group, Laredo, TSi, Limited .............. | 105 | 89 |
| Includes 3.73 axle ratio, auxiliary transmission-oil cooler, special fan drive, special power steering pump. | | |
| Trailer Tow Group III, Laredo, TSi, Limited .................... | 360 | 306 |
| Includes Trailer Tow Prep Group, frame mounted equalizing hitch receptacle. NA 5.9 Limited or with 5.2 liter V-8 engine. | | |
| Trailer Tow Group IV, Laredo, TSi, Limited ................... | 245 | 208 |
| Includes Trailer Tow Prep Group, frame mounted equalizing trailer hitch receptacle. Requires 5.2-liter or 5.9-liter V-8 engine. | | |
| Up Country Suspension Group (4WD only), Laredo ...... | 825 | 701 |

| | Retail Price | Dealer Invoice |
|---|---|---|
| Laredo w/option pkg. | $575 | $489 |
| TSi, Limited | 230 | 196 |

*Skid Plate Group, tow hooks, high-pressure gas shocks, 245/70R15 outlined-white-letter all-terrain tires (Laredo), 225/70R16 Wrangler outlined-white-letter all-terrain tires (TSi, Limited), conventional spare tire, matching fifth wheel.*

## Powertrains

| | | |
|---|---|---|
| 5.2-liter V-8 engine, | | |
| 2WD Laredo w/option pkg., TSi, Limited | 880 | 748 |
| 4WD Laredo w/option pkg. | 1485 | 1262 |
| Quadra-Trac permanent 4WD, 4WD Laredo | 605 | 514 |
| 4WD Laredo w/Up Country Group | 445 | 378 |
| *Requires full-size spare tire.* | | |
| Trac-Lok rear differential, Laredo, TSi, Limited | 285 | 242 |
| *Includes 3.73 axle ratio. Std. 5.9 Limited.* | | |
| Select-Trac full-time 4WD, 4WD TSi, 4WD Limited | NC | NC |
| *NA with 5.2-liter V-8 engine.* | | |

## Comfort and Convenience

| | | |
|---|---|---|
| Power sunroof, Laredo w/Pkg. 26X/28X | 845 | 718 |
| Laredo w/Pkg. 26Y/28Y, Limited, TSi | 760 | 646 |
| *Includes mini overhead console, reading lights, automatic day/night mirror, trip computer.* | | |
| Leather seats, Laredo | 580 | 493 |
| *Requires Pkg. 26Y/28Y.* | | |
| Heated front seats, Laredo, TSi, Limited | 250 | 213 |
| *Laredo requires Pkg. 26Y/28Y, leather seats.* | | |
| AM/FM/cassette/CD player, Laredo | 560 | 476 |
| *Requires option pkg.* | | |
| AM/FM/cassette with Infinity Gold speakers, Laredo | 660 | 561 |
| AM/FM/cassette/CD with Infinity Gold speakers, Laredo | 940 | 799 |
| Laredo Pkg. 26Y/28Y, Limited, TSi | 280 | 238 |

## Appearance and Miscellaneous

| | | |
|---|---|---|
| Theft-deterrent system, Laredo | 150 | 128 |
| Deep-tinted glass, Laredo | 270 | 230 |
| Fog lights, Laredo | 120 | 102 |

## Special Purpose, Wheels and Tires

| | | |
|---|---|---|
| Skid Plate/Tow Hook Group, 4WD | 200 | 170 |
| Full-size spare tire, Laredo, 2WD TSi, 2WD Limited | 160 | 136 |
| 225/75R15 white-letter tires, Laredo | 250 | 213 |
| 225/75R15 white-letter all-terrain tires, Laredo | 315 | 268 |
| Laredo with option pkg. | 65 | 55 |
| *NA with Skid Plate/Tow Hook Group.* | | |

*Prices are accurate at time of publication; subject to manufacturer's change.*

# JEEP WRANGLER

*Jeep Wrangler Sahara*

## SPECIFICATIONS

| | 2-door conv. |
|---|---|
| Wheelbase, in. | 93.4 |
| Overall length, in. | 151.8 |
| Overall width, in. | 66.7 |
| Overall height, in. | 70.2 |
| Curb weight, lbs. | 3092 |
| Cargo vol., cu. ft. | 55.7 |
| Fuel capacity, gals. | 15.0 |
| Seating capacity | 4 |
| Front head room, in. | 42.3 |
| Max. front leg room, in. | 41.1 |
| Rear head room, in. | 40.6 |
| Min. rear leg room, in. | 34.9 |

## ENGINES

| | ohv I-4 | ohv I-6 |
|---|---|---|
| Size, liters/cu. in. | 2.5/150 | 4.0/242 |
| Horsepower @ rpm | 120@ 5400 | 181@ 4600 |
| Torque (lbs./ft.) @ rpm | 140@ 3500 | 222@ 2800 |
| Availability | S[1] | S[2] |
| **EPA city/highway mpg** | | |
| 5-speed OD manual | 18/20 | 17/20 |
| 3-speed automatic | 16/19 | 15/17 |

*1. SE. 2. Sport, Sahara.*

## Jeep Wrangler

| | Retail Price | Dealer Invoice |
|---|---|---|
| SE 2-door convertible | $14090 | $13504 |
| Sport 2-door convertible | 17505 | 15804 |
| Sahara 2-door convertible | 19615 | 17661 |
| Destination charge | 525 | 525 |

## STANDARD EQUIPMENT:

**SE:** 2.5-liter 4-cylinder engine, 5-speed manual transmission, Command-Trac part-time 4WD, driver- and passenger-side air bags, power steering, reclining front vinyl bucket seats, tachometer, voltmeter, trip odometer, oil-pressure and coolant-temperature gauge, front carpeting, mini floor console w/cupholder, dual outside mirrors, dual horn, fender flares, rear bumper, front and rear stabilizer bars, 205/75R15 all-terrain tires, styled steel wheels.

**Sport** adds: 4.0-liter 6-cylinder engine, folding rear bench seat, 2-speaker AM/FM radio, clock, rear carpeting, cargo net, front and rear bumper extensions, 215/75R15 all-terrain tires.

**Sahara** adds: tilt steering wheel, cloth upholstery, Convenience Group, 4-speaker cassette player with rear sound bar and lamp, intermittent wipers, leather-wrapped steering wheel, map pockets, front floormats, fog lights, bodyside steps, upgraded fender flares, extra-capacity fuel tank, spare-tire cover, heavy-duty suspension, Heavy Duty Electrical Group, front tow hooks, 225/75R15 outline white-letter tires, alloy wheels.

## OPTIONAL EQUIPMENT:
### Major Packages

| | | |
|---|---|---|
| Pkg. 22N/23N, SE | 865 | 735 |
| AM/FM radio, high-back bucket seats, back seat. | | |
| Pkg. 25D/24D, Sport | 540 | 459 |
| Tilt steering wheel, intermittent wipers, Convenience Group, extra-capacity fuel tank, full-size spare tire. | | |
| Convenience Group, SE, Sport | 165 | 140 |
| Full storage console w/cupholders, courtesy lights. | | |

### Powertrains

| | | |
|---|---|---|
| 3-speed automatic transmission | 625 | 531 |
| Trac-Loc rear differential | 285 | 242 |
| Requires full-size spare tire. SE and Sport require anti-lock brakes. NA with SE when ordered with 3-speed automatic transmission. | | |
| Dana 44 rear axle, Sport, Sahara | 595 | 506 |
| Requires full-size spare. NA with anti-lock brakes. Includes Trac-Loc rear differential. | | |

### Safety Features

| | | |
|---|---|---|
| Anti-lock brakes, Sport, Sahara | 600 | 510 |

*Prices are accurate at time of publication; subject to manufacturer's change.*

# JEEP

## Comfort and Convenience

| | Retail Price | Dealer Invoice |
|---|---|---|
| Hard top, SE, Sport | $755 | $642 |
| Sahara | 1160 | 986 |

*Includes full metal doors with roll-up windows, rear wiper/washer, deep-tinted glass (Sahara), rear defogger (Sahara), cargo light.*

| | | |
|---|---|---|
| Soft and hard tops, SE, Sport | 1395 | 1186 |
| Sahara | 1800 | 1560 |

*Includes hard doors.*

| | | |
|---|---|---|
| Full metal doors w/roll-up windows | 125 | 106 |
| Air conditioning | 895 | 761 |
| Vinyl rear seat, SE | 595 | 506 |

*Includes rear carpeting.*

| | | |
|---|---|---|
| Cloth/vinyl reclining front bucket seats with rear seat, SE | 745 | 633 |
| SE w/22N/23N, Sport | 150 | 128 |

*SE includes rear carpeting.*

| | | |
|---|---|---|
| Tilt steering wheel, SE, Sport | 195 | 166 |

*Includes intermittent wipers.*

| | | |
|---|---|---|
| Leather-wrapped steering wheel, SE, Sport | 50 | 43 |
| Cruise control, Sahara | 250 | 213 |
| Rear defogger for hardtop, SE, Sport | 165 | 140 |

*Requires Heavy Duty Electrical Group or air conditioning.*

| | | |
|---|---|---|
| AM/FM radio with 2 speakers, SE | 270 | 230 |
| AM/FM/cassette, SE | 715 | 608 |
| SE w/22N/23N | 445 | 378 |
| Sport | 425 | 361 |

*SE includes Sound Group. Sport includes rear sound bar and lamp.*

| | | |
|---|---|---|
| Sound Group, SE | 535 | 455 |
| SE w/22N/23N | 245 | 208 |

*AM/FM radio, four speakers with rear sound bar and lamp.*

| | | |
|---|---|---|
| Four speakers w/rear sound bar and lamp, Sport | 245 | 208 |
| Front floormats, SE, Sport | 30 | 26 |

## Appearance and Miscellaneous

| | | |
|---|---|---|
| Theft-deterrent system | 75 | 64 |
| Add-A-Trunk lockable storage | 125 | 106 |

*SE requires rear seat.*

| | | |
|---|---|---|
| Deep-tinted rear-quarter and liftgate glass, SE, Sport | 405 | 344 |

*Includes rear defogger. Requires hardtop.*

| | | |
|---|---|---|
| Bodyside steps, SE, Sport | 75 | 64 |
| Fog lights, Sport | 120 | 102 |

*Requires Heavy Duty Electrical Group or air conditioning.*

| | | |
|---|---|---|
| Extra-capacity fuel tank, SE, Sport | 65 | 55 |
| Engine block heater | 35 | 30 |
| Spare-tire cover, SE, Sport | 50 | 43 |

*NA with full-size spare tire. NA with SE when ordered with optional tires.*

## Special Purpose Wheels and Tires

| | Retail Price | Dealer Invoice |
|---|---|---|
| Front tow hooks, SE, Sport | $40 | $34 |
| Five 215/75R15 outline white-letter all-terrain tires, SE | 280 | 238 |
|    Sport | 235 | 200 |
|    Sport w/Pkg. 25D/24D | 120 | 102 |
|    *SE requires 5-spoke steel wheels.* | | |
| Five 225/75R15 outline white-letter all-terrain tires, | | |
|    SE | 470 | 400 |
|    Sport | 425 | 361 |
|    Sport w/Pkg. 25D/24D | 310 | 264 |
|    *SE requires 5-spoke steel or alloy wheels.* | | |
| Full-size spare tire, SE, Sport | 115 | 98 |
|    Sahara | 215 | 183 |
| Tire and Wheel Pkg., Sport | 785 | 667 |
|    Sport w/Pkg. 25D/24D | 670 | 570 |
|    Sahara | 360 | 306 |
|    *Five alloy wheels, full-size spare, 30x9.5R15 outline-white-letter tires. Sport includes heavy-duty suspension. NA with optional tires or 5-spoke alloy wheels. Deletes spare-tire cover on Sahara.* | | |
| Five 5-spoke steel wheels, SE | 230 | 196 |
|    *Requires optional tires.* | | |
| 15x7 alloy wheels, Sport | 265 | 225 |
|    *Requires full-size spare or optional tires.* | | |
| Heavy-duty suspension, SE, Sport | 90 | 77 |
|    *SE requires optional tires.* | | |
| Heavy Duty Electrical Group, SE, Sport | 135 | 115 |
|    *Heavy-duty battery and alternator.* | | |

# KIA SPORTAGE

| SPECIFICATIONS | 4-door wagon | 2-door conv. |
|---|---|---|
| Wheelbase, in. | 104.4 | 92.9 |
| Overall length, in. | 159.4 | 148.0 |
| Overall width, in. | 68.1 | 68.1 |
| Overall height, in. | 65.2 | 65.0 |
| Curb weight, lbs. | 3280 | NA |
| Cargo vol., cu. ft. | 55.4 | NA |
| Fuel capacity, gals. | 15.8 | 14.0 |
| Seating capacity | 5 | 4 |
| Front head room, in. | 39.6 | 39.6 |
| Max. front leg room, in. | 44.5 | 44.5 |
| Rear head room, in. | 37.8 | NA |
| Min. rear leg room, in. | 31.1 | NA |

*Prices are accurate at time of publication; subject to manufacturer's change.*

*Kia Sportage*

## ENGINES

|  | dohc I-4 |
|---|---|
| Size, liters/cu. in. | 2.0/122 |
| Horsepower @ rpm | 130@ 5500 |
| Torque (lbs./ft.) @ rpm | 127@ 4000 |
| Availability | S |

**EPA city/highway mpg**

| | |
|---|---|
| 5-speed OD manual | 19/23 |
| 4-speed OD automatic | 19/23 |

| Kia Sportage | Retail Price | Dealer Invoice |
|---|---|---|
| 2WD Base 4-door wagon, 5-speed | $14895 | $13541 |
| 2WD Base 4-door wagon, automatic | 15895 | 14451 |
| 4WD Base 4-door wagon, 5-speed | 16395 | 14770 |
| 4WD Base 4-door wagon, automatic | 17395 | 15680 |
| 2WD EX 4-door wagon, 5-speed | 17295 | 15590 |
| 2WD EX 4-door wagon, automatic | 18295 | 16490 |
| 4WD EX 4-door wagon, 5-speed | 18495 | 16500 |
| 4WD EX 4-door wagon, automatic | 19495 | 17410 |
| Destination charge | 450 | 450 |

## STANDARD EQUIPMENT:

**Base:** 2.0-liter dohc 4-cylinder engine, 5-speed manual or 4-speed automatic transmission, driver- and passenger-side air bags, driver-side knee air bag, variable-assist power steering, tilt steering wheel, cloth reclining front bucket seats w/driver-side lumbar adjuster, console w/armrest, cupholders, split folding rear bench seat, power mirrors, power windows, power door locks, tachometer, digital clock, rear defogger, remote fuel-door release, intermittent wipers, theft-deterrent system, tinted glass, full-size spare with cover, rear spare-tire carrier, 205/75R15 tires, 4WD models add: part-time 4WD, 2-speed transfer case, automatic locking hubs, alloy wheels.

**EX** adds: air conditioning, cruise control, AM/FM/CD player, digital clock, passenger-side visor mirror, variable intermittent wipers, rear wiper/washer, privacy glass, color-keyed outside mirrors, bodyside cladding, roof rack, alloy wheels, 4WD models add: part-time 4WD, 2-speed transfer case, automatic locking hubs.

## OPTIONAL EQUIPMENT:

| | Retail Price | Dealer Invoice |
|---|---|---|
| **Safety Features** | | |
| Anti-lock brakes | $490 | $410 |
| **Comfort and Convenience** | | |
| Air conditioning, Base | 900 | 763 |
| AM/FM/CD, Base | 545 | 430 |
| Leather upholstery, EX | 900 | 760 |
| *Includes leather door-panel inserts, leather-wrapped steering wheel.* | | |
| Floormats w/cargo mat | 119 | 83 |
| **Appearance and Miscellaneous** | | |
| Sport appearance graphics, Base | 95 | 60 |
| Rear spoiler | 189 | 143 |
| Roof rack, Base | 195 | 150 |
| **Special Purpose, Wheels and Tires** | | |
| Alloy wheels, 2WD Base | 340 | 274 |

# LEXUS ES 300

## SPECIFICATIONS

| | 4-door sedan |
|---|---|
| Wheelbase, in. | 105.1 |
| Overall length, in. | 190.2 |
| Overall width, in. | 70.5 |
| Overall height, in. | 54.9 |
| Curb weight, lbs. | 3296 |
| Cargo vol., cu. ft. | 13.0 |
| Fuel capacity, gals. | 18.5 |
| Seating capacity | 5 |
| Front head room, in. | 38.0 |
| Max. front leg room, in. | 43.5 |
| Rear head room, in. | 36.2 |
| Min. rear leg room, in. | 34.4 |

*Prices are accurate at time of publication; subject to manufacturer's change.*

# LEXUS

*Lexus ES 300*

## ENGINES
dohc V-6

| | |
|---|---|
| Size, liters/cu. in. | 3.0/181 |
| Horsepower @ rpm | 200@ 5200 |
| Torque (lbs./ft.) @ rpm | 214@ 4400 |
| Availability | S |

### EPA city/highway mpg
| | |
|---|---|
| 4-speed OD automatic | 19/27 |

| Lexus ES 300 | Retail Price | Dealer Invoice |
|---|---|---|
| Base 4-door sedan | $30790 | $26745 |
| Destination charge | 495 | 495 |

## STANDARD EQUIPMENT:

**Base:** 3.0-liter dohc V-6, 4-speed automatic transmission, driver- and passenger-side air bags, front side-impact air bags, anti-lock 4-wheel disc brakes, variable-assist power steering, tilt steering wheel, cruise control, air conditioning w/automatic climate control, cloth upholstery, power front bucket seats, driver-side power lumbar support, split folding rear seat with trunk pass-through, walnut interior trim, front console with auxiliary power outlet, overhead console, rear cupholder, power windows, power door locks, remote keyless entry, heated power mirrors, AM/FM cassette, tachometer, outside-temperature indicator, rear defogger, variable intermittent wipers, illuminated visor mirrors, remote fuel-door and decklid releases, first-aid kit, automatic headlamps, solar-control tinted glass, theft-deterrent system, fog lights, full-size spare tire, 205/65VR15 tires, alloy wheels.

## OPTIONAL EQUIPMENT:
### Major Packages
| | | |
|---|---|---|
| Leather Trim Pkg. | 1650 | 1320 |
| *Leather upholstery, memory driver seat.* | | |

| **Powertrains** | Retail Price | Dealer Invoice |
|---|---|---|
| Traction control.............................................. | $300 | $240 |
| *Requires Leather Trim Pkg. and all-season tires.* | | |

## Comfort and Convenience

| | | |
|---|---|---|
| Power moonroof ............................................. | 1000 | 800 |
| Heated front seats ......................................... | 420 | 336 |
| *Requires Leather Trim Pkg.* | | |
| Nakamichi premium audio system ................................... | 1600 | 1253 |
| *Includes 6-disc CD changer.* | | |
| 6-disc CD changer........................................... | 1050 | 840 |

## Appearance and Miscellaneous

| | | |
|---|---|---|
| Adaptive Variable Suspension....................................... | 600 | 480 |
| *Requires Leather Trim Pkg.* | | |
| Chrome alloy wheels................................................. | 1700 | 850 |

Other options are available as port installed items.

# LEXUS GS 300/400

*Lexus GS 400*

## SPECIFICATIONS

| | 4-door sedan |
|---|---|
| Wheelbase, in. .............................................................. | 110.2 |
| Overall length, in. ......................................................... | 189.0 |
| Overall width, in. .......................................................... | 70.9 |
| Overall height, in. ......................................................... | 56.7 |
| Curb weight, lbs. .......................................................... | 3690 |
| Cargo vol., cu. ft. ......................................................... | 14.8 |
| Fuel capacity, gals. ...................................................... | 19.8 |
| Seating capacity .......................................................... | 5 |
| Front head room, in. ..................................................... | 39.2 |
| Max. front leg room, in. ................................................. | 44.5 |
| Rear head room, in. ...................................................... | 37.0 |
| Min. rear leg room, in. ................................................... | 34.3 |

*Prices are accurate at time of publication; subject to manufacturer's change.*

# LEXUS

## ENGINES

| | dohc I-6 | dohc V-8 |
|---|---|---|
| Size, liters/cu. in. | 3.0/183 | 4.0/242 |
| Horsepower @ rpm | 225@ 6000 | 300@ 6000 |
| Torque (lbs./ft.) @ rpm | 220@ 4000 | 310@ 4000 |
| Availability | S[1] | S[2] |
| **EPA city/highway mpg** | | |
| 5-speed OD automatic | 20/25 | 17/23 |

1. GS 300. 2. GS 400.

### Lexus GS 300/400

| | Retail Price | Dealer Invoice |
|---|---|---|
| GS 300 4-door sedan | $36800 | $31964 |
| GS 400 4-door sedan | 44800 | 38461 |
| Destination charge | 495 | 495 |

## STANDARD EQUIPMENT:

**GS 300:** 3.0-liter dohc 6-cylinder engine, 5-speed automatic transmission, traction control, dual exhaust, driver- and passenger-side air bags, front side-impact air bags, anti-lock 4-wheel disc brakes, air conditioning w/automatic dual-zone climate control, variable-assist power steering, power tilt/telescopic steering column, cruise control, cloth upholstery, power front bucket seats with power lumbar support, front storage console, rear folding armrest, cupholder, walnut wood trim, power heated outside mirrors, automatic day/night rearview mirror, power windows, power door locks, remote keyless entry, Lexus/Pioneer Audio System with AM/FM/cassette and seven speakers, diversity antenna, rear defogger, digital clock, variable intermittent wipers, two trip odometers, outside-temperature indicator, illuminated visor mirrors, universal garage door opener, remote fuel-door and trunk releases, front and rear reading lights, automatic headlamps, first-aid kit, color-keyed tinted glass, theft-deterrent system, fog lights, tool kit, 215/60VR16 tires, alloy wheels.

**GS 400** adds: 4.0-liter dohc V-8 engine, leather upholstery, leather-wrapped steering wheel, memory system (driver seat, steering wheel, outside mirrors), automatic day/night outside mirrors, 225/55VR16 tires.

## OPTIONAL EQUIPMENT:
### Major Packages

| | | |
|---|---|---|
| Leather Trim Pkg., GS 300 | 1710 | 1368 |

*Leather upholstery, leather-wrapped steering wheel and shifter, memory system (driver seat, steering wheel, outside mirrors).*

### Comfort and Convenience

| | | |
|---|---|---|
| Navigation system | 2250 | 1913 |

*Requires 6-disc CD changer.*

| | Retail Price | Dealer Invoice |
|---|---|---|
| Heated front seats .................................................... | $420 | $336 |
| *GS 300 requires Leather Trim Pkg.* | | |
| Lexus/Nakamichi Premium Audio System...................... | 2250 | 1740 |
| *GS 300 requires Leather Trim Pkg. Includes 6-disc CD changer.* | | |
| 6-disc CD changer..................................................... | 1050 | 840 |
| Power moonroof ......................................................... | 1020 | 816 |

## Appearance and Miscellaneous

| | | |
|---|---|---|
| High intensity headlights................................................ | 500 | 400 |
| Rear spoiler, GS 400 ..................................................... | 420 | 336 |
| Chrome alloy wheels ...................................................... | 1700 | 850 |

Other options are available as port installed items.

# LEXUS LS 400

Lexus LS 400

## SPECIFICATIONS

| | 4-door sedan |
|---|---|
| Wheelbase, in. ...................................................... | 112.2 |
| Overall length, in. ................................................. | 196.7 |
| Overall width, in. ................................................... | 72.0 |
| Overall height, in. ................................................. | 56.5 |
| Curb weight, lbs. ................................................... | 3890 |
| Cargo vol., cu. ft. .................................................. | 13.9 |
| Fuel capacity, gals. ............................................... | 22.5 |
| Seating capacity .................................................... | 5 |
| Front head room, in. .............................................. | 38.9 |
| Max. front leg room, in. ......................................... | 43.7 |
| Rear head room, in. ............................................... | 36.9 |
| Min. rear leg room, in. ........................................... | 36.9 |

## ENGINES

| | dohc V-8 |
|---|---|
| Size, liters/cu. in. .................................................. | 4.0/242 |

*Prices are accurate at time of publication; subject to manufacturer's change.*

# LEXUS

|  | dohc V-8 |
|---|---|
| Horsepower @ rpm | 290@ 6000 |
| Torque (lbs./ft.) @ rpm | 300@ 4000 |
| Availability | S |

**EPA city/highway mpg**

| 5-speed OD automatic | 19/25 |
|---|---|

| **Lexus LS 400** | Retail Price | Dealer Invoice |
|---|---|---|
| Base 4-door sedan | $52900 | $44880 |
| Destination charge | 495 | 495 |

## STANDARD EQUIPMENT:

**Base:** 4.0-liter dohc V-8 engine, 5-speed automatic transmission, traction control, dual exhaust outlets, driver- and passenger-side air bags, front side-impact air bags, anti-lock 4-wheel disc brakes, variable-assist power steering, power tilt/telescopic steering wheel, leather-wrapped steering wheel and shifter, cruise control, air conditioning w/automatic dual-zone climate control, interior air filter, leather upholstery, power front bucket seats with power lumbar support, rear folding armrest, memory system (driver seat, steering wheel, outside mirrors), front storage console with auxiliary power outlet, cupholders, walnut interior trim, heated power mirrors w/passenger-side back-up aid, automatic day/night inside and outside mirrors, power windows, power door locks, remote keyless entry, Lexus/Pioneer AM/FM/cassette with seven speakers, diversity antenna, digital clock, tachometer, two trip odometers, coolant-temperature gauge, outside-temperature indicator, trip computer, rear defogger, remote fuel-door and decklid releases, illuminated visor mirrors, universal garage door opener, front and rear reading lights, speed-sensitive variable intermittent wipers, automatic headlamps, first-aid kit, color-keyed tinted glass, theft-deterrent system, fog lights, tool kit, full-size spare tire, 225/60VR16 tires, alloy wheels.

## OPTIONAL EQUIPMENT:
### Comfort and Convenience

| Navigation system | 3300 | 2753 |
|---|---|---|
| *Includes 6-disc CD changer.* | | |
| Power moonroof | 1120 | 896 |
| Heated front seats | 420 | 336 |
| Lexus/Nakamichi Premium Audio System | 2250 | 1740 |
| *Includes 6-CD auto changer. NA with Navigation system.* | | |
| 6-disc CD changer | 1050 | 840 |
| Woodgrain steering wheel | 330 | 264 |

## Appearance and Miscellaneous

| | Retail Price | Dealer Invoice |
|---|---|---|
| High intensity headlights | $500 | $400 |
| Electronic air suspension | 2970 | 2376 |

*Includes power moonroof. Requires Lexus/Nakamichi Premium Audio System, or Navigation system.*

| | | |
|---|---|---|
| Chrome alloy wheels | 1700 | 850 |

Other options are available as port installed items.

# LEXUS LX 470

Lexus LX 470

## SPECIFICATIONS

| | 4-door wagon |
|---|---|
| Wheelbase, in. | 112.2 |
| Overall length, in. | 192.5 |
| Overall width, in. | 76.4 |
| Overall height, in. | 72.2 |
| Curb weight, lbs. | 5401 |
| Cargo vol., cu. ft. | 97.4 |
| Fuel capacity, gals. | 25.4 |
| Seating capacity | 7 |
| Front head room, in. | 40.3 |
| Max. front leg room, in. | 42.2 |
| Rear head room, in. | 39.4 |
| Min. rear leg room, in. | 34.2 |

## ENGINES

| | dohc V-8 |
|---|---|
| Size, liters/cu. in. | 4.7/285 |
| Horsepower @ rpm | 230@ 4800 |
| Torque (lbs./ft.) @ rpm | 320@ 3400 |

*Prices are accurate at time of publication; subject to manufacturer's change.*

## LEXUS

| | dohc V-8 |
|---|---|
| Availability ............................................................ | S |

**EPA city/highway mpg**

| | |
|---|---|
| 4-speed OD automatic............................................ | 13/16 |

| **Lexus LX 470** | Retail Price | Dealer Invoice |
|---|---|---|
| Base 4-door wagon ...................................... | $48700 | $41809 |
| Destination charge ....................................... | 495 | 495 |

## STANDARD EQUIPMENT:

**Base:** 4.5-liter dohc 6-cylinder engine, 4-speed automatic transmission, full-time 4-wheel drive, driver- and passenger-side air bags, anti-lock 4-wheel disc brakes, air conditioning w/automatic climate control, rear heat duct, variable-assist power steering, tilt steering wheel, leather-wrapped steering wheel and shifter, cruise control, leather upholstery, power front bucket seats with driver-side lumbar support, split folding middle bench seat, retractable rear seats, rear folding armrests, front storage console with cupholders, Lexus/Pioneer AM/FM/cassette with seven speakers, power antenna, digital clock, power mirrors, power windows, power door locks, remote keyless entry, rear defogger, tachometer, voltmeter, coolant-temperature and oil-pressure gauge, illuminated visor mirrors, map lights, variable intermittent wipers, automatic headlamps, remote fuel-door release, first-aid and tool kits, front green-tinted glass, rear privacy glass, sliding rear-quarter windows, theft-deterrent system, full-size spare tire, 275/70HR16 tires, alloy wheels.

## OPTIONAL EQUIPMENT:
### Major Packages

| | | |
|---|---|---|
| Convenience Pkg................................................. | 1039 | 646 |
| *Cargo mat, running boards, roof rack, tow hitch assembly.* | | |

### Powertrains

| | | |
|---|---|---|
| Differential locks............................................... | 900 | 720 |

### Comfort and Convenience

| | | |
|---|---|---|
| Power moonroof ................................................. | 1300 | 1040 |
| 6-disc CD changer.............................................. | 1050 | 840 |

# LEXUS SC 300/400

## SPECIFICATIONS

| | 2-door coupe |
|---|---|
| Wheelbase, in. ........................................................ | 105.9 |

Lexus SC 400

| | 2-door coupe |
|---|---|
| Overall length, in. | 192.5 |
| Overall width, in. | 70.9 |
| Overall height, in. | 53.2 |
| Curb weight, lbs. | 3655 |
| Cargo vol., cu. ft. | 9.3 |
| Fuel capacity, gals. | 20.6 |
| Seating capacity | 4 |
| Front head room, in. | 38.3 |
| Max. front leg room, in. | 44.1 |
| Rear head room, in. | 36.1 |
| Min. rear leg room, in. | 27.2 |

## ENGINES

| | dohc I-6 | dohc V-8 |
|---|---|---|
| Size, liters/cu. in. | 3.0/183 | 4.0/242 |
| Horsepower @ rpm | 225@ 6000 | 300@ 6000 |
| Torque (lbs./ft.) @ rpm | 220@ 4000 | 310@ 4000 |
| Availability | S[1] | S[2] |

**EPA city/highway mpg**

| | | |
|---|---|---|
| 5-speed OD automatic | 19/24 | 19/25 |

1. SC 300.  2. SC 400.

| Lexus SC 300/400 | Retail Price | Dealer Invoice |
|---|---|---|
| SC 300 2-door notchback | $40900 | $35526 |
| SC 400 2-door notchback | 52700 | 45243 |
| Destination charge | 495 | 495 |

## STANDARD EQUIPMENT:

**SC 300:** 3.0-liter dohc 6-cylinder engine, 5-speed automatic transmission, driver- and passenger-side air bags, anti-lock 4-wheel disc brakes, air conditioning w/automatic climate control, variable-assist power steering, tilt/telescoping steering column, leather-wrapped steering wheel, cruise control, cloth upholstery, power front bucket seats, maple wood interior trim, heated power mirrors, power windows, tachometer, power door locks, remote keyless entry, Pioneer Audio System with AM/FM/cassette and seven speakers, diversity antennas, trip computer w/outside-temperature indicator, rear defogger, illuminated visor mirrors, universal garage door opener, remote fuel-door and decklid releases, variable intermittent wipers, automatic day/night inside mirror, cellular phone pre-wiring, automatic on/off headlamps, first aid kit, solar-control tinted glass, theft-deterrent system, fog lights, tool kit, 225/55VR16 performance tires, alloy wheels.

**SC 400** adds: 4.0-liter dohc V-8 engine, leather upholstery and trim, memory driver seat, power tilt/telescoping steering column w/memory, automatic day/night outside mirrors w/memory.

## OPTIONAL EQUIPMENT:

|  | Retail Price | Dealer Invoice |
|---|---|---|

### Major Packages

| | Retail Price | Dealer Invoice |
|---|---|---|
| Leather Trim Pkg., SC 300 | $2050 | $1640 |

*Leather upholstery and trim, automatic day/night outside mirrors w/memory, power tilt/telescoping steering column w/memory, memory driver seat.*

### Powertrains

| | Retail Price | Dealer Invoice |
|---|---|---|
| Traction control system w/heated front seats | 1220 | 976 |

*Requires 225/55VR16 all-season tires. SC 300 requires Leather Trim Pkg.*

### Comfort and Convenience

| | Retail Price | Dealer Invoice |
|---|---|---|
| Power glass moonroof | 1120 | 896 |
| Remote 12-disc CD changer | 1050 | 840 |
| Lexus/Nakamichi Premium Sound System | 2250 | 1740 |

*Includes remote 12-disc CD changer. SC 300 requires Leather Trim Pkg.*

### Appearance and Miscellaneous

| | Retail Price | Dealer Invoice |
|---|---|---|
| Rear spoiler, SC 400 | 420 | 336 |
| Chrome alloy wheels | 1700 | 850 |
| 225/55VR16 all-season tires | NC | NC |

Other options are available as port installed items.

# LINCOLN CONTINENTAL

## SPECIFICATIONS

| | 4-door sedan |
|---|---|
| Wheelbase, in. | 109.0 |
| Overall length, in. | 207.0 |

*Lincoln Continental*

|  | 4-door sedan |
|---|---|
| Overall width, in. | 73.6 |
| Overall height, in. | 56.0 |
| Curb weight, lbs. | 3868 |
| Cargo vol., cu. ft. | 18.9 |
| Fuel capacity, gals. | 20.0 |
| Seating capacity | 6 |
| Front head room, in. | 39.2 |
| Max. front leg room, in. | 41.9 |
| Rear head room, in. | 38.0 |
| Min. rear leg room, in. | 38.0 |

## ENGINES

|  | dohc V-8 |
|---|---|
| Size, liters/cu. in. | 4.6/281 |
| Horsepower @ rpm | 260@ 5750 |
| Torque (lbs./ft.) @ rpm | 270@ 3000 |
| Availability | S |
| **EPA city/highway mpg** | |
| 4-speed OD automatic | 17/24 |

| Lincoln Continental | Retail Price | Dealer Invoice |
|---|---|---|
| Base 4-door sedan | $37830 | $34524 |
| Destination charge | 670 | 670 |

## STANDARD EQUIPMENT:

**Base:** 4.6-liter dohc V-8 engine, 4-speed automatic transmission, traction control, driver- and passenger-side air bags, anti-lock 4-wheel disc brakes, programmable variable-assist power steering, leather-wrapped tilt steering wheel, cruise control, air conditioning w/automatic climate control, interior air-filtration system, leather upholstery, reclining front bucket seats with power lumbar adjusters, 6-way power front seats, center console, burl wal-

*Prices are accurate at time of publication; subject to manufacturer's change.*

nut interior trim, heated power mirrors w/tilt-down back-up aid, power windows, automatic power door locks, 2-driver memory system, rear defogger, automatic day/night rearview mirror w/compass, variable intermittent wipers, tachometer, coolant temperature gauge, AM/FM/cassette, analog clock, remote keyless entry, remote fuel-door and decklid releases, overhead console, systems message center, reading lights, illuminated visor mirrors, automatic headlights, floormats, cargo net, adjustable suspension system, automatic load leveling, solar-control tinted glass, anti-theft alarm system, 225/60R16 tires, alloy wheels.

## OPTIONAL EQUIPMENT:

| | Retail Price | Dealer Invoice |
|---|---|---|
| **Major Packages** | | |
| Personal Security Pkg. | $925 | $796 |
| *Manufacturer's discount price* | 750 | 646 |
| *Securitire with pressure alert, programmable garage-door opener. NA with chrome wheels.* | | |
| Driver Select System | 595 | 512 |
| *Semi-active suspension, selectable ride control, Memory Profile System, steering wheel with touch controls, automatic day/night outside mirrors.* | | |
| **Comfort and Convenience** | | |
| RESCU Pkg. | 2970 | 2554 |
| *Manufacturer's discount price* | 2345 | 2016 |
| *Global-positioning satellite, JBL Audio System, programmable garage-door opener, and voice-activated cellular telephone.* | | |
| RESCU Pkg., ordered w/Personal Security Pkg. | 2850 | 2452 |
| *Manufacturer's discount price* | 2225 | 1914 |
| *Global-positioning satellite, JBL Audio System, programmable garage-door opener, and voice-activated cellular telephone.* | | |
| Power moonroof | 1515 | 1302 |
| *Requires programmable garage-door opener.* | | |
| Front split bench seat | NC | NC |
| Heated seats | 290 | 250 |
| Voice-activated cellular telephone | 790 | 680 |
| *Requires JBL Audio System.* | | |
| JBL Audio System | 565 | 486 |
| *Digital signal processing, subwoofer amplifier, additional speakers.* | | |
| CD changer | 595 | 512 |
| *Requires JBL Audio System.* | | |
| Programmable garage-door opener | 120 | 104 |
| **Appearance and Miscellaneous** | | |
| Tri-coat paint | 365 | 314 |
| Engine block heater | 60 | 52 |
| Double-window chrome wheels | 845 | 726 |
| *NA with Personal Security Pkg.* | | |
| Polished alloy wheels | 350 | 302 |

# LINCOLN MARK VIII

*Lincoln Mark VIII LSC*

## SPECIFICATIONS

| | 2-door coupe |
|---|---|
| Wheelbase, in. | 113.0 |
| Overall length, in. | 207.2 |
| Overall width, in. | 74.8 |
| Overall height, in. | 53.6 |
| Curb weight, lbs. | 3765 |
| Cargo vol., cu. ft. | 14.4 |
| Fuel capacity, gals. | 18.0 |
| Seating capacity | 5 |
| Front head room, in. | 38.1 |
| Max. front leg room, in. | 42.6 |
| Rear head room, in. | 37.5 |
| Min. rear leg room, in. | 35.7 |

## ENGINES

| | dohc V-8 | dohc V-8 |
|---|---|---|
| Size, liters/cu. in. | 4.6/281 | 4.6/281 |
| Horsepower @ rpm | 280@ 5500 | 290@ 5750 |
| Torque (lbs./ft.) @ rpm | 285@ 4500 | 290@ 4500 |
| Availability | S[1] | S[2] |
| **EPA city/highway mpg** | | |
| 4-speed OD automatic | 17/26 | 17/26 |

*1. Base model. 2. LSC.*

| Lincoln Mark VIII | Retail Price | Dealer Invoice |
|---|---|---|
| Base 2-door notchback | $37830 | $34524 |
| LSC 2-door notchback | 39320 | 35850 |
| Destination charge | 670 | 670 |

*Prices are accurate at time of publication; subject to manufacturer's change.*

# LINCOLN

## STANDARD EQUIPMENT:

**Base:** 4.6-liter dohc V-8 280-horsepower engine, traction control, dual exhaust, driver- and passenger-side air bags, anti-lock 4-wheel disc brakes, 4-speed automatic transmission (3.07 final drive ratio), conditioning w/automatic climate control, variable-assist power steering, tilt/telescopic steering wheel, leather-wrapped steering wheel, cruise control, leather upholstery, reclining 6-way power front seats with power lumbar supports and driver-side memory, rear armrest, console with cupholder and storage bin, analog instrumentation with message center and programmable trip functions, tachometer, service interval reminder, heated power mirrors with remote 3-position memory, automatic day/night inside/outside mirrors, power windows, power locks, remote keyless entry, illuminated visor mirrors, rear defogger, remote decklid and fuel-door releases, JBL audio system with AM/FM/cassette, integrated antenna, intermittent wipers, automatic headlamps, solar-control tinted glass, theft-deterrent system, bright grille, bright exterior trim, 225/60VR16 tires, lacy-spoke alloy wheels.

**LSC** adds: 4.6-liter dohc V-8 290-horsepower engine, 4-speed automatic transmission (3.27 final drive ratio), perforated-leather upholstery, upgraded suspension, color-keyed grille, color-keyed exterior trim, chrome directional wheels with locking lug nuts.

## OPTIONAL EQUIPMENT:
### Comfort and Convenience

| | Retail Price | Dealer Invoice |
|---|---|---|
| Power moonroof | $1515 | $1302 |
| Heated seats | 290 | 250 |
| Premium CD player | NC | NC |
| *Replaces standard cassette player.* | | |
| CD changer | 670 | 576 |
| Portable voice-activated cellular telephone | 790 | 680 |
| Universal garage door opener | 120 | 103 |

### Appearance and Miscellaneous

| | | |
|---|---|---|
| Tri-coat paint | 365 | 314 |
| Engine block heater | 60 | 52 |
| Chrome octastar wheels, Base | 845 | 726 |

# LINCOLN NAVIGATOR

## SPECIFICATIONS

| | 4-door wagon |
|---|---|
| Wheelbase, in. | 119.1 |
| Overall length, in. | 204.8 |
| Overall width, in. | 79.9 |

Lincoln Navigator

| | 4-door wagon |
|---|---|
| Overall height, in. | 76.7 |
| Curb weight, lbs. | 5150 |
| Cargo vol., cu. ft. | 116.4 |
| Fuel capacity, gals. | 30.0 |
| Seating capacity | 8 |
| Front head room, in. | 39.8 |
| Max. front leg room, in. | 41.0 |
| Rear head room, in. | 39.8 |
| Min. rear leg room, in. | 39.7 |

## ENGINES

| | ohc V-8 |
|---|---|
| Size, liters/cu. in. | 5.4/330 |
| Horsepower @ rpm | 230@ 4250 |
| Torque (lbs./ft.) @ rpm | 325@ 3000 |
| Availability | S |

**EPA city/highway mpg**

| | |
|---|---|
| 4-speed OD automatic | 13/17[1] |

1. 12/16 with 4WD.

| Lincoln Navigator | Retail Price | Dealer Invoice |
|---|---|---|
| 4-door wagon, 2WD | $39310 | $34333 |
| 4-door wagon, 4WD | 42660 | 37181 |
| Destination charge | 640 | 640 |

## STANDARD EQUIPMENT:

**2WD:** 5.4-liter V-8 engine, 4-speed automatic transmission w/overdrive, anti-lock power 4-wheel disc brakes, driver- and passenger-side air bags, automatic air conditioning, variable-assist power steering, leather-wrapped steering wheel w/radio and climate controls, tilt steering column, cruise

*Prices are accurate at time of publication; subject to manufacturer's change.*

# LINCOLN

control, quad bucket seats, 6-way power front seats w/driver-side memory, third row bench seat, leather upholstery, walnut trim, cupholders, dual heated power mirrors, power windows, power door locks, trip odometer, tachometer, oil-pressure gauge, voltmeter, automatic-on headlights, AM/FM/cassette, digital clock, dual illuminated visor mirrors, floormats, cargo net, intermittent wipers, rear defogger, rear washer/intermittent wiper, remote keyless entry, fog lamps, roof rack, running boards, rear self-leveling suspension, Trailer Towing Group (7-wire harness, hitch, heavy-duty flasher, engine-oil cooler, auxiliary transmission-oil cooler), full-size spare tire, 245/75R16 tires, alloy wheels.

**4WD** adds: Control Trac on-demand 4WD, limited slip differential, front and rear self-leveling suspension, front tow hooks.

| OPTIONAL EQUIPMENT: | Retail Price | Dealer Invoice |
|---|---|---|
| **Powertrains** | | |
| Limited slip differential, 2WD | $255 | $217 |
| *Includes 3.73 axle ratio.* | | |
| **Comfort and Convenience** | | |
| Auxiliary air conditioning | 705 | 599 |
| *NA with moonroof.* | | |
| Power moonroof | 1655 | 1407 |
| *Includes mini overhead console and universal garage door opener. NA with auxiliary air conditioning.* | | |
| Mach AM/FM/cassette | 355 | 302 |
| *Includes 290 watts with seven speakers.* | | |
| 6-disc CD changer | 595 | 506 |
| Automatic day/night mirror | 110 | 94 |
| **Appearance and Miscellaneous** | | |
| Engine block heater | 35 | 30 |
| **Special Purpose, Wheels and Tires** | | |
| Skid plates, 4WD | 105 | 89 |
| 17-inch alloy wheels, 4WD | 235 | 200 |
| *Requires 255/75R17 tires.* | | |
| 17-inch chrome alloy wheels, 4WD | 950 | 808 |
| *Requires 255/75R17 tires.* | | |
| 245/75R16 outline white-letter tires | 130 | 111 |
| *Requires 17-inch wheels.* | | |
| 255/75R17 outline white-letter tires, 4WD | 305 | 259 |
| *Requires 17-inch wheels.* | | |

# LINCOLN TOWN CAR

*Lincoln Town Car*

## SPECIFICATIONS

| | 4-door sedan |
|---|---|
| Wheelbase, in. | 117.7 |
| Overall length, in. | 215.3 |
| Overall width, in. | 78.2 |
| Overall height, in. | 58.0 |
| Curb weight, lbs. | 3860 |
| Cargo vol., cu. ft. | 20.6 |
| Fuel capacity, gals. | 20.0 |
| Seating capacity | 6 |
| Front head room, in. | 39.2 |
| Max. front leg room, in. | 42.6 |
| Rear head room, in. | 37.5 |
| Min. rear leg room, in. | 41.1 |

## ENGINES

| | ohc V-8 | ohc V-8 |
|---|---|---|
| Size, liters/cu. in. | 4.6/281 | 4.6/281 |
| Horsepower @ rpm | 200@ 4500 | 220@ 4500 |
| Torque (lbs./ft.) @ rpm | 265@ 3500 | 275@ 3500 |
| Availability | S[1] | S[2] |

**EPA city/highway mpg**

| | | |
|---|---|---|
| 4-speed OD automatic | 17/25 | 17/25 |

1. Executive, Signature. 2. Cartier; optional Signature.

| **Lincoln Town Car** | Retail Price | Dealer Invoice |
|---|---|---|
| Executive 4-door sedan | $37830 | $34524 |
| Signature 4-door sedan | 39480 | 35992 |

*Prices are accurate at time of publication; subject to manufacturer's change.*

# LINCOLN

|  | Retail Price | Dealer Invoice |
|---|---|---|
| Cartier 4-door sedan | $41830 | $38084 |
| Destination charge | 670 | 670 |

## STANDARD EQUIPMENT:

**Executive:** 4.6-liter V-8, 4-speed automatic transmission, traction assist, driver- and passenger-side air bags, anti-lock 4-wheel disc brakes, variable-assist power steering, tilt steering wheel, leather-wrapped steering wheel, cruise control, air conditioning w/automatic climate control, leather upholstery, 6-way power twin-comfort lounge seats with 2-way front headrests, front and rear armrests, power windows, power door locks, remote keyless entry, heated power mirrors, auxiliary power outlet, automatic headlights, automatic day/night inside and driver-side mirrors, compass, rear defogger, AM/FM/cassette, diversity antenna, coolant-temperature gauge, remote fuel-door and decklid releases, power decklid pulldown, intermittent wipers, digital clock, illuminated visor mirrors, floormats, trunk net, solar-control tinted glass, theft-deterrent system, cornering lamps, 225/60SR16 tires, alloy wheels.

**Signature** adds: memory driver-seat, power lumbar support, power front recliners, memory mirrors, dual footwell lights, front-seat storage with cupholders, steering-wheel radio and climate controls, rear cupholders, programmable garage-door opener.

**Cartier** adds: upgraded leather upholstery, heated front seat, analog clock, 4-way front-seat headrests, Ford JBL Audio System, upgraded door trim panels, gold pkg., dual exhaust.

## OPTIONAL EQUIPMENT:

### Major Packages

| | | |
|---|---|---|
| Touring Pkg., Signature | 500 | 430 |

*Upgraded suspension, performance axle ratio and torque converter, perforated leather upholstery, 225/60TR16 tires, chrome alloy wheels.*

| | | |
|---|---|---|
| Entertainment Pkg., Signature | 2675 | 2300 |
| *Manufacturer's discount price* | 1845 | 1586 |

*JBL Audio system w/CD changer, power moonroof.*

### Comfort and Convenience

| | | |
|---|---|---|
| Power moonroof | 1515 | 1302 |
| *NA Executive.* | | |
| Heated front seats, Signature | 290 | 250 |
| JBL Audio System w/CD changer, Signature | 1160 | 998 |
| *Manufacturer's discount price* | 845 | 728 |
| Trunk-mounted CD changer | 585 | 512 |
| Voice-activated cellular telephone | 790 | 680 |
| *NA Executive.* | | |

## Appearance and Miscellaneous

| | Retail Price | Dealer Invoice |
|---|---|---|
| Tri-coat paint, Signature | $365 | $314 |
| Full-size spare tire | 120 | 104 |
| Chrome alloy wheels, Cartier | 845 | 726 |

# MAZDA 626

*Mazda 626*

## SPECIFICATIONS

| | 4-door sedan |
|---|---|
| Wheelbase, in. | 105.1 |
| Overall length, in. | 186.8 |
| Overall width, in. | 69.3 |
| Overall height, in. | 55.1 |
| Curb weight, lbs. | 2798 |
| Cargo vol., cu. ft. | 14.2 |
| Fuel capacity, gals. | 16.9 |
| Seating capacity | 5 |
| Front head room, in. | 39.2 |
| Max. front leg room, in. | 43.6 |
| Rear head room, in. | 37.0 |
| Min. rear leg room, in. | 34.6 |

## ENGINES

| | dohc I-4 | dohc V-6 |
|---|---|---|
| Size, liters/cu. in. | 2.0/122 | 2.5/152 |
| Horsepower @ rpm | 125@ 5500 | 170@ 5000 |
| Torque (lbs./ft.) @ rpm | 127@ 3000 | 163@ 5000 |
| Availability | S[1] | S[2] |
| **EPA city/highway mpg** | | |
| 5-speed OD manual | 26/33 | 21/27 |

*Prices are accurate at time of publication; subject to manufacturer's change.*

# MAZDA

|  | dohc I-4 | dohc V-6 |
|---|---|---|
| 4-speed OD automatic | 22/29 | 20/26 |

*1. DX, LX. 2. LX V-6, ES V-6.*

## Mazda 626

|  | Retail Price | Dealer Invoice |
|---|---|---|
| DX 4-door sedan | $15695 | $14130 |
| LX 4-cylinder 4-door sedan | 17895 | 16108 |
| LX V-6 4-door sedan | 20795 | 18715 |
| ES V-6 4-door sedan | 23995 | 21592 |
| Destination charge | 450 | 450 |

Prices are for vehicles distributed by Mazda Motor of America, Inc. Prices may be higher in areas served by independent distributors.

## STANDARD EQUIPMENT:

**DX:** 2.0-liter dohc 4-cylinder engine, 5-speed manual transmission, driver- and passenger-side air bags, variable-assist power steering, tilt steering wheel, velour upholstery, reclining front bucket seats w/adjustable thigh support, 60/40 folding rear seat w/folding armrest, storage console with armrest, cupholders, tachometer, coolant-temperature gauge, trip odometer, intermittent wipers, power mirrors, remote fuel-door and decklid releases, rear defogger, passenger-side visor mirror, rear heat ducts, green tinted glass, front mud guards, 185/70SR14 tires, full wheel covers.

**LX** adds: air conditioning, upgraded velour upholstery, power windows, power door locks, cruise control, power mirrors, AM/FM/CD, digital clock, dual visor mirrors w/illuminated passenger-side mirror.

**LX V-6** adds: 2.5-liter dohc V-6 engine, anti-lock 4-wheel disc brakes, variable intermittent wipers, remote keyless entry, illuminated visor mirrors, theft-deterrent system, rear stabilizer bar, dual bright exhaust outlets, 205/60HR15 tires.

**ES** adds: leather upholstery, 8-way power driver seat, leather-wrapped steering wheel and shifter, Bose sound system, power antenna, power moonroof, map lights, floormats, fog lights, alloy wheels.

## OPTIONAL EQUIPMENT:
### Major Packages

| | | |
|---|---|---|
| Convenience Pkg., DX | 1495 | 1196 |

*Air conditioning, AM/FM/CD, floormats.*

| | | |
|---|---|---|
| Luxury Pkg., LX 4-cylinder | 1695 | 1356 |

*Power moonroof, theft-deterrent system, remote keyless entry, floormats, 205/60HR15 tires, alloy wheels.*

| | | |
|---|---|---|
| Premium Pkg., LX V-6 | 1895 | 1516 |

*Power driver seat, power moonroof, Bose sound system, power antenna, floormats, alloy wheels.*

## Powertrains

| | Retail Price | Dealer Invoice |
|---|---|---|
| 4-speed automatic transmission | $800 | $696 |
| *Deletes leather-wrapped shifter on ES.* | | |
| Anti-lock brakes, LX 4-cylinder | 550 | 468 |

## Comfort and Convenience

| | | |
|---|---|---|
| Cassette player | 250 | 213 |
| *DX requires Convenience Pkg.* | | |
| Floormats, DX, LX | 80 | 56 |

# MAZDA MILLENIA

*1998 Mazda Millenia S*

## SPECIFICATIONS

| | 4-door sedan |
|---|---|
| Wheelbase, in. | 108.3 |
| Overall length, in. | 189.8 |
| Overall width, in. | 69.7 |
| Overall height, in. | 54.9 |
| Curb weight, lbs. | 3220 |
| Cargo vol., cu. ft. | 13.3 |
| Fuel capacity, gals. | 18.0 |
| Seating capacity | 5 |
| Front head room, in. | 39.3 |
| Max. front leg room, in. | 43.3 |
| Rear head room, in. | 37.0 |
| Min. rear leg room, in. | 34.1 |

## ENGINES

| | dohc V-6 | Super dohc V-6 |
|---|---|---|
| Size, liters/cu. in. | 2.5/152 | 2.3/138 |
| Horsepower @ rpm | 170@ 5800 | 210@ 4800 |

## MAZDA

| | dohc V-6 | Super dohc V-6 |
|---|---|---|
| Torque (lbs./ft.) @ rpm | 160@ 4800 | 210@ 3500 |
| Availability | S | S[1] |
| **EPA city/highway mpg** | | |
| 4-speed OD automatic | 20/27 | 20/28 |

1. S model.

| Mazda Millenia | Retail Price | Dealer Invoice |
|---|---|---|
| Base 4-door sedan | $28995 | $25562 |
| S 4-door notchback | 36595 | 31514 |
| Destination charge | 450 | 450 |

Prices are for vehicles distributed by Mazda Motor America, Inc. Prices may be higher in areas served by independent distributors.

## STANDARD EQUIPMENT:

**Base:** 2.5-liter dohc V-6 engine, 4-speed automatic transmission, dual exhaust outlets, driver- and passenger-side air bags, anti-lock 4-wheel disc brakes, air conditioning w/automatic climate control, variable-assist power steering, leather-wrapped power tilt steering wheel, cruise control, cloth reclining front bucket seats, 8-way power driver seat, front storage console w/cupholder, folding rear armrest, tachometer, trip odometer, outside-temperature indicator, heated power mirrors, power windows, power door locks, variable intermittent wipers, AM/FM/cassette/CD player, digital clock, integrated diversity antenna, illuminated visor mirrors, rear defogger, auxiliary power outlet, remote fuel-door and decklid releases, floormats, rear heat ducts, theft-deterrent system, tinted glass, fog lights, 205/65HR15 tires, alloy wheels w/locks.

**S adds:** 2.3-liter dohc supercharged V-6 engine, traction control, leather upholstery, 8-way power front passenger seat, remote keyless entry, power moonroof, Bose audio system, heavy-duty starter, 215/55VR16 tires.

## OPTIONAL EQUIPMENT:
### Major Packages

| | | |
|---|---|---|
| Premium Pkg., Base | 4000 | 3189 |

*Leather upholstery, power passenger seat, power moonroof, remote keyless entry.*

| | | |
|---|---|---|
| 4-Seasons Pkg., Base | 600 | 504 |

*Traction control (Base), heated front seats, heavy-duty wipers, heavy-duty battery, extra-capacity windshield-washer tank.*

| | | |
|---|---|---|
| 4-Seasons Package, S | 300 | 252 |

*Traction control (Base), heated front seats, heavy-duty wipers, heavy-duty battery, extra-capacity windshield-washer tank.*

## Comfort and Convenience

|  | Retail Price | Dealer Invoice |
|---|---|---|
| Bose audio system, Base .......................... | $700 | $560 |

## Appearance and Miscellaneous

|  | Retail Price | Dealer Invoice |
|---|---|---|
| White pearl metallic paint......................... | 350 | 294 |
| Polished alloy wheels................................ | 500 | 300 |

# MAZDA MPV

*Mazda MPV*

## SPECIFICATIONS

|  | 4-door van | 4-door van |
|---|---|---|
| Wheelbase, in. ................................... | 110.4 | 110.4 |
| Overall length, in. .............................. | 183.5 | 183.5 |
| Overall width, in. ............................... | 71.9 | 71.9 |
| Overall height, in. .............................. | 68.9 | 71.5 |
| Curb weight, lbs. ............................... | 3790 | 4045 |
| Cargo vol., cu. ft. .............................. | 42.1 | 42.1 |
| Fuel capacity, gals. ........................... | 19.6 | 19.8 |
| Seating capacity................................. | 8 | 8 |
| Front head room, in. ........................... | 40.0 | 40.0 |
| Max. front leg room, in. ...................... | 40.4 | 40.4 |
| Rear head room, in. ........................... | 39.7 | 36.9 |
| Min. rear leg room, in. ........................ | 33.4 | 34.2 |

## ENGINES

|  | ohc V-6 |
|---|---|
| Size, liters/cu. in. ................................................. | 3.0/180 |
| Horsepower @ rpm ............................................... | 155@ 5000 |
| Torque (lbs./ft.) @ rpm ......................................... | 169@ 4000 |

*Prices are accurate at time of publication; subject to manufacturer's change.*

# MAZDA

| | ohc V-6 |
|---|---|
| Availability ................................................................ | S |

**EPA city/highway mpg**
4-speed OD automatic............................................. 16/21[1]

*1. 15/19 w/AWD.*

| **Mazda MPV** | Retail Price | Dealer Invoice |
|---|---|---|
| LX 2WD 3-door van ..................................... | $23095 | $20834 |
| ES 2WD 3-door van ..................................... | 26395 | 23807 |
| LX 4WD 3-door van ..................................... | 26895 | 24258 |
| ES 4WD 3-door van ..................................... | 28895 | 26060 |
| Destination charge ..................................... | 480 | 480 |

All models require a Preferred Equipment Pkg. Prices are for vehicles distributed by Mazda Motor of America, Inc. Prices may be higher in areas served by independent distributors.

## STANDARD EQUIPMENT:

**LX 2WD:** 3.0-liter V-6 engine, 4-speed automatic transmission, driver- and passenger-side air bags, anti-lock 4-wheel disc brakes, variable-assist power steering, tilt steering wheel, cruise control, velour upholstery, 8-passenger seating (reclining front bucket seats, 3-passenger reclining and folding middle bench seat, 3-passenger rear bench seat), power mirrors, power windows, power door locks, tachometer, AM/FM/CD, digital clock, variable intermittent wipers, intermittent rear wiper/washer, rear defogger, remote fuel-door release, rear heat ducts, tinted glass, wheel covers, 195/75R15 tires.

**LX 4WD** adds: part-time 4-wheel drive, 4-Seasons Pkg. (rear heater, large-capacity washer tank, heavy-duty battery), high-capacity cooling fan, All-Sport Pkg. (grille guard, stone guard, eyebrow fender flares, rear bumper guard, roof rack, All-Sport graphics, alloy wheels, 225/70R15 mud and snow tires), special 2-tone paint, full-size spare tire.

**ES 2WD** adds to LX 2WD: leather upholstery, 7-passenger seating (quad captain's chairs, 3-passenger rear bench seat), leather-wrapped steering wheel, Load Leveling Pkg. (automatic load leveling, transmission-oil cooler, high-capacity cooling fan, full-size spare), All-Sport Pkg. (includes 215/65R15 tires), special 2-tone paint, deletes middle bench seat.

**ES 4WD** adds: part-time 4-wheel drive, 4-Seasons Pkg., All-Sport Pkg. (includes 225/70R15 mud and snow tires).

## OPTIONAL EQUIPMENT:
### Major Packages

| | | |
|---|---|---|
| LX Preferred Equipment Group 1, LX............................. | 1550 | 1318 |
| *Manufacturer's discount price*............................................ | 795 | 676 |
| Front air conditioning, remote keyless entry, rear privacy glass, floormats. | | |

| | Retail Price | Dealer Invoice |
|---|---|---|
| LX Preferred Equipment Group 2, LX | $2250 | $1913 |
| *Manufacturer's discount price* | 1495 | 1271 |
| Front and rear air conditioning, remote keyless entry, rear privacy glass, floormats. | | |
| ES Preferred Equipment Group 1, ES | 2250 | 1913 |
| *Manufacturer's discount price* | 1395 | 1186 |
| Front and rear air conditioning, remote keyless entry, rear privacy glass, floormats. | | |
| Load Leveling Pkg., LX 2WD | 595 | 506 |
| LX 4WD | 495 | 421 |
| *Automatic load leveling, transmission-oil cooler, high-capacity cooling fan (2WD), full-size spare tire (2WD).* | | |
| All-Sport Pkg., LX 2WD | 880 | 748 |
| *Grille guard, stone guard, eyebrow fender flares, rear bumper guard, roof rack, All-Sport graphics, alloy wheels, 215/65R15 tires.* | | |

## Comfort and Convenience

| | | |
|---|---|---|
| Quad captain's chairs, LX | 400 | 340 |
| Power moonroof, ES | 1200 | 1020 |
| Cassette player | 250 | 213 |

## Appearance and Miscellaneous

| | | |
|---|---|---|
| Special 2-tone paint, LX 2WD | 350 | 298 |

# MAZDA PROTEGE

## SPECIFICATIONS

| | 4-door sedan |
|---|---|
| Wheelbase, in. | 102.6 |
| Overall length, in. | 174.5 |
| Overall width, in. | 67.3 |
| Overall height, in. | 55.9 |
| Curb weight, lbs. | 2385 |
| Cargo vol., cu. ft. | 13.1 |
| Fuel capacity, gals. | 14.5 |
| Seating capacity | 5 |
| Front head room, in. | 39.2 |
| Max. front leg room, in. | 42.2 |
| Rear head room, in. | 37.4 |
| Min. rear leg room, in. | 35.6 |

## ENGINES

| | dohc I-4 | dohc I-4 |
|---|---|---|
| Size, liters/cu. in. | 1.5/91 | 1.8/110 |

*Prices are accurate at time of publication; subject to manufacturer's change.*

# MAZDA

*Mazda Protege ES*

|  | dohc I-4 | dohc I-4 |
|---|---|---|
| Horsepower @ rpm | 92 @ 5500 | 122@ 6000 |
| Torque (lbs./ft.) @ rpm | 96 @ 4000 | 117@ 4000 |
| Availability | S[1] | S[2] |
| **EPA city/highway mpg** | | |
| 5-speed OD manual | 30/37 | 26/32 |
| 4-speed OD automatic | 25/32 | 23/30 |

*1. DX, LX. 2. ES.*

| **Mazda Protege** | Retail Price | Dealer Invoice |
|---|---|---|
| DX 4-door sedan | $12145 | $11455 |
| LX 4-door sedan | 13545 | 12498 |
| ES 4-door sedan | 15295 | 13956 |
| Destination charge | 450 | 450 |

Prices are for vehicles distributed by Mazda Motor of America, Inc. Prices may be higher in areas served by independent distributors.

## STANDARD EQUIPMENT:

**DX:** 1.5-liter dohc 4-cylinder engine, 5-speed manual transmission, driver- and passenger-side air bags, variable-assist power steering, tilt steering wheel, cloth/vinyl reclining front bucket seats, cupholders, storage console, rear defogger, remote fuel-door release, coolant-temperature gauge, trip odometer, intermittent wipers, auxiliary power outlet, remote outside mirrors, green tinted glass, 175/70R13 tires.

**LX** adds: cruise control, AM/FM/CD, digital clock, velour upholstery, split folding rear seat, remote decklid release, tachometer, power windows, power door locks, power mirrors, map lights, passenger-side vanity mirror, front side storage trays, full wheel covers, 185/65R14 tires.

**ES** adds: 1.8-liter dohc 4-cylinder engine, 4-wheel disc brakes, air conditioning, sport front bucket seats with thigh-support and height adjustment, rear stabilizer bar.

## OPTIONAL EQUIPMENT:

| | Retail Price | Dealer Invoice |
|---|---|---|
| **Major Packages** | | |
| Convenience Pkg., DX | $1575 | $1292 |
| Air conditioning, AM/FM/cassette, floormats. | | |
| Luxury Pkg., LX | 1145 | 939 |
| Air conditioning, raised console armrest (automatic transmission-equipped models), floormats. | | |
| Premium Pkg., ES | 1195 | 956 |
| Alloy wheels with locks, power sunroof. | | |
| Touring Pkg., ES | 105 | 84 |
| Floormats, raised console armrest. Requires automatic transmission. | | |
| **Powertrains** | | |
| 4-speed automatic transmission | 800 | 720 |
| **Safety Features** | | |
| Anti-lock brakes, LX, ES | 800 | 680 |
| **Comfort and Convenience** | | |
| Power sunroof, LX | 700 | 560 |
| Cassette player | 250 | 213 |
| DX requires Convenience Pkg. | | |
| Remote keyless entry, LX, ES | 200 | 160 |
| Includes theft-deterrent system. | | |
| Floormats | 80 | 64 |

# MERCEDES-BENZ C-CLASS AND CLK

## SPECIFICATIONS

| | 4-door sedan | 2-door coupe |
|---|---|---|
| Wheelbase, in. | 105.9 | 105.9 |
| Overall length, in. | 177.4 | 180.2 |
| Overall width, in. | 67.7 | 67.8 |
| Overall height, in. | 56.1 | 53.0 |
| Curb weight, lbs. | 3250 | 3240 |
| Cargo vol., cu. ft. | 12.9 | 11.0 |

*Prices are accurate at time of publication; subject to manufacturer's change.*

# MERCEDES-BENZ

Mercedes-Benz C280

|  | 4-door sedan | 2-door coupe |
|---|---|---|
| Fuel capacity, gals. | 16.4 | 16.4 |
| Seating capacity | 5 | 4 |
| Front head room, in. | 37.2 | 36.9 |
| Max. front leg room, in. | 41.5 | 41.9 |
| Rear head room, in. | 37.0 | 35.6 |
| Min. rear leg room, in. | 32.8 | 31.1 |

## ENGINES

|  | dohc I-4 | ohc V-6 | ohc V-6 |
|---|---|---|---|
| Size, liters/cu. in. | 2.3/140 | 2.8/171 | 3.2/195 |
| Horsepower @ rpm | 148@ 5500 | 194@ 5800 | 215@ 5500 |
| Torque (lbs./ft.) @ rpm | 162@ 4000 | 195@ 3000 | 229@ 3000 |
| Availability | S[1] | S[2] | S[3] |
| **EPA city/highway mpg** | | | |
| 5-speed OD automatic | 23/30 | 21/27 | 21/29 |

1. C230.  2. C280.  3. CLK320.

| Mercedes-Benz C-Class and CLK | Retail Price | Dealer Invoice |
|---|---|---|
| C230 4-door sedan | $30450 | $26490 |
| C280 4-door sedan | 35400 | 30800 |
| CLK 2-door notchback | 39850 | 34670 |
| Destination charge | 595 | 595 |

## STANDARD EQUIPMENT:

**C230:** 2.3-liter dohc 4-cylinder engine, 5-speed automatic transmission, driver- and passenger-side air bags w/automatic child seat recognition

CONSUMER GUIDE™

system, side-impact air bags, anti-lock 4-wheel disc brakes, power steering, leather-wrapped steering wheel and shifter, cruise control, air conditioning w/automatic climate control, cloth 10-way power driver seat, 10-way manual adjustable passenger seat, center storage console, folding rear armrest, cupholders, heated power mirrors w/automatic day/night, burl walnut interior trim, power windows, power door locks, remote keyless entry, remote AM/FM/cassette, digital clock, tachometer, coolant-temperature gauge, trip odometer, outside-temperature indicator, remote decklid release, illuminated visor mirrors, rear defogger, Homelink universal garage-door opener, first-aid kit, floormats, theft-deterrent system, tinted glass, fog lights, 195/65HR15 all-season tires, alloy wheels.

**C280** adds: 2.8-liter ohc 6-cylinder engine, traction control, 10-way power passenger seat, Bose sound system.

**CLK** adds: 3.2-liter ohc 6-cylinder engine, leather upholstery, memory system, dual-zone automatic climate control, interior air filter, 205/55R16 tires.

## OPTIONAL EQUIPMENT:

| | Retail Price | Dealer Invoice |
|---|---|---|
| **Major Packages** | | |
| Option Pkg. C1, C280 | $1890 | $1644 |
| *Electronic Stability Program, heated front seats, headlight washer/wiper.* | | |
| Option Pkg. C2, C230, C280 | 350 | 304 |
| *Split folding rear seat w/pass-through and ski sack.* | | |
| Option Pkg. C3, C230 | 2190 | 1905 |
| C280 | 1990 | 1731 |
| *Leather upholstery, 10-way power passenger seat, power sunroof, rain-sensing wipers (C280).* | | |
| Option Pkg. C6, C280 | 890 | 774 |
| *Leather upholstery, bucket front seats, sport interior trim, telescoping steering wheel, bodyside moldings, sport suspension, 205/55HR16 tires.* | | |
| Option Pkg. K1 | 1495 | 1087 |
| *Integrated mobile cellular telephone, 6-disc CD changer.* | | |
| Option Pkg. K2 | 1895 | 1445 |
| *Integrated portable cellular telephone, 6-disc CD changer.* | | |
| Option Pkg. K3, CLK | 1290 | 1122 |
| *Power glass sunroof, power rear sun shade, automatic day/night rearview and driver side mirrors.* | | |
| Option Pkg. K4, CLK | 1950 | 1696 |
| *Electronic Stability Program, Xenon headlights, rain-sensing wipers.* | | |
| **Powertrains** | | |
| Automatic slip control, C230 | 990 | 861 |
| **Comfort and Convenience** | | |
| Headlamp washer/wipers | 340 | 296 |
| Power glass sunroof | 1100 | 966 |

*Prices are accurate at time of publication; subject to manufacturer's change.*

## MERCEDES-BENZ

| | Retail Price | Dealer Invoice |
|---|---|---|
| Telescopic steering wheel, C230, C280 | $125 | $109 |
| Multi-contour driver seat | 390 | 339 |
| *NA with Option Pkg. C6.* | | |
| Multi-contour power passenger seat | 390 | 339 |
| *NA with Option Pkg. C6.* | | |
| Heated front seats | 595 | 518 |
| Rear seat pass-through, CLK | 175 | 152 |
| *Includes ski sack.* | | |
| Bose sound system, C230 | 570 | 496 |
| Rain-sensing wipers, C230, C280 | 170 | 148 |

### Appearance and Miscellaneous

| | | |
|---|---|---|
| Xenon headlights, C230, C280 | 960 | 835 |
| Metallic paint | 600 | 522 |

# MERCEDES-BENZ E-CLASS

*Mercedes-Benz E320 sedan*

## SPECIFICATIONS

| | 4-door sedan | 4-door wagon |
|---|---|---|
| Wheelbase, in. | 111.5 | 111.5 |
| Overall length, in. | 189.4 | 190.4 |
| Overall width, in. | 70.8 | 70.8 |
| Overall height, in. | 56.7 | 59.3 |
| Curb weight, lbs. | 3460 | 3670 |
| Cargo vol., cu. ft. | 15.3 | 82.6 |
| Fuel capacity, gals. | 21.1 | 18.5 |
| Seating capacity | 5 | 7 |
| Front head room, in. | 37.6 | 38.6 |
| Max. front leg room, in. | 41.3 | 41.3 |

| | 4-door sedan | 4-door wagon |
|---|---|---|
| Rear head room, in. | 37.2 | 37.0 |
| Min. rear leg room, in. | 36.1 | 36.1 |

## ENGINES

| | Turbo dohc I-6 | ohc V-6 | dohc V-8 |
|---|---|---|---|
| Size, liters/cu. in. | 3.0/183 | 3.2/195 | 4.2/256 |
| Horsepower @ rpm | 174@ 5000 | 221@ 5500 | 275@ 5700 |
| Torque (lbs./ft.) @ rpm | 244@ 1600 | 232@ 3000 | 295@ 3900 |
| Availability | S[1] | S[2] | S[3] |
| **EPA city/highway mpg** | | | |
| 5-speed OD automatic | 26/34 | 21/29 | 18/25 |

1. E300 Turbodiesel. 2. E320. 3. E420.

| Mercedes-Benz E-Class | Retail Price | Dealer Invoice |
|---|---|---|
| E300TD 4-door sedan | $41800 | $36370 |
| E320 4-door sedan | 45500 | 39580 |
| E320 4-door wagon | 46500 | 40450 |
| 1997 E420 4-door sedan | 49900 | 43410 |
| Destination charge | 595 | 595 |

## STANDARD EQUIPMENT:

**E300TD:** 3.0-liter dohc 6-cylinder turbocharged diesel engine, 5-speed automatic transmission, ASR (acceleration slip control), front and side air bags, anti-lock 4-wheel disc brakes, variable-assist power steering, automatic climate control, cruise control, cloth upholstery, 10-way power front bucket seats with memory feature, split folding rear seats, cupholders, power tilt/telescopic steering wheel with memory feature, leather-wrapped steering wheel, power windows, power door locks, tachometer, outside-temperature indicator, AM/FM/cassette, power heated outside mirrors with memory feature, automatic day/night inside and driver-side outside mirrors, tinted glass, rear defogger, illuminated visor mirrors, theft-deterrent system, remote keyless entry, remote decklid release, Homelink universal garage-door opener, variable intermittent wipers, reading lights, walnut interior trim, interior air filter, first-aid kit, fog lamps, floormats, 215/55R16 tires, alloy wheels, full-size spare tire.

**E320** adds to E300TD: 3.2-liter OHC V-6 engine, leather upholstery, E320 wagon deletes leather upholstery and adds to sedan: folding third seat, cargo net, cargo cover, rear power outlet, intermittent rear wiper and heated washer, automatic rear load leveling.

**E420** adds to E320 sedan: 4.2-liter dohc V-8 engine, Bose sound system.

*Prices are accurate at time of publication; subject to manufacturer's change.*

## OPTIONAL EQUIPMENT:

| | Retail Price | Dealer Invoice |
|---|---|---|
| **Major Packages** | | |
| E1 Option Pkg., E300TD, E320 | $1950 | $1696 |
| E420 | 760 | 661 |
| *Electronic Stability Program, Xenon headlamps, rain-sensing windshield wipers, heated headlamp washers.* | | |
| E2 Option Pkg., E300TD, E320 | 1350 | 1174 |
| *Bose sound system, power glass sunroof.* | | |
| K2 Option Pkg., E300TD, E320 | 1895 | 1445 |
| *Integrated portable cellular telephone, 6-disc CD changer.* | | |
| E4 Option Pkg., E420 | 1630 | 1418 |
| *Dual multicontour power seats, headlamp washers, Xenon headlamps.* | | |
| E5 Option Pkg. (E420)/K2 Option Pkg. (E300TD, E320) | 1495 | 1087 |
| *Integrated cellular telephone, 6-disc CD changer.* | | |
| E6 Sport Pkg., E420 | 3900 | 3393 |
| *Ground effects, 235/45ZR17 performance tires, monoblock alloy wheels.* | | |
| E7 Option Pkg., E420 | 1950 | 1696 |
| *Electronic Stability Program, headlamp washers, Xenon headlamps.* | | |
| **Powertrains** | | |
| All-wheel-drive system, E320 | 2750 | 2400 |
| **Safety Features** | | |
| Parktronic system, E300TD, E320 | 975 | 848 |
| Electronic Stability Program, E300TD, E320 | 990 | 861 |
| **Comfort and Convenience** | | |
| Power glass sunroof, E300TD, E320 | 1110 | 966 |
| Power glass moonroof, E420 | 1090 | 948 |
| Leather upholstery, E300TD, E320 wagon | 1695 | 1475 |
| Multicontour power driver seat, E300TD, E320 | 390 | 339 |
| E420 | 380 | 331 |
| Multicontour power passenger seat, E300TD, E320 | 390 | 339 |
| E420 | 380 | 331 |
| Heated front seats | 595 | 518 |
| Bose Premium Sound System, E300TD, E320 | 570 | 496 |
| Heated headlamp washers, E300TD, E320 | 340 | 296 |
| Headlamp washers, E420 | 335 | 291 |
| Power rear window sunshade | 395 | 344 |
| *NA station wagon.* | | |
| Xenon headlamps, E300TD, E320 | 960 | 835 |
| E420 | 950 | 826 |
| *Requires heated headlamp washers.* | | |
| Rain-sensing windshield wipers, E300TD, E320 | 170 | 148 |

| **Appearance and Miscellaneous** | Retail Price | Dealer Invoice |
|---|---|---|
| Metallic paint, E300D, E320 | $695 | $605 |
| E420 | NC | NC |
| Luggage rack, E320 wagon | 390 | 339 |

# MERCEDES-BENZ ML320

*Mercedes-Benz ML320*

## SPECIFICATIONS

| | 4-door wagon |
|---|---|
| Wheelbase, in. | 111.0 |
| Overall length, in. | 180.6 |
| Overall width, in. | 73.2 |
| Overall height, in. | 69.9 |
| Curb weight, lbs. | 4200 |
| Cargo vol., cu. ft. | 85.4 |
| Fuel capacity, gals. | 19.0 |
| Seating capacity | 5 |
| Front head room, in. | 39.8 |
| Max. front leg room, in. | 40.3 |
| Rear head room, in. | 39.7 |
| Min. rear leg room, in. | 38.0 |

## ENGINES

| | ohc V-6 |
|---|---|
| Size, liters/cu. in. | 3.2/195 |
| Horsepower @ rpm | 215@ 5500 |
| Torque (lbs./ft.) @ rpm | 233@ 3000 |
| Availability | S |

*Prices are accurate at time of publication; subject to manufacturer's change.*

# MERCEDES-BENZ

**EPA city/highway mpg**
5-speed OD automatic............................................................ 17/21

| **Mercedes-Benz ML320** | Retail Price | Dealer Invoice |
|---|---|---|
| Base 4-door wagon ................................................ | $33950 | $29540 |

## STANDARD EQUIPMENT:

**Base:** 3.2-liter V-6 engine, 5-speed automatic transmission, full-time 4WD, anti-lock 4-wheel disc brakes, driver- and passenger-side air bags, front side-impact air bags, air conditioning, power windows, power door locks, heated power mirrors, rear window defogger, rear wiper/washer, power steering, tilt steering wheel, cruise control, AM/FM/cassette/weatherband with 4 speakers, remote keyless entry, tachometer, temperature gauge, oil pressure gauge, trip odometer, 6-way manual front seats, split folding rear seat, front and rear cupholders, front center armrest with storage, illuminated visor mirrors, cargo cover, illuminated entry, floormats, theft-deterrent system, rear fog lamp, 255/65R16 tires, alloy wheels.

## OPTIONAL EQUIPMENT:
### Major Packages

| | | |
|---|---|---|
| M1 Pkg. .................................................................... | 2950 | 2570 |

*Leather-trimmed seats, leather-wrapped steering wheel and shift knob, walnut interior trim, heated 8-way power front seats, automatic inside rearview mirror, trip computer, outside temperature indicator, lockable safebox, rear privacy glass.*

| | | |
|---|---|---|
| M4 Pkg. .................................................................... | 1595 | 1390 |

*Includes running boards, mud guards, outside-mounted full size spare tire. Requires sunroof.*

| | | |
|---|---|---|
| M7 Pkg., w/cloth upholstery...................................................................... | 900 | 780 |
| w/leather upholstery...................................................................... | 1050 | 910 |

*Includes two third-row bucket seats, power rear quarter windows. Requires sunroof.*

### Comfort and Convenience

| | | |
|---|---|---|
| Power sunroof.................................................................... | 1095 | 950 |
| Bose sound system with 6-disc CD changer.............................................. | 1050 | 910 |

*Includes 6 speakers and subwoofer.*

### Appearance and Miscellaneous

| | | |
|---|---|---|
| Metallic paint ........................................................................ | 475 | 410 |

# MERCEDES-BENZ S-CLASS/CL-CLASS

*Mercedes-Benz S-Class*

| SPECIFICATIONS | 2-door coupe | 4-door sedan | 4-door sedan |
|---|---|---|---|
| Wheelbase, in. | 115.9 | 119.7 | 123.6 |
| Overall length, in. | 199.4 | 201.3 | 205.2 |
| Overall width, in. | 75.3 | 74.3 | 74.3 |
| Overall height, in. | 56.9 | 58.5 | 58.5 |
| Curb weight, lbs. | 4700 | 4480 | 4700 |
| Cargo vol., cu. ft. | 14.2 | 15.6 | 15.6 |
| Fuel capacity, gals. | 26.4 | 26.4 | 26.4 |
| Seating capacity | 5 | 5 | 5 |
| Front head room, in. | 36.5 | 38.0 | 38.0 |
| Max. front leg room, in. | 41.7 | 41.3 | 41.3 |
| Rear head room, in. | 37.2 | 37.8 | 38.5 |
| Min. rear leg room, in. | 31.5 | 36.1 | 39.6 |

| ENGINES | dohc I-6 | dohc V-8 | dohc V-8 | dohc V-12 |
|---|---|---|---|---|
| Size, liters/cu. in. | 3.2/195 | 4.2/256 | 5.0/303 | 6.0/365 |
| Horsepower @ rpm | 228@ 5600 | 275@ 5700 | 315@ 5600 | 389@ 5200 |
| Torque (lbs./ft.) @ rpm | 232@ 3750 | 295@ 3900 | 347@ 3900 | 420@ 3800 |
| Availability | S[1] | S[2] | S[3] | S[4] |
| **EPA city/highway mpg** | | | | |
| 5-speed OD automatic | 17/23 | 15/22 | 15/22[5] | 13/19 |

1. S320.  2. S420.  3. S500, CL500.  4. S600, CL600.  5. 15/21 on S500.

*Prices are accurate at time of publication; subject to manufacturer's change.*

# MERCEDES-BENZ

## Mercedes-Benz S-Class/CL-Class

| | Retail Price | Dealer Invoice |
|---|---|---|
| S320 4-door sedan (119.7-inch wheelbase) | $64000 | $55680 |
| S320 4-door sedan (123.6-inch wheelbase) | 67300 | 58550 |
| S420 4-door sedan | 73900 | 64290 |
| S500 4-door sedan | 87500 | 76120 |
| CL500 2-door notchback | 91900 | 79950 |
| S600 4-door sedan | 132250 | 115060 |
| CL600 2-door notchback | 135300 | 117710 |
| Destination charge | 595 | 595 |

S420/CL500 add Gas Guzzler Tax $1300. S500 add Gas Guzzler Tax $1700. CL600 add Gas Guzzler Tax $2600. S600 add Gas Guzzler Tax $3000.

## STANDARD EQUIPMENT:

**S320:** 3.2-liter dohc 6-cylinder engine, 5-speed automatic transmission, ASR traction control, driver- and passenger-side air bags w/automatic child seat recognition system, front side-impact air bags, anti-lock 4-wheel disc brakes, air conditioning w/dual-zone automatic climate control, variable-assist power steering, power tilt/telescopic steering column w/memory feature, leather-wrapped steering wheel and shift knob, cruise control, power memory mirrors, automatic day/night inside and driver-side outside mirror, power windows, power door locks, leather upholstery, remote keyless entry and decklid release, 12-way power front bucket seats w/memory feature, front storage console, power glass sunroof, Bose AM/FM/cassette, power antenna, tachometer, oil-pressure gauge, trip odometer, rear defogger, headlamp wipers/washers (123.6-inch wheelbase), rain-sensing windshield wipers, Homelink universal garage-door opener, front reading lights, rear reading lights, illuminated front and rear visor mirrors, floormats, cargo net, theft-deterrent system, front and rear fog lights, full-size spare tire, 225/60HR16 tires, alloy wheels.

**S420** adds: 4.2-liter dohc V-8 engine, 235/60HR16 tires.

**S500/CL500** adds: 5.0-liter dohc V-8 engine, automatic rear leveling system, upgraded leather upholstery (CL), heated front seats, heated rear seats (S), Parktronic system (CL), rear storage console (CL), Xenon headlamps.

**S600/CL600** adds: 6.0-liter dohc V-12 engine, upgraded leather upholstery, multicontour power front seats, power rear seats (S), rear dual-zone air conditioner, 6-disc CD changer, portable cellular telephone, power rear-window sunshade, Adaptive Damping System, Electronic Stability Program.

## OPTIONAL EQUIPMENT:
### Comfort and Convenience

| | | |
|---|---|---|
| Dual zone rear air conditioner, S320, S420, S500 | 2010 | 1749 |

| | Retail Price | Dealer Invoice |
|---|---|---|
| Parktronic system, S320, S420, S500, S600 | $975 | $848 |
| Power rear-window sunshade | 495 | 431 |
| Std. S600, CL600. | | |
| Multicontour power front seats, each | 390 | 339 |
| Std. S600, CL600. | | |
| 4-place power seating, S500 4-door, S600 4-door | 5540 | 4820 |
| Power rear seat, S500 | 1750 | 1522 |
| Heated front seats, S320, S420 | 595 | 518 |
| Headlamp washers, S320 (119.7-inch wheelbase) | 340 | 296 |

## Appearance and Miscellaneous

| | Retail Price | Dealer Invoice |
|---|---|---|
| Adaptive Damping System, S500, CL500 | 2270 | 1975 |
| Includes automatic rear leveling system. | | |
| Automatic rear leveling system, S320, S420 | 940 | 818 |
| Electronic Stability Program, S320, S420, S500 | 990 | 861 |
| Xenon headlamps, S320, S420 | 960 | 835 |

# MERCEDES-BENZ SL-CLASS

*Mercedes-Benz SL-Class*

## SPECIFICATIONS

| | 2-door conv. |
|---|---|
| Wheelbase, in. | 99.0 |
| Overall length, in. | 177.1 |
| Overall width, in. | 71.3 |
| Overall height, in. | 51.3 |
| Curb weight, lbs. | 4165 |
| Cargo vol., cu. ft. | 7.9 |

*Prices are accurate at time of publication; subject to manufacturer's change.*

# MERCEDES-BENZ

|  | 2-door conv. |
|---|---|
| Fuel capacity, gals. | 21.1 |
| Seating capacity | 2 |
| Front head room, in. | 37.1 |
| Max. front leg room, in. | 42.4 |
| Rear head room, in. | — |
| Min. rear leg room, in. | — |

## ENGINES

|  | dohc V-8 | dohc V-12 |
|---|---|---|
| Size, liters/cu. in. | 5.0/303 | 6.0/365 |
| Horsepower @ rpm | 315@ 5600 | 389@ 5200 |
| Torque (lbs./ft.) @ rpm | 343@ 3900 | 420@ 3800 |
| Availability | S[1] | S[2] |
| **EPA city/highway mpg** | | |
| 5-speed OD automatic | 16/23 | 14/20 |

1. SL500. 2. SL600.

| Mercedes-Benz SL-Class | Retail Price | Dealer Invoice |
|---|---|---|
| SL500 2-door convertible | $79900 | $69510 |
| SL600 2-door convertible | 125000 | 108750 |
| Destination charge | 595 | 595 |

SL500 add Gas Guzzler Tax $1000. SL600 add Gas Guzzler Tax $2100.

## STANDARD EQUIPMENT:

**SL500:** 5.0-liter dohc V-8 engine, 5-speed automatic transmission, ASR traction control, driver- and passenger-side air bags w/BabySmart automatic child recognition system, side-impact air bags, pop-up roll bar, anti-lock 4-wheel disc brakes, air conditioning w/automatic climate control, interior air filter, power steering, power tilt/telescopic steering column w/memory feature, leather-wrapped steering wheel and shifter, cruise control, leather upholstery, 10-way power front seats w/memory feature, front storage console, Bose AM/FM/cassette, power antenna, heated power mirrors w/memory feature, driver-side mirror w/automatic day/night, power windows, power door locks, remote keyless entry, tachometer, oil-pressure gauges, trip odometer, illuminated visor mirrors, remote decklid and fuel-door release, rear defogger, universal garage-door opener, automatic variable intermittent wipers, automatic day/night rearview mirror w/memory feature, reading lights, floormats, power convertible top, removable hardtop, theft-deterrent system, heated headlamp wipers/washers, front and rear fog lights, 225/55ZR16 tires, alloy wheels.

**SL600** adds: 6.0-liter dohc V-12 engine, upgraded leather upholstery, heated front seats, 6-disc CD changer, portable cellular telephone,

Adaptive Damping System, Electronic Stability Program, Xenon headlights, deletes headlight washer nozzles.

## OPTIONAL EQUIPMENT:

| | Retail Price | Dealer Invoice |
|---|---|---|
| **Major Packages** | | |
| Sport Pkg. | $4970 | $4324 |
| *Ground effects, badging, 245/40ZR18 front tires, 275/35ZR18 rear tires, monoblock alloy wheels.* | | |
| **Comfort and Convenience** | | |
| Heated front seats, SL500 | 595 | 518 |
| Multicontour power front seats, each | 390 | 339 |
| **Appearance and Miscellaneous** | | |
| Removable panorama roof | 3600 | 3132 |
| Xenon headlights, SL500 | 960 | 835 |
| *Deletes headlight washer nozzles.* | | |
| Adaptive Damping System, SL500 | 4390 | 3819 |
| *Includes automatic rear leveling system.* | | |
| Electronic Stability Program, SL500 | 990 | 861 |

# MERCEDES-BENZ SLK230

*Mercedes-Benz SLK*

## SPECIFICATIONS

| | 2-door conv. |
|---|---|
| Wheelbase, in. | 94.5 |
| Overall length, in. | 157.3 |
| Overall width, in. | 67.5 |
| Overall height, in. | 50.7 |
| Curb weight, lbs. | 3036 |
| Cargo vol., cu. ft. | 9.5 |

*Prices are accurate at time of publication; subject to manufacturer's change.*

# MERCEDES-BENZ

| | 2-door conv. |
|---|---|
| Fuel capacity, gals. | 14.0 |
| Seating capacity | 2 |
| Front head room, in. | 37.4 |
| Max. front leg room, in. | 42.7 |
| Rear head room, in. | — |
| Min. rear leg room, in. | — |

## ENGINES

| | Super dohc I-4 |
|---|---|
| Size, liters/cu. in. | 2.3/140 |
| Horsepower @ rpm | 185@ 5300 |
| Torque (lbs./ft.) @ rpm | 200@ 2500 |
| Availability | S |

| Mercedes-Benz SLK230 | Retail Price | Dealer Invoice |
|---|---|---|
| SLK 2-door convertible | $39700 | $34540 |
| Destination charge | 600 | 600 |

## STANDARD EQUIPMENT:

**SLK:** 2.3-liter supercharged dohc 4-cylinder engine, 5-speed automatic transmission, ASR Traction System, driver- and passenger-side air bags with BabySmart automatic child recognition system, door mounted side-impact air bags, anti-lock 4-wheel disc brakes, power steering, air conditioning and dual-zone climate control with dust/pollen filter, cruise control, leather upholstery, cupholders and coinholders, rear window defroster, manually telescoping steering wheel, leather-wrapped steering wheel, power locks, power windows, power heated mirrors, outside temperature readout, integrated garage door opener, AM/FM/cassette, remote keyless entry, remote trunk release, tachometer, power retractable steel hardtop, tinted glass, theft-deterrent system, heated headlight washers, fog lamps, 205/55R16 tires (front), 225/50R16 tires (rear), alloy wheels.

## OPTIONAL EQUIPMENT:
### Comfort and Convenience

| | | |
|---|---|---|
| Heated seats | 595 | 518 |
| K1 Pkg. | 1495 | 1087 |
| *Includes integrated mobile phone and 6-disc CD changer.* | | |
| K2 Pkg. | 1895 | 1445 |
| *Includes integrated portable phone and 6-disc CD changer.* | | |

### Appearance and Miscellaneous

| | | |
|---|---|---|
| Metallic paint | 600 | 522 |

　　　　　　　　　　CONSUMER GUIDE™

# MERCURY GRAND MARQUIS

Mercury Grand Marquis LS

## SPECIFICATIONS

| | 4-door sedan |
|---|---|
| Wheelbase, in. | 114.4 |
| Overall length, in. | 212.0 |
| Overall width, in. | 77.9 |
| Overall height, in. | 56.8 |
| Curb weight, lbs. | 3917 |
| Cargo vol., cu. ft. | 20.6 |
| Fuel capacity, gals. | 19.0 |
| Seating capacity | 6 |
| Front head room, in. | 39.4 |
| Max. front leg room, in. | 42.5 |
| Rear head room, in. | 38.0 |
| Min. rear leg room, in. | 39.6 |

## ENGINES

| | ohc V-8 | ohc V-8 |
|---|---|---|
| Size, liters/cu. in. | 4.6/281 | 4.6/281 |
| Horsepower @ rpm | 200@ 4250[1] | 215@ 4500 |
| Torque (lbs./ft.) @ rpm | 265@ 3000[2] | 275@ 3000 |
| Availability | S | O |
| **EPA city/highway mpg** | | |
| 4-speed OD automatic | 17/25 | 17/25 |

1. 210 hp with dual exhaust. 2. 275 lbs/ft torque with dual exhaust.

| Mercury Grand Marquis | Retail Price | Dealer Invoice |
|---|---|---|
| GS 4-door sedan | $21890 | $20455 |

*Prices are accurate at time of publication; subject to manufacturer's change.*

# MERCURY

| | Retail Price | Dealer Invoice |
|---|---|---|
| LS 4-door sedan | $23790 | $22184 |
| Destination charge | 605 | 605 |

## STANDARD EQUIPMENT:

**GS:** 4.6-liter V-8 engine, 4-speed automatic transmission, driver- and passenger-side air bags, 4-wheel disc brakes, air conditioning, variable-assist power steering, tilt steering wheel, cruise control, cloth front split bench seat, 8-way power driver seat, front folding armrest, power door locks, power windows, power mirrors, oil-pressure and coolant-temperature gauges, voltmeter, trip odometer, AM/FM/cassette, integrated rear-window antenna, digital clock, intermittent wipers, rear defogger, passenger-side visor mirror, automatic headlamps, rear heat ducts, power remote decklid release, floormats, theft-deterrent system, cornering lights, solar-control tinted glass, 225/60R16 tires, wheel covers.

**LS** adds: upgraded upholstery, power driver-seat lumbar adjuster, rear-seat folding armrest, remote keyless entry, illuminated visor mirrors, dual map lights, rear reading lights, body stripes.

## OPTIONAL EQUIPMENT:
### Major Packages

| | | |
|---|---|---|
| Premium Pkg., LS | 1000 | 890 |

*Automatic climate control, power passenger seat w/power lumbar, leather-wrapped steering wheel, automatic day/night rearview mirror, compass, alloy wheels.*

| | | |
|---|---|---|
| Ultimate Pkg., LS | 2400 | 2136 |

*Premium Pkg. plus anti-lock brakes, traction control, electronic instrumentation, premium AM/FM/cassette.*

### Safety Features

| | | |
|---|---|---|
| Anti-lock brakes w/Traction-Assist | 775 | 690 |

### Comfort and Convenience

| | | |
|---|---|---|
| Automatic climate control, LS | 175 | 156 |

*Includes outside-temperature indicator.*

| | | |
|---|---|---|
| Electronic instrumentation, LS | 425 | 379 |

*Digital instrumentation, tripminder computer. Requires Automatic climate control.*

| | | |
|---|---|---|
| Luxury Light Group, GS | 190 | 169 |

*Includes dual dome/map lights, rear reading lights, visors, illuminated visor mirrors.*

| | | |
|---|---|---|
| Keyless entry system, GS | 240 | 213 |
| Universal garage door opener, LS | 115 | 102 |
| Leather upholstery, LS | 735 | 654 |

*Requires Premium Pkg. or Ultimate Pkg.*

| | Retail Price | Dealer Invoice |
|---|---|---|
| CD player, GS | $140 | $124 |
| 6-disc CD player, LS | 350 | 312 |
| *Requires Ultimate Pkg.* | | |

## Appearance and Miscellaneous

| | | |
|---|---|---|
| Engine-block heater | 25 | 23 |
| Striping, GS | 60 | 54 |
| Handling Pkg., GS | 855 | 761 |
| LS | 535 | 476 |
| *Includes rear air suspension, tuned suspension, larger rear stabilizer bar, dual exhaust, 3.27 axle ratio, 225/60R16 handling tires, alloy wheels.* | | |
| Rear air suspension, LS | 270 | 240 |
| *Tuned for softer ride.* | | |
| Full-size spare tire, LS | 105 | 93 |
| LS w/Handling Pkg. | 120 | 107 |
| Alloy wheels, LS | 320 | 285 |

# MERCURY MOUNTAINEER

*Mercury Mountaineer*

## SPECIFICATIONS

| | 4-door wagon |
|---|---|
| Wheelbase, in. | 111.5 |
| Overall length, in. | 188.5 |
| Overall width, in. | 70.2 |
| Overall height, in. | 67.6 |
| Curb weight, lbs. | 4139 |
| Cargo vol., cu. ft. | 81.6 |
| Fuel capacity, gals. | 21.0 |

*Prices are accurate at time of publication; subject to manufacturer's change.*

# MERCURY

| | 4-door wagon |
|---|---|
| Seating capacity | 5 |
| Front head room, in. | 39.9 |
| Max. front leg room, in. | 42.4 |
| Rear head room, in. | 39.3 |
| Min. rear leg room, in. | 37.7 |

## ENGINES

| | ohc V-6 | ohv V-8 |
|---|---|---|
| Size, liters/cu. in. | 4.0/245 | 5.0/302 |
| Horsepower @ rpm | 205@ 5000 | 215@ 4200 |
| Torque (lbs./ft.) @ rpm | 250@ 3000 | 288@ 3300 |
| Availability | S | O |

### EPA city/highway mpg

| | | |
|---|---|---|
| 4-speed OD automatic | | 14/19[2] |
| 5-speed automatic | 15/20[1] | |

*1. 15/19 w/4WD. 2. 14/18 w/AWD.*

| Mercury Mountaineer | Retail Price | Dealer Invoice |
|---|---|---|
| 4-door wagon, 2WD | $26680 | $24118 |
| 4-door wagon, 4WD | 28680 | 25878 |
| 4-door wagon, AWD | 28680 | 25878 |
| Destination charge | 525 | 525 |

All models require a Preferred Equipment Pkg.

## STANDARD EQUIPMENT:

**2WD:** 4.0-liter V-6 engine, 5-speed automatic transmission, driver- and passenger-side air bags, anti-lock 4-wheel disc brakes, air conditioning, power steering, tilt leather-wrapped steering wheel, cruise control, cloth front captain's chairs, split folding rear seat, floor console w/cupholders, power mirrors, power windows, power door locks, tachometer, trip odometer, oil pressure gauge, rear wiper/washer, rear defogger, AM/FM/cassette, digital clock, illuminated visor mirrors, speed-sensitive intermittent wipers, auxiliary power outlets, door map pockets, map lights, theft-deterrent system, front solar-tinted glass, rear privacy glass, dual-note horn, fog lights, full-size spare, 225/70R15 tires, alloy wheels.

**4WD** adds: permanent 4-wheel drive, traction control, skid plates.

**AWD** adds: 5.0-liter V-8 engine, 4-speed automatic transmission, limited-slip differential, 235/75R15 all-terrain outline white-letter tires.

## OPTIONAL EQUIPMENT:

| | Retail Price | Dealer Invoice |
|---|---|---|

### Major Packages

| | Retail Price | Dealer Invoice |
|---|---|---|
| Preferred Equipment Pkg. 650A | $620 | $527 |
| *Manufacturer's discount price* | 115 | 98 |

*Running boards, roof rack, floormats. NA in CA, HI.*

| | | |
|---|---|---|
| Preferred Equipment Pkg. 655A | 2650 | 2253 |
| *Manufacturer's discount price* | 1300 | 1105 |

*Pkg. 650A plus 6-way power front sport bucket seats w/power lumbar support, cassette/CD player, upgraded floor console (includes rear climate and radio controls, cupholders), overhead console (includes outside temperature gauge, compass, reading lamps, storage), Electronics Group (remote keyless entry, theft-deterrent system w/alarm, puddle lights), cargo cover.*

| | | |
|---|---|---|
| Preferred Equipment Pkg. 660A | 4275 | 3634 |
| *Manufacturer's discount price* | 2525 | 2146 |

*Pkg. 655A plus leather upholstery, Appearance Group (2-tone paint, stripes, chrome alloy wheels), Ford Mach audio cassette/CD player w/power antenna.*

| | | |
|---|---|---|
| Electronics Group | 410 | 348 |

*Includes remote keyless entry, theft-deterrent system w/alarm, puddle lights. Requires sport bucket seats.*

| | | |
|---|---|---|
| Appearance Group | 495 | 421 |

*Includes 2-tone paint, stripes, chrome wheels. Requires Pkg. 655A.*

### Powertrains

| | | |
|---|---|---|
| 5.0-liter V-8 engine, 2WD | 465 | 395 |

*Includes 4-speed automatic transmission, limited-slip differential, 3.73 axle ratio, 235/75R15 all-terrain tires. NA 4WD.*

| | | |
|---|---|---|
| Limited-slip differential, 2WD, 4WD | 355 | 302 |

*Includes trailer towing pkg. and 3.73 axle ratio.*

### Comfort and Convenience

| | | |
|---|---|---|
| Cloth sport bucket seats, with Pkg. 650A | 650 | 553 |

*Includes 6-way power front seats and dual power lumbar supports. NA in CA, HI.*

| | | |
|---|---|---|
| Leather sport bucket seats, with Pkg. 655A. | 655 | 557 |

*Includes 6-way power driver's seat and dual power lumbar supports.*

| | | |
|---|---|---|
| Integrated child seats | 200 | 170 |

*Requires leather sport bucket seats.*

| | | |
|---|---|---|
| Automatic day/night rearview mirror | 185 | 158 |

*Includes automatic on/off headlamps. Requires Pkg. 655A, 660A.*

| | | |
|---|---|---|
| Power moonroof | 800 | 680 |

*Requires Pkg. 655A, 660A.*

| | | |
|---|---|---|
| CD player | 150 | 128 |
| Multi-disc CD changer | 370 | 314 |

*Requires Pkg. 655A, 660A.*

*Prices are accurate at time of publication; subject to manufacturer's change.*

| | Retail Price | Dealer Invoice |
|---|---|---|
| Cassette/CD player | $325 | $277 |
| Ford Mach audio cassette/CD player | 475 | 403 |
| *Requires Pkg. 655A.* | | |
| Cargo cover | 80 | 68 |

## Appearance and Miscellaneous
| | | |
|---|---|---|
| Engine block heater | 35 | 30 |

## Special Purpose, Wheels and Tires
| | | |
|---|---|---|
| 235/75R15 all-terrain tires, 2WD, 4WD | 230 | 196 |

# MERCURY MYSTIQUE

*Mercury Mystique LS*

## SPECIFICATIONS

| | 4-door sedan |
|---|---|
| Wheelbase, in. | 106.5 |
| Overall length, in. | 184.8 |
| Overall width, in. | 69.1 |
| Overall height, in. | 54.5 |
| Curb weight, lbs. | 2808 |
| Cargo vol., cu. ft. | 13.9 |
| Fuel capacity, gals. | 14.5 |
| Seating capacity | 5 |
| Front head room, in. | 39.0 |
| Max. front leg room, in. | 42.4 |
| Rear head room, in. | 36.8 |
| Min. rear leg room, in. | 34.4 |

## ENGINES

| | dohc I-4 | dohc V-6 |
|---|---|---|
| Size, liters/cu. in. | 2.0/121 | 2.5/155 |

| | dohc I-4 | dohc V-6 |
|---|---|---|
| Horsepower @ rpm | 125@ 5500 | 170@ 6250 |
| Torque (lbs./ft.) @ rpm | 130@ 4000 | 165@ 4250 |
| Availability | S[1] | S[2] |
| **EPA city/highway mpg** | | |
| 5-speed OD manual | 24/35 | 19/28 |
| 4-speed OD automatic | 24/32 | 21/30 |

1. GS  2. LS

| **Mercury Mystique** | Retail Price | Dealer Invoice |
|---|---|---|
| GS 4-door sedan | $16235 | $14844 |
| LS 4-door sedan | 17645 | 16099 |
| Destination charge | 535 | 535 |

## STANDARD EQUIPMENT:

**GS:** 2.0-liter dohc 4-cylinder engine, 5-speed manual transmission, driver- and passenger-side air bags, air conditioning, cruise control, power mirrors, power windows, power door locks, rear defogger, power steering, tilt steering wheel, cloth reclining front bucket seats, front storage console, tachometer, coolant-temperature gauge, trip odometer, AM/FM/cassette, digital clock, intermittent wipers, remote decklid release, interior air filter, visor mirrors, solar-control tinted glass, 185/70R14 tires, wheel covers.

**LS adds:** 2.5-liter V-6 engine, 4-wheel disc brakes (w/manual transmission), 10-way power driver seat, remote keyless entry, leather upholstery, leather-wrapped steering wheel, 60/40 split folding rear seat, variable intermittent wipers, illuminated passenger-side visor mirror, floormats, fog lights, performance suspension and steering, 205/60R15 tires, polished Mach alloy wheels.

## OPTIONAL EQUIPMENT:
### Major Packages

| | | |
|---|---|---|
| Sport Group, GS | 395 | 352 |

*Leather-wrapped steering wheel, sport floormats, rear spoiler, fog lights, sport badging.*

### Powertrains

| | | |
|---|---|---|
| 4-speed automatic transmission | 815 | 725 |

### Safety Features

| | | |
|---|---|---|
| Anti-lock brakes | 500 | 445 |
| Integrated child seat, GS | 135 | 120 |
| LS | NC | NC |

*NA w/leather upholstery.*

*Prices are accurate at time of publication; subject to manufacturer's change.*

## Comfort and Convenience

| | Retail Price | Dealer Invoice |
|---|---|---|
| Split folding rear seat, GS | $205 | $182 |
| 10-way power driver seat, GS | 350 | 312 |
| Power moonroof | 595 | 530 |
| Remote keyless entry, GS | 190 | 169 |
| Premium cassette player | 135 | 120 |
| CD player | 275 | 245 |
| *Includes premium sound.* | | |
| Power antenna | 95 | 85 |
| Smoker's Pkg. | 15 | 13 |
| *Includes ashtray, cigarette lighter.* | | |
| Floormats, GS | 55 | 49 |

## Appearance and Miscellaneous

| | | |
|---|---|---|
| Rear spoiler, GS, LS | 245 | 218 |
| Engine-block heater | 20 | 18 |
| Mach alloy wheels, GS | 475 | 423 |
| *Includes 205/60R15 tires.* | | |
| Polished Mach alloy wheels, GS | 475 | 423 |
| *Includes 205/60R15 tires.* | | |

# MERCURY SABLE

*Mercury Sable GS wagon*

## SPECIFICATIONS

| | 4-door sedan | 4-door wagon |
|---|---|---|
| Wheelbase, in. | 108.5 | 108.5 |
| Overall length, in. | 199.7 | 199.1 |
| Overall width, in. | 73.0 | 73.0 |
| Overall height, in. | 55.4 | 57.6 |
| Curb weight, lbs. | 3388 | 3536 |
| Cargo vol., cu. ft. | 16.0 | 81.3 |
| Fuel capacity, gals. | 16.0 | 16.0 |
| Seating capacity | 6 | 8 |

| | 4-door sedan | 4-door wagon |
|---|---|---|
| Front head room, in. | 39.4 | 39.3 |
| Max. front leg room, in. | 42.2 | 42.2 |
| Rear head room, in. | 36.6 | 38.9 |
| Min. rear leg room, in. | 38.9 | 38.5 |

## ENGINES

| | ohv V-6 | dohc V-6 |
|---|---|---|
| Size, liters/cu. in. | 3.0/182 | 3.0/181 |
| Horsepower @ rpm | 145@ 5250 | 200@ 5750 |
| Torque (lbs./ft.) @ rpm | 170@ 3250 | 200@ 4500 |
| Availability | S | O |

**EPA city/highway mpg**

| | | |
|---|---|---|
| 4-speed OD automatic | 19/28 | 18/27 |

| Mercury Sable | Retail Price | Dealer Invoice |
|---|---|---|
| GS 4-door sedan | $19445 | $17781 |
| LS 4-door sedan | 20445 | 18761 |
| LS 4-door wagon | 22285 | 20309 |
| LS Premium 4-door sedan | 20445 | 18761 |
| LS Premium 4-door wagon | 22285 | 20309 |
| Destination charge | 550 | 550 |

LS Premium models require Premium Pkg.

## STANDARD EQUIPMENT:

**GS:** 3.0-liter V-6 engine, 4-speed automatic transmission, driver- and passenger-side air bags, air conditioning, variable-assist power steering, cruise control, tilt steering wheel, 6-passenger seating (cloth upholstery, reclining front bucket seats w/center seating console, 60/40 split-folding rear seat), cupholders, front armrest, tachometer, coolant temperature gauge, trip odometer, AM/FM/cassette player w/six speakers, digital clock, power mirrors, power windows, power door locks, variable intermittent wipers, rear defogger, remote decklid release, visor mirrors, rear heat ducts, solar-control tinted glass, 205/65R15 tires, wheel covers.

**LS/LS Premium sedan** add: rear air conditioning, interior air filter, 5-passenger seating (cloth/leather upholstery, reclining front bucket seats w/6-way power driver seat, 60/40 split-folding rear seat), rear armrest, floor console, leather-wrapped steering wheel and shifter, remote keyless entry, remote fuel-door release, Light Group (courtesy, reading, map, and dome lights), alloy wheels.

**LS/LS Premium wagon** add: 4-wheel disc brakes, rear wiper/washer, power antenna, cargo tie-downs, cargo-area light, luggage rack, deletes remote rear decklid release.

*Prices are accurate at time of publication; subject to manufacturer's change.*

## OPTIONAL EQUIPMENT:

| | Retail Price | Dealer Invoice |
|---|---|---|
| **Major Packages** | | |
| Premium Pkg., LS Premium sedan | $825 | $735 |
| LS Premium wagon | 675 | 601 |
| *Duratec 3.0-liter dohc V-6 engine, automatic air conditioning, automatic headlights, illuminated visor mirrors, power antenna (sedan), key pad entry system, theft-deterrent system.* | | |
| **Powertrains** | | |
| Duratec 3.0-liter dohc V-6 engine, GS, LS | 495 | 441 |
| **Safety Features** | | |
| Anti-lock 4-wheel disc brakes, GS | 600 | 534 |
| *Includes 4-wheel disc brakes.* | | |
| Daytime running lights | 40 | 36 |
| *Includes heavy-duty battery.* | | |
| Integrated child seat, wagon | 135 | 120 |
| **Comfort and Convenience** | | |
| Remote keyless entry, GS | 190 | 169 |
| Light Group, GS | 45 | 41 |
| *Courtesy, reading, map, and dome lights.* | | |
| Power moonroof, LS, LS Premium | 740 | 658 |
| Ford Mach audio system, LS | 400 | 357 |
| LS Premium | 320 | 286 |
| *Sedan includes power antenna.* | | |
| 6-disc CD changer | 350 | 312 |
| Leather upholstery, LS, | | |
| LS Premium | 895 | 797 |
| Bucket seats with center console, GS | NC | NC |
| Front split bench seat, | | |
| LS, LS Premium | NC | NC |
| Rear-facing third seat, wagon | 200 | 178 |
| Interior air filter, GS | 30 | 27 |
| Heated mirrors | 35 | 31 |
| Floormats | 55 | 49 |
| Wagon Group, wagon | 140 | 124 |
| *Cargo-area cover, cargo net.* | | |
| **Appearance and Miscellaneous** | | |
| Engine-block heater | 35 | 31 |
| Full-size spare tire | 125 | 112 |
| Alloy wheels, GS | 315 | 280 |
| Chrome alloy wheels, | | |
| LS, LS Premium | 580 | 516 |

# MERCURY TRACER

*Mercury Tracer Trio sedan*

## SPECIFICATIONS

| | 4-door sedan | 4-door wagon |
|---|---|---|
| Wheelbase, in. | 98.4 | 98.4 |
| Overall length, in. | 174.7 | 172.7 |
| Overall width, in. | 67.0 | 67.0 |
| Overall height, in. | 53.3 | 53.9 |
| Curb weight, lbs. | 2469 | 2532 |
| Cargo vol., cu. ft. | 12.8 | 63.4 |
| Fuel capacity, gals. | 12.8 | 12.8 |
| Seating capacity | 5 | 5 |
| Front head room, in. | 39.0 | 38.7 |
| Max. front leg room, in. | 42.5 | 42.5 |
| Rear head room, in. | 36.7 | 39.1 |
| Min. rear leg room, in. | 34.0 | 34.0 |

## ENGINES

| | ohc I-4 |
|---|---|
| Size, liters/cu. in. | 2.0/121 |
| Horsepower @ rpm | 110@ 5000 |
| Torque (lbs./ft.) @ rpm | 125@ 3750 |
| Availability | S |

### EPA city/highway mpg
| | |
|---|---|
| 5-speed OD manual | 28/38 |
| 4-speed OD automatic | 25/34 |

| Mercury Tracer | Retail Price | Dealer Invoice |
|---|---|---|
| GS 4-door sedan | $11355 | $10653 |
| LS 4-door sedan | 12710 | 11886 |
| LS 4-door wagon | 14205 | 13246 |
| Destination charge | 415 | 415 |

*Prices are accurate at time of publication; subject to manufacturer's change.*

## STANDARD EQUIPMENT:

**GS:** 2.0-liter 4-cylinder engine, 5-speed manual transmission, driver- and passenger-side air bags, power steering, cloth and vinyl reclining bucket seats, split folding rear seat, center console with cupholders, passenger-side visor mirror, coolant temperature gauge, trip odometer, AM/FM radio, digital clock, variable intermittent wipers, door pockets, color-keyed body-side moldings, tinted glass, dual outside mirrors, 185/65R14 tires, wheel covers.

**LS sedan** adds: air conditioning, power mirrors, rear defogger, driver door remote keyless entry, upgraded upholstery, tachometer, color-keyed steering wheel, trunk light, bolt-on full wheel covers.

**LS wagon** adds: rear wiper/washer, cargo cover, roof rack.

## OPTIONAL EQUIPMENT:

### Major Packages

| | Retail Price | Dealer Invoice |
|---|---|---|
| Trio Appearance Group, GS | $260 | $232 |
| *Leather-wrapped steering wheel, rear spoiler, badging, chrome wheel covers.* | | |
| Sport Group, LS sedan | 515 | 458 |
| *Cloth sport bucket seats, leather-wrapped steering wheel, rear spoiler, fog lights, bright exhaust tip, alloy wheels.* | | |
| Comfort Group, LS | 365 | 325 |
| *Cruise control, tilt steering wheel, dual visor mirrors, map lights, floormats.* | | |
| Power Group, LS | 395 | 352 |
| *Power windows and door locks, all-door remote keyless entry.* | | |

### Powertrains

| | | |
|---|---|---|
| 4-speed automatic transmission | 815 | 725 |

### Safety Features

| | | |
|---|---|---|
| Anti-lock 4-wheel disc brakes | 400 | 356 |
| Integrated child seat, LS wagon | 135 | 120 |

### Comfort and Convenience

| | | |
|---|---|---|
| Air conditioning, GS | 795 | 708 |
| Rear defogger, GS | 190 | 169 |
| AM/FM/cassette | 185 | 165 |
| *GS requires rear defogger or air conditioning.* | | |
| Premium AM/FM/cassette, LS sedan | 255 | 227 |
| *GS requires rear defogger or air conditioning.* | | |
| AM/FM/cassette w/6-disc CD changer, LS sedan | 515 | 458 |
| *Includes premium sound system.* | | |
| Power mirrors, GS | 95 | 85 |
| Remote keyless entry, GS | 135 | 120 |
| *Driver door only.* | | |

## Appearance and Miscellaneous

| | Retail Price | Dealer Invoice |
|---|---|---|
| Engine block heater | $20 | $18 |
| Alloy wheels, LS | 265 | 236 |

# MERCURY VILLAGER

*Mercury Villager Nautica*

## SPECIFICATIONS

| | 3-door van |
|---|---|
| Wheelbase, in. | 112.2 |
| Overall length, in. | 189.9 |
| Overall width, in. | 73.8 |
| Overall height, in. | 65.6 |
| Curb weight, lbs. | 3815 |
| Cargo vol., cu. ft. | 120.0 |
| Maximum payload, lbs. | 1200 |
| Fuel capacity, gals. | 20.0 |
| Seating capacity | 7 |
| Front head room, in. | 39.4 |
| Max. front leg room, in. | 39.9 |
| Rear head room, in. | 39.7 |
| Min. rear leg room, in. | 36.3 |

## ENGINES

| | ohc V-6 |
|---|---|
| Size, liters/cu. in. | 3.0/181 |
| Horsepower @ rpm | 151@ 4800 |
| Torque (lbs./ft.) @ rpm | 174@ 4400 |
| Availability | S |

**EPA city/highway mpg**

| | |
|---|---|
| 4-speed OD automatic | 17/23 |

*Prices are accurate at time of publication; subject to manufacturer's change.*

# MERCURY

| Mercury Villager | Retail Price | Dealer Invoice |
|---|---|---|
| Cargo 3-door van | $20350 | $18444 |
| GS 3-door van | 20705 | 18755 |
| LS 3-door van | 24975 | 22513 |
| Nautica 3-door van | 26805 | 24123 |
| Destination charge | 580 | 580 |

GS, LS, Nautica require a Preferred Equipment Pkg. Nautica not available in Calif. and Hawaii.

## STANDARD EQUIPMENT:

**Cargo:** 3.0-liter V-6 engine, 4-speed automatic transmission, driver- and passenger-side air bags, anti-lock brakes, power steering, tilt steering column, cloth upholstery, reclining front bucket seats, front carpeting, front headliner, AM/FM/cassette, tachometer, coolant-temperature gauge, trip odometer, visor mirrors, variable-intermittent wipers, rear wiper/washer, rear defogger, floormats, dual outside mirrors, cornering lamps, 205/75R15 tires, wheel covers.

**GS adds:** 5-passenger seating with 3-passenger second-row bench seat, rear carpeting, rear headliner, front and rear cupholders, visor mirrors, rear storage bin, solar-tinted glass, color-keyed bodyside molding, deletes anti-lock brakes and rear defogger.

**LS adds:** anti-lock brakes, front air conditioning, 7-passenger seating (reclining front bucket seats, 3-passenger second-row bench seat, 2-passenger rear bench seat), seatback map pockets, lockable underseat storage bin, rear auxiliary power outlet, power windows, power door locks, power mirrors, Light Group (overhead dual map lights, dual liftgate lights, front door step lights, power rear vent windows, under instrument panel lights with time delay), rear defogger, privacy glass, roof rack, 2-tone paint, color-keyed bodyside molding w/chrome strip.

**Nautica adds:** leather quad captain's chairs, unique exterior paint, color-keyed bodyside molding w/yellow Mylar insert, unique grille, firm-ride suspension, rear stabilizer bar, 215/70R15 tires, alloy wheels.

## OPTIONAL EQUIPMENT:
### Major Packages

| | | |
|---|---|---|
| Base Pkg., GS available in Calif., Hawaii (credit) | (1800) | (1532) |

*Deletes anti-lock brakes, rear air conditioning, 6-way power driver seat, passenger-under-seat storage drawer, remote keyless entry, privacy glass, flip-open liftgate window, roof rack, alloy wheels. Requires Pkg. 692C.*

| | | |
|---|---|---|
| Preferred Equipment Pkg. 691A, GS | 2960 | 2515 |
| *Manufacturer's discount price, GS* | 1600 | 1359 |

*Front air conditioning, cruise control, quad captain's chairs, power windows and door locks, power mirrors, rear defogger. NA CA and HI.*

| | Retail Price | Dealer Invoice |
|---|---|---|
| Preferred Equipment Pkg. 692A/C, GS ......................... | $5715 | $4558 |
| *Manufacturer's discount price*............................................ | 3400 | 2891 |

Front and rear air conditioning, anti-lock brakes, cruise control, Power Group (power windows and door locks, power mirrors), remote keyless entry, 6-way power driver seat, under-passenger-seat storage drawer, quad captain's chairs, rear defogger, flip-open liftgate window, privacy glass, roof rack, alloy wheels.

| | Retail Price | Dealer Invoice |
|---|---|---|
| Preferred Equipment Pkg. 696A, LS............................. | 3935 | 3343 |
| *Manufacturer's discount price*............................................ | 1930 | 1639 |

Rear air conditioning and heater, cruise control, leather quad captain's chairs, 6-way power driver seat, 4-way power front passenger seat, leather-wrapped steering wheel w/radio controls, heated power mirrors, Premium Sound cassette player (rear radio controls with front-seat lockout, dual mini headphone jacks, cassette/CD storage console), remote keyless entry, automatic headlights, illuminated visor mirrors, flip-open liftgate window, deluxe alloy wheels.

| | Retail Price | Dealer Invoice |
|---|---|---|
| Preferred Equipment Pkg. 697A, Nautica ...................... | 2870 | 2439 |
| *Manufacturer's discount price*............................................ | 1500 | 1275 |

Automatic front and rear air conditioning and heater, cruise control, 6-way power driver seat, 4-way power front passenger seat, Premium Sound cassette player (rear radio controls with front-seat lockout, dual mini headphone jacks, cassette/CD storage console), leather-wrapped steering wheel w/radio controls, flip-open liftgate window, heated power mirrors, electronic instrumentation, automatic headlights, remote keyless entry, illuminated visor mirrors.

| | Retail Price | Dealer Invoice |
|---|---|---|
| Gold Sport Pkg., GS............................................................ | 295 | 251 |
| LS.................................................................................... | NC | NC |

Includes heated power mirrors, gold trim badging, color-keyed grille, alloy wheels w/gold accents. Requires Preferred Equipment Group 692A/C. NA with Handling Suspension.

| | Retail Price | Dealer Invoice |
|---|---|---|
| Power Group Delete, GS (credit)...................................... | (670) | (569) |

Power windows and door locks, power mirrors. Requires Preferred Equipment Pkg. 692A/C. NA with remote keyless entry.

| | Retail Price | Dealer Invoice |
|---|---|---|
| Light Group, GS w/Pkg. 692A/C ....................................... | 165 | 140 |

Overhead dual map lights, dual liftgate lights, front-door step lights, power rear vent windows, under instrument panel lights with time delay.

| | Retail Price | Dealer Invoice |
|---|---|---|
| Trailer Towing Pkg., GS, LS, Nautica .............................. | 250 | 213 |

Includes heavy-duty battery, full-size spare tire, 3500-pound trailer rating.

## Safety Features

| | Retail Price | Dealer Invoice |
|---|---|---|
| Anti-lock brakes, GS........................................................ | 590 | 502 |
| Anti-lock brakes (delete), GS w/Pkg. 692A/C (credit) .... | (590) | (502) |

## Comfort and Convenience

| | Retail Price | Dealer Invoice |
|---|---|---|
| Front air conditioning, Cargo............................................ | 855 | 727 |

*Prices are accurate at time of publication; subject to manufacturer's change.*

# MERCURY

| | Retail Price | Dealer Invoice |
|---|---|---|
| Front air conditioning delete, GS (credit) | ($855) | ($727) |
| Rear air conditioning and heater, GS | 465 | 395 |
| Automatic front and rear air conditioning delete, Nautica (credit) | (645) | (548) |
| Automatic air conditioning, LS | 180 | 153 |
| Power window and door locks, Cargo | 570 | 484 |
| Power mirrors, Cargo | 100 | 85 |
| Power moonroof, LS, Nautica | 775 | 659 |
| Quad captain's chairs delete, GS (credit) | (710) | (603) |

*Second row replaced with 3-passenger folding bench seat. Requires Power Group delete. NA with rear air conditioning.*

| | Retail Price | Dealer Invoice |
|---|---|---|
| Leather upholstery delete, LS (credit) | (865) | (735) |
| 7-passenger seating, GS, LS w/leather delete | NC | NC |
| GS w/quad captain's chairs delete | 330 | 281 |
| LS (credit) | (865) | (735) |

*Cloth upholstery, reclining front bucket seats, 3-passenger second-row bench seat, 2-passenger rear bench seat.*

| | Retail Price | Dealer Invoice |
|---|---|---|
| 6-way power driver seat, GS | 395 | 336 |
| Integrated child seats, GS, LS | 240 | 204 |

*Requires 7-passenger seating.*

| | Retail Price | Dealer Invoice |
|---|---|---|
| Premium Sound cassette player, GS w/Pkg. 692A/C | 310 | 263 |

*Includes rear radio controls with front seat lockout, dual mini headphone jacks, cassette/CD storage console.*

Premium Sound cassette/6-disc CD changer,

| | Retail Price | Dealer Invoice |
|---|---|---|
| GS w/Pkg. 692A/C | 680 | 578 |
| LS, Nautica | 370 | 314 |

*Includes rear radio controls with front seat lockout, dual mini headphone jacks, cassette/CD storage console.*

| | Retail Price | Dealer Invoice |
|---|---|---|
| Supersound CD/cassette player, LS, Nautica | 865 | 735 |

*Premium Sound cassette/6-disc CD changer plus subwoofer speaker.*

| | Retail Price | Dealer Invoice |
|---|---|---|
| Electronic instrumentation, LS | 245 | 208 |

*Requires automatic temperature control.*

| | Retail Price | Dealer Invoice |
|---|---|---|
| Remote keyless entry, GS | 175 | 149 |
| Flip-open liftgate window, GS | 115 | 97 |
| Cargo net, GS, LS, Nautica | 30 | 26 |

## Appearance and Miscellaneous

| | Retail Price | Dealer Invoice |
|---|---|---|
| Privacy glass, GS | 415 | 352 |
| Theft-deterrent system, GS, LS, Nautica | 100 | 85 |

*Requires remote keyless entry and anti-lock brakes.*

| | Retail Price | Dealer Invoice |
|---|---|---|
| Roof rack, GS | 175 | 149 |
| 2-tone paint, GS | 295 | 251 |
| Handling suspension, GS, LS | 85 | 73 |

*Includes 215/70R15 performance tires, firm-ride suspension, rear stabilizer bar. GS requires deluxe alloy wheels. NA GS w/Pkg. 691A.*

# MITSUBISHI DIAMANTE

*Mitsubishi Diamante ES*

## SPECIFICATIONS

| | 4-door sedan |
|---|---|
| Wheelbase, in. | 107.1 |
| Overall length, in. | 194.1 |
| Overall width, in. | 70.3 |
| Overall height, in. | 53.9 |
| Curb weight, lbs. | 3494 |
| Cargo vol., cu. ft. | 14.2 |
| Fuel capacity, gals. | 19.0 |
| Seating capacity | 5 |
| Front head room, in. | 37.6 |
| Max. front leg room, in. | 43.6 |
| Rear head room, in. | 36.3 |
| Min. rear leg room, in. | 36.6 |

## ENGINES

| | ohc V-6 |
|---|---|
| Size, liters/cu. in. | 3.5/213 |
| Horsepower @ rpm | 210@ 5000 |
| Torque (lbs./ft.) @ rpm | 231@ 4000 |
| Availability | S |

### EPA city/highway mpg

| | |
|---|---|
| 4-speed OD automatic | 18/24 |

| Mitsubishi Diamante | Retail Price | Dealer Invoice |
|---|---|---|
| ES 4-door sedan | $27650 | $23776 |
| LS 4-door sedan | 33050 | 28087 |
| Destination charge | 470 | 470 |

*Prices are accurate at time of publication; subject to manufacturer's change.*

# MITSUBISHI

## STANDARD EQUIPMENT:

**ES:** 3.5-liter V-6 engine, 4-speed automatic transmission, driver- and passenger-side air bags, anti-lock 4-wheel disc brakes, air conditioning w/automatic climate control, rear heat ducts, power steering, tilt steering column, cruise control, velour upholstery, 7-way adjustable front bucket seats, front console with armrest, cupholders, folding rear armrest, power mirrors, power windows, power door locks, remote keyless entry, remote fuel-door and decklid releases, tachometer, coolant-temperature gauge, trip odometer, variable intermittent wipers, AM/FM/cassette w/six speakers, power and diversity antenna, digital clock, passenger-side illuminated visor mirror, rear defogger, front map light, automatic headlights, floormats, solar-control glass, theft-deterrent system, full-size spare tire, 205/65HR15 tires, wheel covers.

**LS** adds: power driver seat w/memory, leather upholstery, leather-wrapped steering wheel and shift knob, AM/FM/cassette/CD player, power sunroof, driver-side illuminated visor mirror, universal garage door opener, rear map light, fog lights, 215/60VR16 tires, alloy wheels.

## OPTIONAL EQUIPMENT:

|  | Retail Price | Dealer Invoice |
|---|---|---|
| **Major Packages** | | |
| Premium Leather Pkg., ES | $2700 | $2214 |

*Leather upholstery, power driver seat w/memory, leather-wrapped steering wheel and shift knob, bodyside moldings, fog lights, 215/60VR16 tires, wheel locks, alloy wheels.*

| Luxury Group, LS | 3487 | 2859 |
|---|---|---|

*Infinity AM/FM/cassette/CD player w/eight speakers, steering wheel radio controls, remote keyless entry system with seat and mirror memory, power passenger seat, automatic day/night rearview mirror, power trunk and fuel filler release, chrome alloy wheels.*

| **Safety Features** | | |
|---|---|---|
| Integrated child seat, ES | 195 | 160 |
| **Comfort and Convenience** | | |
| Power sunroof, ES | 963 | 790 |

*Includes universal garage door opener.*

| 10-disc CD changer | 797 | 544 |
|---|---|---|

*Includes trunk mat and cargo net.*

| CD player, ES | 399 | 299 |
|---|---|---|

# MITSUBISHI ECLIPSE

## SPECIFICATIONS

|  | 2-door coupe | 2-door conv. |
|---|---|---|
| Wheelbase, in. | 98.8 | 98.8 |

*Mitsubishi Eclipse Spyder GS-T*

| | 2-door coupe | 2-door conv. |
|---|---|---|
| Overall length, in. | 172.4 | 172.4 |
| Overall width, in. | 68.5 | 68.5 |
| Overall height, in. | 49.8 | 52.8 |
| Curb weight, lbs. | 2754 | 2888 |
| Cargo vol., cu. ft. | 16.6 | 5.1 |
| Fuel capacity, gals. | 15.9 | 15.9 |
| Seating capacity | 4 | 4 |
| Front head room, in. | 37.9 | 38.8 |
| Max. front leg room, in. | 43.3 | 43.3 |
| Rear head room, in. | 34.3 | 34.9 |
| Min. rear leg room, in. | 28.4 | 28.4 |

| ENGINES | dohc I-4 | ohc I-4 | Turbo dohc I-4 |
|---|---|---|---|
| Size, liters/cu. in. | 2.0/122 | 2.4/143 | 2.0/122 |
| Horsepower @ rpm | 140@ 6000 | 141@ 5000 | 210@ 6000 |
| Torque (lbs./ft.) @ rpm | 130@ 4800 | 148@ 3000 | 214@ 3000 |
| Availability | S[1] | S[2] | S[3] |
| **EPA city/highway mpg** | | | |
| 5-speed OD manual | 22/33 | 22/30 | 23/31 |
| 4-speed OD automatic | 21/30 | 21/28 | 20/27 |

1. RS, GS. 2. GS Spyder. 3. GS-T, GSX.

| Mitsubishi Eclipse | Retail Price | Dealer Invoice |
|---|---|---|
| RS 2-door hatchback, 5-speed | $15740 | $13671 |
| RS 2-door hatchback, automatic | 16430 | 14289 |
| GS 2-door hatchback, 5-speed | 17880 | 15541 |
| GS 2-door hatchback, automatic | 18580 | 16158 |
| Spyder GS 2-door convertible, 5-speed | 21200 | 18434 |
| Spyder GS 2-door convertible, automatic | 21920 | 19057 |
| GS-T 2-door hatchback, 5-speed | 21960 | 19093 |
| GS-T 2-door hatchback, automatic | 22800 | 19830 |

*Prices are accurate at time of publication; subject to manufacturer's change.*

# MITSUBISHI

| | Retail Price | Dealer Invoice |
|---|---|---|
| Spyder GS-T 2-door convertible, 5-speed | $26660 | $23186 |
| Spyder GS-T 2-door convertible, automatic | 27520 | 23931 |
| GSX 2-door hatchback, 5-speed | 25320 | 21767 |
| GSX 2-door hatchback, automatic | 26170 | 22498 |
| Destination charge | 420 | 420 |

## STANDARD EQUIPMENT:

**RS:** 2.0-liter dohc 4-cylinder engine, 5-speed manual or 4-speed automatic transmission, driver- and passenger-side air bags, variable-assist power steering, tilt steering column, cloth upholstery, reclining front bucket seats, 5-way adjustable driver seat w/memory recline feature, front storage console w/cupholders, folding rear seat, tachometer, coolant-temperature gauge, trip odometer, AM/FM/cassette w/6-speakers, digital clock, map lights, remote fuel-door release, rear defogger, remote hatch release, cargo light, tinted glass, dual outside mirrors, 195/70HR14 tires, wheel covers.

**GS** adds: 4-wheel disc brakes, 6-way adjustable driver seat w/memory feature, split folding rear seat, power mirrors, universal garage-door opener, rear wiper/washer, cargo cover and net, bodyside cladding, low rear spoiler, fog lights, 205/55HR16 tires.

**Spyder GS** adds to RS: 2.4-liter 4-cylinder engine, air conditioning, 6-way adjustable driver seat w/memory recliner feature, power mirrors, power windows, power door locks, AM/FM/CD player, power insulated soft top with glass rear window, vinyl tonneau cover, alloy wheels.

**GS-T** adds to GS: 2.0-liter dohc 4-cylinder turbocharged and intercooled engine, air conditioning, cruise control, oil-pressure gauge, turbo-boost gauge, Infinity 8-speaker AM/FM/cassette/CD player w/amplifier and CD changer controls, power windows, power door locks, dual bright exhaust outlets, high rear spoiler, sport suspension, 205/55HR16 tires, chrome alloy wheels.

**Spyder GS-T** adds: leather-upholstery, leather-wrapped steering wheel and shift knob, remote keyless entry, theft-deterrent system, power insulated soft top with glass rear window, vinyl tonneau cover, 205/55VR16 tires.

**GSX** adds to GS-T: all-wheel drive, leather upholstery, leather-wrapped steering wheel and shift knob, power driver seat, power moonroof, remote keyless entry, theft-deterrent system, 215/50VR17 tires, plain alloy wheels.

## OPTIONAL EQUIPMENT:
### Major Packages

| | | |
|---|---|---|
| Preferred Equipment Pkg. P6, RS | 1498 | 1228 |

*Air conditioning, cargo cover, rear spoiler, alloy wheels.*

| | Retail Price | Dealer Invoice |
|---|---|---|
| Preferred Value Pkg. P1, GS............................................. | $2571 | $2107 |
| *Manufacturer's discount price*....................................... | 1871 | 1757 |
| Air conditioning, power moonroof, power windows and door locks, cruise control. | | |
| Premium Value Pkg. P2, GS............................................. | 3789 | 3106 |
| *Manufacturer's discount price*....................................... | 2789 | 2606 |
| Preferred Value Pkg. P1 plus leather upholstery, Infinity audio system w/CD changer controls, remote keyless entry, theft-deterrent system. | | |
| Premium Value Pkg. P3, GS............................................. | 4505 | 3693 |
| *Manufacturer's discount price*....................................... | 3505 | 3193 |
| Premium Value Pkg. P2 plus anti-lock brakes. | | |
| Appearance Pkg. P1, Spyder GS..................................... | 896 | 735 |
| Rear spoiler, lower bodyside cladding, fog lights, 205/55HR16 tires, special alloy wheels. | | |
| Convenience Pkg. P2, Spyder GS................................... | 691 | 567 |
| Cruise control, universal garage door opener, remote keyless entry system, theft-deterrent system. | | |
| Power Pkg., RS ............................................................... | 755 | 619 |
| Power windows and door locks, cruise control. | | |

## Powertrains

| | | |
|---|---|---|
| Limited-slip differential, GSX ....................................... | 266 | 218 |

## Safety Features

| | | |
|---|---|---|
| Anti-lock brakes, Spyder GS, GS-T, Spyder GS-T, GSX | 716 | 587 |

## Comfort and Convenience

| | | |
|---|---|---|
| Air conditioning, RS ....................................................... | 860 | 705 |
| Power moonroof, RS, GS-T............................................ | 731 | 599 |
| Leather upholstery, GS-T............................................... | 457 | 375 |
| Spyder GS...................................................................... | 567 | 465 |
| Infinity 8-speaker AM/FM/cassette, Spyder GS.............. | 720 | 590 |
| Includes amplifier and CD changer controls. | | |
| CD player, RS, GS......................................................... | 399 | 299 |
| 10-disc CD changer........................................................ | 675 | 465 |
| Remote keyless entry/theft-deterrent system, GS, GS-T | 334 | 274 |

# MITSUBISHI GALANT

## SPECIFICATIONS

| | 4-door sedan |
|---|---|
| Wheelbase, in. ....................................................... | 103.7 |
| Overall length, in. ................................................. | 187.6 |
| Overall width, in. ................................................... | 68.1 |

*Prices are accurate at time of publication; subject to manufacturer's change.*

# MITSUBISHI

*Mitsubishi Galant ES*

|  | 4-door sedan |
|---|---|
| Overall height, in. | 53.1 |
| Curb weight, lbs. | 2778 |
| Cargo vol., cu. ft. | 12.5 |
| Fuel capacity, gals. | 16.9 |
| Seating capacity | 5 |
| Front head room, in. | 39.4 |
| Max. front leg room, in. | 43.3 |
| Rear head room, in. | 37.5 |
| Min. rear leg room, in. | 35.0 |

## ENGINES

|  | ohc I-4 |
|---|---|
| Size, liters/cu. in. | 2.4/143 |
| Horsepower @ rpm | 141@ 5000 |
| Torque (lbs./ft.) @ rpm | 148@ 3000 |
| Availability | S |

**EPA city/highway mpg**

| | |
|---|---|
| 5-speed OD manual | 23/30 |
| 4-speed OD automatic | 22/28 |

| Mitsubishi Galant | Retail Price | Dealer Invoice |
|---|---|---|
| DE 4-door sedan, 5-speed | $15680 | $13952 |
| DE 4-door sedan, automatic | 16550 | 14728 |
| ES 4-door sedan, 5-speed | 17670 | 15565 |
| ES 4-door sedan, automatic | 18450 | 16248 |
| LS 4-door sedan, automatic | 25310 | 21509 |
| Destination charge | 420 | 420 |

## STANDARD EQUIPMENT:

**DE:** 2.4-liter 4-cylinder engine, 5-speed manual or 4-speed automatic transmission, driver- and passenger-side air bags, power steering, tilt steering column, cloth upholstery, 5-way adjustable driver seat, front storage console w/armrest, cupholders, radio prep pkg., digital clock, tinted glass, driver-side visor mirror, tachometer, coolant-temperature gauge, remote fuel-door and decklid releases, rear defogger, intermittent wipers, remote outside mirrors, 185/70HR14 tires, wheel covers.

**ES** adds: air conditioning, cruise control, upgraded cloth upholstery, folding rear seat with center armrest, power windows, power door locks, AM/FM/cassette, power diversity antenna, power mirrors, variable intermittent wipers, passenger-side visor mirror, door map pockets, woodgrain interior trim, floormats, cargo net.

**LS** adds: 4-speed automatic transmission, anti-lock brakes, automatic climate control, power driver seat, leather upholstery, leather-wrapped steering wheel, power sunroof, Infinity audio system w/amplifier, remote keyless entry, Homelink universal garage-door opener, illuminated visor mirrors, seatback map pockets, theft-deterrent system, fog lights, 195/60HR15 tires, alloy wheels.

## OPTIONAL EQUIPMENT:

| | Retail Price | Dealer Invoice |
|---|---|---|
| **Major Packages** | | |
| Premium Pkg., ES | $1805 | $1480 |

*Power sunroof, Homelink universal garage door opener, illuminated visor mirrors, remote keyless entry, theft-deterrent system, fog lights, 195/60HR15 tires, alloy wheels.*

| | Retail Price | Dealer Invoice |
|---|---|---|
| **Safety Features** | | |
| Anti-lock brakes, ES | 965 | 791 |
| **Comfort and Convenience** | | |
| Air conditioning, DE | 902 | 740 |
| AM/FM/cassette, DE | 350 | 247 |
| CD player, ES, LS | 399 | 299 |
| 10-disc CD changer, ES, LS | 675 | 465 |
| Remote keyless entry, ES | 225 | 145 |

# MITSUBISHI MIRAGE

| SPECIFICATIONS | 2-door coupe | 4-door sedan |
|---|---|---|
| Wheelbase, in. | 95.1 | 98.4 |
| Overall length, in. | 168.1 | 173.6 |
| Overall width, in. | 66.5 | 66.5 |
| Overall height, in. | 51.4 | 52.6 |
| Curb weight, lbs. | 2127 | 2227 |
| Cargo vol., cu. ft. | 11.5 | 11.5 |
| Fuel capacity, gals. | 13.2 | 13.2 |
| Seating capacity | 5 | 5 |
| Front head room, in. | 38.6 | 39.8 |

*Prices are accurate at time of publication; subject to manufacturer's change.*

# MITSUBISHI

*Mitsubishi Mirage LS Sedan*

|  | 2-door coupe | 4-door sedan |
|---|---|---|
| Max. front leg room, in. | 43.0 | 43.0 |
| Rear head room, in. | 35.8 | 37.4 |
| Min. rear leg room, in. | 31.1 | 33.5 |

## ENGINES

|  | ohc I-4 | ohc I-4 |
|---|---|---|
| Size, liters/cu. in. | 1.5/90 | 1.8/112 |
| Horsepower @ rpm | 92 @ 5500 | 113@ 5500 |
| Torque (lbs./ft.) @ rpm | 93 @ 3000 | 116@ 4500 |
| Availability | S[1] | S[2] |
| **EPA city/highway mpg** | | |
| 5-speed OD manual | 33/40 | 29/36 |
| 4-speed OD automatic | 28/36 | 26/33 |

*1. DE models. 2. LS models.*

| Mitsubishi Mirage | Retail Price | Dealer Invoice |
|---|---|---|
| DE 2-door coupe, 5-speed | $10830 | $9842 |
| DE 2-door coupe, automatic | 11550 | 10460 |
| DE 4-door sedan, 5-speed | 12360 | 10998 |
| DE 4-door sedan, automatic | 13070 | 11617 |
| LS 2-door coupe, 5-speed | 14330 | 12725 |
| LS 2-door coupe, automatic | 15010 | 13343 |
| LS 4-door sedan, 5-speed | 13300 | 11836 |
| LS 4-door sedan, automatic | 13980 | 12454 |
| Destination charge | 420 | 420 |

## STANDARD EQUIPMENT:

**DE:** 1.5-liter 4-cylinder engine, 5-speed manual or 4-speed automatic transmission, driver- and passenger-side air bags, power steering, cloth front bucket seats, front storage console, passenger-side visor mirror, coolant-temperature gauge, rear defogger, remote fuel-door and decklid release, dual outside mirrors, tinted glass, 175/70R13 tires, wheel covers (sedan).

**LS sedan** adds: 1.8-liter dohc 4-cylinder engine, tilt steering column, height-adjustable driver seat, digital clock, driver-side visor mirror, intermittent wipers.

**LS coupe** adds: air conditioning, split folding rear seat, AM/FM/CD player, tachometer (5-speed), rear spoiler, 185/65R14 tires, alloy wheels, deletes driver-side visor mirror.

## OPTIONAL EQUIPMENT:

| | Retail Price | Dealer Invoice |
|---|---|---|
| **Major Packages** | | |
| Preferred Equipment Pkg., DE coupe | $448 | $367 |
| *Tilt steering wheel, AM/FM/cassette, intermittent wipers, wheel covers.* | | |
| Comfort And Convenience Pkg., DE sedan | 1532 | 1244 |
| *Air conditioning, tilt steering wheel, AM/FM/cassette, intermittent wipers, visor mirrors, split folding rear seat, upgraded upholstery, console armrest, cargo compartment light, floormats, manual remote outside mirrors.* | | |
| Convenience Pkg, LS coupe | 744 | 610 |
| *Cruise control, power windows and door locks, power mirrors, variable intermittent wipers, visor mirrors.* | | |
| Value Pkg., LS sedan | 2538 | 1921 |
| *Manufacturer's discount price* | 1600 | 1491 |
| *Air conditioning, cruise control, AM/FM/cassette w/CD controls, power windows and door locks, power mirrors, split folding rear sport, floormats, variable intermittent wipers, 185/65R14 tires.* | | |
| Premium Pkg., LS sedan | 1190 | 976 |
| *Power sunroof, alloy wheels, wheel locks.* | | |
| **Safety Features** | | |
| Anti-lock brakes, LS | 732 | 600 |
| **Comfort and Convenience** | | |
| Air conditioning, DE | 880 | 720 |
| Power sunroof, LS coupe | 793 | 650 |
| AM/FM/cassette, DE | 352 | 247 |
| CD player, LS sedan | 399 | 299 |
| *LS sedan requires Value Pkg.* | | |
| Remote keyless entry, LS | 248 | 161 |
| *LS coupe requires Convenience Pkg.* | | |
| **Appearance and Miscellaneous** | | |
| Appearance Pkg., LS coupe | 207 | 170 |
| *Fog lamps, air dam.* | | |

Other options are available as port installed items.

*Prices are accurate at time of publication; subject to manufacturer's change.*

# MITSUBISHI MONTERO

*Mitsubishi Montero*

## SPECIFICATIONS

| | 4-door wagon |
|---|---|
| Wheelbase, in. | 107.3 |
| Overall length, in. | 186.6 |
| Overall width, in. | 69.9 |
| Overall height, in. | 74.8 |
| Curb weight, lbs. | 4431 |
| Cargo vol., cu. ft. | 67.1 |
| Fuel capacity, gals. | 24.3 |
| Seating capacity | 7 |
| Front head room, in. | 40.9 |
| Max. front leg room, in. | 40.3 |
| Rear head room, in. | 40.0 |
| Min. rear leg room, in. | 37.6 |

## ENGINES

| | ohc V-6 |
|---|---|
| Size, liters/cu. in. | 3.5/213 |
| Horsepower @ rpm | 200@ 5000 |
| Torque (lbs./ft.) @ rpm | 228@ 3500 |
| Availability | S |

**EPA city/highway mpg**

| | |
|---|---|
| 4-speed OD automatic | 16/19 |

| Mitsubishi Montero | Retail Price | Dealer Invoice |
|---|---|---|
| Base 4-door wagon | $33530 | $28663 |
| Destination charge | 445 | 445 |

## STANDARD EQUIPMENT:

**Base:** 3.5-liter V-6 engine, 4-speed automatic transmission, Active-Trac 4-wheel drive, driver- and passenger-side air bags, anti-lock 4-wheel disc brakes, air conditioning, power steering, leather-wrapped steering wheel, tilt steering column, cruise control, cloth reclining front bucket seats, split folding second-row seat with headrests, split folding third-row seat, front storage console w/cupholders, wood interior trim, power windows, power door locks, power mirrors, trip odometer, tachometer, coolant-temperature gauge, multi-meter (oil-pressure gauge, compass, outside-temperature indicator, voltmeter), map lights, AM/FM/cassette, power diversity antenna, digital clock, rear defogger, variable intermittent wipers, intermittent rear wiper/washer, remote fuel-door release, auxiliary power outlets, visor mirrors, cargo tie-down hooks, rear heat ducts, fog lights, mud guards, side steps, rear privacy glass, sliding rear quarter window, headlamp washers, engine oil cooler, tool kit, front and rear tow hooks, skid plates, full-size spare tire, 265/70R15 tires, alloy wheels.

| OPTIONAL EQUIPMENT: | Retail Price | Dealer Invoice |
|---|---|---|
| **Major Packages** | | |
| Value Pkg. | $2439 | $1631 |
| *Manufacturer's discount price* | 1200 | 1092 |
| *Remote keyless entry, theft-deterrent system, 10-disc CD changer, floormats, cargo mat, cargo cover, roof rack, Spare Tire Pkg. (spare tire cover, wheel locks).* | | |
| Luxury Pkg. | 2787 | 2285 |
| *Leather upholstery, power driver seat, Infinity sound system w/amplifier and CD changer control, power moonroof.* | | |
| Premium Pkg. | 1110 | 910 |
| *Adjustable shocks, sport suspension, chrome alloy wheels.* | | |
| Cold Weather Pkg. | 774 | 635 |
| *Heated front seats, heated mirrors, locking rear differential.* | | |
| **Comfort and Convenience** | | |
| CD player | 399 | 299 |
| **Appearance and Miscellaneous** | | |
| Spare Tire Pkg. | 240 | 156 |
| *Spare tire cover, wheel locks.* | | |
| **Special Purpose, Wheels and Tires** | | |
| Trailer hitch w/harness | 252 | 164 |

*Prices are accurate at time of publication; subject to manufacturer's change.*

# MITSUBISHI MONTERO SPORT

*Mitsubishi Montero Sport LS*

## SPECIFICATIONS

|  | 4-door wagon |
|---|---|
| Wheelbase, in. | 107.3 |
| Overall length, in. | 178.3 |
| Overall width, in. | 66.7 |
| Overall height, in. | 65.6 |
| Curb weight, lbs. | 3980 |
| Cargo vol., cu. ft. | 79.3 |
| Fuel capacity, gals. | 19.5 |
| Seating capacity | 5 |
| Front head room, in. | 38.9 |
| Max. front leg room, in. | 42.8 |
| Rear head room, in. | 37.3 |
| Min. rear leg room, in. | 33.5 |

## ENGINES

|  | ohc I-4 | ohc V-6 |
|---|---|---|
| Size, liters/cu. in. | 2.4/143 | 3.0/181 |
| Horsepower @ rpm | 132@ 5500 | 173@ 5250 |
| Torque (lbs./ft.) @ rpm | 148@ 2750 | 188@ 4000 |
| Availability | S[1] | S[2] |
| **EPA city/highway mpg** | | |
| 5-speed OD manual | 22/25 | 17/20 |
| 4-speed OD automatic | | 19/22[3] |

1. ES. 2. LS, XLS. 3. 18/21 w/4WD.

| Mitsubishi Montero Sport | Retail Price | Dealer Invoice |
|---|---|---|
| ES 2WD 4-door wagon, 5-speed | $18030 | $16219 |
| LS 2WD 4-door wagon, automatic | 22260 | 19361 |
| LS 4WD 4-door wagon, 5-speed | 23920 | 20810 |
| LS 4WD 4-door wagon, automatic | 24780 | 21552 |
| XLS 2WD 4-door wagon, automatic | 28360 | 24670 |
| XLS 4WD 4-door wagon, automatic | 32250 | 28050 |
| Destination charge | 445 | 445 |

## STANDARD EQUIPMENT:

**ES:** 2.4-liter 4-cylinder engine, 5-speed manual transmission, driver- and passenger-side air bags, power steering, tilt steering column, cloth upholstery, front bucket seats, reclining folding rear seat, carpeting, front cupholders, trip odometer, coolant-temperature gauge, tinted glass, AM/FM/CD player w/four speakers, digital clock, rear defogger, intermittent wipers, rear wiper/washer, visor mirrors, map lights, auxiliary power outlet, dual outside mirrors, mud guards, front and rear tow hooks, front-end and fuel-tank skid plates.

**LS 2WD adds:** 3.0-liter V-6 engine, 4-speed automatic transmission, driver seat height adjuster, split folding rear seat, rear cupholders, AM/FM/cassette w/six speakers, power antenna, variable intermittent wipers, rear privacy glass, 225/75R15 mud and snow tires.

**LS 4WD adds:** 5-speed manual or 4-speed automatic transmission, part-time 4-wheel drive, automatic locking front hubs, anti-lock 4-wheel disc brakes, transfer-case skid plates.

**XLS 2WD adds to LS 2WD:** 4-speed automatic transmission, air conditioning, cruise control, leather upholstery, power windows, power door locks, power outside mirrors, power sunroof, Infinity AM/FM/cassette player w/eight speakers, chrome grille accent, fender flares, side steps, 2-tone paint, 265/70R15 mud and snow tires, alloy wheels, deletes 4-wheel disc brakes.

**XLS 4WD adds:** part-time 4WD, automatic locking front hubs, locking rear differential, 4-wheel disc brakes, heated front seats, rear heater, heated mirrors, multi-meter (compass, outside temperature gauge, voltmeter, oil pressure gauge), transfer case skid plates.

## OPTIONAL EQUIPMENT:
### Major Packages

| | | |
|---|---|---|
| Accessory Pkg. 1, LS, XLS | 612 | 405 |
| *Roof rack, rear wind deflector, cargo net and cover, floormats.* | | |
| Accessory Pkg. 2, ES, LS | 755 | 505 |
| *Roof rack, rear wind deflector, side steps. NA power sunroof.* | | |
| Convenience Pkg., LS | 829 | 680 |
| *Cruise control, power windows and door locks, power mirrors.* | | |

*Prices are accurate at time of publication; subject to manufacturer's change.*

| | Retail Price | Dealer Invoice |
|---|---|---|
| Luxury Pkg., LS..................................................... | $1220 | $1000 |
| *Infinity AM/FM/cassette w/eight speakers, power sunroof.* | | |
| Appearance Pkg., LS .......................................... | 1815 | 1488 |
| *Leather-wrapped steering wheel, side steps, bright grille, fender flares, 2-tone paint, 265/70R15 tires, alloy wheels.* | | |
| Limited Slip Axle Pkg., LS 4WD............................ | 744 | 610 |
| *Limited-slip differential, rear heater, multi-meter (includes compass, outside-temperature indicator, voltmeter, oil-pressure gauge).* | | |
| Off-Road Pkg., LS 4WD ....................................... | 1171 | 960 |
| *Limited Slip Axle Pkg. plus rear-mounted spare-tire w/cover, wheel locks.* | | |

## Powertrains

| | | |
|---|---|---|
| Limited slip differential, LS, XLS 2WD............................ | 366 | 300 |

## Comfort and Convenience

| | | |
|---|---|---|
| Air conditioning, ES, LS...................................... | 915 | 750 |
| CD player, LS, XLS.............................................. | 399 | 299 |
| 10-disc CD changer, LS, XLS............................. | 675 | 465 |
| Cargo Kit............................................................. | 200 | 131 |
| *Floormats, cargo cover and net.* | | |

## Appearance and Miscellaneous

| | | |
|---|---|---|
| Theft-deterrent system, LS, XLS ....................... | 345 | 224 |
| *Includes alarm and remote keyless entry. LS requires Convenience Pkg.* | | |
| Side steps, ES, LS.............................................. | 350 | 245 |
| Roof rack, ES, LS w/o sunroof ........................... | 260 | 165 |

## Special Purpose, Wheels and Tires

| | | |
|---|---|---|
| Trailer hitch w/harness........................................ | 252 | 164 |
| Alloy wheels, LS.................................................. | 427 | 350 |

Other options are available as port installed items.

# NISSAN 200SX

## SPECIFICATIONS

| | 2-door coupe |
|---|---|
| Wheelbase, in. ................................................................. | 99.8 |
| Overall length, in. ............................................................ | 170.1 |
| Overall width, in. ............................................................. | 66.6 |
| Overall height, in. ............................................................ | 54.2 |
| Curb weight, lbs. .............................................................. | 2363 |
| Cargo vol., cu. ft. ............................................................. | 10.4 |
| Fuel capacity, gals. .......................................................... | 13.2 |

*Nissan 200SX SE-R*

|  | 2-door coupe |
|---|---|
| Seating capacity | 4 |
| Front head room, in. | 39.1 |
| Max. front leg room, in. | 42.3 |
| Rear head room, in. | 35.4 |
| Min. rear leg room, in. | 31.4 |

## ENGINES

|  | dohc I-4 | dohc I-4 |
|---|---|---|
| Size, liters/cu. in. | 1.6/97 | 2.0/122 |
| Horsepower @ rpm | 115@ 6000 | 140@ 6400 |
| Torque (lbs./ft.) @ rpm | 108@ 4000 | 132@ 4800 |
| Availability | S[1] | S[2] |
| **EPA city/highway mpg** | | |
| 5-speed OD manual | 29/39 | 23/31 |
| 4-speed OD automatic | 27/36 | 23/30 |

*1. Base and SE. 2. SE-R.*

| Nissan 200SX | Retail Price | Dealer Invoice |
|---|---|---|
| Base 2-door coupe, 5-speed | $13149 | $12520 |
| Base 2-door coupe, automatic | 13949 | 13282 |
| SE 2-door coupe, 5-speed | 15399 | 14025 |
| SE 2-door coupe, automatic | 16199 | 14754 |
| SE-R 2-door coupe, 5-speed | 16749 | 15255 |
| SE-R 2-door coupe, automatic | 17549 | 15984 |
| Destination charge | 470 | 470 |

## STANDARD EQUIPMENT:

**Base:** 1.6-liter dohc 4-cylinder, 5-speed manual or 4-speed automatic transmission, driver- and passenger-side air bags, cupholders, power steering, tilt steering column, cloth upholstery, reclining front bucket seats, power mirrors, tachometer, coolant temperature gauge, trip odometer, rear defogger, intermittent wipers, remote decklid and fuel-door releases, tinted glass, rear spoiler, 175/70R13 tires, wheel covers.

**SE** adds: air conditioning, cruise control, upgraded cloth upholstery, front sport bucket seats, split folding rear seat, AM/FM/CD, digital clock, power windows, power door locks, fog lights, color-keyed bodyside moldings and door handles, 175/65R14 tires, alloy wheels.

**SE-R** adds: 2.0-liter dohc 4-cylinder engine, limited-slip differential, 4-wheel disc brakes, remote keyless entry, leather-wrapped steering wheel and shifter, theft-deterrent system, 195/55R15 tires.

## OPTIONAL EQUIPMENT:

| | Retail Price | Dealer Invoice |
|---|---|---|
| **Major Packages** | | |
| Base Option Pkg., Base | $999 | $858 |
| *Air conditioning, AM/FM/CD.* | | |
| SE-R Option Pkg., SE-R | 999 | 858 |
| *Power moonroof, cassette/CD player, remote keyless entry, theft-deterrent system.* | | |
| **Safety Features** | | |
| Anti-lock brakes, SE, SE-R | 499 | 450 |
| *SE includes 4-wheel disc brakes.* | | |
| **Comfort and Convenience** | | |
| Power moonroof, SE | 449 | 386 |
| Armrest | 59 | 37 |
| Rosewood trim | 319 | 221 |
| Floormats | 79 | 52 |
| **Appearance and Miscellaneous** | | |
| Mudguards, Base, SE | 89 | 62 |

# NISSAN ALTIMA

## SPECIFICATIONS

| | 4-door sedan |
|---|---|
| Wheelbase, in. | 103.1 |
| Overall length, in. | 183.1 |
| Overall width, in. | 69.1 |
| Overall height, in. | 55.9 |
| Curb weight, lbs. | 2859 |
| Cargo vol., cu. ft. | 13.8 |
| Fuel capacity, gals. | 15.9 |
| Seating capacity | 5 |
| Front head room, in. | 39.4 |
| Max. front leg room, in. | 42.0 |

*Nissan Altima GLE*

|  | 4-door sedan |
|---|---|
| Rear head room, in. | 37.7 |
| Min. rear leg room, in. | 33.9 |

## ENGINES

|  | dohc I-4 |
|---|---|
| Size, liters/cu. in. | 2.4/146 |
| Horsepower @ rpm | 150@ 5600 |
| Torque (lbs./ft.) @ rpm | 154@ 4400 |
| Availability | S |
| **EPA city/highway mpg** | |
| 5-speed OD manual | 24/31 |
| 4-speed OD automatic | 22/30 |

| Nissan Altima | Retail Price | Dealer Invoice |
|---|---|---|
| XE 4-door sedan, 5-speed | $14990 | $14265 |
| XE 4-door sedan, automatic | 15790 | 15025 |
| GXE 4-door sedan, 5-speed | 17190 | 15646 |
| GXE 4-door sedan, automatic | 17990 | 16373 |
| SE 4-door sedan, 5-speed | 18490 | 16638 |
| SE 4-door sedan, automatic | 19290 | 17358 |
| GLE 4-door sedan, automatic | 19890 | 17897 |
| Destination charge | 420 | 420 |

## STANDARD EQUIPMENT:

**XE:** 2.4-liter 4-cylinder engine, 5-speed manual or 4-speed automatic transmission, driver- and passenger-side air bags, power steering, tilt steering wheel, rear defogger, cupholders, remote fuel door and decklid release, cloth reclining bucket seats, power windows, power mirrors, tachometer, coolant-temperature gauge, trip odometer, intermittent wipers, passenger-side visor mirror, tinted glass, 195/65R15 tires, wheel covers.

**GXE adds:** air conditioning, cruise control, power door locks, 4-speaker AM/FM/CD, digital clock, illuminated entry, lockable glove compartment, woodgrain trim, split folding rear seat, dual visor mirrors.

*Prices are accurate at time of publication; subject to manufacturer's change.*

# NISSAN

**SE** adds: 4-wheel disc brakes, front sport seats, leather-wrapped steering wheel and manual shift knob, white-faced gauges, 6-speaker AM/FM/cassette/CD, power/diversity antenna, remote keyless entry, sport-tuned suspension, theft-deterrent system, fog lights, rear spoiler, 205/60R15 tires, alloy wheels, deletes woodgrain trim.

**GLE** adds to GXE: 4-speed automatic transmission, leather upholstery, leather-wrapped steering wheel, 8-way power driver seat with adjustable lumbar support, rear center armrest with trunk pass-through, 6-speaker AM/FM/cassette/CD, power/diversity antenna, remote keyless entry, variable intermittent wipers, illuminated visor mirrors, theft-deterrent system.

## OPTIONAL EQUIPMENT:

| | Retail Price | Dealer Invoice |
|---|---|---|
| **Major Packages** | | |
| XE Option Pkg., XE | $1899 | $1632 |
| *AM/FM/cassette with digital clock, air conditioning, cruise control.* | | |
| GXE Security and Convenience Pkg., GXE | 549 | 472 |
| *6-speaker AM/FM/cassette/CD, remote keyless entry, theft-deterrent system.* | | |
| **Safety Features** | | |
| Anti-lock brakes | 499 | 450 |
| *XE requires Option Pkg.* | | |
| **Comfort and Convenience** | | |
| Leather upholstery, SE | 1299 | 1116 |
| *Includes 8-way power driver seat with adjustable lumbar support, rear center armrest with trunk pass-through.* | | |
| Power sunroof | 849 | 730 |
| *NA XE. GXE requires option pkg.* | | |
| Cassette player, GXE | NC | NC |
| *Deletes std. CD player.* | | |
| Floormats | 79 | 52 |
| **Appearance and Miscellaneous** | | |
| Rear spoiler, XE, GXE, GLE | 409 | 287 |
| Mud guards | 89 | 59 |
| Alloy wheels, GLE | 299 | 257 |
| Polished alloy wheels, GXE | 599 | 415 |

# NISSAN MAXIMA

## SPECIFICATIONS

| | 4-door sedan |
|---|---|
| Wheelbase, in. | 106.3 |
| Overall length, in. | 187.7 |

*Nissan Maxima GLE*

| | 4-door sedan |
|---|---|
| Overall width, in. | 69.7 |
| Overall height, in. | 55.7 |
| Curb weight, lbs. | 3001 |
| Cargo vol., cu. ft. | 14.5 |
| Fuel capacity, gals. | 18.5 |
| Seating capacity | 5 |
| Front head room, in. | 40.1 |
| Max. front leg room, in. | 43.9 |
| Rear head room, in. | 37.4 |
| Min. rear leg room, in. | 34.3 |

## ENGINES

| | dohc V-6 |
|---|---|
| Size, liters/cu. in. | 3.0/181 |
| Horsepower @ rpm | 190@ 5600 |
| Torque (lbs./ft.) @ rpm | 205@ 4000 |
| Availability | S |

**EPA city/highway mpg**

| | |
|---|---|
| 5-speed OD manual | 22/27 |
| 4-speed OD automatic | 21/28 |

| Nissan Maxima | Retail Price | Dealer Invoice |
|---|---|---|
| GXE 4-door sedan, 5-speed | $21499 | $19470 |
| GXE 4-door sedan, automatic | 23249 | 20814 |
| SE 4-door sedan, 5-speed | 23499 | 20916 |
| SE 4-door sedan, automatic | 24499 | 21806 |
| GLE 4-door sedan, automatic | 26899 | 23943 |
| Destination charge | 490 | 490 |

## STANDARD EQUIPMENT:

**GXE:** 3.0-liter dohc V-6 engine, 5-speed manual or 4-speed automatic transmission, driver- and passenger-side air bags, 4-wheel disc brakes, air conditioning, power steering, cruise control, cloth reclining front bucket seats, multi-adjustable driver seat w/lumbar support, front storage console, cupholders, folding rear armrest w/trunk pass-through, power windows, power door locks, power mirrors, tilt steering column, tinted glass, tachometer, coolant-temperature gauge, dual trip odometers, digital clock, 4-speaker AM/FM/cassette, diversity antenna, visor mirrors, intermittent wipers, rear defogger, remote decklid and fuel-door releases, map light, bright grille, 205/65R15 tires, wheel covers, deluxe 6-speaker audio system with AM/FM/cassette/CD player, leather-wrapped steering wheel and shifter.

**SE** adds: sport-tuned suspension, fog lamps, rear spoiler, bright exhaust outlet, color-keyed grille, 215/55R15 tires, alloy wheels.

**GLE** adds to GXE: 4-speed automatic transmission, automatic air conditioning, 8-way power driver seat, 4-way power passenger seat, leather upholstery, leather-wrapped steering wheel and shifter, simulated-wood interior trim, remote keyless entry, illuminated visor mirrors, variable intermittent wipers, remote keyless entry system with trunk release, theft-deterrent system, Bose 6-speaker audio system with AM/FM/cassette/CD player, Homelink universal garage-door opener, simulated-leather door panels, bright exhaust outlet, 205/65HR15 tires, alloy wheels.

## OPTIONAL EQUIPMENT:

|  | Retail Price | Dealer Invoice |
|---|---|---|
| **Major Packages** | | |
| Leather Trim Pkg., SE | $1349 | $1159 |
| *Includes leather seats, 4-way power front passenger seat, automatic climate control, simulated-leather door panels. Requires Security and Convenience Pkg. and Bose audio system.* | | |
| Deluxe Seating Pkg., SE, GLE | 449 | 386 |
| *Front-seat side air bags, heated front seats, heated mirrors, low washer fluid warning light, heavy-duty battery. GLE requires anti-lock brakes. SE requires anti-lock brakes, Bose audio system, Leather Trim Pkg., and Security and Convenience Pkg.* | | |
| Security and Convenience Pkg., GXE | 699 | 615 |
| SE | 1690 | 1488 |
| *Includes 8-way power driver seat, power sunroof (SE), remote keyless entry system, power trunk release, security system, illuminated visor vanity mirrors, variable intermittent wipers, Homelink universal garage door opener (SE). NA GXE with 5-speed manual transmission.* | | |
| **Safety Features** | | |
| Anti-lock brakes | 499 | 450 |
| **Comfort and Convenience** | | |
| Bose audio system, SE | 899 | 790 |
| *Requires Security and Convenience Pkg.* | | |
| Power sunroof, GXE, GLE | 899 | 772 |
| *GXE requires automatic transmission and Security and Convenience Pkg.* | | |

| | Retail Price | Dealer Invoice |
|---|---|---|
| Sunroof wind deflector | $49 | $39 |
| Burlwood trim, GXE, SE | 429 | 292 |
| *NA GXE with rear spoiler.* | | |
| Floormats | 79 | 52 |

### Appearance and Miscellaneous

| | | |
|---|---|---|
| Rear spoiler, GXE, GLE | 429 | 308 |
| *NA GXE with burlwood trim.* | | |
| Alloy wheels, GXE | 849 | 555 |

# NISSAN PATHFINDER

*Nissan Pathfinder LE*

## SPECIFICATIONS

| | 4-door wagon |
|---|---|
| Wheelbase, in. | 106.3 |
| Overall length, in. | 178.3 |
| Overall width, in. | 68.7 |
| Overall height, in. | 67.1 |
| Curb weight, lbs. | 3675 |
| Cargo vol., cu. ft. | 85.0 |
| Fuel capacity, gals. | 20.8 |
| Seating capacity | 5 |
| Front head room, in. | 39.5 |
| Max. front leg room, in. | 41.7 |
| Rear head room, in. | 37.5 |
| Min. rear leg room, in. | 31.8 |

## ENGINES

| | ohc V-6 |
|---|---|
| Size, liters/cu. in. | 3.3/201 |
| Horsepower @ rpm | 168@ 4800 |
| Torque (lbs./ft.) @ rpm | 196@ 2800 |

# NISSAN

|  | ohc V-6 |
|---|---|
| Availability ........................................................................ | S |

**EPA city/highway mpg**
| | |
|---|---|
| 5-speed OD manual............................................................ | 17/19[1] |
| 4-speed OD automatic........................................................ | 16/20[2] |

*1. 16/18 w/4WD. 2. 15/19 w/4WD.*

## Nissan Pathfinder

| | Retail Price | Dealer Invoice |
|---|---|---|
| XE 2WD 4-door wagon, 5-speed ................................. | $23999 | $21610 |
| XE 2WD 4-door wagon, automatic ............................... | 24999 | 22510 |
| XE 4WD 4-door wagon, 5-speed ................................. | 25999 | 23410 |
| XE 4WD 4-door wagon, automatic ............................... | 26999 | 24311 |
| SE 4WD 4-door wagon, 5-speed ................................. | 29099 | 26202 |
| SE 4WD 4-door wagon, automatic ............................... | 30099 | 27103 |
| LE 2WD 4-door wagon, automatic ............................... | 30449 | 27418 |
| LE 4WD 4-door wagon, automatic ............................... | 32849 | 29580 |
| Destination charge ....................................................... | 490 | 490 |

## STANDARD EQUIPMENT:

**XE:** 3.3-liter V-6 engine, 5-speed manual or 4-speed automatic transmission, driver- and passenger-side air bags, anti-lock brakes, power steering, air conditioning, cloth upholstery, reclining front bucket seats, 60/40 split folding rear seat with reclining seatback and head restraints, center storage console with armrest, cupholders, tilt steering column, AM/FM/CD player, diversity antenna, digital clock, tachometer, coolant-temperature gauge, trip odometer, tinted glass, dual outside mirrors, passenger-side visor mirror, rear defogger, variable intermittent wipers, rear intermittent wiper/washer, remote fuel-door release, auxiliary power outlets, concealed storage bin, map lights, chrome upper bumpers, front and rear tow hooks, 235/70R15 tires, chromed steel wheels, full-size spare tire, 4WD models add: part-time 4WD, cargo cover.

**SE** adds: part-time 4WD, cruise control, automatic air conditioning, moquette upholstery, multi-adjustable driver seat, rear folding armrest, heated power mirrors, power door locks, power windows, remote keyless entry, theft-deterrent system, power antenna, privacy glass, illuminated visor mirrors, luggage rack, tubular step rail, cargo net and cover, fog lamps, rear wind deflector, fender flares, bright grille and bumper, mud guards, 265/70R15 tires, 6-spoke alloy wheels.

**LE** deletes fender flares and tubular step rail and adds: 4-speed automatic transmission, leather upholstery, leather-wrapped steering wheel, wood-grain interior trim, simulated-leather door trim, digital compass and outside-temperature gauge, Bose AM/FM/cassette/CD player, Homelink universal garage-door opener, bright running boards, 235/70R15 tires, lacy-spoke alloy wheels, deletes part-time 4WD (2WD), 4WD adds: part-time 4WD, limited slip differential, heated front seats.

## OPTIONAL EQUIPMENT:
### Major Packages

| | Retail Price | Dealer Invoice |
|---|---|---|
| Convenience Pkg., XE | $1449 | $1245 |

*Cruise control, power windows and door locks, heated power mirrors, remote keyless entry and theft-deterrent system, cargo cover and net, luggage rack.*

| | | |
|---|---|---|
| Sport Pkg., XE 2WD | 1099 | 944 |
| XE 4WD | 499 | 428 |

*Includes limited slip differential (4WD), black fender flares (2WD), fog lights, rear wind deflector, step rails (2WD), luggage rack, 265/70R15 tires (2WD), six-spoke alloy wheels (2WD). Requires Convenience Pkg.*

| | | |
|---|---|---|
| Leather Trim Pkg., SE | 1399 | 1201 |

*Includes leather upholstery, leather-wrapped steering wheel, heated front seats, simulated leather door trim, compass, outside temperature gauge.*

| | | |
|---|---|---|
| Off-Road Pkg., SE | 249 | 214 |

*Limited-slip rear differential, black bumpers. Requires Bose/Moonroof Pkg.*

| | | |
|---|---|---|
| Luxury Pkg., LE | 1299 | 1116 |

*Power moonroof, power front seats.*

| | | |
|---|---|---|
| Bose/Moonroof Pkg., SE | 1549 | 1331 |

*Power moonroof, Bose AM/FM/cassette/CD player, power antenna, Homelink universal garage door opener. Requires Sport Pkg.*

### Comfort and Convenience

| | | |
|---|---|---|
| Burlwood interior trim, XE, SE | 369 | 252 |

*XE requires Convenience Pkg.*

| | | |
|---|---|---|
| Floormats | 79 | 52 |

### Appearance and Miscellaneous

| | | |
|---|---|---|
| Rear wind deflector, XE | 89 | 68 |

### Special Purpose, Wheels and Tires

| | | |
|---|---|---|
| Alloy wheels, XE 2WD | 849 | 588 |
| Spare tire carrier, XE, SE | 299 | 257 |

*XE requires Sport Pkg. SE requires Off-Road Pkg.*

| | | |
|---|---|---|
| Tow hitch | 389 | 292 |

# NISSAN QUEST

## SPECIFICATIONS

| | 3-door van |
|---|---|
| Wheelbase, in. | 112.2 |
| Overall length, in. | 189.9 |
| Overall width, in. | 73.7 |

*Prices are accurate at time of publication; subject to manufacturer's change.*

# NISSAN

*Nissan Quest GXE*

|  | 3-door van |
|---|---|
| Overall height, in. | 65.6 |
| Curb weight, lbs. | 3865 |
| Cargo vol., cu. ft. | 114.8 |
| Fuel capacity, gals. | 20.0 |
| Seating capacity | 7 |
| Front head room, in. | 39.5 |
| Max. front leg room, in. | 39.9 |
| Rear head room, in. | 39.7 |
| Min. rear leg room, in. | 36.3 |

## ENGINES

|  | ohc V-6 |
|---|---|
| Size, liters/cu. in. | 3.0/181 |
| Horsepower @ rpm | 151@ 4800 |
| Torque (lbs./ft.) @ rpm | 174@ 4400 |
| Availability | S |

**EPA city/highway mpg**

| 4-speed OD automatic | 17/23 |
|---|---|

| Nissan Quest | Retail Price | Dealer Invoice |
|---|---|---|
| XE 3-door van | $23099 | $20560 |
| GXE 3-door van | 26049 | 23186 |
| Destination charge | 490 | 490 |

## STANDARD EQUIPMENT:

**XE:** 3.0-liter V-6 engine, 4-speed automatic transmission, driver- and passenger-side air bags, front air conditioning, power steering, tilt steering column, cruise control, cloth upholstery, reclining front bucket seats, 2-passenger second-row bench seat and 3-passenger rear bench seat, front storage console, underseat storage, tachometer, trip odometer, coolant-temperature gauge, AM/FM/cassette/CD player, rear audio controls, diversity antenna, digital clock, heated power mirrors, power front windows, power door locks, remote keyless entry, rear defogger, intermittent rear wiper/washer, visor mirrors, variable intermittent wipers, floormats, privacy glass, theft-deterrent system, roof rack, cornering lamps, 205/75R15 tires, wheel covers.

**GXE** adds: anti-lock 4-wheel disc brakes, rear air conditioning, rear climate controls, upgraded cloth upholstery, 8-way power driver seat w/height and lumbar adjustment, second row captain's chairs, power rear quarter windows, illuminated visor mirrors, leather-wrapped steering wheel w/audio controls, power antenna, map lights, automatic headlamps, rear auxiliary power outlets, cargo net, 215/70R15 tires, alloy wheels.

## OPTIONAL EQUIPMENT:

| | Retail Price | Dealer Invoice |
|---|---|---|
| **Major Packages** | | |
| Power And Convenience Pkg. delete, XE (credit) | ($1898) | ($825) |
| *Deletes power windows and door locks, heated power mirrors, cruise control, rear radio controls, remote keyless entry, theft-deterrent system, rear privacy glass, roof rack. NA with rear air conditioning, anti-lock brakes, second-row captain's chairs, or integrated child seats.* | | |
| GLE Leather Pkg., GXE | 1299 | 1116 |
| *Leather upholstery, power passenger seat, badging. Requires Luxury Pkg.* | | |
| Luxury Pkg., GXE | 1249 | 1074 |
| *Semi-automatic air conditioning, 6-disc CD changer, power sunroof.* | | |
| Handling Pkg., GXE | 549 | 472 |
| *Upgraded shock absorbers and suspension, rear stabilizer bar, trailer wiring harness, full-size spare tire. Requires Luxury Pkg.* | | |
| **Safety Features** | | |
| Anti-lock 4-wheel disc brakes, XE | 499 | 428 |
| Integrated child seats | 199 | 170 |
| *XE requires rear air conditioning, anti-lock brakes. Middle bench replaces captain's chairs on GXE. NA with GLE Leather Pkg.* | | |
| **Comfort and Convenience** | | |
| Rear air conditioning, XE | 649 | 558 |
| Second-row captain's chairs, XE | 599 | 514 |
| *Requires rear air conditioning.* | | |
| **Appearance and Miscellaneous** | | |
| 2-tone paint | 299 | 257 |

# NISSAN SENTRA

## SPECIFICATIONS

| | 4-door sedan |
|---|---|
| Wheelbase, in. | 99.8 |

*Prices are accurate at time of publication; subject to manufacturer's change.*

*Nissan Sentra SE*

| | 4-door sedan |
|---|---|
| Overall length, in. | 171.1 |
| Overall width, in. | 66.6 |
| Overall height, in. | 54.5 |
| Curb weight, lbs. | 2315 |
| Cargo vol., cu. ft. | 10.7 |
| Fuel capacity, gals. | 13.2 |
| Seating capacity | 5 |
| Front head room, in. | 39.1 |
| Max. front leg room, in. | 42.3 |
| Rear head room, in. | 36.5 |
| Min. rear leg room, in. | 32.4 |

## ENGINES

| | dohc I-4 | dohc I-4 |
|---|---|---|
| Size, liters/cu. in. | 1.6/97 | 2.0/122 |
| Horsepower @ rpm | 115@ 6000 | 140@ 6400 |
| Torque (lbs./ft.) @ rpm | 108@ 4000 | 132@ 4800 |
| Availability | S | S[1] |

**EPA city/highway mpg**

| | | |
|---|---|---|
| 5-speed OD manual | 29/39 | 23/31 |
| 4-speed OD automatic | 27/36 | 23/30 |

1. SE.

| Nissan Sentra | Retail Price | Dealer Invoice |
|---|---|---|
| Base 4-door sedan, 5-speed | $11499 | $10950 |
| XE 4-door sedan, 5-speed | 13699 | 12761 |
| XE 4-door sedan, automatic | 14499 | 13506 |
| GXE 4-door sedan, 5-speed | 14899 | 13494 |
| GXE 4-door sedan, automatic | 15699 | 14218 |
| GLE 4-door sedan, 5-speed | 15749 | 14263 |
| GLE 4-door sedan, automatic | 16549 | 14987 |
| SE 4-door sedan, 5-speed | 16749 | 15168 |
| SE 4-door sedan, automatic | 17549 | 15892 |
| Destination charge | 490 | 490 |

## STANDARD EQUIPMENT:

**Base:** 1.6-liter dohc 4-cylinder engine, 5-speed manual transmission, driver- and passenger-side air bags, cloth reclining front bucket seats, front console, cupholders, tilt steering column, coolant-temperature gauge, trip odometer, rear defogger, auxiliary power outlet, tinted glass, driver-side outside mirror, 155/80R13 tires.

**XE** adds: 5-speed manual or 4-speed automatic transmission, power steering, air conditioning, AM/FM/cassette, digital clock, intermittent wipers, remote decklid and fuel-door releases, dual outside mirrors, 175/70R13 tires, wheel covers.

**GXE** adds: cruise control, split folding rear seat, upgraded cloth upholstery, power windows, power door locks, power mirrors, passenger-side visor mirror, cargo light, bodyside moldings.

**GLE** adds: velour upholstery, fold front armrest (w/automatic), remote keyless entry, CD/cassette player, tachometer, theft-deterrent system, 175/65R14 tires, alloy wheels.

**SE** adds: 2.0-liter dohc 4-cylinder engine, variable-assist power steering, leather-wrapped steering wheel, floormats, front air dam, rear spoiler, lower bodyside moldings, fog lights, 195/55R15 tires, deletes CD player.

## OPTIONAL EQUIPMENT:

| | Retail Price | Dealer Invoice |
|---|---|---|
| **Major Packages** | | |
| SE Option Pkg., SE | $899 | $772 |
| *Includes power moonroof, AM/FM/cassette/CD player, remote keyless entry, theft-deterrent system.* | | |
| **Safety Features** | | |
| Anti-lock brakes, GXE, GLE, SE | 499 | 450 |
| *Includes 4-wheel disc brakes.* | | |
| **Comfort and Convenience** | | |
| Power moonroof, GLE | 449 | 386 |
| 3-disc CD changer, XE, GXE, SE | 559 | 408 |
| CD player, XE, GXE, SE | 469 | 307 |
| Rosewood trim, Base, XE, GXE, GLE | 319 | 221 |
| **Appearance and Miscellaneous** | | |
| Rear spoiler, Base, XE, GXE, GLE | 339 | 246 |

# OLDSMOBILE AURORA

## SPECIFICATIONS

| | 4-door sedan |
|---|---|
| Wheelbase, in. | 113.8 |

*Prices are accurate at time of publication; subject to manufacturer's change.*

# OLDSMOBILE

*Oldsmobile Aurora*

|  | 4-door sedan |
|---|---|
| Overall length, in. | 205.4 |
| Overall width, in. | 74.4 |
| Overall height, in. | 55.4 |
| Curb weight, lbs. | 3967 |
| Cargo vol., cu. ft. | 16.1 |
| Fuel capacity, gals. | 20.0 |
| Seating capacity | 5 |
| Front head room, in. | 38.4 |
| Max. front leg room, in. | 42.6 |
| Rear head room, in. | 36.9 |
| Min. rear leg room, in. | 38.4 |

## ENGINES

|  | dohc V-8 |
|---|---|
| Size, liters/cu. in. | 4.0/244 |
| Horsepower @ rpm | 250@ 5600 |
| Torque (lbs./ft.) @ rpm | 260@ 4400 |
| Availability | S |
| **EPA city/highway mpg** |  |
| 4-speed OD automatic | 17/26 |

| Oldsmobile Aurora | Retail Price | Dealer Invoice |
|---|---|---|
| Base 4-door sedan | $35960 | $32543 |
| Destination charge | 665 | 665 |

## STANDARD EQUIPMENT:

**Base:** 4.0-liter dohc V-8 engine, 4-speed automatic transmission, traction control, driver- and passenger-side air bags, anti-lock 4-wheel disc brakes, air conditioning w/automatic climate control system, inside/outside temperature indicator, variable-assist power steering, tilt steering wheel, leather-wrapped steering wheel, steering-wheel climate and radio, cruise control, leather upholstery, power front bucket seats with power lumbar support and driver-side 2-position memory, center storage console with leather-wrapped shifter, interior wood trim, auxiliary power source, overhead storage console, folding rear armrest with trunk pass-through, power memory mirrors with defoggers, power windows, automatic programmable door locks, remote keyless illuminated entry/exit system, automatic day/night rearview mirror with compass, AM/FM/cassette/CD player, integrated antenna, illuminated visor mirrors, power fuel-door and deck-lid release, intermittent wipers, Driver Information System, tachometer, engine-coolant temperature gauge, trip odometer, oil-level sensor, universal garage-door opener, rear defogger, Twilight Sentinel automatic headlamp control, cargo net, floormats, solar-control tinted glass, Pass-Key theft-deterrent system, fog lights, cornering lamps, dual exhaust outlets, 235/60R16 tires, alloy wheels.

## OPTIONAL EQUIPMENT:

| | Retail Price | Dealer Invoice |
|---|---|---|
| **Major Packages** | | |
| Autobahn Pkg. | $395 | $352 |
| *Includes 3.71 axle ratio and 235/60VR16 tires.* | | |
| **Comfort and Convenience** | | |
| OnStar System | 895 | 761 |
| *Includes global positioning system, voice-activated cellular telephone, roadside assistance, emergency services. Requires dealer installation charge and monthly service charges.* | | |
| Power sunroof | 995 | 886 |
| Heated driver and front passenger seats | 295 | 263 |
| Bose Acoustimass Sound System | 871 | 775 |
| 12-disc CD changer | 460 | 409 |
| **Appearance and Miscellaneous** | | |
| Engine-block heater | 20 | 18 |
| White diamond paint | 395 | 352 |
| Chrome wheels | 800 | 712 |

# OLDSMOBILE BRAVADA

## SPECIFICATIONS

| | 4-door wagon |
|---|---|
| Wheelbase, in. | 107.0 |
| Overall length, in. | 183.7 |
| Overall width, in. | 67.8 |
| Overall height, in. | 63.2 |
| Curb weight, lbs. | 4049 |
| Cargo vol., cu. ft. | 37.3 |
| Fuel capacity, gals. | 18.0 |
| Seating capacity | 5 |
| Front head room, in. | 39.6 |

*Prices are accurate at time of publication; subject to manufacturer's change.*

*Oldsmobile Bravada*

|  | 4-door wagon |
|---|---|
| Max. front leg room, in. | 42.4 |
| Rear head room, in. | 38.2 |
| Min. rear leg room, in. | 36.3 |

## ENGINES

|  | ohv V-6 |
|---|---|
| Size, liters/cu. in. | 4.3/262 |
| Horsepower @ rpm | 190@ 4400 |
| Torque (lbs./ft.) @ rpm | 250@ 2800 |
| Availability | S |

**EPA city/highway mpg**

| 4-speed OD automatic | 16/21 |
|---|---|

| Oldsmobile Bravada | Retail Price | Dealer Invoice |
|---|---|---|
| Base 4-door wagon | $30645 | $27734 |
| Destination charge | 515 | 515 |

## STANDARD EQUIPMENT:

**Base:** 4.3-liter V-6 engine, 4-speed automatic transmission, automatic 4-wheel drive with active electronic transfer case, locking rear differential, driver- and passenger-side air bags, anti-lock 4-wheel disc brakes, daytime running lamps, air conditioning w/automatic climate control, variable-assist power steering, tilt steering wheel, cruise control, leather upholstery, front reclining bucket seats with power lumbar adjustment, 6-way power driver's seat w/power recliner, split folding rear bench seat, center console with storage armrest, cupholders, overhead storage console (trip computer, compass, reading lamps, outside temperature gauge, universal garage-door opener), AM/FM/cassette with six speakers, power antenna, digital clock, rear defogger, rear wiper/washer, automatic day/night mirror, tachometer, oil-pressure, coolant-temperature gauges, voltmeter, trip odometer, power mirrors w/heated driver-side, power windows, power door locks, remote keyless entry, illuminated visor mirrors, intermittent wipers, automatic headlights, auxiliary power outlets, cargo net and cover, floormats, theft-deterrent system, solar-control windshield, tinted windows, fog lamps, luggage rack, striping, front tow hooks, full-size spare tire, 235/70R15 all-season tires, alloy wheels.

## OPTIONAL EQUIPMENT:

| | Retail Price | Dealer Invoice |
|---|---|---|

### Major Packages

| | Retail Price | Dealer Invoice |
|---|---|---|
| Value Pkg. | $70 | $60 |

Heated front seats, CD/cassette player, Towing Pkg. NA with cloth upholstery.

| | | |
|---|---|---|
| Towing Pkg. | 210 | 181 |

Heavy-duty suspension and hazard lights, 8-wire electrical harness, platform hitch, engine oil cooler.

### Comfort and Convenience

| | | |
|---|---|---|
| Heated front seats | 225 | 194 |

NA with cloth upholstery.

| | | |
|---|---|---|
| Power sunroof | 695 | 598 |
| CD/cassette player | 200 | 172 |

### Appearance and Miscellaneous

| | | |
|---|---|---|
| Engine block heater | 33 | 28 |

### Special Purpose, Wheels and Tires

| | | |
|---|---|---|
| White letter tires | 135 | 116 |

# OLDSMOBILE CUTLASS

## SPECIFICATIONS

| | 4-door sedan |
|---|---|
| Wheelbase, in. | 107.0 |
| Overall length, in. | 192.0 |
| Overall width, in. | 69.4 |
| Overall height, in. | 56.9 |
| Curb weight, lbs. | 2982 |
| Cargo vol., cu. ft. | 17.0 |
| Fuel capacity, gals. | 15.2 |
| Seating capacity | 5 |
| Front head room, in. | 39.4 |
| Max. front leg room, in. | 42.2 |

*Prices are accurate at time of publication; subject to manufacturer's change.*

# OLDSMOBILE

*Oldsmobile Cutlass GLS*

|  | 4-door sedan |
|---|---|
| Rear head room, in. | 37.6 |
| Min. rear leg room, in. | 38.0 |

## ENGINES

|  | ohv V-6 |
|---|---|
| Size, liters/cu. in. | 3.1/191 |
| Horsepower @ rpm | 155@ 4800 |
| Torque (lbs./ft.) @ rpm | 180@ 3200 |
| Availability | S |

**EPA city/highway mpg**

| 4-speed OD automatic | 20/29 |
|---|---|

| Oldsmobile Cutlass | Retail Price | Dealer Invoice |
|---|---|---|
| GL 4-door sedan | $17800 | $16287 |
| GLS 4-door sedan | 19425 | 17773 |
| Destination charge | 525 | 525 |

## STANDARD EQUIPMENT:

**GL:** 3.1-liter V-6 engine, 4-speed automatic transmission, driver- and passenger-side air bags, anti-lock brakes, daytime running lights, air conditioning, power steering, tilt steering column, cruise control, cloth upholstery, reclining front bucket seats, split folding rear seat w/trunk passthrough, storage console w/armrest, front and rear cupholders, power door locks, tachometer, coolant-temperature gauge, trip odometer, tinted glass, AM/FM/cassette, digital clock, rear defogger, remote decklid release, visor mirrors, auxiliary power outlets, map/reading lights, intermittent wipers, automatic headlamps, floormats, dual outside mirrors w/driver-side remote, Pass-Lock II theft-deterrent system, fog lights, 215/60R15 tires, bolt-on wheel covers.

**GLS** adds: leather upholstery, 6-way power driver seat, power windows, power mirrors, remote keyless entry, illuminated passenger-side visor mirror, passenger-assist handles, cargo net, alloy wheels.

## OPTIONAL EQUIPMENT:

| | Retail Price | Dealer Invoice |
|---|---|---|
| **Major Packages** | | |
| Convenience Pkg., GL | $625 | $556 |
| *Power windows and mirrors, remote keyless entry, cargo net.* | | |
| **Comfort and Convenience** | | |
| 6-way power driver seat, GL | 305 | 271 |
| Sunroof, GLS | 595 | 530 |
| Cassette/CD player | 200 | 178 |
| Remote keyless entry, GL | 150 | 134 |
| **Appearance and Miscellaneous** | | |
| Engine-block heater | 20 | 18 |
| Alloy wheels, GL | 315 | 280 |

# OLDSMOBILE EIGHTY EIGHT/LSS/REGENCY

*Oldsmobile LSS*

## SPECIFICATIONS

| | 4-door sedan |
|---|---|
| Wheelbase, in. | 110.8 |
| Overall length, in. | 200.4 |
| Overall width, in. | 74.1 |
| Overall height, in. | 55.7 |
| Curb weight, lbs. | 3455 |
| Cargo vol., cu. ft. | 18.0 |
| Fuel capacity, gals. | 18.0 |
| Seating capacity | 6 |
| Front head room, in. | 38.7 |
| Max. front leg room, in. | 42.5 |
| Rear head room, in. | 38.3 |
| Min. rear leg room, in. | 38.7 |

## ENGINES

| | ohv V-6 | Supercharged ohv V-6 |
|---|---|---|
| Size, liters/cu. in. | 3.8/231 | 3.8/231 |

*Prices are accurate at time of publication; subject to manufacturer's change.*

# OLDSMOBILE

| | ohv V-6 | Supercharged ohv V-6 |
|---|---|---|
| Horsepower @ rpm .................................. | 205@ 5200 | 240@ 5200 |
| Torque (lbs./ft.) @ rpm ................................. | 230@ 4000 | 280@ 3200 |
| Availability ........................................ | S | O[1] |
| **EPA city/highway mpg** | | |
| 4-speed OD automatic...................................... | 19/29 | 18/27 |

*1. LSS.*

| Oldsmobile Eighty Eight/LSS/Regency | Retail Price | Dealer Invoice |
|---|---|---|
| Base 4-door sedan ................................................ | $22795 | $20857 |
| LS 4-door sedan ................................................ | 24195 | 22138 |
| LSS 4-door sedan ................................................ | 28095 | 25706 |
| Regency 4-door sedan ................................................ | 28395 | 25981 |
| Destination charge ...................................... | 605 | 605 |

## STANDARD EQUIPMENT:

**Base:** 3.8-liter V-6 engine, 4-speed automatic transmission, driver- and passenger-side air bags, anti-lock brakes, daytime running lamps, power steering, tilt steering wheel, cruise control, air conditioning, 55/45 cloth front seat with reclining seatback, storage armrest w/cupholders, 8-way power driver seat, power windows, power door locks, rear defogger, AM/FM/cassette player w/6-speaker sound system, digital clock, power antenna, auxiliary power outlet, remote decklid release, coolant-temperature gauge, trip odometer, courtesy/reading lights, visor mirrors, intermittent wipers, Twilight Sentinel headlight control, floormats, left remote and right manual outside mirrors, tinted glass with solar-control windshield and rear window, Pass-Key theft-deterrent system, tool kit, 205/70R15 tires, bolt-on wheel covers.

**LS** adds: traction control system, front bucket seats, remote keyless entry, programmable door locks, power mirrors, illuminated visor mirrors, 215/65R15 touring tires, alloy wheels.

**LSS** adds: dual-zone air conditioning with inside/outside temperature indicator, variable-assist power steering, leather upholstery, manual lumbar support, 8-way power passenger seat, floor console, overhead storage console, rear seat w/trunk pass-through, rear-seat storage armrest, tachometer, leather-wrapped steering wheel w/radio and climate controls, cassette/CD player, automatic day/night rearview and driver-side outside mirror, illuminated entry/exit, fog lights, cargo net, automatic load-leveling touring suspension, 225/60R16 tires.

**Regency** adds to Base: traction control system, dual-zone air conditioner with inside/outside temperature indicator, leather upholstery, 6-way power front seats with power recliners and lumbar-support adjusters, front and rear storage armrests w/cupholders, overhead storage console w/reading lamps, power mirrors, automatic day/night inside mirror w/compass, driver seat, and outside-mirror memory controls, automatic day/night heated driver-side outside mirror, AM/FM/cassette/CD player, leather-wrapped steering wheel w/radio and climate controls, remote keyless entry, illuminated visor mirrors, illuminated entry/exit system, cargo net, automatic load-leveling touring suspension, 205/70R15 whitewall tires, alloy wheels.

## OPTIONAL EQUIPMENT:

| | Retail Price | Dealer Invoice |
|---|---|---|
| **Powertrains** | | |
| Supercharged 3.8-liter V-6 engine, LSS | $1022 | $909 |
| **Comfort and Convenience** | | |
| 8-way power passenger seat, LS | 350 | 312 |
| Power sunroof, LSS, Regency | 995 | 886 |
| Leather upholstery, LS | 515 | 458 |
| Remote keyless entry, Base | 225 | 200 |
| Cassette/CD player, LS | 200 | 178 |
| **Appearance and Miscellaneous** | | |
| Engine block heater | 20 | 18 |
| Alloy wheels, Base | 330 | 294 |
| 16-inch alloy wheels, LS | 150 | 134 |
| *Includes 225/60R16 tires.* | | |
| Chrome alloy wheels, LSS | 600 | 534 |

# OLDSMOBILE INTRIGUE

## SPECIFICATIONS

| | 4-door sedan |
|---|---|
| Wheelbase, in. | 109.0 |
| Overall length, in. | 195.6 |
| Overall width, in. | 73.6 |
| Overall height, in. | 56.6 |
| Curb weight, lbs. | 3455 |
| Cargo vol., cu. ft. | 16.0 |
| Fuel capacity, gals. | 18.0 |
| Seating capacity | 5 |
| Front head room, in. | 39.3 |
| Max. front leg room, in. | 42.4 |
| Rear head room, in. | 37.4 |
| Min. rear leg room, in. | 36.9 |

## ENGINES

| | ohv V-6 |
|---|---|
| Size, liters/cu. in. | 3.8/231 |

*Prices are accurate at time of publication; subject to manufacturer's change.*

# OLDSMOBILE

*Oldsmobile Intrigue GL*

|  | ohv V-6 |
|---|---|
| Horsepower @ rpm | 195@ 5200 |
| Torque (lbs./ft.) @ rpm | 220@ 4000 |
| Availability | S |
| **EPA city/highway mpg** | |
| 4-speed OD automatic | 19/30 |

| Oldsmobile Intrigue | Retail Price | Dealer Invoice |
|---|---|---|
| Base 4-door sedan | $20700 | $18941 |
| GL 4-door sedan | 22100 | 20222 |
| Destination charge | 550 | 550 |

## STANDARD EQUIPMENT:

**Base:** 3.8-liter V-6 engine, 4-speed automatic transmission, traction control, anti-lock 4-wheel disc brakes, driver- and passenger side air bags, daytime running lamps, shoulder belt adjusters, childproof rear door locks, variable-effort power steering, air conditioning, AM/FM/cassette, cruise control on steering wheel, cloth reclining front bucket seats, tilt steering wheel, center console, front and rear cupholders, power door locks, power windows, power mirrors, remote trunk and fuel door release, map pockets, auxiliary electrical outlets, reading lights, Pass-Lock theft-deterrent system, 225/60SR16 tires, alloy wheels.

**GL** adds: Comfort and Security Pkg. (remote keyless entry, illuminated entry, tire inflation monitor), automatic dual-zone air conditioning, heated power outside mirrors, 6-way power driver seat, leather-wrapped steering wheel/armrest/shifter, 6-speaker sound system, rear window grid-antenna, split-folding rear seat, illuminated visor mirrors, trunk cargo net, fog lamps.

## OPTIONAL EQUIPMENT:

| | Retail Price | Dealer Invoice |
|---|---|---|
| **Major Packages** | | |
| Autobahn Pkg., GL | $230 | $205 |
| *Heavy-duty brakes, 225/60HR16 tires.* | | |
| **Comfort and Convenience** | | |
| Sunroof | 695 | 619 |
| 6-way power driver seat, Base | 305 | 271 |
| CD/cassette player, Base | 270 | 240 |
| GL | 200 | 178 |
| *Includes six speakers, seek/scan, digital clock.* | | |
| Bose CD/cassette player | 500 | 445 |
| *Includes eight speakers, seek/scan, automatic tone control, amplifier, digital clock.* | | |
| 12-disc CD changer | 460 | 409 |
| Six speaker sound system, Base | 70 | 62 |
| Steering wheel radio controls, GL | 125 | 111 |
| Remote keyless entry, Base | 150 | 134 |
| Leather-wrapped steering wheel, Base | 120 | 107 |
| *Includes leather shifter and armrest.* | | |
| Leather upholstery, GL | 995 | 886 |
| Split folding rear seat, Base | 150 | 134 |
| **Appearance and Miscellaneous** | | |
| Rear spoiler | 150 | 134 |
| *Base requires rear window grid-antenna.* | | |
| Chrome alloy wheels, GL | 600 | 534 |

# OLDSMOBILE SILHOUETTE

| SPECIFICATIONS | 4-door van | 4-door van |
|---|---|---|
| Wheelbase, in. | 112.0 | 120.0 |
| Overall length, in. | 187.4 | 201.4 |
| Overall width, in. | 72.2 | 72.2 |
| Overall height, in. | 67.4 | 68.1 |
| Curb weight, lbs. | 3746 | 3942 |
| Cargo vol., cu. ft. | 133.0 | 155.9 |
| Fuel capacity, gals. | 20.0 | 25.0 |
| Seating capacity | 8 | 8 |
| Front head room, in. | 39.9 | 39.9 |
| Max. front leg room, in. | 39.9 | 39.9 |
| Rear head room, in. | 39.3 | 39.3 |
| Min. rear leg room, in. | 36.9 | 39.0 |

*Prices are accurate at time of publication; subject to manufacturer's change.*

# OLDSMOBILE

*Oldsmobile Silhouette*

## ENGINES

| | ohv V-6 |
|---|---|
| Size, liters/cu. in. | 3.4/207 |
| Horsepower @ rpm | 180@ 5200 |
| Torque (lbs./ft.) @ rpm | 205@ 4000 |
| Availability | S |

**EPA city/highway mpg**

| | |
|---|---|
| 4-speed OD automatic | 18/25 |

| Oldsmobile Silhouette | Retail Price | Dealer Invoice |
|---|---|---|
| GL 4-door van, extended | $23965 | $21688 |
| GS 4-door van, SWB | 24430 | 22109 |
| GLS 4-door van, extended | 27165 | 24584 |
| Destination charge | 570 | 570 |

SWB denotes short wheelbase.

## STANDARD EQUIPMENT:

**GL:** 3.4-liter V-6 engine, 4-speed automatic transmission, driver- and passenger-side air bags, front side-impact air bags, anti-lock brakes, daytime running lights, front air conditioning, interior air filter, power steering, tilt steering wheel, cruise control, power sliding passenger-side door, reclining front bucket seats w/lumbar adjustment and folding armrests, 4-way adjustable driver seat, second-row 60/40 split-folding bench seat, third-row 50/50 split-folding bench seat, front storage console, under-passenger-seat storage drawer, overhead console w/map lights, front and rear cupholders, power mirrors, power windows, power door locks, tachometer, coolant-temperature gauge, trip odometer, AM/FM/cassette, integrated antenna, digital clock, intermittent wipers, rear wiper/washer, rear defogger, automatic headlights, visor mirrors, rear reading lights, front and rear auxiliary power outlets, cargo net, floormats, sliding driver-side door, solar control windshield, deep-tinted glass, theft-deterrent system, fog lights, roof rack, 215/70R15 tires, wheel covers.

**GS** adds: remote keyless entry, 6-way power front seats, overhead storage console (includes compass, outside temperature indicator, driver information center), illuminated visor mirrors, 205/70R15 tires, deletes under-passenger-seat storage drawer.

**GLS** adds: traction control, leather upholstery, second-row captain's chairs, leather-wrapped steering wheel w/radio controls, rear-seat radio controls, rear air conditioning and heater controls, touring suspension w/automatic load leveling, air inflation kit, 215/70R15 touring tires, alloy wheels.

## OPTIONAL EQUIPMENT:

| | Retail Price | Dealer Invoice |
|---|---|---|

### Major Packages

| | Retail Price | Dealer Invoice |
|---|---|---|
| Rear Convenience Pkg., GL | $540 | $464 |
| *Rear air conditioning and heater, rear-seat radio controls.* | | |
| Towing Pkg., GL, GS | 355 | 305 |
| GLS | 85 | 73 |
| *Includes touring suspension and automatic load leveling (GL, GS), engine-oil cooler, heavy-duty radiator, 5-lead wiring harness, 215/70R15 touring tires (GS).* | | |

### Powertrains

| | Retail Price | Dealer Invoice |
|---|---|---|
| Traction control, GL, GS | 195 | 168 |

### Comfort and Convenience

| | Retail Price | Dealer Invoice |
|---|---|---|
| OnStar System | 895 | 761 |
| *Includes Global Positioning System, voice-activated cellular telephone, roadside assistance, emergency services. Requires dealer installation charge and monthly service charges.* | | |
| Rear air conditioning, GLS | 450 | 387 |
| *Includes rear heater.* | | |
| 6-way power front seats, GL | 575 | 495 |
| Leather upholstery, GS | 870 | 748 |
| *Includes leather-wrapped steering wheel.* | | |
| Two center-row captain's chairs, GL, GS | 250 | 215 |
| 8-passenger seating, GL, GS | 235 | 202 |
| *Includes 3 center-row bucket seats, 3-passenger split-folding rear bench seat.* | | |
| Integrated child seat, GL, GS | 125 | 108 |
| Dual integrated child seats, GL, GS | 225 | 194 |
| CD player | 100 | 86 |
| *Includes automatic tone control.* | | |
| Cassette/CD player | 200 | 172 |
| *Includes automatic tone control.* | | |
| Steering wheel radio controls, GS | 125 | 108 |
| Rear radio controls, GL, GS | 90 | 77 |
| Remote keyless entry, GL | 150 | 129 |

*Prices are accurate at time of publication; subject to manufacturer's change.*

## Appearance and Miscellaneous

| | Retail Price | Dealer Invoice |
|---|---|---|
| Engine block heater | $20 | $17 |
| Touring suspension, GL, GS | 270 | 232 |

*Includes automatic load leveling, air inflater, 215/70R15 touring tires (GS).*

| | | |
|---|---|---|
| Alloy wheels, GL, GS | 285 | 245 |

# PLYMOUTH BREEZE

*Plymouth Breeze*

## SPECIFICATIONS

| | 4-door sedan |
|---|---|
| Wheelbase, in. | 108.0 |
| Overall length, in. | 186.7 |
| Overall width, in. | 71.7 |
| Overall height, in. | 51.9 |
| Curb weight, lbs. | 2929 |
| Cargo vol., cu. ft. | 15.7 |
| Fuel capacity, gals. | 16.0 |
| Seating capacity | 5 |
| Front head room, in. | 38.1 |
| Max. front leg room, in. | 42.3 |
| Rear head room, in. | 36.8 |
| Min. rear leg room, in. | 37.8 |

## ENGINES

| | ohc I-4 | dohc I-4 |
|---|---|---|
| Size, liters/cu. in. | 2.0/122 | 2.4/148 |
| Horsepower @ rpm | 132@ 6000 | 150@ 5200 |
| Torque (lbs./ft.) @ rpm | 129@ 5000 | 167@ 4000 |
| Availability | S | O |

**EPA city/highway mpg**

| | | |
|---|---|---|
| 5-speed OD manual | 27/37 | 21/30 |

| | ohc I-4 | dohc I-4 |
|---|---|---|
| 4-speed OD automatic | 23/33 | |

| **Plymouth Breeze** | Retail Price | Dealer Invoice |
|---|---|---|
| Base 4-door sedan | $14675 | $13476 |
| | | |
| Destination charge | 535 | 535 |

## STANDARD EQUIPMENT:

**Base:** 2.0-liter 4-cylinder engine, 5-speed manual transmission, driver- and passenger-side air bags, air conditioning, power steering, cloth reclining front bucket seats, folding rear seat, tilt steering column, center storage console, trip odometer, tachometer, voltmeter, oil-pressure gauge, coolant-temperature gauge, 4-speaker AM/FM radio, digital clock, cupholders, rear defogger, speed-sensitive intermittent wipers, auxiliary power outlet, remote decklid release, visor mirrors, front floormats, dual remote mirrors, tinted glass, 195/70R14 tires, wheel covers.

## OPTIONAL EQUIPMENT:
### Major Packages

| | | |
|---|---|---|
| Pkg. 21B/22B/24B | 760 | 676 |
| *Manufacturer's discount price* | 685 | 609 |
| *4-way manual driver-seat height adjuster, power heated mirrors, power door locks and windows, rear floormats.* | | |
| Expresso Pkg. | 375 | 334 |
| *Manufacturer's discount price* | 275 | 245 |
| *Cassette player, body stripes, badging, special wheel covers.* | | |

### Powertrains

| | | |
|---|---|---|
| 2.4-liter dohc 4-cylinder engine | 450 | 401 |
| *Requires automatic transmission.* | | |
| 4-speed automatic transmission | 1050 | 935 |
| *Includes cruise control.* | | |

### Safety Features

| | | |
|---|---|---|
| Anti-lock 4-wheel disc brakes | 565 | 503 |
| Integrated child seat | 100 | 89 |
| *Includes fixed rear seat.* | | |

### Comfort and Convenience

| | | |
|---|---|---|
| Power sunroof | 695 | 619 |
| *Includes map lights, illuminated visor mirrors. Requires Pkg. 21B/22B/24B.* | | |
| Remote keyless entry | 170 | 151 |
| *Requires Pkg. 21B/22B/24B.* | | |
| Cassette player | 180 | 160 |
| Premium CD player | 380 | 338 |
| *w/Expresso Pkg.* | 200 | 178 |

*Prices are accurate at time of publication; subject to manufacturer's change.*

| | Retail Price | Dealer Invoice |
|---|---|---|
| Premium AM/FM/cassette and 6-disc CD changer ........ | $730 | $650 |
| w/Expresso Pkg. ................................................ | 550 | 490 |
| Smoker's Pkg. ...................................................... | 20 | 18 |
| *Lighter, ashtray.* | | |

## Appearance and Miscellaneous

| | | |
|---|---|---|
| Candy-apple red paint ............................................... | 200 | 178 |
| Full-size spare ........................................................ | 125 | 111 |

# PLYMOUTH VOYAGER

*Plymouth Voyager SE*

## SPECIFICATIONS

| | 3-door van | 4-door van |
|---|---|---|
| Wheelbase, in. ............................................ | 113.3 | 119.3 |
| Overall length, in. ..................................... | 186.3 | 199.6 |
| Overall width, in. ....................................... | 76.8 | 76.8 |
| Overall height, in. ...................................... | 68.5 | 68.5 |
| Curb weight, lbs. ....................................... | 3516 | 3683 |
| Cargo vol., cu. ft. ...................................... | 142.9 | 168.5 |
| Fuel capacity, gals. .................................... | 20.0 | 20.0 |
| Seating capacity........................................ | 7 | 7 |
| Front head room, in. .................................. | 39.8 | 39.8 |
| Max. front leg room, in. ............................. | 40.6 | 40.6 |
| Rear head room, in. ................................... | 40.0 | 40.0 |
| Min. rear leg room, in. ............................... | 42.3 | 39.6 |

## ENGINES

| | dohc I-4 | ohc V-6 | ohv V-6 |
|---|---|---|---|
| Size, liters/cu. in. ......................... | 2.4/148 | 3.0/181 | 3.3/202 |
| Horsepower @ rpm ....................... | 150@ 5200 | 150@ 5200 | 158@ 4850 |
| Torque (lbs./ft.) @ rpm .................. | 167@ 4000 | 176@ 4000 | 203@ 3250 |
| Availability ................................... | S[1] | S[2] | O |

**EPA city/highway mpg**

| | | | |
|---|---|---|---|
| 3-speed automatic | 20/26 | 19/24 | |
| 4-speed OD automatic | | 19/26 | 18/24 |

*1. Base. 2. SE, optional Base.*

| Plymouth Voyager | Retail Price | Dealer Invoice |
|---|---|---|
| Base 3-door van, SWB | $17415 | $15845 |
| Base Grand 4-door van | 20125 | 18270 |
| SE 4-door van, SWB | 21290 | 19255 |
| Grand SE 3-door van | 22285 | 20171 |
| Destination charge | 580 | 580 |

SWB denotes short wheelbase.

## STANDARD EQUIPMENT:

**Base SWB:** 2.4-liter dohc 4-cylinder engine, 3-speed automatic transmission, driver- and passenger-side air bags, power steering, cloth reclining front bucket seats, 3-passenger rear bench seat, AM/FM radio, digital clock, trip odometer, variable intermittent wipers, variable intermittent rear wiper/washer, visor mirrors, auxiliary power outlet, tinted glass, dual exterior mirrors, 205/75R14 tires, wheel covers.

**Base Grand** adds: 3.0-liter V-6 engine, sliding driver side door, folding 2-passenger middle bench seat, folding 3-passenger rear bench seat.

**SE** adds: 4-speed automatic transmission, anti-lock brakes, folding 2-passenger middle bench seat with armrest (SWB), deluxe cloth upholstery, cassette player, tachometer, storage drawer below passenger seat, dual horns, additional sound insulation, cargo net, 215/65R15 tires.

## OPTIONAL EQUIPMENT:
### Major Packages

| | | |
|---|---|---|
| Pkg. 22T/24T/28T, Base SWB | 1610 | 1369 |
| *Manufacturer's discount price* | 375 | 319 |

    *Air conditioning, CYE 7-passenger Seating Group (folding 2-passenger middle bench seat, folding 3-passenger rear bench seat) (SWB), rear sound insulation, storage drawer below passenger seat, dual horns.*

| | | |
|---|---|---|
| Pkg. 22T/24T/28T, Base Grand | 885 | 752 |
| *Manufacturer's discount price* | 25 | 21 |

    *Air conditioning, CYE 7-passenger Seating Group (folding 2-passenger middle bench seat, folding 3-passenger rear bench seat) (SWB), rear sound insulation, storage drawer below passenger seat, dual horns.*

| | | |
|---|---|---|
| Pkg. 25B/25B/28B, SE | 1205 | 1024 |
| *Manufacturer's discount price* | 195 | 165 |

    *Air conditioning, CYN 7-passenger Deluxe Seating Group (reclining/folding 2-passenger middle bench seat and 3-passenger rear bench seat with adjustable headrests), rear defogger.*

| | Retail Price | Dealer Invoice |
|---|---|---|
| Pkg. 25C/28C (Expresso), SE ......................................... | $2080 | $1768 |
| *Manufacturer's discount price.........................................* | *885* | *752* |
| Pkg. 25B/26B/28B plus Expresso Pkg. (solar-control glass, Expresso decals, striping, AM/FM/CD). Requires 3.3-liter V-6 engine. | | |
| Pkg. 25D/26D/28D, SE..................................................... | 2240 | 1904 |
| *Manufacturer's discount price.........................................* | *930* | *790* |
| Pkg. 25B/26B/28B plus tilt steering wheel, cruise control, heated power mirrors, power windows and door locks, Light Group (courtesy lights, illuminated ignition w/time delay), illuminated visor mirrors, added sound insulation, floormats. | | |
| Pkg. 28E (Expresso), SE ................................................. | 3115 | 2648 |
| *Manufacturer's discount price.........................................* | *1620* | *1377* |
| Pkg. 25D/26D/28D plus Expresso Pkg. Requires 3.3-liter V-6 engine. | | |
| Pkg. 25L/28L, SE............................................................. | 3545 | 3013 |
| *Manufacturer's discount price.........................................* | *2235* | *1899* |
| Pkg. 25D/26D/28D plus CYS Deluxe 7-passenger Seating Group (reclining/folding middle bucket seats, and rear 3-passenger bench seat with adjustable headrests), premium cloth upholstery, 8-way power driver seat, overhead console w/trip computer, intermediate map/courtesy lights. Requires 3.3-liter V-6 engine. | | |
| Pkg. 25N/28N (Expresso), SE ......................................... | 4420 | 2925 |
| *Manufacturer's discount price.........................................* | *2925* | *2486* |
| Pkg. 28L plus Expresso Pkg. Requires 3.3-liter V-6 engine. | | |
| Climate Group 2............................................................... | 450 | 383 |
| *Solar-control glass, windshield wiper de-icer. Requires option pkg.* | | |
| Climate Group 3, Grand SE w/Pkg. 25B/26B/28B......... | 1130 | 961 |
| Grand SE w/Pkg. 25C/28C............................................. | 680 | 578 |
| *Requires Pkg. 25D/26D/28D, 28E, 28L, or 28N.* | | |
| 10-speaker cassette/CD w/equalizer, SE....................... | 720 | 612 |
| *Requires Pkg. 25D/26D/28D, 28E, 28L, or 28N.* | | |
| Climate Group 3, Grand SE w/Pkg. 25D/26D/28D | 1020 | 867 |
| Grand SE w/Pkg. 28E..................................................... | 570 | 485 |
| Grand SE w/Pkg. 28L..................................................... | 940 | 799 |
| Grand SE w/Pkg. 25N/28N ............................................. | 490 | 417 |
| *Rear heater and air conditioning, overhead console.* | | |
| Convenience/Security Group 1, Base............................. | 435 | 370 |
| *Cruise control, tilt steering column, power mirrors. Requires option pkg.* | | |
| Convenience/Security Group 2, Base............................. | 750 | 638 |
| SE .................................................................................. | 315 | 268 |
| *Group 1 plus power locks. Requires option pkg.* | | |
| Convenience/Security Group 3, SE................................. | 685 | 582 |
| *Group 1 plus power windows and rear quarter vent windows. Requires option pkg.* | | |

| | Retail Price | Dealer Invoice |
|---|---|---|
| Convenience/Security Group 4, SE.................... | $235 | $200 |

*Remote keyless entry, illuminated entry, headlight-off delay. Requires Pkg. 24D/28D, 28E, 28L, or 28N.*

| | | |
|---|---|---|
| Convenience/Security Group 5, SE.................... | 385 | 327 |

*Group 3 plus theft-deterrent system. Requires Pkg. 25D/26D/28D, 28E, 28L, or 28N.*

| | | |
|---|---|---|
| Loading & Towing Group 2, SE ..................... | 180 | 153 |

*Group 1 plus heavy load/firm ride suspension. Requires option pkg.*

| | | |
|---|---|---|
| Loading & Towing Group 3, Grand SE.................... | 445 | 378 |
| ordered w/Climate Group III.................... | 380 | 323 |

*Group 2 plus Heavy Duty Trailer Tow Group (heavy-duty battery, alternator, brakes, and radiator, heavy-duty transmission-oil cooler, trailer wiring harness). Requires Pkg. 28D, 28E, 28L, or 28N. Requires 3.3-liter V-6 engine.*

## Powertrains

| | | |
|---|---|---|
| 3.0-liter V-6 engine, Base SWB .................... | 770 | 655 |

*NA with 4-speed automatic transmission. Base requires option pkg. NA SE Pkgs. 28C, 28E, 28L, or 28N.*

| | | |
|---|---|---|
| 3.3-liter V-6 engine, Base SWB .................... | 970 | 825 |
| Base Grand, SE.................... | 200 | 170 |

*Requires 4-speed automatic transmission (std. on SE) and option pkg.*

| | | |
|---|---|---|
| 4-speed automatic transmission, Base .................... | 250 | 213 |

*Requires 3.3-liter V-6 engine and option pkg.*

## Safety Features

| | | |
|---|---|---|
| Anti-lock brakes, Base.................... | 565 | 480 |

## Comfort and Convenience

| | | |
|---|---|---|
| CYE 7-passenger Seating Group, Base SWB .................... | 350 | 298 |

*Folding 2-passenger middle bench seat, folding 3-passenger rear bench seat.*

| | | |
|---|---|---|
| CYK 7-passenger Seating Group, Base .................... | 285 | 242 |

*Reclining/folding 2-passenger middle bench seat with two integrated child seats and adjustable headrests, folding 3-passenger rear bench seat. Requires option pkg.*

| | | |
|---|---|---|
| CYR Deluxe 7-passenger Seating Group, SE .................... | 225 | 191 |

*CYN Deluxe 7-passenger Seating Group with two integrated child seats in middle bench. Requires option pkg. (NA with Pkg. 28L or 28N).*

| | | |
|---|---|---|
| CYS Deluxe 7-passenger Seating Group, SE.................... | 650 | 553 |

*Reclining/folding middle bucket seats and rear 3-passenger bench seat with adjustable headrests. Requires Pkg. 24D/28D or 28E. Requires sliding driver-side door.*

| | | |
|---|---|---|
| Air conditioning.................... | 860 | 731 |
| Rear defogger, Base w/o Convenience/Security Group | 195 | 166 |

*Prices are accurate at time of publication; subject to manufacturer's change.*

|  | Retail Price | Dealer Invoice |
|---|---|---|
| Base w/Convenience/Security Group, SE | $230 | $196 |
| *Includes windshield wiper de-icer.* | | |
| Sliding driver-side door, Base SWB | 595 | 506 |
| *Requires option pkg.* | | |
| AM/FM/cassette, Base | 180 | 153 |
| *Requires option pkg.* | | |
| 10-speaker cassette player w/equalizer, SE | 325 | 276 |
| *Requires Pkg. 25D/28D, 28E, 28L, or 28N.* | | |

## Appearance and Miscellaneous

|  |  |  |
|---|---|---|
| Roof rack | 175 | 149 |
| *Requires option pkg.* | | |
| Smoker's Group | 20 | 17 |
| *Cigarette lighter, ashtrays.* | | |
| Engine-block heater | 35 | 30 |
| Load-leveling suspension, Grand SE | 290 | 247 |
| *Requires Pkg. 25D/26D/28D, 28E, 28L, or 28N.* | | |
| Alloy wheels, Grand SE | 415 | 353 |
| *Requires Pkg. 25B/26B/28B, 25D/26D/28D, or 28L.* | | |
| Full-size spare tire | 110 | 94 |

# PONTIAC BONNEVILLE

*Pontiac Bonneville SE*

## SPECIFICATIONS

|  | 4-door sedan |
|---|---|
| Wheelbase, in. | 110.8 |
| Overall length, in. | 200.5 |
| Overall width, in. | 74.5 |
| Overall height, in. | 55.7 |
| Curb weight, lbs. | 3446 |
| Cargo vol., cu. ft. | 18.0 |
| Fuel capacity, gals. | 18.0 |
| Seating capacity | 6 |

| | 4-door sedan |
|---|---|
| Front head room, in. | 39.2 |
| Max. front leg room, in. | 42.6 |
| Rear head room, in. | 38.3 |
| Min. rear leg room, in. | 38.0 |

## ENGINES

| | ohv V-6 | Super ohv V-6 |
|---|---|---|
| Size, liters/cu. in. | 3.8/231 | 3.8/231 |
| Horsepower @ rpm | 205@ 5200 | 240@ 5200 |
| Torque (lbs./ft.) @ rpm | 230@ 4000 | 280@ 3200 |
| Availability | S | O[1] |
| **EPA city/highway mpg** | | |
| 4-speed OD automatic | 19/28 | 17/27 |

1. SSE.

| Pontiac Bonneville | Retail Price | Dealer Invoice |
|---|---|---|
| SE 4-door sedan | $22390 | $20487 |
| SSE 4-door sedan | 29390 | 26892 |
| Destination charge | 605 | 605 |

## STANDARD EQUIPMENT:

**SE:** 3.8-liter V-6 engine, 4-speed automatic transmission, driver- and passenger-side air bags, anti-lock brakes, daytime running lamps, air conditioning, power steering, tilt steering wheel, cruise control, cloth 45/55 split bench seat with storage armrest, cupholders, power windows, power door locks, 4-speaker AM/FM radio, digital clock, coolant-temperature gauge, oil-pressure gauge, voltmeter, tachometer, trip odometer, rear defogger, intermittent wipers, visor mirrors, Twilight Sentinel, Lamp Group (includes rear courtesy lights, rear assist handles, headlamp-on warning, trunk light), floormats, tinted glass, left remote and right manual outside mirrors, Pass-Key II theft-deterrent system, fog lights, decklid spoiler, 215/65R15 touring tires, bolt-on wheel covers.

**SSE** adds: traction control, dual exhaust, automatic climate control w/outside temperature indicator, variable-assist power steering, 45/45 leather bucket seats with center storage console, 6-way power driver seat, power passenger seat, rear vents, rear armrest w/cupholders, overhead console with power outlet, heated power mirrors, automatic day/night inside mirror, CD player with equalizer and Bose 8-speaker sound system, leather-wrapped steering wheel with radio controls, power antenna, EyeCue Head-up instrument display, Driver Information Center, remote keyless entry, illuminated entry, remote decklid release, illuminated visor mirrors, cargo net, electronic load leveling, theft-deterrent system w/alarm, lower-body cladding, emergency road kit (includes spot light, first aid kit, air hose, windshield scraper, gloves), 225/60R16 touring tires, 3-spoke alloy wheels.

## OPTIONAL EQUIPMENT:

| | Retail Price | Dealer Invoice |
|---|---|---|
| **Major Packages** | | |
| Option Group 2, 1SB, SE | $1125 | $1001 |
| *Variable-effort power steering, illuminated entry, remote keyless entry, cassette player, 6-way power driver's seat, illuminated visor mirrors, power mirrors, remote decklid release, cargo net.* | | |
| Option Group 3, 1SC, SE | 2030 | 1807 |
| *Group 1SB plus bucket seats, Radio Enhancement Pkg. (leather-wrapped steering wheel w/radio controls, 6-speaker sound system), 225/60R16 tires, alloy wheels.* | | |
| Option Group 4, 1SD, SE | 3135 | 2790 |
| *Group 1SC plus automatic climate control, power antenna, leather upholstery.* | | |
| SLE Special Edition Pkg., SE | 1100 | 946 |
| *Manufacturer's discount price* | 600 | 516 |
| *Fog lights, special bumpers and grille, dual exhausts.* | | |
| **Powertrains** | | |
| SSEi Supercharger Pkg., SSE | 1170 | 1041 |
| *Includes supercharged 3.8-liter V-6 engine, driver selectable shift, boost gauge, unique floormats, 225/60HR16 tires.* | | |
| Traction control, SE | 175 | 156 |
| *Requires option group, bucket seats, and alloy wheels.* | | |
| **Comfort and Convenience** | | |
| Power glass sunroof, SE | 995 | 886 |
| SE with bucket seats, SSE | 980 | 872 |
| *SE includes illuminated visor mirrors. SE requires alloy wheels.* | | |
| Cloth 45/45 bucket seats, SE | 220 | 196 |
| *Includes center storage console and rear vents, illuminated visor mirrors, overhead console w/power outlet.* | | |
| Leather 45/45 bucket seats, SE with Group 1SB | 1345 | 1197 |
| SE with Group 1SC | 850 | 757 |
| *Includes center storage console and rear vents, rear seat storage armrest, leather-wrapped steering wheel, overhead console with power outlet.* | | |
| 45/45 articulating leather bucket seats, SSE | 245 | 218 |
| 6-way power passenger seat, SE | 305 | 271 |
| *SE requires option group and alloy wheels when ordered with group 1SC.* | | |
| Radio Enhancement Pkg., SE w/Group 1SB | 275 | 245 |
| *Includes leather-wrapped steering wheel w/radio controls, 6-speaker sound system. Requires alloy wheels.* | | |

| | Retail Price | Dealer Invoice |
|---|---|---|
| Cassette player, SE | $220 | $196 |
| *Includes graphic equalizer and Radio Enhancement Pkg.* | | |
| CD player, SE | 320 | 285 |
| *Includes graphic equalizer and Radio Enhancement Pkg.* | | |
| Power antenna, SE | 85 | 76 |
| *Requires option group.* | | |

## Appearance and Miscellaneous

| | | |
|---|---|---|
| Theft-deterrent system w/alarm, SE | 190 | 169 |
| *Includes locking fuel filler door. Requires Group 1SD.* | | |
| Engine block heater | 20 | 18 |
| Computer Command Ride, SSE | 380 | 338 |
| Computer Command Ride/Handling Pkg., SSE | NA | NA |
| *Computer Command Ride, 3.05 rear axle ratio, 225/60HR16 touring tires.* | | |
| 16-inch 5-blade alloy wheels, SE | 325 | 289 |
| *Requires 225/60R16 tires.* | | |
| 16-inch gold or silver crosslace alloy wheels, SE | 325 | 289 |
| *Requires 225/60R16 tires.* | | |
| 16-inch Chrome Torque Star alloy wheels, SE | 920 | 819 |
| SE w/Group 1SD, SSE | 595 | 530 |
| *SE requires 225/60R16 tires.* | | |
| 225/60R16 blackwall touring tires, SE | 85 | 76 |
| *Requires alloy wheels.* | | |

# PONTIAC FIREBIRD

*Pontiac Firebird Trans Am convertible*

## SPECIFICATIONS

| | 2-door hatchback | 2-door conv. |
|---|---|---|
| Wheelbase, in. | 101.1 | 101.1 |
| Overall length, in. | 193.4 | 193.4 |
| Overall width, in. | 74.5 | 74.5 |
| Overall height, in. | 52.0 | 52.7 |

*Prices are accurate at time of publication; subject to manufacturer's change.*

# PONTIAC

| | 2-door hatchback | 2-door conv. |
|---|---|---|
| Curb weight, lbs. | 3340 | 3492 |
| Cargo vol., cu. ft. | 33.7 | 12.9 |
| Fuel capacity, gals. | 15.5 | 15.5 |
| Seating capacity | 4 | 4 |
| Front head room, in. | 37.2 | 37.2 |
| Max. front leg room, in. | 43.0 | 43.0 |
| Rear head room, in. | 35.3 | 35.3 |
| Min. rear leg room, in. | 28.9 | 28.9 |

## ENGINES

| | ohv V-6 | ohv V-8 | ohv V-8 |
|---|---|---|---|
| Size, liters/cu. in. | 3.8/231 | 5.7/346 | 5.7/346 |
| Horsepower @ rpm | 200@ 5200 | 305@ 5200 | 320@ 5200 |
| Torque (lbs./ft.) @ rpm | 225@ 4000 | 335@ 4000 | 345@ 4400 |
| Availability | S[1] | S[2] | O[2] |

### EPA city/highway mpg

| | | | |
|---|---|---|---|
| 5-speed OD manual | 19/30 | | |
| 6-speed OD manual | | 17/26 | 16/26 |
| 4-speed OD automatic | 19/29 | 18/24 | 18/24 |

1. Base. 2. Formula, Trans Am.

| Pontiac Firebird | Retail Price | Dealer Invoice |
|---|---|---|
| Base 2-door coupe | $18015 | $16484 |
| Base 2-door coupe Consumer Marketing Initiative w/Group 1SG | 19825 | 18281 |
| Base 2-door coupe Consumer Marketing Initiative w/Group 1SH | 21825 | 20121 |
| Base 2-door convertible | 24305 | 22239 |
| Formula 2-door coupe | 22865 | 20921 |
| Trans Am 2-door coupe | 25975 | 23767 |
| Trans Am 2-door convertible | 29715 | 27189 |
| Destination charge | 525 | 525 |

Consumer Marketing Initiative models available in Calif., Ore., Wash., Idaho. CMI prices include destination charge.

## STANDARD EQUIPMENT:

**Base coupe:** 3.8-liter V-6 engine, 5-speed manual transmission, driver- and passenger-side air bags, anti-lock 4-wheel disc brakes, daytime running lights, air conditioning, power steering, tilt steering wheel, cruise control, cloth reclining front bucket seats, folding rear bench seat, center console (storage, auxiliary power outlet, cupholder), 4-speaker AM/FM/CD with equalizer, intermittent wipers, coolant-temperature and oil-pressure gauges, tachometer, voltmeter, trip odometer, dual reading lamps, visor mirrors, remote hatch release, rear defogger, floormats, tinted glass, left remote and right manual mirrors, Pass-Key II theft-deterrent system, fog lights, front air dam, decklid spoiler, 215/60R16 touring tires, alloy wheels.

**Base coupe Consumer Marketing Initiative w/Group 1SG** adds: 4-speed automatic transmission, power windows, power door locks, power mirrors, power antenna.

**Base coupe Consumer Marketing Initiative w/Group 1SH** adds: limited slip differential, 3.42 axle ratio, premium AM/FM/CD w/ten speakers, 6-way power driver seat, remote keyless entry, theft-deterrent system w/alarm, upgraded steering, dual exhaust, 235/55R16 tires.

**Base convertible** adds to Base coupe: power door locks, power windows, power mirrors, leather-wrapped steering wheel w/radio controls, leather-wrapped shifter and handbrake, premium AM/FM/CD w/six speakers, rear decklid release, power top with glass rear window and rear window defogger.

**Formula** adds to base coupe: 5.7-liter V-8 engine, 4-speed automatic transmission, air conditioning, power mirrors, power windows, power door locks, leather-wrapped steering wheel w/radio controls, leather-wrapped shifter and parking brake, premium AM/FM/CD w/ten speakers, power antenna, performance suspension, 245/50ZR16 touring tires.

**Trans Am coupe** adds to Formula: 6-way power driver seat, leather upholstery, remote keyless entry, removable hatch roof, theft-deterrent system w/alarm.

**Trans Am convertible** adds: power top with rear glass window, 6-speaker sound system, rear decklid release, deletes removable hatch roof.

# OPTIONAL EQUIPMENT:
## Major Packages

| | Retail Price | Dealer Invoice |
|---|---|---|
| Option Group 1SB, Base coupe | $1510 | $1344 |
| *4-speed automatic transmission, power mirrors, power windows, power door locks, power antenna. Requires 235/55R16 tires.* | | |
| Option Group 1SC, Base coupe | 2450 | 2181 |
| *Group 1SB plus premium AM/FM/CD w/ten speakers, leather-wrapped steering wheel w/radio controls, 6-way power driver seat, remote keyless entry, theft-deterrent system w/alarm.* | | |
| Option Group 1SB, Formula | 1505 | 1339 |
| *4-speed automatic transmission, removable hatch roof, 6-way power driver seat, remote keyless entry, power antenna, theft-deterrent system w/alarm.* | | |
| 1LE Performance Pkg., Formula | — | — |
| *Ram Air Performance and Handling Pkg. plus 6-speed manual transmission, stiffer front and rear control arm bushings, double adjustable shock absorbers.* | | |

*Prices are accurate at time of publication; subject to manufacturer's change.*

# PONTIAC

|  | Retail Price | Dealer Invoice |
|---|---|---|
| 3800 Performance Pkg., Base | $440 | $392 |

*Limited slip differential, faster ratio steering gear, dual exhaust, 3.42 rear axle ratio (with automatic transmission), 235/55R16 tires.*

| WS6 Ram Air Performance and Handling Pkg., Formula, Trans Am | 3100 | 2759 |
|---|---|---|

*Ram air induction system, functional hood scoops, upgraded suspension, power steering fluid cooler, bright exhaust outlets, 275/40ZR17 tires, high-polished alloy wheels. Formula requires option group.*

| Sport Appearance Pkg., Base | 990 | 881 |
|---|---|---|

*Specific Aero Appearance Pkg., dual exhaust. Coupe requires option group.*

| Security Pkg., Base coupe, Formula | 240 | 214 |
|---|---|---|

*Remote keyless entry, theft-deterrent system w/alarm. Base requires Group 1SB.*

## Powertrains

| 5-speed manual transmission, Base coupe, (credit) | (815) | (725) |
|---|---|---|

*Requires option group.*

| 6-speed manual transmission, Formula, Trans Am | NC | NC |
|---|---|---|
| 4-speed automatic transmission, Base | 815 | 725 |
| Traction control, Formula, Trans Am | 450 | 401 |
| Rear performance axle, Formula, Trans Am | 225 | 200 |

*Includes 3.23 axle ratio. Requires 4-speed automatic transmission and 245/50ZR16 tires.*

## Comfort and Convenience

| Premium cassette player, Base coupe w/Group 1SB | 330 | 294 |
|---|---|---|
| Base coup w/Group 1SC, Formula, Trans Am (credit) | (100) | (89) |

*Includes 10-speaker sound system (coupes), 6-speaker sound system (convertibles), leather-wrapped steering wheel with radio controls (Base coupe).*

| Premium CD player, Base coupe w/Group 1SB | 430 | 383 |
|---|---|---|

*Includes 10-speaker sound system, leather-wrapped steering with radio controls.*

| 12-disc CD changer | 595 | 530 |
|---|---|---|

*Base requires Group 1SC.*

| Leather upholstery, Base, Formula | 650 | 579 |
|---|---|---|

*Base coupe requires Group 1SC. Formula requires Group 1SB.*

| Articulating bucket seats, Trans Am | 155 | 138 |
|---|---|---|
| 6-way power driver seat, Base coupe, Formula | 270 | 240 |

## Appearance and Miscellaneous

| Removable locking hatch roof, Base coupe, Formula | 995 | 886 |
|---|---|---|

*Includes sunshades, lock, and stowage.*

| 235/55R16 touring tires, Base | 135 | 120 |
|---|---|---|

| | Retail Price | Dealer Invoice |
|---|---|---|
| 245/50ZR16 high performance tires, Formula, Trans Am | $225 | $200 |
| Chromed alloy wheels | 595 | 530 |

*Base coupe and Formula require option group. NA with Ram Air Performance and Handling Pkg.*

# PONTIAC GRAND AM

*Pontiac Grand Am GT coupe*

## SPECIFICATIONS

| | 2-door coupe | 4-door sedan |
|---|---|---|
| Wheelbase, in. | 103.4 | 103.4 |
| Overall length, in. | 186.9 | 186.9 |
| Overall width, in. | 68.3 | 68.3 |
| Overall height, in. | 53.5 | 53.5 |
| Curb weight, lbs. | 2835 | 2877 |
| Cargo vol., cu. ft. | 13.4 | 13.4 |
| Fuel capacity, gals. | 15.2 | 15.2 |
| Seating capacity | 5 | 5 |
| Front head room, in. | 37.8 | 37.8 |
| Max. front leg room, in. | 43.1 | 43.1 |
| Rear head room, in. | 36.5 | 37.0 |
| Min. rear leg room, in. | 33.9 | 34.9 |

## ENGINES

| | dohc I-4 | ohv V-6 |
|---|---|---|
| Size, liters/cu. in. | 2.4/146 | 3.1/191 |
| Horsepower @ rpm | 150@ 6000 | 155@ 5200 |
| Torque (lbs./ft.) @ rpm | 155@ 4400 | 185@ 4000 |
| Availability | S | O |

### EPA city/highway mpg

| | | |
|---|---|---|
| 5-speed OD manual | 22/33 | |
| 4-speed OD automatic | 22/32 | 20/29 |

*Prices are accurate at time of publication; subject to manufacturer's change.*

## Pontiac Grand Am

| | Retail Price | Dealer Invoice |
|---|---|---|
| SE 2-door notchback | $14874 | $13610 |
| SE 4-door sedan | 15024 | 13746 |
| GT 2-door notchback | 16324 | 14936 |
| GT 4-door sedan | 16474 | 15074 |
| Destination charge | 525 | 525 |

## STANDARD EQUIPMENT:

**SE:** 2.4-liter dohc 4-cylinder engine, 5-speed manual transmission, driver- and passenger-side air bags, anti-lock brakes, daytime running lamps, air conditioning, power steering, cloth reclining front bucket seats, center console (armrest, storage, cupholders), overhead compartment, rear-seat headrests, AM/FM radio, power door locks, remote fuel-door and decklid release, tachometer, coolant-temperature gauge, trip odometer, illuminated entry, visor mirrors, floormats, left remote and right manual outside mirrors, Passlock theft-deterrent system, tinted glass, fog lights, 195/70R14 tires, wheel covers.

**GT** adds: leather-wrapped steering wheel, shifter, parking-brake handle, tilt steering wheel, intermittent wipers, dual exhaust, decklid spoiler, 205/55R16 performance tires, alloy wheels.

## OPTIONAL EQUIPMENT:
### Major Packages

| | | |
|---|---|---|
| Option Group 1SB, SE | 545 | 485 |
| *Cassette player, rear defogger, spoiler.* | | |
| Option Group 1SC, SE | 995 | 886 |
| *Group 1SB plus 4-speed automatic transmission, tilt steering wheel, cruise control, intermittent wipers.* | | |
| Option Group 1SD, SE 2-door | 1870 | 1664 |
| SE 4-door | 1935 | 1722 |
| *Group 1SC plus 3.1-liter V-6 engine, power mirrors, power windows, CD player, remote keyless entry, 195/65R15 tires.* | | |
| Option Group 1SE, SE 2-door | 2575 | 2292 |
| SE 4-door | 2640 | 2350 |
| *Group 1SD plus split folding rear seat, steering-wheel radio controls, 205/55R16 tires, alloy wheels.* | | |
| Option Group 1SB, GT | 375 | 324 |
| *Cassette player, rear defogger, spoiler.* | | |
| Option Group 1SC, GT 2-door | 1415 | 1259 |
| GT 4-door | 1480 | 1317 |
| *Group 1SB plus 3.1-liter V-6 engine, 4-speed automatic transmission, variable-assist power steering, CD player, power windows, power mirrors, cruise control, remote keyless entry.* | | |
| Option Group 1SD, GT 2-door | 2470 | 2198 |

| | Retail Price | Dealer Invoice |
|---|---|---|
| GT 4-door .................................................. | $2535 | $2256 |

*Group 1SC plus sunroof, steering-wheel radio controls, Sport Interior Group (upgraded cloth upholstery, driver seat lumbar adjuster, seat back pockets, map lights), split folding rear seat.*

| | | |
|---|---|---|
| Sport Interior Group, GT............................... | 170 | 151 |

*Upgraded cloth upholstery, driver-seat lumbar adjuster, seat back pockets, map lights. Requires Group 1SC.*

Sport Interior Group w/leather upholstery,

| | | |
|---|---|---|
| GT w/Group 1SC ...................................... | 810 | 721 |
| GT w/Group 1SD ...................................... | 475 | 423 |

*Includes split folding back seat.*

## Powertrains

| | | |
|---|---|---|
| 3.1-liter V-6 engine, SE............................... | 450 | 401 |

*Requires 4-speed automatic transmission. Requires Option Group 1SB or 1SC.*

| | | |
|---|---|---|
| 4-speed automatic transmission .................... | 810 | 721 |

*Includes traction control. Requires Option Group 1SB.*

## Comfort and Convenience

| | | |
|---|---|---|
| Rear defogger ............................................. | 180 | 160 |
| 6-way power driver's seat, GT ....................... | 340 | 303 |

*Requires Group 1SD.*

| | | |
|---|---|---|
| Power sunroof ............................................ | 595 | 530 |

*SE requires Group 1SD or 1SE. GT requires Group 1SB or 1SC.*

| | | |
|---|---|---|
| Cassette player with equalizer, with option group .......... | 110 | 98 |

*Includes six speakers.*

CD player with equalizer,

| | | |
|---|---|---|
| with option group ..................................... | 210 | 187 |

*Includes six speakers.*

Cassette and CD players with equalizer,

| | | |
|---|---|---|
| SE w/Group 1SB or 1SC, GT w/Group 1SB .............. | 405 | 360 |
| SE w/Group 1SD or 1SE, GT w/Group | | |
| 1SC or 1SD ............................................. | 195 | 174 |
| Smoker's Pkg............................................. | 170 | 151 |

*Lighter, ashtray.*

## Appearance and Miscellaneous

| | | |
|---|---|---|
| Engine block heater ..................................... | 20 | 18 |
| 195/65R15 touring tires, SE........................... | 135 | 120 |

*Requires Group 1SB or 1SC.*

| | | |
|---|---|---|
| 205/55R16 touring tires, SE........................... | 225 | 200 |

*Requires Group 1SD and 16-inch alloy wheels*

| | | |
|---|---|---|
| 15-inch crosslace alloy wheels, SE ................. | 300 | 267 |
| 16-inch alloy wheels, SE.............................. | 325 | 289 |

*Prices are accurate at time of publication; subject to manufacturer's change.*

# PONTIAC GRAND PRIX

*Pontiac Grand Prix GT sedan*

## SPECIFICATIONS

| | 2-door coupe | 4-door sedan |
|---|---|---|
| Wheelbase, in. | 110.5 | 110.5 |
| Overall length, in. | 196.5 | 196.5 |
| Overall width, in. | 72.7 | 72.7 |
| Overall height, in. | 54.7 | 54.7 |
| Curb weight, lbs. | 3396 | 3414 |
| Cargo vol., cu. ft. | 16.0 | 16.0 |
| Fuel capacity, gals. | 18.0 | 18.0 |
| Seating capacity | 5 | 6 |
| Front head room, in. | 38.3 | 38.3 |
| Max. front leg room, in. | 42.4 | 42.4 |
| Rear head room, in. | 36.5 | 36.7 |
| Min. rear leg room, in. | 36.1 | 35.8 |

## ENGINES

| | ohv V-6 | ohv V-6 | Super ohv V-6 |
|---|---|---|---|
| Size, liters/cu. in. | 3.1/191 | 3.8/231 | 3.8/231 |
| Horsepower @ rpm | 160@ 5200 | 195@ 5200 | 240@ 5200 |
| Torque (lbs./ft.) @ rpm | 185@ 4000 | 220@ 4000 | 280@ 3200 |
| Availability | S[1] | S[2] | O[3] |
| **EPA city/highway mpg** | | | |
| 4-speed OD automatic | 20/29 | 19/30 | 18/27 |

*1. SE. 2. GT; optional, SE. 3. GT.*

| Pontiac Grand Prix | Retail Price | Dealer Invoice |
|---|---|---|
| SE 4-door sedan | $18795 | $17197 |
| GT 2-door coupe | 20415 | 18680 |
| GT 4-door sedan | 20665 | 18908 |
| Destination charge | 550 | 550 |

## STANDARD EQUIPMENT:

**SE:** 3.1-liter V-6 engine, 4-speed automatic transmission, Enhanced Traction System, anti-lock 4-wheel disc brakes, driver- and passenger-side air bags, daytime running lights, air conditioning, power steering, cloth front bucket seats, front floor console, auxiliary power outlet, integrated rear seat headrests, AM/FM radio, power windows, power door locks, tachometer, trip odometer, coolant temperature gauge, Driver Information Center, tilt steering wheel, power mirrors, visor mirrors, door map pockets, tinted glass, intermittent wipers, rear window defogger, fog lights, bright exhaust outlets, 205/70R15 tires, wheel covers.

**GT** adds: 3.8-liter V-6 engine, dual exhaust outlets, Magnasteer variable-effort steering, cruise control, cassette player, leather-wrapped steering wheel, remote decklid release, overhead console, 225/60R16 tires, 5-spoke alloy wheels.

## OPTIONAL EQUIPMENT:
### Major Packages

| | Retail Price | Dealer Invoice |
|---|---|---|
| Option Group 1SB, SE | $540 | $481 |
| *Cruise control, rear-seat pass-through, cassette player, remote decklid release.* | | |
| Option Group 1SC, SE | 1665 | 1482 |
| *Group 1SB plus overhead console, leather-wrapped steering wheel with radio controls, 6-way power driver's seat, cargo net, remote keyless entry, 225/60R16 tires, machine-faced alloy wheels.* | | |
| Option Group 1SD, SE | 2905 | 2585 |
| *Group 1SC plus MAGNASTEER variable-effort power steering, trip computer, Eyecue head-up instrument display, automatic air conditioning, leather upholstery.* | | |
| Option Group 1SB, GT | 755 | 672 |
| *Rear-seat pass-through, steering-wheel radio controls, 6-way power driver's seat, cargo net, remote keyless entry.* | | |
| Option Group 1SC, GT 2-door | 2085 | 1856 |
| GT 4-door | 2115 | 1882 |
| *Group 1SB plus trip computer, Eyecue Head-up instrument display, automatic air conditioning, leather upholstery, Premium Lighting Pkg.* | | |
| GTP Performance Pkg., GT w/Group 1SB | 1610 | 1433 |
| GT w/Group 1SC | 1410 | 1255 |
| *3.8-liter supercharged V-6 engine, 4-speed automatic transmission, full-function traction control, trip computer, rear decklid spoiler, 225/60R16 performance tires, silver 5-spoke alloy wheels.* | | |
| Premium Lighting Pkg., 4-door | 215 | 191 |
| 2-door | 185 | 165 |
| *Lighted visor mirrors, front-door courtesy lamps, rear reading lamps, assist grip, automatic day/night rearview mirror. SE requires Group 1SD. GT requires Group 1SB.* | | |

*Prices are accurate at time of publication; subject to manufacturer's change.*

| | Retail Price | Dealer Invoice |
|---|---|---|
| **Powertrains** | | |
| 3.8-liter V-6 engine, SE w/option group | $415 | $369 |
| **Safety Features** | | |
| Child seat, GT | 125 | 111 |
| SE w/option group, GT w/option group | 75 | 67 |
| **Comfort and Convenience** | | |
| Automatic air conditioning, GT w/Group 1SB | 195 | 174 |
| 6-way power driver seat, SE w/Group 1SB | 270 | 240 |
| Power driver seat lumbar support adjuster | 100 | 89 |
| *Includes heated driver seat when ordered with leather upholstery. Requires option group and bucket seats.* | | |
| Leather seats, SE w/Group 1SC, GT w/Group 1SB | 475 | 423 |
| Heated driver seat | 50 | 45 |
| *Requires bucket seats.* | | |
| Cassette player w/graphic equalizer | 190 | 169 |
| *Includes steering-wheel radio controls, premium sound system. Requires option group. NA SE w/Group 1SB.* | | |
| CD player | 140 | 125 |
| *Requires option group.* | | |
| CD player w/graphic equalizer | 290 | 258 |
| *Requires option group. NA SE w/Group 1SB.* | | |
| Multi-disc CD changer | 595 | 530 |
| *Requires option group. NA SE w/Group 1SB.* | | |
| Premium sound system | 125 | 111 |
| *Requires cassette or CD player. SE requires Group 1SC or 1SD.* | | |
| Overhead console, SE w/Group 1SB | 80 | 71 |
| *NA with power sunroof.* | | |
| Power sunroof | 650 | 579 |
| with overhead console | 570 | 507 |
| *SE requires option group. Deletes overhead console.* | | |
| Remote keyless entry, SE w/Group 1SB | 150 | 134 |
| Theft-deterrent system | 60 | 53 |
| *Requires option group.* | | |
| **Appearance and Miscellaneous** | | |
| Rear decklid spoiler | 175 | 156 |
| *SE requires option group.* | | |
| Machine faced alloy wheels, SE w/Group 1SB | 260 | 231 |
| *Requires 225/60R16 tires.* | | |
| Crosslace alloy wheels, SE | 260 | 231 |
| *SE requires option group, 225/60R16 tires.* | | |
| 5-spoke high-polished alloy wheels, GT | 325 | 289 |
| 5-spoke white alloy wheels, GT | NC | NC |
| *Requires white exterior paint.* | | |
| 225/60R16 tires, SE | 160 | 142 |

# PONTIAC SUNFIRE

*1998 Pontiac Sunfire SE convertible*

## SPECIFICATIONS

| | 2-door coupe | 4-door sedan | 2-door conv. |
|---|---|---|---|
| Wheelbase, in. | 104.1 | 104.1 | 104.1 |
| Overall length, in. | 181.9 | 181.9 | 181.9 |
| Overall width, in. | 67.4 | 67.3 | 68.4 |
| Overall height, in. | 53.0 | 54.7 | 53.9 |
| Curb weight, lbs. | 2637 | 2674 | 2868 |
| Cargo vol., cu. ft. | 12.4 | 13.1 | 9.9 |
| Fuel capacity, gals. | 15.2 | 15.2 | 15.2 |
| Seating capacity | 5 | 5 | 4 |
| Front head room, in. | 37.6 | 38.9 | 38.8 |
| Max. front leg room, in. | 42.1 | 42.1 | 42.1 |
| Rear head room, in. | 36.6 | 37.2 | 38.5 |
| Min. rear leg room, in. | 32.6 | 34.3 | 32.6 |

## ENGINES

| | ohv I-4 | dohc I-4 |
|---|---|---|
| Size, liters/cu. in. | 2.2/133 | 2.4/146 |
| Horsepower @ rpm | 115@ 5000 | 150@ 5600 |
| Torque (lbs./ft.) @ rpm | 135@ 3600 | 155@ 4400 |
| Availability | S[1] | S[2] |

### EPA city/highway mpg

| | | |
|---|---|---|
| 5-speed OD manual | 24/34 | 23/33 |
| 3-speed automatic | 23/29 | |
| 4-speed OD automatic | 23/31 | 22/32 |

1. SE.  2. GT; optional, SE.

| Pontiac Sunfire | Retail Price | Dealer Invoice |
|---|---|---|
| GT 2-door coupe | $15495 | $14332 |
| SE 2-door coupe | 12495 | 11558 |
| SE 2-door coupe Consumer Marketing Initiative | 14695 | 13630 |
| SE 4-door sedan | 12495 | 11558 |

*Prices are accurate at time of publication; subject to manufacturer's change.*

# PONTIAC

|  | Retail Price | Dealer Invoice |
|---|---|---|
| SE 4-door sedan Consumer Marketing Initiative .......... | $14695 | $13630 |
| SE 2-door convertible ................................................ | 19495 | 18033 |
| SE convertible Consumer Marketing Initiative .............. | 21495 | 19920 |
| Destination charge ....................................................... | 500 | 500 |

Consumer Marketing Initiative models available in Calif., Ore., Wash., Idaho. CMI prices include destination charge.

## STANDARD EQUIPMENT:

**SE sedan/coupe:** 2.2-liter 4-cylinder engine, 5-speed manual transmission, driver- and passenger-side air bags, anti-lock brakes, daytime running lamps, power steering, cloth reclining front bucket seats, center console with storage armrest, folding rear seat w/headrests, AM/FM radio, tachometer, coolant-temperature and oil-pressure gauges, trip odometer, visor mirrors, rear heat ducts, floormats, tinted glass, left remote and right remote outside mirrors, Pass-Lock theft-deterrent system, rear spoiler (2-door), 195/70R14 tires, bolt-on wheel covers.

**SE convertible** adds: 4-speed automatic transmission, traction control, air conditioning, power top, cruise control, tilt steering wheel, CD player, rear defogger, intermittent wipers, Convenience Pkg. (overhead storage console, remote decklid release, assist handles, trunk net, reading lights), rear spoiler, 195/65R15 tires.

**GT** adds to SE 2-door: 2.4-liter dohc 4-cylinder engine, air conditioning, tilt steering wheel, CD player, rear defogger, 205/55R16 tires, alloy wheels.

**SE sedan/coupe Consumer Marketing Initiative** adds: 3-speed automatic transmission, air conditioning, tilt steering wheel, CD player, rear defogger.

## OPTIONAL EQUIPMENT:
### Major Packages

|  | Retail Price | Dealer Invoice |
|---|---|---|
| Option Group 1SB, SE sedan/coupe .............................. | $2130 | $1896 |

*Air conditioning, 3-speed automatic transmission, CD player, tilt steering wheel, rear defogger.*

|  | | |
|---|---|---|
| Option Group 1SC, SE coupe .......................................... | 3015 | 2683 |
| SE sedan................................................................ | 3055 | 2719 |

*Group 1SB plus cruise control, intermittent wipers, Convenience Pkg. (cargo net, overhead console, map lights), power door locks, remote keyless entry, rear spoiler, 195/65R15 tires.*

|  | | |
|---|---|---|
| Option Group 1SD, SE coupe .......................................... | 3700 | 3293 |
| SE sedan................................................................ | 3740 | 3329 |

*Group 1SC plus 4-speed automatic transmission, traction control, alloy wheels.*

|  | | |
|---|---|---|
| Option Group 1SE, SE coupe............................................ | 4655 | 4143 |

| | | |
|---|---|---|
| SE sedan...................................................................... | 4760 | 4236 |

*Group 1SD plus 2.4-liter 4-cylinder engine, power windows, power mirrors, steering-wheel radio controls.*

| | | |
|---|---|---|
| Option Group 1SB, SE convertible.................................. | 1800 | 1602 |
| GT............................................................................. | 1740 | 1549 |

*2.4-liter 4-cylinder engine, steering-wheel radio controls, power windows, power door locks, remote keyless entry, power mirrors, sport bucket seats, leather-wrapped steering wheel, driver seat lumbar adjustment.*

| | | |
|---|---|---|
| Option Group 1SC, GT..................................................... | 2245 | 1998 |

*Group 1SB plus power windows, power mirrors, steering-wheel radio controls, sport bucket seats, leather-wrapped steering wheel, driver seat lumbar adjustment.*

## Powertrains

| | | |
|---|---|---|
| 3-speed automatic transmission, SE coupe, sedan....... | 600 | 534 |

*NA with option groups.*

| | | |
|---|---|---|
| 4-speed automatic transmission, GT.............................. | 810 | 721 |
| SE sedan/coupe w/Group 1SC ..................................... | 210 | 187 |

*Includes traction control.*

## Comfort and Convenience

| | | |
|---|---|---|
| Air conditioning, SE sedan/coupe.................................. | 830 | 739 |
| Rear defogger, SE sedan/coupe ................................... | 180 | 160 |
| Cassette player, SE sedan/coupe ................................ | 195 | 174 |
| SE sedan/coupe w/option group (credit).................... | (175) | (156) |
| Power sunroof, GT ....................................................... | 595 | 530 |
| SE coupe w/Group 1SB/1SC, GT w/Group 1SB ....... | 556 | 495 |

*Replaces overhead console when ordered with Convenience Pkg.*

## Appearance and Miscellaneous

| | | |
|---|---|---|
| Alloy wheels, SE sedan/coupe ...................................... | 295 | 263 |

*Requires 195/65R15 tires and Group 1SC.*

| | | |
|---|---|---|
| 195/65R15 touring tires, SE sedan/coupe ..................... | 135 | 120 |

# PONTIAC TRANS SPORT

| SPECIFICATIONS | 3-door van | 4-door van |
|---|---|---|
| Wheelbase, in. .................................... | 112.0 | 120.0 |
| Overall length, in. ............................... | 187.3 | 201.3 |
| Overall width, in. ................................ | 72.7 | 72.7 |
| Overall height, in. ............................... | 67.4 | 68.1 |
| Curb weight, lbs. ................................ | 3730 | 3942 |
| Cargo vol., cu. ft. ............................... | 126.6 | 155.9 |

*Prices are accurate at time of publication; subject to manufacturer's change.*

*Pontiac Trans Sport Montana*

| | 3-door van | 4-door van |
|---|---|---|
| Fuel capacity, gals. | 20.0 | 25.0 |
| Seating capacity | 8 | 8 |
| Front head room, in. | 39.9 | 39.9 |
| Max. front leg room, in. | 39.9 | 39.9 |
| Rear head room, in. | 39.3 | 39.3 |
| Min. rear leg room, in. | 36.9 | 39.0 |

## ENGINES

| | ohv V-6 |
|---|---|
| Size, liters/cu. in. | 3.4/207 |
| Horsepower @ rpm | 180@ 5200 |
| Torque (lbs./ft.) @ rpm | 205@ 4000 |
| Availability | S |

**EPA city/highway mpg**

| | |
|---|---|
| 4-speed OD automatic | 18/25 |

| Pontiac Trans Sport | Retail Price | Dealer Invoice |
|---|---|---|
| SWB 3-door van | $20840 | $18860 |
| SWB 4-door van | 22380 | 20254 |
| Extended wheelbase 4-door van | 23090 | 20896 |
| Destination charge | 570 | 570 |

SWB denotes standard wheelbase.

## STANDARD EQUIPMENT:

**SWB 3-door:** 3.4-liter V-6 engine, 4-speed automatic transmission, driver- and passenger-side side air bags, front side-impact air bags, anti-lock brakes, daytime running lights, power steering, tilt steering wheel, front air conditioning, interior air filter, cloth upholstery, 7-passenger seating (front reclining bucket seats w/manual lumbar adjustment, second- and third-row bench seats), front storage console, cupholders, power mirrors, power door locks, tachometer, coolant-temperature gauge, voltmeter, trip odometer,

AM/FM radio, integrated antenna, under-passenger-seat storage, visor mirrors, intermittent wipers, rear wiper/washer, front and rear auxiliary power outlets, Lamp Group (includes front map lights, rear reading lights, cargo-area lights, underhood light), automatic headlights, floormats, tinted glass with solar-control windshield, fog lamps, 205/70R15 tires, wheel covers.

**SWB 4-door** adds: sliding driver-side door, cruise control, cassette player, perimeter lighting, cargo net.

**Extended** adds: rear split reclining bench seats, 215/70R15 tires.

## OPTIONAL EQUIPMENT:

| | Retail Price | Dealer Invoice |
|---|---|---|
| **Major Packages** | | |
| Option Pkg. 1SB, 3-door | $460 | $409 |
| *Cruise control, cassette player, cargo net.* | | |
| Option Pkg. 1SC, 3-door | 1450 | 1291 |
| *Group 1SB plus power windows, power rear quarter windows, deep-tint glass, remote keyless entry, rear defogger, perimeter lighting.* | | |
| Option Pkg. 1SD, 3-door | 2495 | 2221 |
| *Group 1SC plus power driver seat, rear split reclining bench seats (SWB), overhead console (storage, outside-temperature indicator, compass), illuminated visor mirrors, roof rack.* | | |
| Option Pkg. 1SC, 4-door | 930 | 828 |
| *Power windows, power rear quarter windows, deep-tinted glass, remote keyless entry, rear defogger, perimeter lighting.* | | |
| Option Pkg. 1SD, 4-door | 1640 | 1460 |
| *Group 1SC plus power driver seat, overhead console, (storage, outside-temperature indicator, compass), illuminated visor mirrors, roof rack.* | | |
| Montana Pkg., SWB 4-door w/Pkg. 1SC | 1225 | 1090 |
| SWB 4-door w/Pkg. 1SD | 1050 | 935 |
| Extended w/Pkg. 1SC | 1185 | 1055 |
| Extended w/Pkg. 1SD | 1010 | 899 |
| *Traction control, automatic level control, rear split reclining bench seats (SWB), unique exterior appearance, saddle-bag storage, roof rack, sport suspension, self-sealing 215/70R15 outline-white-letter tires, alloy wheels.* | | |
| Safety and Security Pkg. | 210 | 187 |
| Ordered w/Montana Pkg. or 215/70R15 self-sealing touring tires | 60 | 53 |
| *Theft-deterrent system, 215/70R15 self-sealing touring tires. Requires Option Pkg. 1SD.* | | |
| Trailer Pkg. | 150 | 134 |
| *Trailer wiring harness, heavy-duty cooling, heavy-duty flasher. Requires automatic level control, 215/70R15 touring tires.* | | |
| **Powertrains** | | |
| Traction control | 195 | 174 |
| *Requires automatic level control.* | | |

*Prices are accurate at time of publication; subject to manufacturer's change.*

# PONTIAC

## Safety Features

| | Retail Price | Dealer Invoice |
|---|---|---|
| Integrated child seat | $125 | $111 |
| *NA w/captain's chairs.* | | |
| Two integrated child seats | 225 | 200 |
| *NA w/captain's chairs.* | | |

## Comfort and Convenience

| | | |
|---|---|---|
| Rear air conditioning, extended | 460 | 409 |
| Extended w/Montana Pkg. or automatic level control | 450 | 401 |
| *Includes saddle-bag storage, rear heater.* | | |
| Power sliding side door | 385 | 343 |
| *Includes power rear-quarter windows. 3-door requires Pkg. 1SC, remote keyless entry.* | | |
| Power driver seat | 270 | 240 |
| Power front seats | 305 | 271 |
| *Requires rear modular bucket seats, second-row captain's chairs w/split reclining third-row bench seat, or 8-passenger seating.* | | |
| Rear split reclining bench seats, SWB | 335 | 298 |
| Rear modular bucket seats, SWB | 450 | 401 |
| SWB w/Pkg. 1SD or Montana Pkg. | 115 | 102 |
| Extended | 115 | 102 |
| Second-row captain's chairs w/split reclining | | |
| third-row bench seat, SWB | 600 | 534 |
| SWB w/Pkg. 1SD or Montana Pkg. | 265 | 236 |
| Extended | 265 | 236 |
| 8-passenger seating, SWB | 600 | 534 |
| SWB w/Pkg. 1SD or Montana Pkg. | 265 | 236 |
| Extended | 265 | 236 |
| Leather upholstery | 1055 | 939 |
| *Includes leather-wrapped steering wheel w/radio controls. Requires power driver's seat.* | | |
| Power windows | 325 | 289 |
| *Includes rear quarter vents.* | | |
| Overhead console | 175 | 156 |
| *Includes storage, outside temperature indicator, driver information center, illuminated visor mirrors. Requires Pkg. 1SC and remote keyless entry.* | | |
| Cassette player, 3-door | 195 | 174 |
| Cassette player w/equalizer | 350 | 312 |
| Ordered w/leather upholstery | 165 | 147 |
| *Includes rear-seat audio controls and earphone jacks, leather-wrapped steering wheel w/radio controls, extended-range coaxial speakers.* | | |
| CD player | 100 | 89 |
| *Requires option pkg.* | | |
| CD player w/equalizer | 450 | 401 |

| | Retail Price | Dealer Invoice |
|---|---|---|
| Ordered w/leather upholstery.................................. | $265 | $236 |

*Includes rear-seat audio controls and earphone jacks, leather-wrapped steering wheel w/radio controls, extended-range coaxial speakers. Requires option pkg.*

| | | |
|---|---|---|
| Cassette/CD player w/equalizer ....................................... | 550 | 490 |
| Ordered w/leather upholstery.................................. | 365 | 325 |

*Includes rear-seat audio controls and earphone jacks, leather-wrapped steering wheel w/radio controls, extended-range coaxial speakers. Requires option pkg.*

| | | |
|---|---|---|
| Leather-wrapped steering wheel w/radio controls.......... | 185 | 165 |
| Rear defogger ................................................................. | 180 | 160 |
| Remote keyless entry....................................................... | 150 | 134 |

## Appearance and Miscellaneous

| | | |
|---|---|---|
| Deep-tint glass ................................................................ | 275 | 245 |
| Roof rack ......................................................................... | 175 | 156 |
| 2-tone paint ..................................................................... | 125 | 111 |

*NA w/Montana Pkg.*

| | | |
|---|---|---|
| Automatic level control .................................................... | 180 | 160 |

*Includes saddle-bag storage, 215/70R15 touring tires.*

| | | |
|---|---|---|
| 215/70R15 touring tires, SWB | 75 | 67 |
| 215/70R15 self-sealing touring tires................................ | 150 | 134 |
| Alloy wheels .................................................................... | 280 | 249 |

*Requires 215/70R15 touring tires.*

# SAAB 900

*Saab 900 convertible*

## SPECIFICATIONS

| | 2-door hatchback | 4-door hatchback | 2-door conv. |
|---|---|---|---|
| Wheelbase, in. .................................... | 102.4 | 102.4 | 102.4 |

*Prices are accurate at time of publication; subject to manufacturer's change.*

# SAAB

| | 2-door hatchback | 4-door hatchback | 2-door conv. |
|---|---|---|---|
| Overall length, in. | 182.6 | 182.6 | 182.6 |
| Overall width, in. | 67.4 | 67.4 | 67.4 |
| Overall height, in. | 56.6 | 56.6 | 56.5 |
| Curb weight, lbs. | 2980 | 2980 | 3090 |
| Cargo vol., cu. ft. | 24.0 | 24.0 | 10.0 |
| Fuel capacity, gals. | 18.0 | 18.0 | 18.0 |
| Seating capacity | 5 | 5 | 4 |
| Front head room, in. | 39.3 | 39.3 | 39.0 |
| Max. front leg room, in. | 42.3 | 42.3 | 42.3 |
| Rear head room, in. | 37.8 | 37.8 | 37.9 |
| Min. rear leg room, in. | 34.1 | 34.1 | 33.0 |

## ENGINES

| | dohc I-4 | Turbo dohc I-4 |
|---|---|---|
| Size, liters/cu. in. | 2.3/140 | 2.0/121 |
| Horsepower @ rpm | 150@ 5700 | 185@ 5500 |
| Torque (lbs./ft.) @ rpm | 155@ 4300 | 194@ 2100 |
| Availability | S[1] | S[2] |

### EPA city/highway mpg

| | | |
|---|---|---|
| 5-speed OD manual | 22/28 | 20/27 |
| 4-speed OD automatic | 20/26 | |

*1. S 4-door and S convertible. 2. S 2-door and SE.*

| Saab 900 | Retail Price | Dealer Invoice |
|---|---|---|
| S Turbo 2-door hatchback | $24500 | $23610 |
| S 4-door hatchback | 26955 | 24273 |
| S 2-door convertible | 36395 | 32665 |
| SE Turbo 2-door hatchback | 30995 | 27911 |
| SE Turbo 4-door hatchback | 31995 | 28811 |
| SE Turbo 2-door convertible | 42195 | 37765 |
| Destination charge | 550 | 550 |

Add $230 mandatory fees.

## STANDARD EQUIPMENT:

**S:** 2.3-liter dohc 4-cylinder engine (4-door hatchback, convertible), 2.0-liter turbocharged dohc 4-cylinder engine w/intercooler (2-door hatchback), driver- and passenger-side air bags, anti-lock 4-wheel disc brakes, daytime running lights, 5-speed manual transmission, air conditioning, interior air filter, power steering, leather-wrapped steering wheel and shifter (convertible), telescopic steering wheel, cruise control, velour upholstery (hatchbacks), leather upholstery (convertible), heated reclining front bucket seats, driver-seat lumbar adjustment, folding rear seat w/trunk passthrough, power convertible top (convertible), cupholder, heated power mirrors, power windows, power door locks, remote keyless entry, tachometer, turbo boost gauge (2-door hatchback), trip odometer, coolant temperature gauge, 6-speaker AM/FM/cassette w/weather band and anti-theft, power antenna, analog clock, rear defogger, intermittent wipers, illuminated visor mirrors, rear wiper/washer (hatchbacks), automatic headlights, floormats, theft-deterrent system, solar-control tinted glass (hatchbacks), headlamp wipers/washers, front and rear fog lamps, front spoiler, rear spoiler (2-door), tool kit, 195/60VR15 tires, alloy wheels.

**SE Turbo** adds: 2.0-liter turbocharged dohc 4-cylinder engine w/intercooler, automatic air conditioning, leather upholstery, leather-wrapped steering wheel and shifter, power front seats w/driver-seat memory, power sunroof (hatchbacks), turbo-boost gauge, 8-speaker upgraded audio system, 6-disc CD changer (convertible), trip computer, walnut-trimmed instrument panel (convertible), rear spoiler (4-door hatchback), lower sport chassis, 205/50ZR16 tires.

## OPTIONAL EQUIPMENT:

|  | Retail Price | Dealer Invoice |
|---|---|---|
| **Powertrains** | | |
| 4-speed automatic transmission | $1020 | $877 |
| **Safety Features** | | |
| Integrated child seats, 4-doors | 270 | 232 |
| **Comfort and Convenience** | | |
| Power sunroof, S hatchbacks | 1020 | 877 |
| Leather Pkg., S hatchbacks | 1315 | 1131 |

*Leather upholstery, leather-wrapped steering wheel.*

# SATURN COUPE

## SPECIFICATIONS

|  | 2-door coupe |
|---|---|
| Wheelbase, in. | 102.4 |
| Overall length, in. | 180.0 |
| Overall width, in. | 67.3 |
| Overall height, in. | 52.4 |
| Curb weight, lbs. | 2308 |
| Cargo vol., cu. ft. | 11.4 |
| Fuel capacity, gals. | 12.1 |
| Seating capacity | 4 |
| Front head room, in. | 38.5 |
| Max. front leg room, in. | 42.6 |
| Rear head room, in. | 35.7 |
| Min. rear leg room, in. | 31.0 |

*Prices are accurate at time of publication; subject to manufacturer's change.*

*Saturn SC1*

## ENGINES

| | ohc I-4 | dohc I-4 |
|---|---|---|
| Size, liters/cu. in. | 1.9/116 | 1.9/116 |
| Horsepower @ rpm | 100@ 5000 | 124@ 5600 |
| Torque (lbs./ft.) @ rpm | 114@ 2400 | 122@ 4800 |
| Availability | S[1] | S[2] |
| **EPA city/highway mpg** | | |
| 5-speed OD manual | 28/39 | 26/36 |
| 4-speed OD automatic | 27/37 | 24/34 |

1. SC1.  2. SC2.

| Saturn Coupe | Retail Price | Dealer Invoice |
|---|---|---|
| SC1 2-door coupe, 5-speed | $12595 | $11336 |
| SC1 2-door coupe, automatic | 13455 | 12110 |
| SC2 2-door coupe, 5-speed | 14855 | 13370 |
| SC2 2-door coupe, automatic | 15715 | 14144 |
| Destination charge | 440 | 440 |

## STANDARD EQUIPMENT:

**SC1:** 1.9-liter 4-cylinder engine, 5-speed manual or 4-speed automatic transmission, driver- and passenger-side air bags, daytime running lights, power steering, tilt steering wheel, cloth reclining front bucket seats w/lumbar support, 60/40 split folding rear seatback, front and rear consoles, cupholders, coolant-temperature gauge, trip odometer, AM/FM radio, digital clock, tachometer, rear defogger, intermittent wipers, remote fuel-door and decklid releases, passenger-side visor mirror, tinted glass, dual remote outside mirrors, 175/70R14 tires, wheel covers.

**SC2** adds: 1.9-liter dohc engine, air conditioning, variable-assist power steering, driver-seat height adjustment, locking storage armrest, sport suspension, rear spoiler, fog lights, striping, 195/60HR15 tires.

## OPTIONAL EQUIPMENT:

| | Retail Price | Dealer Invoice |
|---|---|---|

### Major Packages

Option Pkg. 1, SC1............................................................ $1930 $1737

*Air conditioning, cruise control, power windows and door locks, remote keyless entry, theft-deterrent system, power passenger-side outside mirror.*

Option Pkg. 2, SC2............................................................ 1320 1188

*Cruise control, power windows and door locks, remote keyless entry, theft-deterrent system, power passenger-side outside mirror, alloy wheels.*

### Safety Features

Anti-lock brakes........................................./............................ 695 626

*Includes traction control. SC2 also includes 4-wheel disc brakes.*

### Comfort and Convenience

| | | |
|---|---|---|
| Air conditioning, SC1 | 960 | 864 |
| Power sunroof | 695 | 626 |
| Cassette player | 260 | 234 |
| Cassette player w/equalizer and premium speakers | 390 | 351 |
| CD player w/equalizer and premium speakers | 510 | 459 |
| Cruise control | 290 | 261 |
| Leather upholstery, SC2 | 700 | 630 |

*Includes leather-wrapped steering wheel.*

Floormats........................................................................... 60 54

### Appearance and Miscellaneous

Rear spoiler, SC1............................................................... 245 221

Double-fin alloy wheels, SC1............................................ 450 405

*Includes 185/65R15 touring tires.*

Teardrop II alloy wheels, SC2.......................................... 350 305

# SATURN SEDAN/WAGON

| SPECIFICATIONS | 4-door sedan | 4-door wagon |
|---|---|---|
| Wheelbase, in. | 102.4 | 102.4 |
| Overall length, in. | 176.9 | 176.9 |
| Overall width, in. | 66.7 | 66.7 |
| Overall height, in. | 54.5 | 54.9 |
| Curb weight, lbs. | 2326 | 2392 |
| Cargo vol., cu. ft. | 12.1 | 24.9 |
| Fuel capacity, gals. | 12.1 | 12.1 |
| Seating capacity | 5 | 5 |
| Front head room, in. | 39.3 | 39.3 |

*Prices are accurate at time of publication; subject to manufacturer's change.*

# SATURN

*Saturn SL2*

| | 4-door sedan | 4-door wagon |
|---|---|---|
| Max. front leg room, in. | 42.5 | 42.5 |
| Rear head room, in. | 38.0 | 38.7 |
| Min. rear leg room, in. | 32.8 | 32.8 |

## ENGINES

| | ohc I-4 | dohc I-4 |
|---|---|---|
| Size, liters/cu. in. | 1.9/116 | 1.9/116 |
| Horsepower @ rpm | 100@ 5000 | 124@ 5600 |
| Torque (lbs./ft.) @ rpm | 114@ 2400 | 122@ 4800 |
| Availability | S[1] | S[2] |
| **EPA city/highway mpg** | | |
| 5-speed OD manual | 28/39 | 26/36 |
| 4-speed OD automatic | 27/37 | 24/34 |

1. SL, SL1, SW1. 2. SL2, SW2.

## Saturn Sedan/Wagon

| | Retail Price | Dealer Invoice |
|---|---|---|
| SL 4-door sedan, 5-speed | $10595 | $9536 |
| SL1 4-door sedan, 5-speed | 11295 | 10166 |
| SL1 4-door sedan, automatic | 12155 | 10940 |
| SL2 4-door sedan, 5-speed | 12755 | 11480 |
| SL2 4-door sedan, automatic | 13615 | 12254 |
| SW1 4-door wagon, 5-speed | 12295 | 11065 |
| SW1 4-door wagon, automatic | 13155 | 11840 |
| SW2 4-door wagon, 5-speed | 14255 | 12402 |
| SW2 4-door wagon, automatic | 15115 | 13150 |
| Destination charge | 440 | 440 |

## STANDARD EQUIPMENT:

**SL:** 1.9-liter 4-cylinder engine, 5-speed manual transmission, driver- and passenger-side air bags, daytime running lamps, cloth reclining front bucket seats w/lumbar support, 60/40 split folding rear seat, front console, cupholders, tilt steering wheel, tachometer, coolant-temperature gauge, trip odometer, AM/FM radio, digital clock, rear defogger, intermittent wipers, remote fuel-door and decklid releases, passenger-side visor mirror, tinted glass, 175/70R14 tires, wheel covers.

**SL1** adds: 5-speed manual or 4-speed automatic transmission, power steering, upgraded interior trim, dual outside mirrors.

**SL2** adds: 1.9-liter 4-cylinder dohc engine, air conditioning, variable-assist power steering, upgraded upholstery, driver-seat height adjustment, sport suspension, 185/65TR15 touring tires.

**SW1** adds to SL1: rear wiper/washer, remote liftgate release.

**SW2** adds to SW1: 1.9-liter dohc engine, air conditioning, variable-assist power steering, driver-seat height adjustment, cargo cover, sport suspension, upgraded upholstery, 185/65R15 touring tires.

## OPTIONAL EQUIPMENT:

| | Retail Price | Dealer Invoice |
|---|---|---|
| **Major Packages** | | |
| Option Pkg. 1, SL1, SW1 | $2055 | $1788 |
| SW2 | 1095 | 953 |
| *Air conditioning (SL1, SW1), cruise control, power windows and door locks, power passenger-side outside mirror.* | | |
| Option Pkg. 2, SL2 | 1445 | 1257 |
| *Cruise control, power mirrors, power windows and door locks, alloy wheels.* | | |
| **Safety Features** | | |
| Anti-lock brakes | 695 | 626 |
| *Includes traction control. SL2 also includes 4-wheel disc brakes.* | | |
| **Comfort and Convenience** | | |
| Air conditioning, SL, SL1, SW1 | 960 | 836 |
| Power sunroof, SL1, SL2 | 695 | 626 |
| Cassette player, SL | 290 | 252 |
| SL1, SL2, SW1, SW2 | 260 | 226 |
| Cassette player w/equalizer and premium speakers, SL | 420 | 365 |
| SL1, SL2, SW1, SW2 | 390 | 339 |
| CD player w/equalizer and premium speakers, SL | 540 | 473 |
| SL1, SL2, SW1, SW2 | 495 | 446 |
| Power door locks | 370 | 324 |
| *Includes remote keyless entry, theft-deterrent system. NA on SL.* | | |
| Cruise control | 290 | 252 |
| *NA on SL.* | | |
| Leather upholstery, SL2, SW2 | 700 | 626 |
| *Includes leather-wrapped steering wheel.* | | |
| **Appearance and Miscellaneous** | | |
| Rear spoiler, SL2 | 205 | 185 |
| Fog lamps, SL2, SW2 | 160 | 144 |
| Alloy wheels, SL2, SW2 | 350 | 305 |

*Prices are accurate at time of publication; subject to manufacturer's change.*

# SUBARU FORESTER

*Subaru Forester S*

## SPECIFICATIONS

| | 4-door wagon |
|---|---|
| Wheelbase, in. | 99.4 |
| Overall length, in. | 175.2 |
| Overall width, in. | 68.3 |
| Overall height, in. | 65.0 |
| Curb weight, lbs. | 3020 |
| Cargo vol., cu. ft. | 64.6 |
| Fuel capacity, gals. | 15.9 |
| Seating capacity | 5 |
| Front head room, in. | 40.6 |
| Max. front leg room, in. | 43.0 |
| Rear head room, in. | 39.6 |
| Min. rear leg room, in. | 33.4 |

## ENGINES

| | dohc Flat-4 |
|---|---|
| Size, liters/cu. in. | 2.5/150 |
| Horsepower @ rpm | 165@ 5600 |
| Torque (lbs./ft.) @ rpm | 162@ 4000 |
| Availability | S |

**EPA city/highway mpg**

| | |
|---|---|
| 5-speed OD manual | 21/27 |
| 4-speed OD automatic | 21/26 |

| Subaru Forester | Retail Price | Dealer Invoice |
|---|---|---|
| Base 4-door wagon | $18695 | $17454 |
| L 4-door wagon | 19995 | 18034 |

| | Retail Price | Dealer Invoice |
|---|---|---|
| S 4-door wagon | $22195 | $19925 |
| Destination charge | 495 | 495 |

Prices are for vehicles distributed by Subaru of North America. Prices may be higher in areas serviced by independent distributors.

## STANDARD EQUIPMENT:

**Base:** 2.5-liter dohc 4-cylinder engine, 5-speed manual transmission, full-time all-wheel drive, driver- and passenger-side air bags, rear seat head-rests, air conditioning, variable-assist power steering, tilt steering wheel, reclining cloth bucket seats, reclining split folding rear seat, 4-speaker AM/FM/cassette, cupholders, storage bins, overhead console (map lights, digital clock, and sunglasses storage), tachometer, power windows, inter-mittent wipers, rear wiper/washer, rear defogger, power outlets, tinted glass, dual manual outside mirrors, 2-tone paint, fog lights, roof rack, body-side moldings, trailer harness connector, 205/70R15 tires.

**L** adds: anti-lock brakes, power door and liftgate locks, floormats, mud guards, rear bumper step pad.

**S** adds: 4-wheel disc brakes, cruise control, power mirrors, upgraded cloth upholstery, front seatback pockets, driver and passenger vanity mirrors, coat hooks, chrome grille, 215/60R16 tires, alloy wheels.

## OPTIONAL EQUIPMENT:
### Major Packages

| | | |
|---|---|---|
| Cold Weather Pkg., S | 300 | 266 |
| *Includes heated front seats, heated outside mirrors.* | | |

### Powertrains

| | | |
|---|---|---|
| 4-speed automatic transmission, L, S | 800 | 711 |

### Comfort and Convenience

| | | |
|---|---|---|
| Cruise control, Base, L | 340 | 222 |
| Leather upholstery | 1295 | 975 |
| CD player | 420 | 315 |
| CD changer | 689 | 517 |
| Remote keyless entry | 225 | 146 |

### Appearance and Miscellaneous

| | | |
|---|---|---|
| Grille guard | 375 | 282 |

### Special Purpose, Wheels and Tires

| | | |
|---|---|---|
| Differential protector | 159 | 104 |
| Trailer hitch | 295 | 192 |
| Alloy wheels, Base, L | 595 | 447 |

*Prices are accurate at time of publication; subject to manufacturer's change.*

# SUBARU IMPREZA

*Subaru Impreza 2.5 RS*

## SPECIFICATIONS

| | 2-door coupe | 4-door sedan | 4-door wagon | 4-door wagon |
|---|---|---|---|---|
| Wheelbase, in. | 99.2 | 99.2 | 99.2 | 99.2 |
| Overall length, in. | 172.2 | 172.2 | 172.2 | 172.2 |
| Overall width, in. | 67.1 | 67.1 | 67.1 | 67.1 |
| Overall height, in. | 55.5 | 55.5 | 55.5 | 60.0 |
| Curb weight, lbs. | 2720 | 2690 | 2795 | 2835 |
| Cargo vol., cu. ft. | 11.1 | 11.1 | 25.51 | 25.51 |
| Fuel capacity, gals. | 13.2 | 13.2 | 13.2 | 13.2 |
| Seating capacity | 5 | 5 | 5 | 5 |
| Front head room, in. | 39.2 | 39.2 | 39.2 | 39.2 |
| Max. front leg room, in. | 43.1 | 43.1 | 43.1 | 43.1 |
| Rear head room, in. | 36.7 | 36.7 | 37.4 | 37.4 |
| Min. rear leg room, in. | 32.5 | 32.5 | 32.4 | 32.4 |

## ENGINES

| | ohc Flat-4 | dohc Flat-4 |
|---|---|---|
| Size, liters/cu. in. | 2.2/135 | 2.5/150 |
| Horsepower @ rpm | 137@ 5400 | 165@ 5600 |
| Torque (lbs./ft.) @ rpm | 145@ 4000 | 162@ 4000 |
| Availability | S[1] | S[2] |

### EPA city/highway mpg

| | | |
|---|---|---|
| 5-speed OD manual | 23/30 | 22/28 |
| 4-speed OD automatic | 23/30 | 22/28 |

1. L, Outback Sport. 2. 2.5 RS.

| Subaru Impreza | Retail Price | Dealer Invoice |
|---|---|---|
| L 2-door coupe | $15895 | $14445 |
| L 4-door sedan | 15895 | 14445 |
| L 4-door wagon | 16295 | 14804 |

| | Retail Price | Dealer Invoice |
|---|---|---|
| Outback Sport | | |
| 4-door wagon | $17995 | $16321 |
| 2.5 RS 2-door coupe | 19195 | 17404 |
| Destination charge | 495 | 495 |

Prices are for vehicles distributed by Subaru of America. Prices may be higher in areas served by independent distributors.

## STANDARD EQUIPMENT:

**L:** 2.2-liter 4-cylinder engine, 5-speed manual transmission, permanent all-wheel drive, driver- and passenger-side air bags, air conditioning, variable-assist power steering, tilt steering wheel, cloth upholstery, reclining front bucket seats, split folding rear seat (wagon), front storage console, cupholder, AM/FM/cassette, digital clock, power mirrors, power windows, power door locks, rear defogger, remote decklid release (sedan and 2-door), auxiliary power outlet, cargo cover (wagon), rear wiper/washer (wagon), passenger-side visor mirror, tinted glass, rear spoiler (2-door), 195/60H15 tires, wheel covers.

**Outback Sport** adds to L wagon: anti-lock brakes, cargo tray, raised heavy-duty suspension, roof rack, mud guards, 2-tone paint, rear bumper cover, 205/60S15 outlined white-letter tires.

**2.5 RS** adds to L 2-door: 2.5-liter dohc 4-cylinder engine, leather-wrapped steering wheel, sport bucket seats, reading lights, power sunroof, sport suspension, bodyside moldings, tailpipe cover, 205/55H16 tires, alloy wheels.

## OPTIONAL EQUIPMENT:

### Powertrains

| | | |
|---|---|---|
| 4-speed automatic transmission | 800 | 717 |

### Comfort and Convenience

| | | |
|---|---|---|
| Cruise control | 357 | 232 |
| CD player | 420 | 315 |
| Remote keyless entry | 225 | 146 |

### Appearance and Miscellaneous

Fog lights, L,

| | | |
|---|---|---|
| Outback Sport | 245 | 160 |
| Roof rack, L wagon | 239 | 156 |

Alloy wheels, L,

| | | |
|---|---|---|
| Outback Sport | 550 | 413 |

Other options are available as port installed items.

*Prices are accurate at time of publication; subject to manufacturer's change.*

# SUBARU LEGACY

*Subaru Legacy Outback Limited*

## SPECIFICATIONS

| | 4-door sedan | 4-door wagon | 4-door wagon |
|---|---|---|---|
| Wheelbase, in. | 103.5 | 103.5 | 103.5 |
| Overall length, in. | 181.5 | 184.5 | 185.8 |
| Overall width, in. | 67.5 | 67.5 | 67.5 |
| Overall height, in. | 55.3 | 57.1 | 63.0 |
| Curb weight, lbs. | 2885 | 2975 | 3155 |
| Cargo vol., cu. ft. | 12.6 | 36.1 | 36.5 |
| Fuel capacity, gals. | 15.9 | 15.9 | 15.9 |
| Seating capacity | 5 | 5 | 5 |
| Front head room, in. | 38.9 | 39.5 | 40.2 |
| Max. front leg room, in. | 43.3 | 43.3 | 43.3 |
| Rear head room, in. | 36.7 | 38.8 | 39.2 |
| Min. rear leg room, in. | 34.6 | 34.8 | 34.8 |

## ENGINES

| | ohc Flat-4 | dohc Flat-4 |
|---|---|---|
| Size, liters/cu. in. | 2.2/135 | 2.5/150 |
| Horsepower @ rpm | 137@ 5400 | 165@ 5600 |
| Torque (lbs./ft.) @ rpm | 145@ 4000 | 162@ 4000 |
| Availability | S[1] | S[2] |

**EPA city/highway mpg**

| | | |
|---|---|---|
| 5-speed OD manual | 23/30 | 21/27 |
| 4-speed OD automatic | 23/30 | 21/26 |

*1. Brighton, L. 2. GT, GT Limited, Outback, and Outback Limited.*

## Subaru Legacy

| | Retail Price | Dealer Invoice |
|---|---|---|
| Brighton 4-door wagon | $16895 | $15788 |
| L 4-door sedan | 19195 | 17278 |
| L 4-door wagon | 19895 | 17898 |

| | Retail Price | Dealer Invoice |
|---|---|---|
| Outback 4-door wagon | $22495 | $20183 |
| Outback Limited 4-door wagon | 24595 | 22049 |
| GT 4-door sedan | 22795 | 20453 |
| GT 4-door wagon | 23495 | 21073 |
| GT Limited 4-door wagon | 24895 | 22314 |
| Destination charge | 495 | 495 |

Prices are for vehicles distributed by Subaru of America. Prices may be higher in areas served by independent distributors.

## STANDARD EQUIPMENT:

**Brighton:** 2.2-liter 4-cylinder engine, 5-speed manual transmission, full-time all-wheel drive, driver- and passenger-side air bags, child safety rear door locks, cloth reclining front bucket seats, split folding rear seat, air conditioning, storage console, cupholder, variable-assist power steering, tilt steering column, 2-speaker AM/FM/cassette, digital clock, trip odometer, temperature gauge, rear defogger, rear wiper/washer, intermittent wipers, remote fuel door and decklid releases, tinted glass, bodyside moldings, 185/70SR14 tires, wheel covers.

**L adds:** anti-lock 4-wheel disc brakes, cruise control, power mirrors, power windows, power door locks, map light, 4-speaker AM/FM/cassette, right side visor mirror, deletes rear wiper/washer (sedan).

**Outback adds:** 2.5-liter dohc 4-cylinder engine, upgraded cloth interior, overhead console, cargo hooks, cargo area power outlet, cargo tray, floormats, hood scoop, mudguards, roof rack, fog lights, 2-tone paint, rear headrests, heavy-duty suspension, tail pipe cover, 205/70SR15 white-letter tires, alloy wheels.

**Outback Limited adds:** Cold Weather Pkg. (heated front seats, heated power outside mirrors, windshield wiper de-icer), leather upholstery, leather-wrapped steering wheel and shifter, AM/FM/cassette/CD, power antenna, woodgrain interior trim, gold badging, special alloy wheels.

**GT adds to L:** 2.5-liter dohc 4-cylinder engine, power moonroof w/sunshade, power antenna, leather-wrapped steering wheel and shifter, variable intermittent wipers, illuminated vanity mirror, woodgrain trim, sport suspension, fog lights, hood scoop, rear spoiler, ground effects, roof rack (wagon), 205/55HR16 tires, alloy wheels.

**GT Limited adds:** 4-speed automatic transmission, leather upholstery, 6-speaker CD player.

## OPTIONAL EQUIPMENT:
### Major Packages

| | | |
|---|---|---|
| Cold Weather Pkg., Outback | 400 | 358 |

*Includes heated front seats, dual heated outside mirrors, windshield wiper de-icer.*

*Prices are accurate at time of publication; subject to manufacturer's change.*

## Powertrains

| | Retail Price | Dealer Invoice |
|---|---|---|
| 4-speed automatic transmission, Brighton, L, Outback, Outback Limited, GT ............... | $800 | $714 |

## Comfort and Convenience

| | Retail Price | Dealer Invoice |
|---|---|---|
| Dual power moonroofs, Outback Limited........................ | 1200 | 1059 |
| *Requires automatic transmission.* | | |
| Cruise control, Brighton ...................................................... | 334 | 218 |
| CD player, Brighton, L, Outback, GT ............................... | 420 | 315 |
| CD changer, Brighton, L, Outback, GT ........................... | 689 | 517 |
| Outback Limited, GT Limited ...................................... | 497 | 373 |
| Remote keyless entry............................................................. | 225 | 146 |
| *NA Brighton.* | | |
| Leather upholstery, Outback, GT ..................................... | 1295 | 975 |

## Appearance and Miscellaneous

| | | |
|---|---|---|
| Body-colored rear spoiler, Brighton, L wagon, Outback, Outback Limited ........... | 295 | 192 |
| L sedan................................................................ | 375 | 282 |
| 7-spoke alloy wheels, Brighton, L..................................... | 595 | 199 |
| Cross spoke alloy wheels, Brighton, L ............................. | 635 | 199 |

# SUZUKI ESTEEM/SWIFT

*Suzuki Esteem wagon*

## SPECIFICATIONS

| | 2-door hatchback | 4-door sedan | 4-door wagon |
|---|---|---|---|
| Wheelbase, in. ..................................... | 93.1 | 97.6 | 97.6 |
| Overall length, in. ............................. | 149.4 | 165.2 | 171.1 |
| Overall width, in. ................................ | 62.6 | 65.7 | 66.5 |
| Overall height, in. .............................. | 54.7 | 53.9 | 55.9 |
| Curb weight, lbs. ................................. | 1895 | 2227 | 2359 |
| Cargo vol., cu. ft. ................................ | 8.4 | 12.0 | 24.0 |
| Fuel capacity, gals. ............................ | 10.3 | 13.5 | 13.5 |
| Seating capacity ................................. | 4 | 5 | 5 |

| | 2-door hatchback | 4-door sedan | 4-door wagon |
|---|---|---|---|
| Front head room, in. | 39.1 | 39.1 | 38.8 |
| Max. front leg room, in. | 42.5 | 42.3 | 42.3 |
| Rear head room, in. | 36.0 | 37.2 | 38.0 |
| Min. rear leg room, in. | 32.2 | 34.1 | 36.6 |

## ENGINES

| | | ohc I-4 | ohc I-4 |
|---|---|---|---|
| Size, liters/cu. in. | | 1.3/79 | 1.6/97 |
| Horsepower @ rpm | | 79@ 6000 | 95@ 6000 |
| Torque (lbs./ft.) @ rpm | | 75@ 3000 | 99@ 3000 |
| Availability | | S[1] | S[2] |

**EPA city/highway mpg**

| | | | |
|---|---|---|---|
| 5-speed OD manual | | 39/43 | 30/37 |
| 3-speed automatic | | 30/34 | |
| 4-speed OD automatic | | | 27/34 |

1. Swift. 2. Esteem.

## Suzuki Esteem/Swift

| | Retail Price | Dealer Invoice |
|---|---|---|
| Swift 2-door hatchback, 5-speed | $9099 | $8462 |
| Swift 2-door hatchback, automatic | 9749 | 9066 |
| Esteem GL 4-door sedan, 5-speed | 11999 | 11397 |
| Esteem GL 4-door sedan, automatic | 12999 | 12349 |
| Esteem GL 4-door wagon, 5-speed | 12499 | 11874 |
| Esteem GL 4-door wagon, automatic | 13499 | 12824 |
| Esteem GLX 4-door sedan, 5-speed | 13099 | 12444 |
| Esteem GLX 4-door sedan, automatic | 14099 | 13394 |
| Esteem GLX 4-door wagon, 5-speed | 13599 | 12919 |
| Esteem GLX 4-door wagon, automatic | 14599 | 13869 |
| Esteem GLX Plus 4-door sedan, automatic | 14899 | 14154 |
| Esteem GLX Plus 4-door wagon, automatic | 15599 | 14819 |
| Destination charge: Swift | 380 | 380 |
| Destination charge: Esteem | 430 | 430 |

## STANDARD EQUIPMENT:

**Swift:** 1.3-liter 4-cylinder engine, 5-speed manual or 3-speed automatic transmission, driver- and passenger-side air bags, daytime running lights, cloth reclining front bucket seats, folding rear seat, front console, intermittent wipers, rear defogger, trip odometer, cargo cover, tinted glass, dual outside mirrors, 155/80R13 tires, wheel covers.

**Esteem GL** adds: 1.6-liter 4-cylinder engine, 5-speed manual or 4-speed automatic transmission, air conditioning, power steering, cupholders, AM/FM/cassette, rear wiper/washer (wagon), remote fuel-door and decklid releases, bodyside moldings and mud guards (wagon), roof rails (wagon), 175/70R13 tires, deletes wheel covers.

*Prices are accurate at time of publication; subject to manufacturer's change.*

## SUZUKI

**Esteem GLX** adds: power mirrors, power windows, power door locks, remote keyless entry, split folding rear seat, tachometer, passenger-side visor mirror, trunk light, theft-deterrent system, rear spoiler (wagon), mud guards, bodyside moldings, 185/60R14 tires, wheel covers.

**Esteem GLX Plus** adds: 4-speed automatic transmission, anti-lock brakes, cruise control, power sunroof (wagon).

## OPTIONAL EQUIPMENT:
### Safety Features

| | Retail Price | Dealer Invoice |
|---|---|---|
| Anti-lock brakes, Swift | $560 | $504 |

Other options are available as dealer-installed accessories.

# SUZUKI SIDEKICK

*Suzuki Sidekick JLX Sport*

## SPECIFICATIONS

| | 2-door conv. | 4-door wagon | 4-door wagon |
|---|---|---|---|
| Wheelbase, in. | 86.6 | 97.6 | 97.6 |
| Overall length, in. | 143.7 | 158.7 | 162.4 |
| Overall width, in. | 65.2 | 64.4 | 66.7 |
| Overall height, in. | 64.3 | 65.7 | 66.3 |
| Curb weight, lbs. | 2337 | 2624 | 2811 |
| Cargo vol., cu. ft. | 32.9 | 32.9 | 46.0 |
| Fuel capacity, gals. | 11.1 | 14.5 | 18.5 |
| Seating capacity | 4 | 4 | 4 |
| Front head room, in. | 39.5 | 40.6 | 40.6 |
| Max. front leg room, in. | 42.1 | 42.1 | 42.1 |
| Rear head room, in. | 39.0 | 40.0 | 38.6 |
| Min. rear leg room, in. | 31.7 | 32.7 | 32.7 |

## ENGINES

| | ohc I-4 | dohc I-4 |
|---|---|---|
| Size, liters/cu. in. | 1.6/97 | 1.8/112 |
| Horsepower @ rpm | 95 @ 5600 | 120@ 6500 |

| | ohc I-4 | dohc I-4 |
|---|---|---|
| Torque (lbs./ft.) @ rpm | 98 @ 4000 | 114@ 3500 |
| Availability | S[1] | S[2] |
| **EPA city/highway mpg** | | |
| 5-speed OD manual | 24/26 | 23/25 |
| 3-speed automatic | 23/24 | |
| 4-speed OD automatic | | 21/24 |

1. 2-door, 4-door. 2. Sport.

## Suzuki Sidekick

| | Retail Price | Dealer Invoice |
|---|---|---|
| JS 2WD 2-door convertible, 5-speed | $13099 | $12444 |
| JS 2WD 2-door convertible, automatic | 13699 | 13014 |
| JS 2WD 4-door wagon, 5-speed | 14399 | 13391 |
| JS 2WD 4-door wagon, automatic | 15349 | 14274 |
| JX 4WD 2-door convertible, 5-speed | 14869 | 13828 |
| JX 4WD 2-door convertible, automatic | 15469 | 14386 |
| JX 4WD 4-door wagon, 5-speed | 15999 | 14559 |
| JX 4WD 4-door wagon, automatic | 16949 | 15423 |
| JS Sport 2WD 4-door wagon, 5-speed | 16899 | 15378 |
| JS Sport 2WD 4-door wagon, automatic | 17899 | 16288 |
| JX Sport 4WD 4-door wagon, 5-speed | 17899 | 16288 |
| JX Sport 4WD 4-door wagon, automatic | 18899 | 17198 |
| JLX Sport 4WD 4-door wagon, 5-speed | 19399 | 17653 |
| JLX Sport 4WD 4-door wagon, automatic | 20399 | 18563 |
| Destination charge, 2-door | 420 | 420 |
| Destination charge, 4-door | 430 | 430 |

## STANDARD EQUIPMENT:

**JS 2-door:** 1.6-liter 4-cylinder engine, 5-speed manual or 3-speed automatic transmission, driver- and passenger-side air bags, daytime running lights, cloth reclining front bucket seats, folding rear seat, cupholders, dual outside mirrors, trip odometer, intermittent wipers, carpeting, folding canvas top, tinted glass, fuel-tank skid plate, spare-tire carrier w/full-size spare tire, 195/75R15 tires.

**JX 2-door** adds: power steering, tachometer, 205/75R15 tires, 4WD models add: part-time 4WD, 2-speed transfer case.

**JS/JX 4-door** adds: 5-speed manual or 4-speed automatic transmission, split folding rear seat, AM/FM/cassette, rear defogger, 195/75R15 tires (JS), 205/75R15 tires (JX), deletes folding canvas top, 4WD models add: part-time 4-wheel drive, 2-speed transfer case.

**JS/JX Sport** adds: 1.8-liter dohc 4-cylinder engine, air conditioning, power windows, power door locks, power mirrors, passenger-side visor mirror, remote fuel-door release, theft-deterrent system, map lights, 215/65R16 tires, 4WD models add: part-time 4-wheel drive, 2-speed transfer case.

*Prices are accurate at time of publication; subject to manufacturer's change.*

**JLX Sport** adds: part-time 4-wheel drive, 2-speed transfer case, automatic locking front hubs, anti-lock brakes, cruise control, cloth door trim, rear wiper/washer, spare-tire cover w/wheel lock, alloy wheels.

## OPTIONAL EQUIPMENT:
### Safety Features

| | Retail Price | Dealer Invoice |
|---|---|---|
| Anti-lock brakes, JS, JX, JS/JX Sport ............................ | $600 | $540 |

Other options are available as dealer-installed accessories.

# TOYOTA AVALON

*Toyota Avalon XLS*

## SPECIFICATIONS

| | 4-door sedan |
|---|---|
| Wheelbase, in. ....................................................... | 107.1 |
| Overall length, in. .................................................. | 191.9 |
| Overall width, in. ................................................... | 70.5 |
| Overall height, in. .................................................. | 56.7 |
| Curb weight, lbs. ................................................... | 3340 |
| Cargo vol., cu. ft. .................................................. | 15.4 |
| Fuel capacity, gals. ............................................... | 18.5 |
| Seating capacity ................................................... | 6 |
| Front head room, in. .............................................. | 39.1 |
| Max. front leg room, in. ......................................... | 44.1 |
| Rear head room, in. ............................................... | 37.8 |
| Min. rear leg room, in. ........................................... | 38.3 |

## ENGINES

| | dohc V-6 |
|---|---|
| Size, liters/cu. in. ................................................. | 3.0/183 |
| Horsepower @ rpm ................................................ | 200@ 5200 |
| Torque (lbs./ft.) @ rpm .......................................... | 214@ 4400 |
| Availability ........................................................... | S |

**EPA city/highway mpg**

| | |
|---|---|
| 4-speed OD automatic .......................................... | 21/30 |

| Toyota Avalon | Retail Price | Dealer Invoice |
|---|---|---|
| XL 4-door sedan, front bucket seats ............................... | $24278 | $21254 |
| XL 4-door sedan, front bench seat ................................. | 25108 | 21981 |
| XLS 4-door sedan ................................................................ | 28128 | 24336 |
| Destination charge ............................................................ | 420 | 420 |

Prices are for vehicles distributed by Toyota Motor Sales, U.S.A., Inc. The dealer invoice and destination charge may be higher in areas served by independent distributors.

## STANDARD EQUIPMENT:

**XL:** 3.0-liter dohc V-6 engine, 4-speed automatic transmission, driver- and passenger-side air bags, front side-impact air bags, anti-lock 4-wheel disc brakes, heated power mirrors, air conditioning, power steering, reading lights, tilt steering wheel, cruise control, cloth 6-way adjustable front bucket seats or power split bench seat with storage armrest, cupholders, tachometer, AM/FM/cassette, power windows, power door locks, power mirrors, remote fuel-door and decklid releases, illuminated visor mirrors, intermittent wipers, automatic headlamps, rear defogger, tinted glass, full-size spare tire, 205/65HR15 tires, wheel covers.

**XLS** adds: automatic climate control, outside temperature display, 7-way power front bucket seats or power split bench seat with storage armrest, leather-wrapped steering wheel, premium CD player, remote keyless entry, variable intermittent wipers, fog lights, theft-deterrent system, alloy wheels.

## OPTIONAL EQUIPMENT:
### Major Packages

| | | |
|---|---|---|
| Leather Trim Pkg., XL with bucket seats......................... | 1910 | 1562 |
| XL with bench seat...................................................... | 1060 | 848 |
| XLS.............................................................................. | 1005 | 804 |
| *Leather upholstery, simulated-leather door trim. XL adds leather-wrapped steering wheel.* | | |
| Leather Trim Pkg. w/memory, XLS with bucket seats.... | 1310 | 1048 |
| XLS with bench seat.................................................... | 1255 | 1004 |
| *Leather Trim Pkg. plus driver seat memory.* | | |
| Leather Trim Pkg. w/memory and heat, | | |
| XLS with bucket seats................................................. | 1555 | 1288 |
| XLS with bench seat.................................................... | 1555 | 1244 |
| *Leather Trim Pkg. w/memory plus heated front seats.* | | |

### Powertrains

| | | |
|---|---|---|
| Traction control............................................................... | 300 | 240 |

### Comfort and Convenience

| | | |
|---|---|---|
| 7-way power front bucket seats, XL with bucket seats .. | 850 | 714 |

*Prices are accurate at time of publication; subject to manufacturer's change.*

## TOYOTA

|  | Retail Price | Dealer Invoice |
|---|---|---|
| Power moonroof, XL | $1000 | $800 |
| XLS | 980 | 784 |
| Premium cassette player, XL | 290 | 218 |
| CD player, XL | 100 | 75 |
| Premium CD player, XL | 390 | 293 |
| Premium cassette/CD player, XL | 570 | 428 |
| XLS | 180 | 135 |
| Heated power mirrors, XL | 30 | 24 |

### Appearance and Miscellaneous

|  | | |
|---|---|---|
| Theft-deterrent system, XL | 320 | 256 |
| Mud guards | 60 | 48 |
| Diamond white pearlescent paint | 210 | 179 |
| Alloy wheels, XL | 435 | 348 |

# TOYOTA CAMRY

*Toyota Camry LE*

## SPECIFICATIONS

|  | 4-door sedan |
|---|---|
| Wheelbase, in. | 105.2 |
| Overall length, in. | 188.5 |
| Overall width, in. | 70.1 |
| Overall height, in. | 55.4 |
| Curb weight, lbs. | 3042 |
| Cargo vol., cu. ft. | 14.1 |
| Fuel capacity, gals. | 18.5 |
| Seating capacity | 5 |
| Front head room, in. | 38.6 |
| Max. front leg room, in. | 43.5 |
| Rear head room, in. | 37.6 |
| Min. rear leg room, in. | 35.5 |

## ENGINES

| | dohc I-4 | dohc V-6 |
|---|---|---|
| Size, liters/cu. in. | 2.2/132 | 3.0/183 |
| Horsepower @ rpm | 133@ 5200 | 194@ 5200 |
| Torque (lbs./ft.) @ rpm | 147@ 4400 | 209@ 4400 |
| Availability | S[1] | S[2] |

### EPA city/highway mpg

| | | |
|---|---|---|
| 5-speed OD manual | 23/32 | 20/28 |
| 4-speed OD automatic | 23/30 | 19/27 |

1. 4-cylinder models. 2. V-6 models.

## Toyota Camry

| | Retail Price | Dealer Invoice |
|---|---|---|
| CE 4-cylinder 4-door sedan, 5-speed | $16938 | $15003 |
| CE 4-cylinder 4-door sedan, automatic | 17738 | 15712 |
| CE V-6 4-door sedan, 5-speed | 19828 | 17563 |
| LE 4-cylinder 4-door sedan, automatic | 20218 | 17699 |
| LE V-6 4-door sedan, automatic | 22558 | 19848 |
| XLE 4-cylinder 4-door sedan, automatic | 22628 | 19810 |
| XLE V-6 4-door sedan, automatic | 24868 | 21771 |
| Destination charge | 420 | 420 |

Prices are for vehicles distributed by Toyota Motor Sales, U.S.A., Inc. The dealer invoice and destination charge may be higher in areas served by independent distributors.

## STANDARD EQUIPMENT:

**CE:** 2.2-liter dohc 4-cylinder or 3.0-liter dohc V-6 engine, 5-speed manual or 4-speed automatic transmission, anti-lock 4-wheel disc brakes (V-6), driver- and passenger-side air bags, power steering, split folding rear seat w/armrest, cloth reclining front bucket seats, front and rear storage consoles, overhead storage console, front and rear cupholders, tilt steering column, tachometer, coolant-temperature gauge, two trip odometers, AM/FM radio w/four speakers, tinted glass, dual remote outside mirrors, remote fuel-door and trunk releases, rear defogger, illuminated visor mirrors, auxiliary power outlet, 205/65HR15 tires (V-6), 195/70R14 tires (4-cylinder), wheel covers.

**LE** adds: 4-speed automatic transmission, anti-lock brakes, 4-wheel disc brakes (V-6), power door locks, air conditioning, cruise control, power windows, power mirrors, cassette player, integrated antenna, intermittent wipers.

**XLE** adds to LE: power front seats, driver-seat manual lumbar support, CD player, variable intermittent wipers, theft-deterrent system, alloy wheels.

*Prices are accurate at time of publication; subject to manufacturer's change.*

# TOYOTA

## OPTIONAL EQUIPMENT:

| | Retail Price | Dealer Invoice |
|---|---|---|
| **Major Packages** | | |
| Black Pearl Elite Pkg. | $820 | $452 |
| *Black Pearl Emblems, wood dashboard, floormats, trunk mat.* | | |
| Gold Elite Pkg. | 835 | 475 |
| *Gold badging, wood dashboard, floormats, trunk mat.* | | |
| Leather Trim Pkg., LE | 1100 | 880 |
| XLE | 1005 | 804 |
| *Leather upholstery, driver-seat lumbar support, leather-wrapped steering wheel and shifter, seatback map pockets. NA with integrated child seat.* | | |
| Power Pkg., CE | 780 | 624 |
| *Power windows, door locks, and mirrors.* | | |
| **Powertrains** | | |
| Traction control, LE V-6, XLE V-6 | 300 | 240 |
| **Safety Features** | | |
| Anti-lock 4-wheel disc brakes, CE w/4-cylinder engine | 550 | 473 |
| Side-impact air bags | 250 | 215 |
| *CE requires Power Pkg.* | | |
| Integrated child seat | 125 | 100 |
| *NA w/Leather Trim Pkg.* | | |
| **Comfort and Convenience** | | |
| Air conditioning, CE | 1005 | 804 |
| Cruise control, CE | 290 | 232 |
| Power moonroof, LE, XLE | 1000 | 800 |
| *Includes map lights, sunshade.* | | |
| Premium AM/FM/cassette, LE | 220 | 165 |
| *Includes six speakers, diversity antenna.* | | |
| Premium CD player, CE, LE | 320 | 240 |
| *NA with Premium AM/FM/cassette* | | |
| Premium cassette/CD player, LE | 500 | 375 |
| XLE | 180 | 135 |
| *Includes six speakers, equalizer, diversity antenna.* | | |
| 6-disc CD autochanger | 550 | 385 |
| Remote keyless entry, CE, LE | 299 | 149 |
| Wood dashboard | 499 | 335 |
| **Appearance and Miscellaneous** | | |
| Theft-deterrent system, LE | 540 | 432 |
| Fog lamps | 399 | 249 |
| Rear spoiler | 539 | 329 |
| Alloy wheels, CE 4-cylinder | 755 | 560 |
| LE 4-cylinder | 415 | 332 |
| LE V-6 | 435 | 348 |

# TOYOTA COROLLA

*Toyota Corolla LE*

## SPECIFICATIONS

| | 4-door sedan |
|---|---|
| Wheelbase, in. | 97.0 |
| Overall length, in. | 174.0 |
| Overall width, in. | 66.7 |
| Overall height, in. | 54.5 |
| Curb weight, lbs. | 2414 |
| Cargo vol., cu. ft. | 12.1 |
| Fuel capacity, gals. | 13.2 |
| Seating capacity | 5 |
| Front head room, in. | 39.3 |
| Max. front leg room, in. | 42.5 |
| Rear head room, in. | 36.9 |
| Min. rear leg room, in. | 33.2 |

## ENGINES

| | dohc I-4 |
|---|---|
| Size, liters/cu. in. | 1.8/110 |
| Horsepower @ rpm | 120@ 5600 |
| Torque (lbs./ft.) @ rpm | 122@ 4400 |
| Availability | S |

**EPA city/highway mpg**

| | |
|---|---|
| 5-speed OD manual | 31/38 |
| 3-speed automatic | 28/33 |
| 4-speed OD automatic | 28/36 |

| Toyota Corolla | Retail Price | Dealer Invoice |
|---|---|---|
| VE 4-door sedan, 5-speed | $11908 | $10854 |
| VE 4-door sedan, automatic | 12408 | 11309 |
| CE 4-door sedan, 5-speed | 13788 | 12568 |

*Prices are accurate at time of publication; subject to manufacturer's change.*

# TOYOTA

|  | Retail Price | Dealer Invoice |
|---|---|---|
| CE 4-door sedan, automatic | $14588 | $13298 |
| LE 4-door sedan, 5-speed | 14798 | 13107 |
| LE 4-door sedan, automatic | 15598 | 13816 |
| Destination charge | 420 | 420 |

Prices are for vehicles distributed by Toyota Motor Sales, U.S.A., Inc. The dealer invoice and destination charge may be higher in areas served by independent distributors.

## STANDARD EQUIPMENT:

**VE:** 1.8-liter dohc 4-cylinder engine, 5-speed manual or 3-speed automatic transmission, driver- and passenger-side air bags, daytime running lights, power steering, cloth reclining front bucket seats w/lumbar support, front storage console with storage, cupholders, visor mirrors, trip odometer, automatic headlights, remote fuel door release, 175/65R14 tires.
**CE** adds: 5-speed manual or 4-speed automatic transmission, air conditioning, power windows, power door locks, AM/FM/cassette w/four speakers, digital clock, intermittent wipers, rear defogger, 60/40 split folding rear seat w/headrests, remote trunk release, dual remote mirrors, wheel covers.
**LE** adds: power mirrors, tachometer, variable intermittent wipers, outside temperature display, color-keyed bodyside moldings, 185/65R14 tires.

## OPTIONAL EQUIPMENT:
### Major Packages

| | | |
|---|---|---|
| All-Weather Guard Pkg., VE | 265 | 215 |
| CE, LE | 80 | 67 |
| *Heavy-duty rear defogger, starter, and heater, rear heater ducts.* | | |
| Touring Pkg., CE | 290 | 232 |
| LE | 140 | 112 |
| *Front stabilizer bar, mud guards, rocker panel extensions, tachometer (CE), 185/65SR14 tires.* | | |
| Touring Pkg. w/alloy wheels, LE | 555 | 444 |
| *Front stabilizer bar, mud guards, rocker panel extensions, tachometer (CE), 185/65SR14 tires.* | | |
| Power Pkg., CE | 640 | 512 |
| *Power windows and door locks, power mirrors.* | | |

### Safety Features

| | | |
|---|---|---|
| Anti-lock brakes | 550 | 473 |
| Side impact air bags | 250 | 215 |
| Integrated child seat, CE, LE | 125 | 100 |

### Comfort and Convenience

| | | |
|---|---|---|
| Air conditioning, VE | 950 | 760 |

| | Retail Price | Dealer Invoice |
|---|---|---|
| Power sunroof, LE | $735 | $588 |
| Rear defogger, VE | 185 | 148 |
| Cruise control, CE, LE | 290 | 232 |
| Radio Prep Pkg., VE | 100 | 75 |
| *Includes four speakers, wiring harness, antenna.* | | |
| AM/FM/cassette, VE | 450 | 338 |
| *Requires Radio Prep Pkg.* | | |
| AM/FM/CD, VE | 550 | 413 |
| CE, LE | 100 | 75 |
| *Requires Radio Prep Pkg.* | | |
| 3-disc CD changer | 641 | 449 |
| *Requires AM/FM/cassette or CD.* | | |
| 6-disc CD autochanger | 550 | 338 |
| *Requires AM/FM/cassette or CD.* | | |
| Remote keyless entry, CE, LE | 229 | 149 |
| *Requires Power Pkg.* | | |
| Burlwood dashboard, VE, CE | 325 | 215 |
| CE w/Power Pkg., LE | 425 | 275 |

## Appearance and Miscellaneous

| | | |
|---|---|---|
| Theft-deterrent system, CE, LE | 399 | 249 |
| Rear Spoiler | 499 | 299 |
| Alloy wheels, VE, CE | 755 | 560 |
| LE | 415 | 332 |

Other options are available as port installed items.

# TOYOTA RAV4

| SPECIFICATIONS | 2-door wagon | 4-door wagon |
|---|---|---|
| Wheelbase, in. | 86.6 | 94.9 |
| Overall length, in. | 147.6 | 163.8 |
| Overall width, in. | 66.7 | 66.7 |
| Overall height, in. | 65.2 | 65.4 |
| Curb weight, lbs. | 2701 | 2789 |
| Cargo vol., cu. ft. | 34.7 | 57.9 |
| Fuel capacity, gals. | 15.3 | 15.3 |
| Seating capacity | 4 | 4 |
| Front head room, in. | 40.0 | 40.3 |
| Max. front leg room, in. | 39.5 | 39.5 |
| Rear head room, in. | 38.6 | 39.0 |
| Min. rear leg room, in. | 33.9 | 33.9 |

*Prices are accurate at time of publication; subject to manufacturer's change.*

# TOYOTA

*Toyota RAV4 4-door*

## ENGINES

|  | dohc I-4 |
|---|---|
| Size, liters/cu. in. | 2.0/122 |
| Horsepower @ rpm | 127@ 5400 |
| Torque (lbs./ft.) @ rpm | 132@ 4600 |
| Availability | S |

**EPA city/highway mpg**

| | |
|---|---|
| 5-speed OD manual | 24/29[1] |
| 4-speed OD automatic | 24/29[1] |

*1. 22/26 w/4WD.*

| Toyota RAV4 | Retail Price | Dealer Invoice |
|---|---|---|
| 2WD 2-door wagon, 5-speed | $15388 | $14026 |
| 2WD 2-door wagon, automatic | 16438 | 14983 |
| 2WD 4-door wagon, 5-speed | 16248 | 14809 |
| 2WD 4-door wagon, automatic | 17298 | 15768 |
| 4WD 2-door wagon, 5-speed | 16798 | 15052 |
| 4WD 4-door wagon, 5-speed | 17658 | 15822 |
| 4WD 4-door wagon, automatic | 18708 | 16763 |
| Destination charge | 420 | 420 |

Prices are for vehicles distributed by Toyota Motor Sales, U.S.A., Inc. The dealer invoice and destination charge may be higher in areas served by independent distributors.

## STANDARD EQUIPMENT:

**Base:** 2.0-liter dohc 4-cylinder engine, 5-speed manual or 4-speed automatic transmission, driver- and passenger-side air bags, power steering, tilt steering wheel (4-door), reclining cloth front bucket seats, split folding and reclining rear seat, front storage console, cupholders, tachometer, trip odometer, coolant-temperature gauge, digital clock, rear defogger, intermittent front and rear wipers, rear auxiliary power outlet, dual outside mirrors, front tow hook, 215/70R16 tires, 4WD models add: permanent 4WD.

## OPTIONAL EQUIPMENT:
### Major Packages

| | Retail Price | Dealer Invoice |
|---|---|---|
| Value Pkg. 1, 4-door ................................................ | $1672 | $1505 |
| *Air conditioning, AM/FM/cassette player, tilt steering wheel, cruise control, power windows, doors, and mirrors, carpeted floormats, trunk mat.* | | |
| Value Pkg. 2, 4-door ................................................ | 1772 | 1595 |
| *Pkg. 1 plus AM/FM/CD player, cloth front and rear headrests, spare tire cover, body cladding graphic.* | | |
| Upgrade Pkg., 4-door ................................................ | 930 | 744 |
| *Power windows, door locks, and mirrors. Requires AM/FM/cassette or CD player.* | | |
| All-Weather Guard Pkg. .......................................... | 70 | 59 |
| *Heavy-duty battery, rear heater ducts, heavy-duty starter motor, large windshield washer reservoir.* | | |

### Powertrains

| | | |
|---|---|---|
| Limited slip differential, 4WD............................................ | 375 | 309 |

### Safety Features

| | | |
|---|---|---|
| Anti-lock brakes.................................................. | 590 | 507 |

### Comfort and Convenience

| | | |
|---|---|---|
| Air conditioning...................................................... | 985 | 788 |
| Power moonroof, 4-door ...................................... | 915 | 732 |
| Cruise control ........................................................ | 290 | 232 |
| Tilt steering wheel, 2-door .................................. | 170 | 145 |
| AM/FM/CD player .................................................. | 450 | 338 |
| AM/FM/cassette player.......................................... | 350 | 263 |

### Appearance and Miscellaneous

| | | |
|---|---|---|
| Privacy glass, 2-door.............................................. | 220 | 176 |
| 4-door.............................................. | 295 | 236 |

### Special Purpose, Wheels and Tires

| | | |
|---|---|---|
| Alloy wheels .......................................................... | 685 | 548 |
| Alloy wheels w/fender flares, 4WD............................ | 1140 | 912 |

# TOYOTA SIENNA

## SPECIFICATIONS

| | 3-door van |
|---|---|
| Wheelbase, in. ........................................................ | 114.2 |
| Overall length, in. .................................................. | 193.5 |
| Overall width, in. .................................................... | 73.4 |

*Prices are accurate at time of publication; subject to manufacturer's change.*

# TOYOTA

*Toyota Sienna XLE*

| | 3-door van |
|---|---|
| Overall height, in. | 67.3 |
| Curb weight, lbs. | 3759 |
| Cargo vol., cu. ft. | 143.0 |
| Fuel capacity, gals. | 21.0 |
| Seating capacity | 7 |
| Front head room, in. | 40.6 |
| Max. front leg room, in. | 41.9 |
| Rear head room, in. | 37.7 |
| Min. rear leg room, in. | 34.0 |

## ENGINES

| | dohc V-6 |
|---|---|
| Size, liters/cu. in. | 3.0/183 |
| Horsepower @ rpm | 194@ 5200 |
| Torque (lbs./ft.) @ rpm | 209@ 4400 |
| Availability | S |

**EPA city/highway mpg**

| | |
|---|---|
| 4-speed OD automatic | 18/24 |

| Toyota Sienna | Retail Price | Dealer Invoice |
|---|---|---|
| CE 3-door van | $21140 | $18724 |
| LE 3-door van | 23500 | 20573 |
| LE 4-door van | 23975 | 20989 |
| XLE 4-door van | 27100 | 23514 |
| Destination charge | 420 | 420 |

## STANDARD EQUIPMENT:

**CE:** 3.0-liter dohc V-6 engine, 4-speed automatic transmission, driver- and passenger-side air bags, anti-lock brakes, air conditioning, variable-assist

CONSUMER GUIDE™

power steering, tilt steering wheel, cloth reclining front bucket seats, console with storage, overhead console, 2-passenger second-row seat, 3-passenger split-folding third row seat, cupholders, AM/FM/cassette, digital clock, visor mirrors, auxiliary power outlets, variable intermittent wipers, automatic headlights, tinted glass, dual outside mirrors, 205/70R15 tires, wheel covers.

**LE** adds: front side-impact air bags, front and rear air conditioning, power windows, power door locks, power mirrors, cruise control, rear defogger, tachometer, illuminated visor mirrors, privacy glass.

**XLE** adds: power driver seat, heated power mirrors, CD player, quad captain's chairs, leather-wrapped steering wheel, remote keyless entry, floormats, roof rack, theft-deterrent system, full-size spare tire, 215/65R15 tires, alloy wheels.

## OPTIONAL EQUIPMENT:

| | Retail Price | Dealer Invoice |
|---|---|---|
| **Major Packages** | | |
| Pkg. 1, LE | $430 | $333 |
| _Cassette player, privacy glass, roof rack._ | | |
| Pkg. 2, LE | 1690 | 1341 |
| _Pkg. 2 plus captain's chairs, alloy wheels._ | | |
| Pkg. 3, XLE | 2390 | 1912 |
| _Leather upholstery, power sunroof._ | | |
| Leather Pkg., XLE | 1410 | 1128 |
| _Leather upholstery._ | | |
| Security Pkg., LE | 440 | 352 |
| _Theft-deterrent system, remote keyless entry._ | | |
| Power Pkg., CE | 895 | 716 |
| _Cruise control, power windows and door locks._ | | |
| Towing Pkg., CE | 600 | 480 |
| LE, XLE | 150 | 120 |
| _Includes rear air conditioning. Requires full-size spare tire._ | | |
| Towing Pkg. 2, CE | 150 | 120 |
| _Not available with rear air conditioning. Requires full-size spare tire._ | | |
| **Safety Features** | | |
| Integrated child seat, CE, LE | 250 | 200 |
| _NA with quad captain's chairs._ | | |
| **Comfort and Convenience** | | |
| Rear air conditioning, CE | 450 | 360 |
| Power mirrors, CE | 180 | 144 |
| Heated power mirrors, CE | 180 | 144 |
| Rear defogger, CE | 195 | 156 |
| Remote keyless entry | 229 | 149 |
| _CE requires Power Pkg._ | | |
| Cassette player, CE | 231 | 162 |

_Prices are accurate at time of publication; subject to manufacturer's change._

## TOYOTA

|  | Retail Price | Dealer Invoice |
|---|---|---|
| CD player, CE, LE | $335 | $235 |
| 3-disc CD player, CE, LE | 641 | 449 |
| Power sliding door, LE, XLE | 375 | 300 |
| *Requires Security Pkg.* | | |
| Quad captain's chairs, LE | 650 | 520 |
| Power sunroof, XLE | 980 | 784 |

### Appearance and Miscellaneous

| | | |
|---|---|---|
| Rear privacy glass, CE, LE | 360 | 288 |
| Roof rack, CE, LE | 210 | 168 |
| Deluxe theft-deterrent system | 399 | 249 |
| *CE requires Power Pkg.* | | |
| Alloy wheels, LE | 610 | 488 |

Other options are available as port installed items.

# TOYOTA 4RUNNER

*Toyota 4Runner Limited*

## SPECIFICATIONS

|  | 4-door wagon |
|---|---|
| Wheelbase, in. | 105.3 |
| Overall length, in. | 178.7 |
| Overall width, in. | 66.5 |
| Overall height, in. | 67.5 |
| Curb weight, lbs. | 3850 |
| Cargo vol., cu. ft. | 79.7 |
| Fuel capacity, gals. | 18.5 |
| Seating capacity | 5 |
| Front head room, in. | 39.2 |
| Max. front leg room, in. | 43.1 |
| Rear head room, in. | 38.7 |
| Min. rear leg room, in. | 34.9 |

## ENGINES

| | dohc I-4 | dohc V-6 |
|---|---|---|
| Size, liters/cu. in. | 2.7/164 | 3.4/207 |
| Horsepower @ rpm | 150@ 4800 | 183@ 4800 |
| Torque (lbs./ft.) @ rpm | 177@ 4000 | 217@ 3600 |
| Availability | S[1] | S[2] |

### EPA city/highway mpg

| | dohc I-4 | dohc V-6 |
|---|---|---|
| 5-speed OD manual | 19/24[3] | 16/19 |
| 4-speed OD automatic | 20/24[4] | 17/21[5] |

1. Base. 2. SR5, Limited. 3. 17/21 w/4WD. 4. 19/22 w/4WD. 5. 17/20 w/4WD.

| Toyota 4Runner | Retail Price | Dealer Invoice |
|---|---|---|
| Base 2WD 4-door wagon, 5-speed | $20558 | $17997 |
| Base 2WD 4-door wagon, automatic | 21458 | 18785 |
| Base 4WD 4-door wagon, 5-speed | 22708 | 19881 |
| Base 4WD 4-door wagon, automatic | 23608 | 20668 |
| SR5 2WD 4-door wagon, automatic | 25118 | 21990 |
| SR5 4WD 4-door wagon, 5-speed | 26268 | 22997 |
| SR5 4WD 4-door wagon, automatic | 27168 | 23784 |
| Limited 2WD 4-door wagon, automatic | 32248 | 28233 |
| Limited 4WD 4-door wagon, automatic | 34618 | 30307 |
| Destination charge | 420 | 420 |

Prices are for vehicles distributed by Toyota Motor Sales, U.S.A., Inc. The dealer invoice and destination charge may be higher in areas served by independent distributors.

## STANDARD EQUIPMENT:

**Base:** 2.7-liter dohc 4-cylinder engine, 5-speed manual or 4-speed automatic transmission, driver- and passenger-side air bags, power steering, cloth bucket seats, 50/50 split folding rear seat, oil-pressure gauge, front and rear cupholders, tachometer, voltmeter, trip odometer, AM/FM radio with four speakers, power tailgate window, intermittent wipers, passenger-side visor mirror, remote fuel-door release, tinted glass, mudguards, 225/75R15 tires, 4WD models add: 4WDemand part-time 4WD.

**SR5** adds: 3.4-liter dohc V-6 engine, anti-lock brakes, tilt steering wheel, power door locks, power mirrors, cassette player, spring rear antenna, digital clock, rear defogger, rear wiper/washer, rear cupholders, variable intermittent wipers, map and courtesy lights, privacy glass, chrome bumpers and grille, 4WD models add: 4WDemand part-time 4WD.

**Limited** adds: 4-speed automatic transmission, air conditioning, cruise control, power front sport seats, leather upholstery, premium CD player with six speakers, power antenna, leather-wrapped steering wheel and shift knob, power windows, illuminated passenger-side visor mirror, wood

# TOYOTA

interior trim, tonneau cover, floormats, bodyside cladding, fender flares, running boards, 265/70R16 tires, alloy wheels, 4WD adds: 4WDemand part-time 4WD, One-Touch Hi-4 4WD, remote 4-wheel drive selector, All-Weather Guard Pkg. (heavy-duty battery, heavy-duty wiper motor and starter motor, large windshield washer reservoir).

## OPTIONAL EQUIPMENT:

| | Retail Price | Dealer Invoice |
|---|---|---|
| **Major Packages** | | |
| Upgrade Pkg., Base | $2275 | $1805 |
| *Air conditioner, cruise control, power windows and door locks, power mirrors, deluxe cassette, power antenna, additional lighting, floormats.* | | |
| Preferred Equipment Group 1, SR5 | 2720 | 2165 |
| *Air conditioning, power windows, premium cassette player with six speakers, power antenna, alloy wheels with 31-inch tires (265/70R16 tires).* | | |
| Preferred Equipment Group 2, SR5 | 2105 | 1673 |
| *Group 1 without 31-inch tires.* | | |
| Convenience Pkg., Base | 705 | 577 |
| SR5 | 375 | 300 |
| *Tilt steering wheel, variable intermittent wipers, digital clock, intermittent rear wiper/washer (Base), rear defogger, map light.* | | |
| Power Pkg. #1, Base | 810 | 648 |
| *Power door locks, power mirrors, additional lighting.* | | |
| Power Pkg. #2, Base | 920 | 736 |
| SR5 | 505 | 404 |
| *Power windows and door locks, power mirrors, power antenna. SR5 requires premium cassette player or cassette/CD player.* | | |
| Sports Pkg., SR5 | 1760 | 1422 |
| *Sports Seat Pkg., leather-wrapped steering wheel, leather-wrapped shifter (5-speed), fender flares, P265/70R16 tires, alloy wheels.* | | |
| Sports Pkg. w/locking rear differential, 4WD SR5 w/automatic | 2085 | 1690 |
| Sports Seat Pkg, SR5 | 685 | 548 |
| *Cloth sport seats, cruise control, upgraded door trim, leather-wrapped steering wheel, leather-wrapped shift knob (4WD SR5 w/5-speed).* | | |
| Leather Trim Pkg., SR5 | 1535 | 1228 |
| *Leather sports seats, leather door trim, leather-wrapped steering wheel, leather-wrapped shift knob (4WD SR5 w/5-speed), cruise control.* | | |
| **Powertrains** | | |
| Locking rear differential, Base 4WD, SR5 4WD w/5-speed, Limited 4WD | 325 | 268 |
| *Base requires styled steel wheels or alloy wheels w/31-inch tires (265/70R16 tires). 4WD SR5 w/5-speed requires alloy wheels w/31-inch tires, Sports Pkg., or Group 1.* | | |
| Alloy wheels w/locking rear differential, SR5 4WD w/automatic | 1355 | 1092 |

| Safety Features | Retail Price | Dealer Invoice |
|---|---|---|
| Anti-lock brakes, Base | $590 | $507 |

## Comfort and Convenience

| | | |
|---|---|---|
| Air conditioning, Base, SR5 | 985 | 788 |
| Rear heater | 165 | 132 |
| *Includes rear storage console w/cupholders.* | | |
| Cruise control, Base, SR5 | 290 | 232 |
| Tilt steering column, Base | 235 | 201 |
| *Includes variable intermittent wipers.* | | |
| Rear defogger, wiper/washer, Base | 365 | 292 |
| Power sunroof, SR5, Limited | 915 | 732 |
| Tonneau cover, Base, SR5 | 85 | 68 |
| Premium cassette player, SR5 | 220 | 165 |
| *Includes six speakers. Requires Power Pkg. #2.* | | |
| Deluxe CD player, Base, SR5 | 100 | 75 |
| *Includes four speakers.* | | |
| Premium CD player, SR5 | 320 | 240 |
| *Requires Power Pkg. #2.* | | |
| Premium Cassette/CD player, SR5 | 500 | 375 |
| Limited | 180 | 135 |
| *Includes six speakers. Requires Power Pkg. #2.* | | |

## Appearance and Miscellaneous

| | | |
|---|---|---|
| Privacy glass, Base | 295 | 236 |

## Special Purpose, Wheels and Tires

| | | |
|---|---|---|
| Styled steel wheels, Base | 600 | 480 |
| *Includes 265/70R16 tires, 4.56 axle ratio. 2WD requires anti-lock brakes.* | | |
| Alloy wheels w/31-inch tires | 1030 | 824 |
| *Includes 265/70R16 tires. Base 2WD requires anti-lock brakes.* | | |
| Alloy wheels, Base, SR5 | 415 | 332 |

# VOLKSWAGEN PASSAT

| SPECIFICATIONS | 4-door sedan |
|---|---|
| Wheelbase, in. | 106.4 |
| Overall length, in. | 184.1 |
| Overall width, in. | 68.5 |
| Overall height, in. | 57.4 |
| Curb weight, lbs. | 3120 |
| Cargo vol., cu. ft. | 15.0 |
| Fuel capacity, gals. | 18.5 |

*Prices are accurate at time of publication; subject to manufacturer's change.*

# VOLKSWAGEN

*Volkswagen Passat GLS sedan*

|  | 4-door sedan |
|---|---|
| Seating capacity | 5 |
| Front head room, in. | 39.7 |
| Max. front leg room, in. | 41.5 |
| Rear head room, in. | 37.8 |
| Min. rear leg room, in. | 35.3 |

## ENGINES

|  | Turbo dohc I-4 | Turbodiesel ohc I-4 | dohc V-6 |
|---|---|---|---|
| Size, liters/cu. in. | 1.8/109 | 1.9/116 | 2.8/169 |
| Horsepower @ rpm | 150@ 5700 | 90@ 4000 | 200@ 6000 |
| Torque (lbs./ft.) @ rpm | 155@ 1750 | 149@ 1900 | 207@ 3200 |
| Availability | S[1] | S[2] | S[3] |
| **EPA city/highway mpg** | | | |
| 5-speed OD manual | 23/32 | 39/50 | 20/29 |
| 4-speed OD automatic | | 31/44 | |
| 5-speed OD automatic | 21/31 | | 18/29[4] |

1. GLS.  2. TDI.  3. GLS V-6, GLX.  4. 17/26 w/Syncro.

| Volkswagen Passat | Retail Price | Dealer Invoice |
|---|---|---|
| GLS 4-door sedan | $20750 | $18676 |
| GLS TDI 4-door sedan | 21200 | 19078 |
| GLS V-6 4-door sedan | 23190 | 20855 |
| GLX 4-door sedan | 26250 | 23589 |
| Destination charge | 500 | 500 |

## STANDARD EQUIPMENT:

**GLS:** 1.8-liter 4-cylinder engine, 5-speed manual transmission, traction control, driver- and passenger-side air bags, front side-impact air bags, anti-lock 4-wheel disc brakes, daytime running lights, air conditioning, interior air filter, rear heat ducts, power steering, tilt steering wheel, cruise control, cloth reclining front bucket seats w/adjustable lumbar support and headrests, 60/40 folding rear seat, rear armrest, front storage console, cupholders, heated power mirrors, power windows, power door locks, remote keyless entry, map lights, tachometer, coolant-temperature gauge, trip odometer, trip computer, outside temperature indicator, AM/FM/cassette w/CD controls, digital clock, rear defogger, power remote decklid release, variable intermittent wipers, illuminated visor mirrors, floormats, theft-deterrent system, tinted glass, fog lights, full-size spare tire, 195/65HR15 tires, wheel covers.

**GLS TDI** adds: 1.9-liter turbodiesel 4-cylinder engine.

**GLS V-6** adds to GLS: 2.8-liter V-6 engine, wood interior trim.

**GLX** adds: leather upholstery, leather-wrapped steering wheel and shifter, heated 8-way power front seats w/driver seat memory, automatic temperature control, power moonroof, heated windshield washer nozzles.

## OPTIONAL EQUIPMENT:

| | Retail Price | Dealer Invoice |
|---|---|---|
| **Major Packages** | | |
| All-Weather Pkg., GLS, GLS TDI, GLS V-6 | $325 | $284 |
| *Includes heated front seats and windshield washer nozzles.* | | |
| **Powertrains** | | |
| 5-speed Tiptronic automatic transmission, GLS, GLS V-6, GLX | 1075 | 1063 |
| 4-speed automatic transmission, GLS TDI | 875 | 856 |
| **Comfort and Convenience** | | |
| Leather upholstery, GLS, GLS TDI, GLS V-6 | 950 | 829 |
| *Includes leather-wrapped steering wheel and shifter, leather and wood door trim.* | | |
| Power moonroof, GLS, GLS TDI, GLS V-6 | 1000 | 873 |
| 6-disc CD changer | NA | NA |

# VOLVO S70/V70

## SPECIFICATIONS

| | 4-door sedan | 4-door wagon |
|---|---|---|
| Wheelbase, in. | 104.9 | 104.9 |
| Overall length, in. | 185.9 | 185.9 |
| Overall width, in. | 69.3 | 69.3 |
| Overall height, in. | 55.2 | 56.2 |
| Curb weight, lbs. | 3152 | 3259 |
| Cargo vol., cu. ft. | 15.1 | 77.2 |
| Fuel capacity, gals. | 18.5 | 18.5 |

*Prices are accurate at time of publication; subject to manufacturer's change.*

*Volvo S70 GLT*

| | 4-door sedan | 4-door wagon |
|---|---|---|
| Seating capacity | 5 | 5 |
| Front head room, in. | 39.1 | 39.1 |
| Max. front leg room, in. | 41.4 | 41.4 |
| Rear head room, in. | 37.8 | 37.9 |
| Min. rear leg room, in. | 35.2 | 35.2 |

## ENGINES

| | dohc I-5 | Turbo dohc I-5 | Turbo dohc I-5 |
|---|---|---|---|
| Size, liters/cu. in. | 2.4/149 | 2.4/149 | 2.3/141 |
| Horsepower @ rpm | 168@ 6100 | 190@ 5200 | 236@ 5100 |
| Torque (lbs./ft.) @ rpm | 162@ 4700 | 199@ 1800 | 243@ 2100 |
| Availability | S[1] | S[2] | S[3] |

**EPA city/highway mpg**

| | | | |
|---|---|---|---|
| 5-speed OD manual | 20/29 | | 19/25 |
| 4-speed OD automatic | 20/28 | 19/27 | 18/25 |

1. Base, GT.  2. GLT, AWD, XC AWD.  3. T-5, R.

| Volvo S70/V70 | Retail Price | Dealer Invoice |
|---|---|---|
| Base 4-door sedan, 5-speed | $26985 | $24785 |
| Base 4-door sedan, automatic | 27960 | 25760 |
| Base 4-door wagon, 5-speed | 28285 | 26085 |
| Base 4-door wagon, automatic | 29260 | 27060 |
| GT 4-door sedan, 5-speed | 29540 | 27240 |
| GT 4-door sedan, automatic | 30515 | 28215 |
| GT 4-door wagon, 5-speed | 30840 | 28540 |
| GT 4-door wagon, automatic | 31815 | 29515 |
| GLT 4-door sedan | 32440 | 30040 |
| GLT 4-door wagon | 33740 | 31340 |
| AWD 4-door wagon | 34420 | 31720 |
| AWD 4-door wagon w/moonroof | 35620 | 32920 |
| XC AWD 4-door wagon | 36420 | 33470 |
| XC AWD 4-door wagon w/moonroof | 37620 | 34670 |
| T-5 4-door sedan, 5-speed | 34010 | 31060 |

# VOLVO

| | Retail Price | Dealer Invoice |
|---|---|---|
| T-5 4-door sedan, automatic | $34985 | $32035 |
| T-5 4-door wagon, 5-speed | 35310 | 32360 |
| T-5 4-door wagon, automatic | 36285 | 33335 |
| R AWD 4-door wagon | 40995 | 36795 |
| Destination charge | 575 | 575 |

## STANDARD EQUIPMENT:

**Base:** 2.4-liter dohc 5-cylinder engine, 5-speed manual or 4-speed automatic transmission, driver- and passenger-side air bags, front side-impact air bags, anti-lock 4-wheel disc brakes, daytime running lights, child-proof rear door locks, air conditioning w/dual manual climate control, variable-assist power steering, cruise control, intermittent wipers, velour upholstery, reclining front bucket seats, 8-way manually adjustable driver seat, fully folding passenger seat, 60/40 split folding rear seat, rear-seat trunk pass-through (sedan), front armrest w/cupholder, tilt/telescoping steering column, power windows, power door locks, remote keyless entry, remote decklid/tailgate release, heated power mirrors, coolant temperature gauge, trip odometer, tachometer, digital clock, outside temperature indicator, 6-speaker AM/FM/cassette w/anti-theft, power antenna (sedan), integrated window antenna (wagon), rear defogger, rear wiper/washer (wagon), illuminated visor mirrors, front and rear reading lights, floormats, theft-deterrent system, tinted glass, rear fog lights, front mud guards, tool kit, 195/60VR15 tires, wheel covers.

**GT** adds: power glass moonroof, 8-way power driver's seat w/memory feature, 6-spoke alloy wheels.

**GLT** adds: 2.4-liter dohc turbocharged 5-cylinder 190-horsepower engine, 4-speed automatic transmission, automatic climate control, premium AM/FM/cassette.

**AWD** adds to GLT wagon: automatic 4-wheel drive, locking rear differential, traction control, heated front seats, automatic load leveling suspension, headlight wipers/washers, 205/55R16 tires, deletes power moonroof.

**XC AWD** adds: leather-wrapped steering wheel, trip computer, leather and cloth upholstery, AM/FM/cassette w/3-disc CD changer, cargo net, raised suspension, roof rack, front fog lights.

**T-5** adds to GLT: 2.3-liter dohc turbocharged 5-cylinder 236 horsepower engine, 5-speed manual or 4-speed automatic transmission, CD player, leather-wrapped steering wheel, trip computer, 205/50ZR16 tires, 5-spoke alloy wheels.

**R AWD** adds to XC AWD: 2.3-liter dohc turbocharged 5-cylinder 236-horsepower engine, power moonroof, leather and suede upholstery, leather and suede-wrapped steering wheel, 8-way power passenger seat, alloy instrument panel inserts, front spoiler, deletes raised suspension.

# VOLVO

## OPTIONAL EQUIPMENT:

| | Retail Price | Dealer Invoice |
|---|---|---|
| **Major Packages** | | |
| Touring Pkg., Base, GT, GLT ............................ | $395 | $315 |
| *Trip computer, leather-wrapped steering wheel.* | | |
| Grand Touring Pkg., Base ................................ | 1780 | 1420 |
| GT, GLT ........................................................ | 1285 | 1025 |
| *8-way power driver's seat w/memory feature (Base), power passenger seat, CD player, burled walnut interior trim.* | | |
| Sport Pkg., Base, GT, GLT, T-5 ........................ | 595 | 475 |
| *Front fog lights, rear spoiler.* | | |
| TRACS/Cold Weather Pkg., | | |
| Base, GT, GLT, T-5 ...................................... | 785 | 625 |
| *Traction control, heated front seats, headlight wiper/washer.* | | |

### Comfort and Convenience

| | | |
|---|---|---|
| AM/FM/cassette/CD, | | |
| Base, GT, GLT, AWD, XC AWD .................................. | 485 | 385 |
| Dolby Pro Logic sound system, R AWD ...................... | 595 | 475 |
| Leather upholstery, Base, GT, GLT, T-5 .................. | 1195 | 955 |
| XC AWD ...................................................... | 595 | 475 |
| 8-way power driver's seat w/memory feature, Base ...... | 495 | 395 |
| Burled walnut interior trim, T-5 ........................ | 575 | 460 |
| R AWD ........................................................ | NC | NC |
| *Replaces alloy dash inserts on R AWD.* | | |

### Appearance and Miscellaneous

| | | |
|---|---|---|
| Automatic load leveling, 2WD wagons ...................... | 495 | 395 |
| Sport suspension, Base, GT, GLT, T-5 ..................... | 175 | 140 |
| Alloy wheels, Base .......................................... | 450 | 360 |
| 205/50ZR16 high performance tires, T-5 ................... | NC | NC |